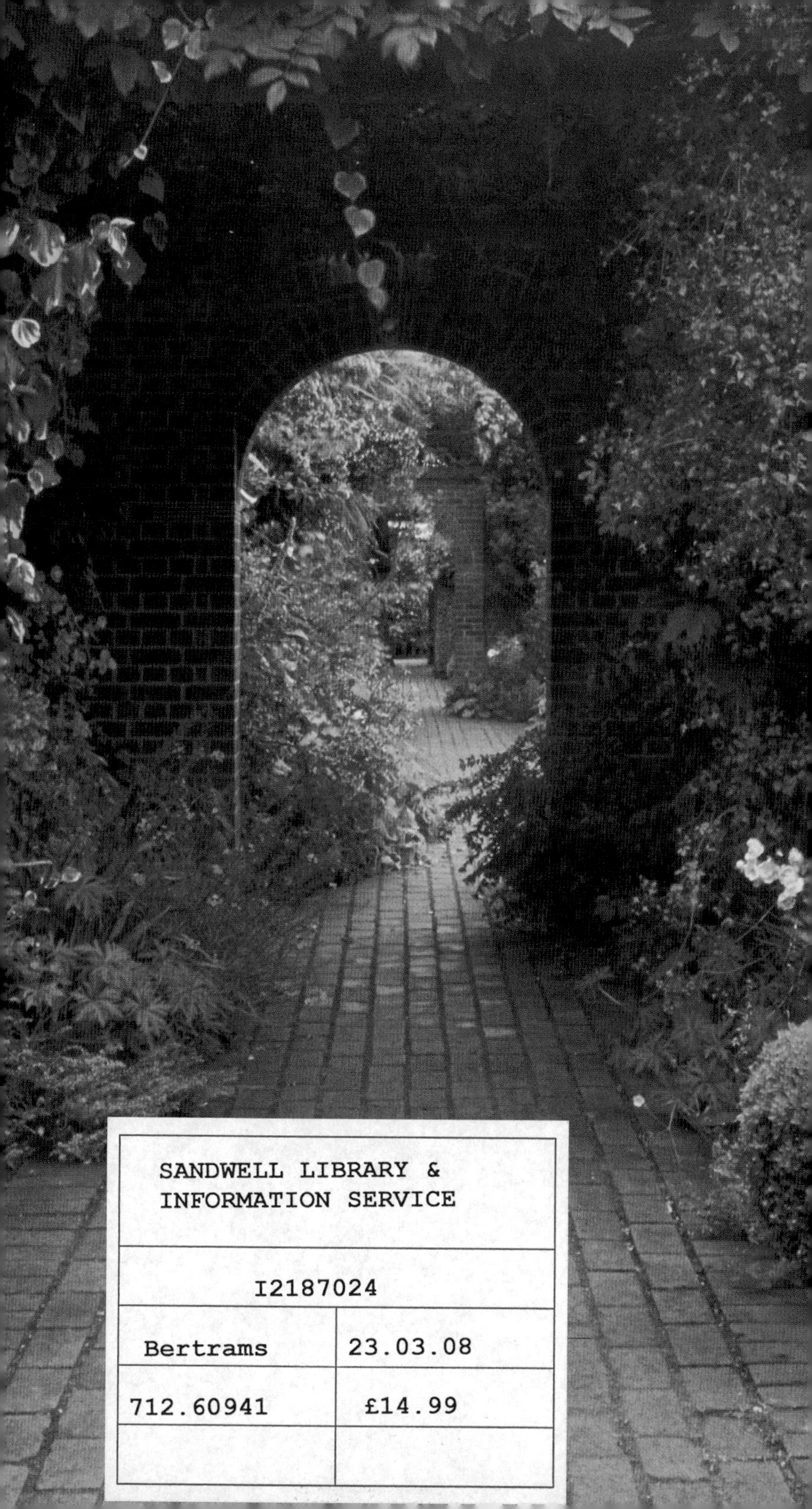

LONDON, NEW YORK, MUNICH, MELBOURNE, DELHI

For Caroline, with all love

Project Editor	Andrea Bagg
Project Designer	Elly King
Production Controller	Wendy Penn
Managing Editor	Anna Kruger
Managing Art Editor	Alison Donovan
Cartography	Iorwerth Watkins

First published in 2008 by
Dorling Kindersley Limited
80 Strand, London WC2R 0RL
A Penguin Company

2 4 6 8 10 9 7 5 3 1

Colour reproduction by GRB Editrice, Italy

Printed by L-Rex, China

Discover more at
www.dk.com

CONTENTS

SOUTH-WEST ENGLAND

SOUTH-CENTRAL ENGLAND

SOUTH-EAST ENGLAND

BRITAIN AND IRELAND HAVE A GREATER NUMBER AND RANGE OF NOTABLE SURVIVING GARDENS THAN ANY REGION OF COMPARABLE SIZE IN THE WORLD. WE HAVE EXCELLED IN THE ART OF THE GARDEN TO A MUCH GREATER DEGREE THAN IN THE VISUAL ARTS OF PAINTING AND SCULPTURE.

Despite our excellence in the art of gardening, ordinarily cultivated people often know little about gardens. This book describes a wide range of the best, and most enjoyable, of them. All the gardens included reflect my personal taste – I have visited them all, most of them repeatedly, and have come to love them. I have interpreted the word "garden" broadly to include arboreta, botanic gardens and landscape parks as well as the formal flower gardens which are the most characteristic type of British garden. All are regularly open to the public. They include great and famous gardens like Chatsworth and Stourhead, as well as smaller private gardens like Bury Court or Herterton House, and charming oddities like the Gnome Reserve. Among them are most of the gardens generally considered masterpieces of their kind, such as Crathes Castle, Powerscourt, Powis Castle and Rousham. These fine gardens are, for the most part, complete, and well maintained, but I have also included some which,

The Temple of Flora at Stourhead

although fragmentary, retain potent atmosphere. Reversals of fortune, or genteel decay, can sometimes bring magic to a landscape. The poignant remains of Lyveden New Bield are, to my taste, one of the most movingly beautiful sights of any garden. The windswept coastal site of Downhill Castle, with its suavely classical temple/library teetering among crying gulls on a cliff high above the Atlantic, is dramatic, mysterious and poignant. Such fragmentary remains touch the heart and fire the imagination in a way that immaculate borders and pristine lawns sometimes fail to do.

The one type of garden which is not thoroughly covered in this book is the commonest of all – the kind of garden that most people have behind their houses. These vernacular gardens, as often as not governed by a passion for plants, are a key indicator of horticultural health – just as, in those countries with high standards of food, it is the quality of ordinary, everyday fare

The maze at Chatsworth

that is far more significant than the kind of food served in the temples of gastronomy. The thousands of gardens that are open to the public and described in the Yellow Book of the National Gardens Scheme (*Gardens of England and Wales Open for Charity*) and in the Yellow Book of the Scotland Gardens Scheme (*Gardens of Scotland*) cover the whole range of vernacular gardens (and some that are much grander). Many are the keen gardeners whose early inspiration came from visiting Yellow Book gardens.

The Flower Garden at Herterton House

Much of the historical information in this book comes from a series of priceless sources: the *English Heritage Register of Parks and Gardens of Special Historic Interest*; the Scottish *Inventory of Gardens and Designed Landscapes* (produced jointly by Scottish Natural Heritage and Historic Scotland); and the Cadw/ICOMOS *Register of Landscapes, Parks and Gardens of Special Historic Interest in Wales*. If a garden is included in any of these, I indicate it. The very detailed descriptions in the Registers and the Inventory are of huge value as a primary source of information about historic

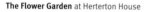

landscapes or gardens. In addition, the English and Welsh Registers grade gardens according to their importance, in exactly the same way as historic buildings are listed (Grades I, II* and II), and I include these grades – though it should be emphasised that the grading is an indication of historical importance rather than horticultural excellence. (A garden may be listed Grade I, for example, simply because it has some very rare feature, such as a medieval garden wall.) Tudor terraces, the traces of 17th-century avenues in a deer park, splendid surviving 18th-century parkland

The front garden at Docwra's Manor

trees or a temple on a wooded eminence are all thrilling ingredients of the landscape, but they are more than that: they are also part of the long, complicated and fascinating story of the way in which people have laid out gardens.

TYPES OF GARDEN

The range of different types of garden in Britain and Ireland is immense. Of the earliest gardens, dating from the middle ages and the Tudor period, nothing survives completely intact. It is not until the 18th century that we find many extant examples of complete period gardens. These, for the most part landscape parks, are remarkable creations of trees, sculptures and ornamental buildings, and of water, in particular lakes and cascades. The great gardens at Bramham, Stourhead, Stowe, Petworth and Audley End all display great landscapes of superlative quality in this tradition. The greatest gardens of the 19th century are, arguably, the woodland gardens which were created to display the dazzling new

flowering shrubs that were being introduced from far flung places in that period. Arduaine, Caerhays Castle, Crarae, Inverewe, Trebah, Trewithen and other gardens of the period display magnificent collections of plants as well as magical landscapes. Of gardens of the early 20th century, usually of the Arts and Crafts tradition, there are many exceptional surviving examples. Athelhampton, Hestercombe, Hidcote Manor, Iford Manor and Sissinghurst Castle are all marvellous survivals from this period. Accurate recreations and

The walled garden at Saling Hall

restorations of period gardens are a relatively new, and very welcome, development. The charming medieval garden at Tretower Court, the dazzling and deeply researched restoration of the 17th-century Privy Garden at Hampton Court Palace, the Marchioness of Salisbury's Knot Garden at Hatfield House and the meticulous restoration of Gertrude Jekyll's design for the Manor House, Upton Grey are welcome and precious gardens in this tradition.

It is a matter of some puzzlement, and regret, that so few gardens in Britain and Ireland are today inspired by innovative ideas about design. Some of the happy exceptions are described – Christopher Bradley-Hole's garden at Bury Court, Jacques and Peter Wirtz's garden at Alnwick Castle and Piet Oudolf's outstanding design for the Scampston Walled Garden. It is curious that the National Trust, the guardian of so many exceptional gardens, should only in 2003 have commissioned an entirely new garden. This first departure, still unfinished in 2007, is the West Garden designed by Arne Maynard for Dyrham Park – "a contemporary garden with echoes of the past".

Patrick Taylor

Patrick Taylor

USING THIS BOOK

The Guide is divided into regions and the gardens are listed alphabetically within each group. Opening times are given, but please note that these are subject to change, so it is essential to phone or email the garden if you are planning a long journey. The three most valuable guides, which are updated every year, are the Yellow Book for England and Wales, the Yellow Book for Scotland, and *Hudson's Historic Houses and Gardens*.

SCOTLAND

IRELAND

NORTH of
ENGLAND

HEART of
ENGLAND

EAST of
ENGLAND

WALES &
WEST of
ENGLAND

SOUTH-
CENTRAL
ENGLAND

SOUTH-EAST
ENGLAND

SOUTH-
WEST ENGLAND

Who's Who

LISTED HERE ARE KEY ARCHITECTS, GARDEN DESIGNERS AND GARDEN MAKERS MENTIONED IN THIS BOOK.

Note: all the gardens mentioned below are described in this book.

SIR REGINALD BLOMFIELD (1856-1942)

Architect and garden designer practising in a lively Arts and Crafts manner. Godinton House, Mellerstain and Sulgrave Manor are among his best surviving works, all of which are in excellent order.

CHARLES BRIDGEMAN (*d.*1738)

Rather enigmatic garden designer very little of whose work survives. He made early designs for some outstanding estates, among them Blenheim Palace, Castle Hill, Rousham, Stowe and Wimpole Hall, all magnificent.

LANCELOT "CAPABILITY" BROWN (1716-83)

Architect and the greatest landscape designer of his time. He made the informal English landscape park the most fashionable type of garden of the day – with serpentine lakes, belts and clumps of trees, and occasional ornamental buildings. Audley End, Chatsworth, Corsham Court, Petworth, Warwick Castle, Weston Park, and Wrest Park are some of his best and most diverse designs.

PERCY CANE (1881-1976)

Garden designer and knowledgeable plantsman. Excellent examples of his work may be seen at Dartington Hall and Falkland Palace.

THE HON. CHARLES HAMILTON (1704-86)

Anglo-Irish garden designer who laid out the great garden at Painshill. He also advised his friend Henry Hoare in the garden at Stourhead and the Marquess of Lansdowne at Bowood.

GERTRUDE JEKYLL (1843-1932)

Plantswoman, garden designer and garden author, among the most important of her time. The superbly restored Manor House garden at Upton Grey is a magnificent example of Gertrude Jekyll's work. Elsewhere she often worked in collaboration with Sir Edwin Lutyens – Hestercombe is one of their finest designs.

SIR GEOFFREY JELLICOE (1900-96)

Landscape architect and garden designer, one of the great figures of his time. Excellent work by him may be seen at Cliveden, Mottisfont Abbey, Shute House and Wisley.

WILLIAM KENT (*c.*1685-1748)

Architect and garden designer. At Rousham he laid out a pioneer early romantic landscape, one of the best gardens of its time. His work also survives at Chiswick House and at Stowe, both enchanting.

GEORGE LONDON (*c.*1640-1713)

Great designer of formal gardens, sometimes in partnership with Henry Wise (1653-1738). Their joint work may be seen at Chatsworth, Hampton Court and Melbourne Hall.

SIR EDWIN LUTYENS (1869-1944)

Great architect with a particular interest in gardens, often working in collaboration with Gertrude Jekyll. Great Dixter, Greywalls, Hestercombe and Heywood are among his best works.

THOMAS MAWSON (1861-1933)

Garden designer practising in an elaborate Arts and Crafts style. Dyffryn is an excellent example of his work.

The Rock Garden at Mount Stuart displays his work in quieter mood.

WILLIAM ANDREWS NESFIELD (1793-1881)

Garden designer practising in a High Victorian formal style. His work may be seen at Castle Howard, the Royal Botanic Garden Kew, Shugborough, Somerleyton Hall (one of his best) and Sudeley Castle. A remarkable talent.

PIET OUDOLF (*b.*1945)

Dutch nurseryman and brilliant modern garden designer with a particular love of naturalistic plantings of herbaceous perennials. Excellent work by him may be seen at Bury Court, Scampston Walled Garden, Trentham Gardens and Wisley.

SIR JOSEPH PAXTON (1803-65)

Gardener, architect and garden designer – one of the 19th century's greatest garden figures. His dazzling and varied work survives at Chatsworth (where he was head gardener), Lismore Castle and Tatton Park.

HAROLD PETO (1854-1933)

Architect and garden designer working in a refined Arts and Crafts style. Among his best work are Buscot Park, Heale House, Iford Manor (his own house), Ilnacullin and West Dean.

Paxton's Italian garden at Tatton Park

HUMPHRY REPTON (1752-1818)

Distinguished garden designer who inherited the mantle of "Capability" Brown. Among his surviving works are Antony House, Corsham Court, Kenwood House, Sheringham Park, Tatton Park and Wimpole Hall.

LANNING ROPER (1912-83)

American garden designer who lived and practised in England, often designing lavish mixed borders in the English style. His work may be seen at Claverton House, Broughton Castle, Waddesdon Manor, Penshurst Place, Scotney Castle and Wisley.

FRANCIS INIGO THOMAS (1866-1950)

Outstanding architect and garden designer practising in Arts and Crafts style. Athelhampton is his masterpiece.

SIR JOHN VANBRUGH (1664-1726)

English architect practising in a dramatic Baroque style, who also designed landscapes. He worked at Blenheim Palace, Castle Howard and Grimsthorpe Castle.

JACQUES WIRTZ (*b.*1924)

Outstanding Flemish garden designer with a love of formality and flowers, often working in partnership with his son Peter. Their work is magnificently displayed at Alnwick Castle and Ascott.

SOUTH-WEST ENGLAND

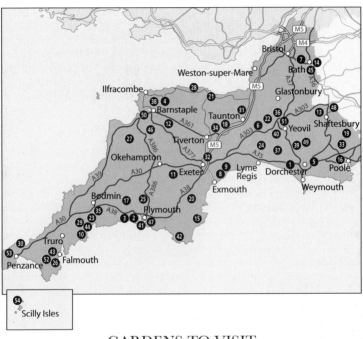

Scilly Isles

GARDENS TO VISIT

1. Abbotsbury Subtropical Gardens
2. Antony House
3. Antony Woodland Garden
4. Arlington Court
5. Athelhampton House Gardens
6. Barrington Court
7. Bath Botanical Gardens
8. Bicton College of Agriculture
9. Bicton Park Gardens
10. Caerhays Castle
11. Castle Drogo
12. Castle Hill
13. Chiffchaffs

14. Claverton Manor
15. Coleton Fishacre Garden
16. Compton Acres
17. Cotehele
18. Cothay Manor
19. Cranborne Manor Gardens
20. Dartington Hall
21. Dunster Castle
22. East Lambrook Manor
23. The Eden Project
24. Forde Abbey
25. The Garden House
26. Glendurgan Garden
27. Gnome Reserve
28. Greencombe

29. Heligan
30. Barbara Hepworth Garden
31. Hestercombe
32. Killerton
33. Kingston Lacy
34. Knightshayes Court
35. Lanhydrock
36. Lytes Cary Manor
37. Mapperton House Gardens
38. Marwood Hill Gardens
39. Minterne
40. Montacute House
41. Mount Edgcumbe
42. Overbeck's Garden

43. Penjerrick
44. Pine Lodge Gardens
45. Prior Park Landscape Garden
46. Rosemoor Garden
47. Saltram House
48. Shute House
49. Sticky Wicket
50. Tapeley Park
51. Tintinhull House
52. Trebah
53. Trengwainton Garden
54. Tresco Abbey Gardens

Image *Tresco Abbey Gardens*

Abbotsbury Subtropical Gardens

A GREAT JUNGLE OF RARE PLANTS THAT TAKES ADVANTAGE OF AN UNUSUAL MICROCLIMATE

Few gardens display such an extraordinary collection of exotic plants in such thrilling surroundings as Abbotsbury. The impression is of a benign jungle in which species from many of the world's subtropical climates flourish in splendid harmony. The microclimate here is unusual. On the Dorset coast, right by the Chesil bank, there is seldom any frost and old tree plantations provide good protection from the wind. The sea is very deep close to the shore and acts as a permanent storage heater, warding off the coldest temperatures. It also adds to the air humidity, giving the moisture needed for such plants as tree ferns. The rainfall is around 30in/75cm per annum, providing enough for the many Asiatic shrubs but not drowning plants from drier regions.

The land here came to the Strangways family after the dissolution of the monastic estates in 1541. In the 18th century a walled kitchen garden was built and, in the early 19th century, a woodland garden. William Fox-Strangways (1795–1865), the 4th Earl of Ilchester and a distinguished gentleman botanist, started the plant collection for which the gardens became famous. By the end of the 19th century well over 4,000 species were cultivated here. The gardens remain in the ownership of the Ilchester Estate, which maintains them to high standards and continues to introduce new plants.

MICROCLIMATES

The gardens, disposed on the gently undulating slopes of a valley, are irrigated by a stream which is dammed to form ornamental pools. Skilful use is made of different microclimates within the garden: a south-facing steeply pitched bank is filled with tender plants from the Mediterranean or from subtropical regions – cistuses, lavenders and myrtles from the Mediterranean; succulents from Mexico; leucadendrons and stately watsonias from South Africa. Down by the stream, in wooded shade, is a long walk of hydrangeas, one of the best groups of the giant *Gunnera manicata* in England, and beautifully grown tree ferns. The high canopy of countless mature trees and the larger shrubs also give protection to other plants. New plants are constantly being added – a pair of South American jelly palms (*Butia capitata*) flourish by the restaurant. Abbotsbury is a botanic garden of importance as well as a landscape of rare enchantment.

The water garden at Abbotsbury

INFORMATION

Location Abbotsbury, nr Weymouth DT3 4LA, Dorset; ½m W of Abbotsbury, 9m NW of Weymouth by B3157
Tel 01305 871412/871344
Fax 01305 871092
Email info@abbotsbury-tourism.co.uk
Owner Ilchester Estates
Open daily 10–5 (dusk in winter); closed 25 Dec
Area 30 acres/12 hectares

Antony House

GRAND FORMAL GARDENS, A HUMPHRY REPTON LANDSCAPE AND A BEAUTIFUL SETTING ON PLYMOUTH SOUND

Once seen, the ensemble of breathtakingly beautiful house – early 18th-century, built of silver Pentewan stone – and serene landscape is unlikely to be forgotten. Under Reginald Pole Carew in the late 18th century many changes took place, with much planting of new trees. Humphry Repton was consulted and produced a Red Book for Antony in 1792. Although not all his recommendations were adopted, his advice to remove the walled garden that lay directly in front of the north façade of the house and plant trees to form vistas running through woods led to the creation of the most memorable views today. Below the north terrace of the house a giant lawn is embellished with a single tree, a beautiful American black walnut (*Juglans nigra*) with a dramatically spreading crown. It is known that Reginald Pole Carew had seeds of trees from North America and this could have been planted by him. Far beyond the walnut, parkland slopes gently down to the Tamar estuary with openings in the woodland revealing glimpses of the shimmering water of the estuary and, to the east, the arches of the Tamar bridge.

Antony House from the woodland

FORMAL GARDENS

The gardens to the west of the house match the stately formality of the house. A conical fountain by William Pye echoes a gigantic cone of yew nearby, whose interior has been partly hollowed out to form a summerhouse. A broad turf walk is enclosed in castellated yew hedges, ending in a bench and two 18th-century statues in niches cut into the yew. To the south is a wonderful cork oak (*Quercus suber*) with deeply fissured bark and a magnificent crown. Cornwall is a great county for these cork oak trees and this is one of the best. A finely contrived knot garden of box and germander (*Teucrium lucidrys*) and a formal flower garden are enclosed in yew hedges. Scattered about the garden is a very large collection of daylilies – a National Collection of around 600 cultivars.

There is a plenty to admire in the garden at Antony but the things that particularly stick in the mind are the beautifully tailored yew hedges close to the house and the sight of the shimmering water of the Tamar at the end of the long tree-lined walks.

INFORMATION

Location Torpoint PL11 2QA, Cornwall; 5m W of Plymouth by Torpoint car ferry and A374
Tel 01752 812191
Email antony@nationaltrust.org.uk English
English Heritage Register Grade II*
Owner The National Trust
Open Apr to Oct, Tue, Wed, Thur and Bank Hol Mon (Jun to Aug, also Sun) 1.30–5.30
Area 25 acres/10 hectares

Antony Woodland Garden

A SECRET GARDEN OF TREES AND SHRUBS ENRICHED WITH MODERN SCULPTURES AND FINE VIEWS

The woodland garden immediately adjacent to Antony House gardens was established in separate ownership by the Carew Pole family. The entrance from the National Trust garden is low-key and charming – an inconspicuous gate with an honesty box opens onto a path fringed in summer with cow parsley and buttercups. This was the special preserve of Sir John Carew Pole who died in 1993 and started the woodland garden just before World War II, although his father, Sir Reginald, had already begun planting hybrid rhododendrons in this area.

Wildflowers and exotics in Antony Woodland Garden

In this woodland garden, exotics – especially camellias, outstanding magnolias and large numbers of rhododendrons – look marvellously at home, with waves of bluebells, wild garlic and wood anemones lapping at their feet in Spring. Old oaks and Scots pines form much of the background planting but many young plantings include, for example, sweet chestnut and flowering shrubs. *Michelia doltsopa*, a close relation of the magnolia, gives off its sweetly exotic scent in May. Everywhere there are good trees – Japanese maples, Gingko biloba, Himalayan birches, a cut-leafed walnut (*Juglans regia* 'Laciniata') and much else. Walks lead through the woods to the banks of the river Lynher with idyllic glimpses across to the castellated silhouette of Ince Castle. A curiosity here, in the western part of the garden, is an 18th-century bath house, partly open to the sky and filled with salt water from the tidal river Lynher.

Sir John's son, Richard, has continued to cherish the garden, and add to it. A rocky mount on Jupiter Point is now crowned with an upright slab of stone designed and lettered by Tom Perkins with the words "and still a garden by the water blows" on one side and "Remember John and Cynthia Carew Pole who loved the garden" on the other.

MODERN SCULPTURE

Below the mount, in a circle mown into the long grass, a mossy boulder is cut neatly into two, its inside faces carved with a maze-like pattern – the work of Peter Randall Page. Further round the coast is a graceful sweep of curved bronze by Eilis O'Connell. The charm of this woodland garden lies in its essentially wild character, while the occasional sculpture, distant views of the great house and walks along the very edge of the water make it an altogether delightful place.

INFORMATION

Location Torpoint PL11 2QA, Cornwall; 5m W of Plymouth by Torpoint car ferry and A374
English Heritage Register Grade II*
Owner Carew Pole Garden Trust
Open Mar to Oct, Tues to Thurs, Sat and Sun (open Bank Hol Mon) 11–5.30
Area 100 acres/40 hectares

Arlington Court

A VICTORIAN FLOWER GARDEN AND GREENHOUSE, AND A WOODLAND WALK TO A MYSTERIOUS LAKE

Arlington Court is not a place for horticultural hijinks but it does possess the memorably harmonious character of a well-run and delightful estate. The house was built between 1820 and 1823, to the designs of Thomas Lee, for Colonel John Palmer Chichester whose family had lived here since the 16th century. There is no evidence of early gardens here.

The Victorian garden with its terraced lawns to the east of the house has all the character of its period. A splendid pair of cast-iron herons with worms wriggling in their beaks – the crest of the Chichester family – flank the steps, and the roof of a glasshouse is again crowned with the Chichester heron. Double borders on each side of the glasshouse include vigorous thickets of the unusual *Cautleya spicata* 'Robusta', a member of the ginger family, with maroon and yellow flowers in late summer. Below the glasshouse a pool with a fountain is flanked by arbours garlanded with roses and honeysuckle; young monkey puzzles – that archetypal mid-Victorian tree – stand on either side. Beds enclosed in metalwork edging (Hardenberg baskets) are planted with bedding schemes of annuals.

ROSALIE CHICHESTER

The parish church of St James lies within the grounds of Arlington Park and is worth visiting for the Chichester memorials – especially a charming plaque to Miss Rosalie Chichester (who died in 1949) decorated with ferns and shells and designed by John Piper. It was she who was responsible for the quirky collections of ships, shells, pewter and so forth still preserved in the house. That has nothing to do with gardening but it does bring to mind the continuity of ownership and careful stewardship that enabled places like Arlington Court to flourish and survive.

In the wooded valley at some distance to the west of the house a lake was created in 1850 by damming the river Yeo. At this time, too, there was a plan to create a new entrance drive which would have swept across the lake on a great bridge. Only the stone piers were completed and they remain, gaunt and forlorn, by the banks of the lakes. Nearby is a neo-classical urn, with an inscription by Reynolds Stone, erected in memory of Rosalie Chichester – an atmospheric arcadian scene.

The Victorian garden at Arlington

INFORMATION

Location Arlington, nr Barnstaple EX31 4LP, Devon; 7m NE of Barnstaple by A39
Tel 01271 850296 **Fax** 01271 850711
English Heritage Register Grade II*
Owner The National Trust
Open mid March to June, Sept to Oct, daily except Sat 10.30–5; Jul to Aug, daily 10.30–5
Area 25 acres/10 hectares

Athelhampton House Gardens

A MASTERPIECE OF ARTS AND CRAFTS DESIGN – MAGNIFICENT TOPIARY, WALLED ENCLOSURES AND SUPERB STONEWORK

The garden at Athelhampton is one of the most beautiful examples of the English architectural garden. The house, dating from the late middle ages, was substantially rebuilt in the 16th and 17th centuries, although it still has enough of its original charm for Pevsner to describe it as "the *beau idéal* of the late medieval manor house". Nothing is known about earlier gardens on the site but Alfred Cart de Lafontaine commissioned the architect Francis Inigo Thomas to lay out new gardens between 1891 and 1893. Inigo Thomas created a beguiling sequence of enclosed spaces in which architectural ornament made the use of plants almost superfluous. What he designed took its cue, as is the case with all successful garden designs, from the character of the house as well as its setting in the landscape.

WALLED ENCLOSURES

At the heart of the garden is the Corona, a circular walled enclosure with a parapet of gracefully sweeping curves separated by slender obelisks.

The Corona at Athelhampton House

Curved beds run along the walls planted in blues, purples and whites. A pool at its centre has an urn and a water jet, and decorative stone piers flank wrought-iron gates which lead into other enclosures. The Great Court with its twelve unforgettable pyramids of clipped yew, rising over 35ft/10m high, is overlooked by a raised walk with stone balustrades and dashing summerhouses – the effect is at once serene and dramatic. The restraint of a slender lily pool running arrow-straight from the east façade of the house is spectacularly enlivened by a superlative old cedar of Lebanon spreading over the garden walls. In Inigo Thomas's last enclosure, east of the Corona, a fountain and pool are embraced by a moss-nibbled Gothic niche. Here there was originally a chaste parterre, but the enclosure now overflows with boisterous modern plantings of tender exotics.

Further gardens have since been added to Inigo Thomas's design but, alas, they seem incoherent and clumsy by comparison and bear little relevance to the site. In any other context their merits might have shone, but here they cannot compete with the well-conceived pattern of Inigo Thomas's layout and the beautiful execution of its detail. Athelhampton is a model of its kind, a garden that causes visiting gardeners to resolve to create light and order in their own muddled plots at home.

INFORMATION

Location Athelhampton DT2 7LG, Dorset; 5m NE of Dorchester on A35
Tel 01305 848363
Email enquiry@athelhampton.co.uk
English Heritage Register Grade I
Owner Patrick Cooke
Open Mar to Oct, Sun to Thurs 10.30–5; Nov to Feb, Sun 10.30–5
Area 15 acres/6 hectares

Barrington Court

A GRAND TUDOR HOUSE WITH DECORATIVE EARLY 20TH-CENTURY GARDENS INFLUENCED BY GERTRUDE JEKYLL

The great house at Barrington and its splendid outhouses are a handsome mixture of Tudor, 17th-century and early 20th-century Arts and Crafts architecture. The estate seems to have been bought from the Daubeney family in 1552 by William Clifton who built the splendid house we can see today. But the garden is almost entirely 20th-century, made after Colonel Lyle took a tenancy of the ruinous house from the National Trust in 1920.

Barrington Court from the park

FORBES AND JEKYLL

Lyle recruited the architect J.E. Forbes to restore the house and its fine outhouses and it is his work that has had the greatest influence on the character of the garden. Gertrude Jekyll was asked to advise on the planting but did not visit the site and worked only from Forbes's plans.

Traces of Jekyll's style of planting survive (such as the use of bergenias as emphatic structural plants) but, it must be said, not much of her spirit. In the walled Lily Garden she had specified banks of hydrangeas in raised beds flanking the long sides of the scalloped lily pond – azaleas have taken their place. For the corners she chose a favourite plant of emphatic architectural form, *Yucca gloriosa* – these now have clumps of pink *Crinum* x *powellii*. In 2007 a garish spring combination of orange-red tulips and yellow, purple and orange wallflowers exploded at each end of the pool, while deep beds that surround the garden had a vigorous colour scheme of yellow and red – all very jolly, but is it Jekyll?

Alongside the walled garden a formal rose garden with modern bedding varieties is partly enclosed by a humped hedge of box; and nearby, spreading its branches expansively over the old calf-pens, is the most beautiful plant in the garden, a majestic old ash. Another beauty of the garden is the pattern of virtuoso paths of narrow bricks laid in endlessly inventive patterns, now basket-weave, now herringbone, and always beautifully cambered to shed water. The most intricate one runs south of the house, with intermingled patterns of wonderful virtuosity. Here, an open expanse of lawn, with a scattering of old oaks, gives one of the best views at Barrington, back to the great house, with its gables, barley-sugar chimney stacks and finials, looking serenely outwards over lovely parkland.

INFORMATION

Location Barrington, nr Ilminster TA19 0NQ, Somerset; 5m NE of Ilminster off A303
Tel 01460 241938
Email barringtoncourt@nationaltrust.org.uk
English Heritage Register Grade II*
Owner The National Trust
Open Mar to Oct, daily except Wed, phone for times; 1 Dec to mid Dec, Sat and Sun 11–4
Area 9 acres/3.6 hectares

Bath Botanical Gardens

IN THE CENTRE OF GEORGIAN BATH, AN EXCELLENT, WELL MAINTAINED COLLECTION OF PLANTS IN A FINE SETTING

As soon as you enter the Bath Botanical Gardens from the south-western gate you see splendid trees – a huge pendent silver lime (*Tilia petiolaris*), an elegant *Cornus controversa* 'Variegata' and a wide-spreading golden catalpa (*Catalpa bignonioides* 'Aurea'). They give an immediate foretaste of the character of these exceptionally attractive public gardens, laid out in 1840 to form an extension to the Royal Victoria Park.

The site slopes gently southwards and is enlivened by a serpentine pool and stream. There are many fine trees, some of them rare (such as the Chinese *Catalpa fargesii f. duclouxii* with spectacular pink flowers) and some of them especially fine specimens of less rare plants – among them several beautiful, and venerable, magnolias and an outstanding *Cornus kousa* var. *chinensis*. Much of the planting is attractively informal, of which an exceptional example is the meadow planting beneath old Japanese maples by the rock garden. Here in spring is an enchanting sight – wood anemones, bluebells, scillas and snake's head fritillaries growing in marvellous profusion. Although there are polite, and more or less conventional borders, much use is made of species roses which also give a touch of wildness.

A 19th-century urn in Bath Botanical Gardens

THE DELL GARDEN

On the northern side of the garden, separated by the Royal Victoria Park carriage drive and on the site of a former quarry, is a garden of different character: the Dell garden, shaded by lugubrious conifers. In an atmospheric clearing, a memorial to Shakespeare, placed here in 1864 to celebrate the tercentenary of his birth, is in the shape of a Roman votive altar. Hidden away, is a monument of an altogether more extravagant kind: John Osborne's statue of Jupiter (1839), a fierce and boldly modelled head mounted on a very tall plinth, rivalling the trees for height.

The gardens are one of the few public parks still maintained by the municipality, rather than by the cheapest available contractor, and look all the better for it. They perfectly fulfil their two functions of providing an agreeable place in which to do nothing and displaying a wonderful collection of often unfamiliar plants for the delectation and education of gardeners. Until I came here I had never seen the beautiful slender *Malus trilobata* with its distinguished grey three-lobed leaves, white flowers and shapely but compact presence – the perfect ornamental tree for a garden of modest size.

INFORMATION

Location Royal Victoria Park, Upper Bristol Road, Bath BA1 2NQ, Somerset; W of city centre by Upper Bristol Road
English Heritage Register Grade II
Owner City of Bath
Open daily 9–sunset
Area 3 acres/1.2 hectares

Bicton College of Agriculture

OUTSTANDING TREES, TENDER SHRUBS, SALVIAS AND SUPERB COLLECTIONS OF AGAPANTHUS AND PITTOSPORUMS

This is the other surviving part of Bicton Park (*see page 24*). Bicton College is a college of agriculture and horticulture and although there is little garden design to be seen there are many memorable plants and occasional good planting. The park entrance starts off with a splendid Victorian trumpet-blast, not to everyone's taste: an avenue of monkey puzzles lining the upper part of the drive. This avenue was planted in 1843–44 under the supervision of the famous Exeter nurseryman James Veitch and J.C. Loudon, the greatest garden writer and expert of his day.

EXCEPTIONAL TREES

Parkland on either side, with grazing cattle or sheep, has many exceptional trees – among them superb examples of a local tree *Quercus x lucombeana* 'William Lucombe', named after the man who started the nursery of Lucombe & Plince in Exeter in 1720 and who spotted a chance seedling of a hybrid of the Turkey oak (*Q. cerris*) and the cork oak (*Q. suber*). There are immense tulip trees (*Liriodendron tulipifera*) with giant

gnarled stems and some beautiful common limes (*Tilia x europaea*).

At the head of the drive the house, built in 1800 by James Wyatt but rebuilt in dapper Edwardian style by Sir Walter Tapper in 1908 and 1909, faces south over land that slopes gently down across the tree-studded park to a lake fringed with fine trees, and the old pinetum on the far bank. To one side of the house are the college's walled gardens, glasshouses and a small nursery with some good plants. A large garden spread out in front of a glasshouse has island beds with bedding roses and annual bedding schemes. It also has an astonishing thicket of agapanthus with tufts of *Eucomis comosa* thrusting through. Bicton College keeps National Collections of agapanthus (90 species and cultivars) and pittosporum (70 species and cultivars). Two beds of ornamental grasses also have attractive combinations of plants. The walled Yard Garden is lined with deep mixed borders of tender plants such as *Michelia doltsopa* and dozens of species of salvias, few of which would survive a winter in most English gardens. In the car park you will see a magnificent Lucombe oak and as you leave you will inevitably stop to admire the majestic trees on either side of the drive.

Agapanthus and grasses at Bicton College

INFORMATION

Location East Budleigh, Budleigh Salterton EX9 7DP, Devon; 6m NE of Exmouth by A376
Tel 01395 562427
Email enquiries@bicton.ac.uk
Website www.bicton.ac.uk
English Heritage Register Grade I
Owner Bicton College
Open daily 10–4.30
Area 19 acres/7.7 hectares

Bicton Park Gardens

18TH-CENTURY FORMAL GARDENS, VICTORIAN EXUBERANCE AND A WONDERFUL EARLY GLASSHOUSE

Great gardens survive by different means. In the case of the ancient Bicton Park estate it has meant that the two major parts of the garden have gone their separate ways (the other half now belongs to Bicton College). This was the estate of the ancient Rolle family who came by it in the early 17th century by marriage to a Dennys heiress. Two Rolles played a vital role in the evolution of the gardens here: Henry, the 1st Lord Rolle, who laid out the Italian Gardens in about 1735, and his nephew, John, who was responsible for the great garden works, especially tree planting, that took place in the first half of the 19th century. The family died out and in 1935 Bicton Park became a girls' school. In 1957 the estate was dismembered and the chief part of the garden now belongs to Simon Lister and is run very much as a tourist attraction, with a miniature railway running through the woods. If this is the only means by which a great garden may survive in some form, then who can complain?

The Italian Garden at the heart of Bicton is partly walled on three sides and slopes gently downhill, with a pedimented stone conservatory, flanked by glasshouses, following the curve of the wall at the top. It is a jolly Victorian scene – two fountain pools surrounded by many small beds cut into a lawn and filled with silver *Senecio cineraria*, scarlet pelargoniums, mop-headed marigolds and rich purple verbenas. At the foot of the hill are the remains of the 1st Lord Rolle's formal gardens. Rumour, but no more than that, has attached the name of André Le Nôtre to this scheme – but he died in 1700. Here, a handsome rectangular pool has a great tiered fountain spouting a plume of three jets high into the air, and a curious amphitheatre-like shape cut into the turf banks with, aligned on it, a distant obelisk revealed in a gap between trees. Empty plinths surround the pool where in the recent past there had been some fine statues. There are other exceptionally attractive and unusual features in the garden. To the east are the

The Palm House at Bicton

Shell House and American garden. The Shell House, dating from about 1840, is a hermitage-like stubby tower fashioned of roughly shaped lumps of flinty stone; stones line the paths and the interior has a display of exotic shells arranged on shelves lining the wall. An American Garden was made in about 1832 during the time when Robert Glendinning was head gardener, and it is one of the few surviving examples of a type of garden that was fashionable in the second half of the 18th century when new North American plants were coming to England in increasing numbers. A few American trees can still be seen: *Catalpa bignonioides*, tulip tree (*Liriodendron tulipifera*), tupelo (*Nyssa sylvatica*) and Wellingtonia.

THE GREAT PALM HOUSE

Above the Italian Garden is a garden building so beautiful that it alone would have made Bicton famous: the Palm House is one of the earliest surviving glasshouses in the country, dating from around 1820. Built against a wall and three-lobed in shape, it has a framework of cast-iron with very thin glazing bars and overlapping fish-scale glass panes. Restored in 1985, it is in marvellous condition and houses a collection of palms, with a particularly shapely date palm (*Phoenix dactylifera*) occupying the central area.

THE PINETUM

The Pinetum was started in around 1839 under Robert Glendinning's surpervision, with the help of J.C. Loudon, and although the storm of 1990 destroyed many trees, what remains is remarkable – a huge collection of conifers, one of the most atmospheric in the country, with countless fine specimens, many of them rare. Beyond is the Hermitage, an octagonal rustic summerhouse dating from 1839 with, as Barbara Jones records in her *Follies & Grottoes* (1974), "a knucklebone floor and an uncommon basketwork lining nicely free of the spiders and earwigs that usually attend the rustic style". There is much to relish at Bicton, with or without miniature railways.

INFORMATION

Location East Budleigh, Budleigh Salterton EX9 7BJ, Devon; 6m NE of Exmouth by A376
Tel 01395 568465
Email valerie@bictongardens.co.uk
English Heritage Register Grade I
Owner Simon Lister
Open daily (except 25 and 26 December) 10–6 (closes 5 in winter)
Area 50 acres/20 hectares

Caerhays Castle

EXTRAVAGANTLY PICTURESQUE CASTLE, MARVELLOUSLY SITED,
WITH ONE OF THE FINEST PLANT COLLECTIONS IN CORNWALL

The castle at Caerhays is the work of John Nash and was built between 1805 and 1807 for the Trevanion family who bankrupted themselves in the process. It fits into its already dramatic landscape to perfection – a low-lying castellated mansion with splendid trees crowding all about except on the slopes below it where there are unimpeded views southwards down the wide valley to Porthluney Bay. Humphry Repton, who sometimes worked with Nash, is rumoured to have had a hand in the shaping of the landscape here, but there is no record of it. He would certainly have loved it – but could he have added to its beauties?

Wild garlic and azaleas at Caerhays

ASIATIC SHRUBS

The estate was bought in 1854 by Michael Williams II, a Cornish mine-owner, whose grandson, John Charles Williams, established Caerhays as an outstanding plantsman's garden. He was a subscriber to several great plant-hunting expeditions, in particular those of George Forrest, Reginald Farrer, Frank Kingdon Ward and E.H. Wilson. Through them, vast numbers of rhododendrons, magnolias, and camellias made their way to Caerhays. By 1917, for example, there were 264 species and wild varieties of rhododendron in cultivation here. J.C. Williams's name is commemorated in the beautiful *Rhododendron williamsianum* and also in hybrid camellias, *C. x williamsii*. J.C., as he was known, also took a great interest in exotic trees and built up collections of southern hemisphere Nothofagus and Asian Lithocarpus. Exceptional old specimens of many trees survive in the garden, including several so-called "champions", the largest known examples of their species in the country.

For the plant lover the great attraction of Caerhays is the very large number of Asiatic flowering shrubs, often venerable and beautiful specimens of the earliest introductions to European gardens, but for those who just enjoy beautiful landscape the pleasures are no less intense. There is, in truth, little design at Caerhays, and nothing as obvious as the contrived plant associations, least of all the studious colour combinations, of tamer gardens. One of the charms of Caerhays is the intermingling of native plants, among them exceptional old beeches and great waves of bluebells and wild garlic, with rare exotics. The landscape is marvellous too, and when a milky-white sea mist rolls in off the bay you could easily imagine yourself on an expedition with Frank Kingdon Ward in the Himalayan foothills.

INFORMATION

Location nr Gorran FA1 7DE, Cornwall; in Caerhays village, 10m S of St Austell by minor roads
Tel 01872 501310
Email estateoffice@caerhays.co.uk
Website www.caerhays.co.uk
English Heritage Register Grade II*
Owner F.J. Williams
Open mid Feb to early June, daily 10–5
Area 100 acres/40 hectares

Castle Drogo

DRAMATIC EARLY 20TH-CENTURY CASTLE BY EDWIN LUTYENS, ADORNED WITH A FINE FLOWER GARDEN

No 20th-century country house in England has such striking presence in its landscape as Castle Drogo. Sir Edwin Lutyens designed it for Julius Drewe and it was built in 1910–30. The great granite house dominates a bluff overlooking the Teign valley on the edge of Dartmoor. Its resemblance to some early medieval fortress is made more cheerful by high, intricate stone-mullioned windows. Drewe wanted to keep the approach to his castle informal and unfussy. The winding drive passes between ramparts of clipped yew and a grove of holm oaks (*Quercus ilex*), and Gertrude Jekyll advised on a naturalistic planting scheme of birch, blackthorn, holly, Scots pine and wild roses here.

The garden is quite detached from the castle, against the wishes of Lutyens who had wanted it firmly related to the house. In the 1920s a garden of formal character with a Lutyens flavour but unrelated to the castle was eventually made by George Dillestone of Tunbridge Wells. Hidden behind walls of yew north-east of the house, it is an admirable design with two sharply contrasting enclosures. The first is a vast sunken garden of subtly contrived changes of level. In each corner *Parrotia persica* is trained to form a spacious leafy arbour – especially beautiful in early spring with the extraordinary scarlet stamens of its flowers, and in autumn the crimson and gold of its foliage. In the shade of the parrotias, beds of ferns are edged with the gleaming foliage of *Asarum europaeum*. Two central lawns are surrounded by terraces flanked by mixed borders, between which scalloped paths of Mughal influence thread their way, with beds of modern roses running round the lawns. In late spring a vast, beautifully trained wisteria snakes along the crest of a retaining wall.

A CIRCULAR LAWN

A path between a walk with azaleas, enkianthus, magnolias and Japanese maples leads to the second enclosure, one of Lutyens's most marvellous garden conceits. A high yew hedge encloses a circular lawn, 150ft/45m in diameter, originally a tennis court but now used for croquet. The deep green drum of yew surrounding the pale green of fine turf has an aura of mystery and splendour, like the temple of some forgotten religion.

Changing levels at Castle Drogo

INFORMATION

Location Drewsteignton EX6 6PB, Devon; 21m W of Exeter by A30

Tel 01647 433306

Email castledrogo@ nationaltrust.org.uk

English Heritage Register Grade II*

Owner The National Trust

Open mid Mar to 4 Nov daily 10.30–5.30 (or dusk); phone for out of season openings

Area 12 acres/4.8 hectares

Castle Hill

A MAGNIFICENT 18TH-CENTURY LANDSCAPE ON THE GRAND SCALE WITH MARVELLOUS WOODLAND PLANTING

The view of Castle Hill as it is approached by road is one of the most memorable and attractive in south-west England. The long, low creamy-yellow house topped with green domes lies on rising land. Behind the house wooded parkland spreads uphill to an 18th-century castellated Gothic mock castle. Immediately in front of the house are terraces enlivened with columns of clipped yew, stone urns and stone sphinxes. Below the terraces a river snakes across meadows. The Fortescue family (of which Lady Arran is a member) came to live here in the early 18th century, built the house and laid out a giant landscape park animated with ornamental buildings.

WOODLAND PLANTING

A much later addition is the woodland planting to the north-west of the house. Here, a picturesque stream flows down a valley decorated with a rustic temple and an even more rustic stone arched bridge – Ugley Bridge – with camellias, rhododendrons and magnolias along its banks. The steep eastern slope is richly clad in trees and flowering shrubs (in particular many fine magnolias)

Water sculpture by Giles Rayner

splendidly underplanted with sheets of daffodils followed by bluebells. Paths rise through the woods to the gothic castle flanked with holm oaks (*Quercus ilex*) and guarded by a row of cannons pointing southwards across the river valley with a grand view of the Triumphal Arch on the far horizon. Walking back down the precipitous hill of the woodland garden in spring, delicious views of flowering shrubs are seen between the trunks of leafless trees, with the stream shimmering below.

It is the setting of Castle Hill in its superb parkland, and the beauty of the woodland garden, that are the great garden features here – both are outstanding. A new garden close to the entrance was laid out to celebrate the millennium. This, designed by Xa Tollemache, intermingles formality – lollipops of clipped holm oak, hedges of laurustinus and *Osmanthus* x *burkwoodii* – with lively herbaceous borders. However, it scarcely suits the sobriety and nobility of its ancient surroundings nor does it seem to form a suitable entrance for visitors. On the other hand, no doubt, in summer it gives floriferous colour when the sublime drama of the woodland garden is no longer in action.

INFORMATION

Location Filleigh, nr Barnstaple EX32 0RH, Devon; 6m SE of Barnstaple off A361

Tel 01598 760421

Email ladyarran@castlehill-devon.com

Website www.castlehilldevon.co.uk

English Heritage Register Grade I

Owner The Earl and Countess of Arran

Open Feb to Sept, daily except Sat 11–5

Area c.617 acres/250 hectares

Chiffchaffs

THE ESSENTIAL COTTAGE GARDEN, WITH BEAUTIFULLY KEPT FLOWER GARDEN AND WOODLAND GARDEN OF CHARACTER

The idea of the cottage garden may be interpreted in many different ways; its commonest use is as a licence for more or less amiable chaos. The Potts came here in 1977 and although their charming house is undeniably a cottage their garden is as unchaotic as could be. Everything is bursting with vigour and the garden is impeccably maintained – you will search in vain for a weed.

The cherry avenue at Chiffchaffs

In the month of April you will be greeted by the exhilarating fanfare of an avenue of Japanese cherries in full flower – the lovely white *Prunus* 'Shirotae' and a single rogue pink-flowered *P. sargentii*. The gardens about the house fill a gently south-west facing slope with an irrepressible array of plants and carefully made enclosures. The slope is terraced, with stone retaining walls and a network of paved or gravel paths. A crescent of lawn is embraced by mixed borders in which the smaller conifers jostle with azaleas (and other small rhododendrons), roses and viburnums –all lavishly underplanted for spring and summer.

SKILFUL USE OF SPACE

Although the area is relatively small the planting is skilfully orchestrated with bold use of trees and shrubs to create a landscape that seems much larger than it is and in which nothing is out of place. The keen visitor will soon notice that every corner must be scrutinised. A stepped pool in a shady corner is planted about with snake's head fritillaries and bloodroot (*Sanguinaria canadensis*). There are elaborately clipped yew hedges, and at the top of

the garden, a pergola of clematis and roses leads to a little kitchen garden that is charmingly hidden away in a corner.

At a little distance from the house – the walk is delightful – is a woodland garden where paths running along the upper contours look down on magnolias and rhododendrons underplanted with drifts of narcissi, primulas and shuttlecock ferns. The slopes are punctuated with ornamental trees and shrubs – camellias, cherries, pieris and many maples – while beautiful old oaks, a great ornament of the landscape in these parts, rise imperturbably above. Kenneth Potts's nursery, Abbey Plants, sells a wide range of plants almost entirely propagated on the premises.

INFORMATION

Location Chaffeymoor, Bourton, nr Gillingham SP8 5BY, Dorset; at W end of Bourton village, 3m E of Wincanton off A303
Tel 01747 840841
Owner Mr and Mrs K.R. Potts
Open Apr to Oct, Wed and Thur (and on other days for the NGS) 2–5
Area 11 acres/4.5 hectares

Claverton Manor

A RARE GARDEN OF AMERICAN FLAVOUR FOR A GEORGIAN MANSION THAT HOUSES THE AMERICAN MUSEUM IN BRITAIN

The old manor at Claverton was built in about 1580 at the centre of an elaborate terraced garden and close to the church. The terraces remain, still with some of the garden walls, intricate stone balustrades and old gate piers capped with openwork obelisks, but the house was demolished in 1820 and an entirely new Bath stone mansion was built for John Vivian to Sir Jeffry Wyatville's design. It occupies a fine position on raised ground with broad views across the Avon valley.

The Mount Vernon Garden at Claverton

AN AMERICAN FLAVOUR

There had been 19th-century pleasure grounds about the house, and good trees along the drive survive from this time, but the gardens took on an entirely new life in 1961 when the estate was acquired as the American Museum in Britain. The new garden was given a pronounced American flavour, and an arboretum of North American trees and shrubs is a vivid reminder to British gardeners of the debt owed to America. Close to the house is a collection of medicinal, culinary and dying herbs used in colonial times, with a straw-covered bee skep at the centre. The walls of the house are garlanded with excellent roses, among them 'Climbing Mrs Herbert Stevens', 'Zéphirine Drouhin' and the exquisite pale apricot 'Climbing Lady Hillingdon', all seen to perfection against honey-coloured Bath stone. A fine mixed border, against high terrace walls, was designed by the American garden designer Lanning Roper. Here, tall clipped Irish yews trained hard against the walls rise like

pilasters to the parapet high above, whose stone urns seem to crown them. Beyond the house a curious little 19th-century Dutch summer house looks across the valley. At a lower level, a copy of part of George Washington's garden at Mount Vernon has a parterre-like arrangement of box- or brick-edged beds. Shrub roses fill some of the beds, and herbaceous plants, many of them American, fill the others, with domes of clipped *Prunus glandulosa* soaring above. A facsimile of a Washingtonian octagonal pavilion with pepper-pot roof mounts guard in a corner, and a white-painted paling fence encloses two sides of the garden.

INFORMATION

Location Claverton, nr Bath BA2 7BD, Somerset 4m SE of Bath by A36
Tel 01225 460503
Fax 01225 480726
Email info@americanmuseum.org
Website www.americanmuseum.org
English Heritage Register Grade II
Owner The American Museum in Britain
Open end Mar to early Nov, daily except Mon 1–6 (Sat and Sun 12–6; Bank Hol Sun and Mon 11–6)
Area 10 acres/4 hectares

Coleton Fishacre Garden

REMOTE AND IRRESISTIBLE, A VALLEY GARDEN IN A HIDDEN CORNER OF DEVON, WITH EXCELLENT PLANTS

Coleton Fishacre has a remote feel to it, isolated at the tip of a promontory with the river Dart to the west and the sea to the south and east. It sits in a shallow valley which runs down to the sea at Pudcombe Cove, and a stream flowing through it is dammed from time to time to form pools. The soil is acid, the rainfall around 40in/100cm per annum and the coastal position creates a very mild microclimate. The handsome stone Arts and Crafts house, built in 1926 for Rupert D'Oyly Carte to the designs of Oswald Milne, faces down the valley. The design for the layout of the garden, but probably not the planting, was the work of Edward White of the firm Milner White.

TENDER PLANTS

Terracing on the south side of the house makes an especially protected site for such tender shrubs as *Beschorneria yuccoides*, the autumn-flowering *Camellia sasanqua*, the rare banana-scented Chinese *Michelia figo*, and other exotic things that need cosseting. The house itself on this side is shrouded in tender exotics, and the little walled Rill Garden also provides shelter for tender plants.

Paths run down the valley on either side of the stream, edged with notable and often rare plants. Here are excellent trees – a noble tulip tree (*Liriodendron tulipifera*), *Metasequoia glyptostroboides*, *Ailanthus altissima* and many Japanese maples. Appropriate planting continues along the banks of the stream – bamboos, ferns, *Gunnera manicata*, hostas and rheum. If you love plants – and it would be madness to come here if you do not – you will want to walk slowly along each path, with the National Trust plant list in hand. Spring is the prime season, with rhododendrons filling the air with scent and providing shamelessly glamorous blossom, but any season has its beauties of one kind or another. At the foot of the valley a gate leads into wild woodland that gives out onto a narrow coastal path with a vertiginous view of Pudcome Cove, the definitive smuggler's hideaway. When you have had your fill of the garden you may walk up the hill to the Gazebo, from which there are lovely views to the sea and the sinister Eastern Black Rock.

The Rill Garden at Coleton Fishacre

INFORMATION

Location Coleton, Kingswear, Dartmouth TQ6 0EQ, Devon; 4m S of Brixham off B3205
Tel 01803 752466
Email coletonfishacre@ntrust.org.uk
English Heritage Register Grade II*
Owner The National Trust
Open mid Mar to Oct, Wed to Sun (open Bank Hol Mon) 10.30–5
Area 20 acres/8 hectares

Compton Acres

A CLIFFTOP COLLECTION OF THEMED GARDENS, ALL VERY DIFFERENT, CARRIED OUT WITH PANACHE

A dizzying anthology of garden styles clinging to the cliffs on the Dorset coast sounds an alarming prospect. The experience of visiting Compton Acres is, however, simultaneously soothing, exhilarating and, just occasionally, wince-making. Thomas William Simpson came here just after World War I, built a new house and started a garden in which ingredients of very different periods and types would be linked together with a walk that ambled along the contours of the slopes. When he started work the coast was less built up than it is now and the site offered marvellous gardening possibilities.

VARYING AUTHENTICITY

During World War II the garden fell into neglect but is now well cared for and has for many years opened as a self-contained tourist attraction. Several new features have been added since Simpson's time, some of them in keeping with the spirit of the place and

others (a deer sanctuary?) rather less so. The features also vary in their authenticity: for example, the Roman Garden dazzles the eye with wildly inauthentic bedding plants while the Japanese Garden is wholly convincing. Built by Japanese craftsmen in 1920, its setting is a rocky valley with a cascade and tall stone pagoda at its head and a backdrop of largely coniferous planting. A scarlet teahouse, clasped by wisterias, stands at the side of a pool ornamented with bronze cranes and snow lanterns. The Italian Garden has a long lily pool and fountains with a temple, mounds of golden yew, statues and ornaments, gravel walks and summer and winter bedding schemes. Not authentically Italian but on a summer's evening when the light is low and the fountains are playing, it has a very agreeable effect.

There is good planting throughout the garden, with plants chosen for their site. Several species of eucalyptus decorate sun-baked slopes, and hydrangeas and rhododendron relish the shade of fine trees. The spirit evoked by Compton Acres seems to me to be that of the lively public-minded municipal park of Victorian times. There is plenty to see, you can sit on a bench at a viewpoint and eat an ice-cream; or, notebook and occasionally binoculars in hand, you can get down to some serious plant-spotting.

The Japanese Garden at Compton Acres

INFORMATION

Location Canford Cliffs Road, Poole BH13 7ES, Dorset; 1½m W of Bournemouth by A35 and B3065
Tel 01202 700778
Email events@comptonacres.co.uk
Website www.comptonacres.co.uk
English Heritage Register Grade II*
Owner Bernard Merna
Open Mar to Oct, daily 9–6; Nov to Feb, daily 10–4
Area 10 acres/4 hectares

Cotehele

THE ANCIENT ESTATE OF THE EDGCUMBES IN LOVELY CORNISH COUNTRYSIDE, WITH RICHLY ATMOSPHERIC GARDENS

The wooded country of the upper reaches of the river Tamar is one of the most beautiful parts of Cornwall and Devon. This is the lovely setting for the marvellously romantic Cotehele House where the Edgcumbe family lived from 1353. When the Edgcumbes moved to their grander estate at Mount Edgcumbe (*see page 58*) in 1553, Cotehele was left to potter on as a secondary residence, which it remained until the 6th Earl of Mount Edgcumbe handed over the estate to the National Trust in 1947.

Spring in the woodland garden at Cotehele

It seems that there was never much ornamental gardening at Cotehele though it was famous for its ancient trees. When the National Trust took over the garden, these fine old trees were the chief ornament of the estate and most of the interesting planting has been made since 1947.

FINE CLIMBING PLANTS

The grey granite walls of the house and outhouses give protection for several fine climbing plants – among them the beautiful Macartney rose (*Rosa bracteata*) and the tender pale yellow *Jasminum mesnyi*. In the upper garden, on the slopes above the house, are beautifully detailed high yew hedges, with fine topiary. A square pool is overhung with the unusual ash *Fraxinus excelsior* 'Jaspidea' whose foliage in early spring and in autumn is butter yellow. Here, too, is a handsome tulip tree (*Liriodendron tulipifera*), grass bright in spring with daffodils, and a mixed border running along the boundary wall.

On the far side of the house the sloping ground has been terraced and is embellished with beautiful magnolias. At the foot of the terraced garden a hidden passage leads under the road to a surprise – a woodland garden studded with fine trees and shrubs (camellias, enkianthus, hoherias, hydrangeas and maples) which runs down to the banks of the Tamar. A rare domed dovecote with a stone-tiled roof looms above a pool with azaleas, flowering cherries and rich red tree rhododendrons (*R. arboreum*). At the bottom of the garden a path leads to the family chapel of Saints George and Thomas à Becket.

The garden at Cotehele, with its lovely ancient setting, is one of intermittent but very definite pleasures rather than a blindingly revelatory horticultural experience. But who wants blinding revelations every day?

INFORMATION

Location St Dominick, nr Saltash PL12 6TA, Cornwall; 8m SW of Tavistock off A390
Infoline 01579 352739 **Tel** 01579 351346
Email cotehele@nationaltrust.org.uk
English Heritage Register Grade II
Owner The National Trust
Open daily 10.30–dusk
Area 11 acres/4.4 hectares

Cothay Manor

BEAUTIFUL MEDIEVAL HOUSE WITH RESTORED 20TH-CENTURY GARDEN OF COMPARTMENTS WITH EXCELLENT PLANTING

The manor at Cothay is a rare house, remarkably complete and unchanged from the late 15th century, and well cared for. Its rural setting is exceedingly beautiful – a countryside of high hedgerows, narrow lanes and rolling pasture land. Between the wars Colonel Reginald Cooper lived here. He was a brilliant garden designer, a friend and confidant of Lawrence Johnston at Hidcote and of Harold Nicolson at Sissinghurst Castle. At Cothay he laid out a long yew walk running parallel to the western façade of the house and linking various hedged enclosures, one of which is an unusual and striking box parterre.

When the present owners came here in 1993 the garden needed much revitalisation; this they have provided with great energy and, above all, a real feeling for the horticultural spirit of the place. They have restored Cooper's magnificent yew hedges and filled the garden with planting of beauty and distinction. Mary-Anne Robb is a knowledgeable plantswoman and she and her husband, Alastair, are accomplished practical gardeners. A striking quality of the planting is the way in which it is sensitively deployed in different contexts. The gatehouse, for example, a bold, castellated building like the entrance to an Oxford or Cambridge college, is swathed in *Vitis coignetiae* whose huge heart-shaped leaves tumble down to intermingle with *Magnolia grandiflora*, and is flanked with *Ampelopsis glandulosa* var. *brevipedunculata* whose jewel-like fruit in autumn are as brilliant as medieval stained glass. Within the entrance courtyard the planting is restricted to apricot, red and yellow, with *Campsis radicans* garlanding the wall. Below the western windows of the house a sea of *Erigeron karvinskianus*,

The west terrace at Cothay Manor

Geranium palmatum and *Sisyrinchium californicum* on a paved terrace gives an air of sprightly informality.

NEW ADDITIONS

The Robbs have also added new areas, among them a bog garden by the banks of the river Tone, which flows through the grounds; a long formal avenue of mop-headed acacias (*Robinia pseudoacacia* 'Umbraculifera') with underplanted with thousands of 'White Triumphator' tulips and clouds of catmint; a gravel garden; a finely planted lake; and a mount overlooking an exquisite meadow garden. Cothay was fortunate to find new owners who respected its character and yet were bold enough to put their own sympathetic stamp on it.

INFORMATION

Location Greenham, nr Wellington TA21 0JR, Somerset; 5m W of Wellington by A38 (signed on A38 4m W of Wellington)
Tel 01823 672283
Email cothaymanor@btinternet.co.uk
Website www.cothaymanor.co.uk
Owner Mr and Mrs A.H.B. Robb
Open Easter to Sept, Wed, Thur, Sun and Bank Hol Mon 2–6
Area 5 acres/2 hectares

Cranborne Manor Gardens

THE ANCIENT HOUSE OF THE CECILS, WITH ROMANTIC LATE 20TH-CENTURY GARDENS IN A CHARMING SETTING

Built as a royal hunting lodge in the early 13th century, Cranborne Manor is one of the most beguiling houses imaginable. It was rebuilt by Robert Cecil (later Earl of Salisbury) between 1608 and 1611 when he was also building the great house at Hatfield (*see page 244*). Cranborne Manor is built on a more modest, domestic scale but as at Hatfield John Tradescant the Elder worked on the garden, planting trees, in 1610 and 1611.

Of Tradescant's time the only garden survival is the mount to the west of the house; the design of the garden today is largely the work of the Dowager Marchioness of Salisbury who as Viscountess Cranborne came to live here in 1954. The mount, crowned with a sundial, is now at the centre of a formal garden of box-edged beds of lavishly underplanted shrub roses, with tall Irish yews marking the outer edges. An informal area of simple but memorable character has fine old beeches and long grass, enlivened by a majestic giant bronze head by Elizabeth Frink on a tall plinth, and a stone figure of a crouching wild boar in the grass.

ENCLOSED IN HEDGES

Beyond the brick entrance lodges formal gardens are enclosed in hedges. An intricate four-part knot of box, its compartments filled with herbs, surrounds an octagonal pool; a broad grass path leads between mixed borders given structure by towers of *Clematis tangutica* or hop (*Humulus lupulus*) and the occasional substantial tree (such as a *Cercis siliquastrum*) or shrub (*Osmanthus* x *burkwoodii*), generously underplanted. The southern border is backed by a yew hedge clipped into swooping shapes and with "windows" cut out to give views of pasture and woodland. A gate leads to a further garden quartered by grass paths, a sundial at its centre, and eight beds edged in santolina and filled with shrub roses and culinary herbs.

Cranborne Manor lies on the edge of the village of Cranborne, where the square tower of the parish church of St Mary and St Bartholomew can be seen rising above the garden enclosures. The garden reflects the orderliness of the village while allowing views of rural landscape, with the house doing a perfect balancing act between the two.

Elizabeth Frink's bronze head at Cranborne

INFORMATION

Location nr Wimborne BH21 5PP, Dorset; in Cranborne village, 16½m SW of Salisbury by A354 and B3081
Tel and Fax 01725 517248
Website www.cranborne.co.uk
English Heritage Register Grade II*
Owner The Marquess and Marchioness of Salisbury
Open Mar to Sept, Wed 9–5
Area 10 acres/4 hectares

Dartington Hall

NOBLE GARDENS WITH EXCELLENT TREES AND SHRUBS FOR A MAGNIFICENT MEDIEVAL HOUSE

Dartington Hall is a beautiful 14th-century house at the heart of an estate that was bought in 1925 by Leonard and Dorothy Elmhirst who were filled with idealistic plans for the regeneration of the rural economy and for education. When they came here house and grounds were in a terrible state and desperately needed attention. They restored the marvellous medieval house, created distinguished new gardens while preserving the earlier landscape, and commissioned new architecture in the very latest International Modern style in the grounds. A prime example of this is the former headmaster's house, High Cross House, designed by William Lescaze, and built in 1931–32. Now housing an

excellent collection of art and crafts and open to the public it is well worth visiting for a flavour of the modernist impulses that inspired the Elmhirsts. All this makes Dartington a most exciting place to visit.

GRASS TERRACES

The garden, to the west of the house, lies in a beautiful undulating site; at its centre are the curious and dramatic grassy terraces of the Tournament Ground with its row of twelve apostles – tall clipped yews planted in the 19th century. The origins of the Tournament Ground are obscure; it has been described as a medieval "tiltyard" but is much more likely to date from the early 18th century and is probably related to similar turf terraces at Bicton Park (also in Devon) and the amphitheatre at

Grass terraces at Dartington Hall

Claremont Park (Surrey). Whatever its origins, it is full of atmosphere and a delightful place in which to wander.

In refashioning the gardens the Elmhirsts had the advice of three people: H. Avray Tipping, Percy Cane and Beatrix Farrand. The work they did is not only harmonious but also makes the best of the existing landscape. Tipping's work was chiefly to do with preserving and enhancing the existing fine features, like the Tournament Ground. The ground here was leveled and the turf terraces leading down to it restored. For the terraces Percy Cane devised two breathtaking stone staircases. Both have shallow steps of York stone which follow the descending slopes of the turf terraces and are generously broad – anything narrower would have looked mean in this setting. Cane's planting is skilfully chosen – one flight of steps is edged with waves of epimediums with cream, pink and yellow azaleas rising above; the other is overshadowed by huge old specimens of *Magnolia* x *soulangeana* and its dark-purple flowered cultivar 'Lennei'. On the sloping land to the west of the Tournament Ground the planting is informal, of a woodland kind, and here Beatrix Farrand made her "wilderness" with long walks that follow the contours of the land among trees, and lined them with camellias or rhododendrons. She also redesigned the great courtyard overlooked by the medieval house. Inspired by the courtyards of Cambridge colleges she laid out a beguiling pattern of paths made of pebbles with a few carefully positioned trees.

Fountain pool at Dartington Hall

WOODLAND PLANTING

Everywhere there are memorable plantings: fine specimens of Chinese dogwoods (especially *Cornus kousa*), *Davidia involucrata* and *Cercidiphyllum japonicum*; beautiful groups of Chinese crab-apples (*Malus hupehensis*), an exuberant froth of white blossom in spring; an aristocratic procession of venerable sweet chestnuts with, at their end, a Henry Moore sculpture of a reclining woman gazing back into the woodland. The sculpture, carved of beautiful warm brown Hornton stone, was placed here in 1945. It was Moore's intention that the curves of the figure should echo those of the distant hills. He also wrote that "I wanted the figure to have a quiet stillness and a sense of permanence as though it could stay there forever."

This feeling of permanence, and the continuity of the past, pervades the atmosphere here. There is nothing modish here; the place has entirely its own character and atmosphere. Nor is there anything ungenerous or fiddly at Dartington; everything is of the right scale and character, taking its cue from the noble house and powerful landscape. All good gardens give pleasure on any day of the year – this is true at Dartington and the pleasure is exceptional. Today it is particularly well cared for and, although not particularly well known, one of the finest landscapes in the country. Few gardens have so much to offer the visitor.

INFORMATION

Location Dartington, Totnes TQ9 6EL, Devon; 2m NW of Totnes by A384
Tel 01803 862367
Website www.dartingtonhall.org.uk
Email trust@dartingtonhall.org.uk
English Heritage Register Grade II*
Owner Dartington Hall Trust
Open daily dawn–dusk
Area 30 acres/12 hectares

Dunster Castle

HIGH ON A WOODED HILL ON THE SOMERSET COAST, TENDER PLANTS FLOURISH ON THE CASTLE SLOPES

Luttrells, one of the oldest Somerset families, first lived here in the 14th century and remained until Colonel Walter Luttrell gave the estate to the National Trust in 1975. The climate is very mild, the nearby coast well warmed by the Gulf Stream Drift, and the south and west slopes of the castle tor have an especially benign microclimate. The western terraces date back to at least the 18th century, when they were planted as vineyards, and since at least the mid 19th century a lemon tree has been cultivated here, planted out against the south wall of the castle and protected when necessary by movable lights.

The slopes below the castle walls are today densely planted with shrubs, with much self-sown laurustinus, and with paths ambling along the contours. The drainage is sharp and the south terrace provides the perfect site for many other tender plants – the common mimosa (*Acacia dealbata*), the Mexican *Beschorneria yuccoides*, the shrimp bush (*Justicia brandegeeana*), olive trees and many others. The south-facing wall of the castle is clothed in such climbers as *Clianthus puniceus* (white and red), *Rosa banksiae* 'Lutea', *Solanum jasminoides* and thickets of such tender shrubs as *Salvia rutilans*. A remarkable National Collection of strawberry trees (*Arbutus*) is kept here, with 9 species and 6 cultivars.

PANORAMIC VIEWS

The Keep Garden to the west of the castle – a bowling green in the 18th century – is overlooked by an octagonal gazebo. There are good shrubs here too: the tender *Acca sellowiana*, *Drimys winteri*, several magnolias, myrtles, pittosporums and the beautiful pink rose of wild Himalayan parentage, *Rosa* 'Anemone'. Not the least charm of this

The Mill Walk at Dunster

part of the garden is the delicious panoramic view that is to be had – of the castle park, the village and magnificent sea views opening out.

At the southern foot of the tor, along the banks of the river Avill, is a garden of quite different character. The Mill Walk, at the foot of vertiginous paths zigzagging down the castle ramparts, is a woodland garden that takes advantage of the lime-free soil to grow magnificent camellias, dogwoods, eucryphias, hydrangeas, pieris and rhododendrons, with much herbaceous underplanting of acanthus, comfrey, ferns, gunneras and hostas. The river is crossed by a picturesque 18th-century rustic bridge above a cascade.

INFORMATION

Location Dunster, nr Minehead TA24 6SL, Somerset; 3m SE of Minehead by A396
Infoline 01643 823004 **Tel** 01643 821314
Email dunstercastle@nationaltrust.org.uk
English Heritage Register Grade I
Owner The National Trust
Open Jan to Mar, Oct to Dec, daily 11–4; Apr to Sept, daily 10–5 (closed 25–29 Dec)
Area 17 acres/7 hectares

East Lambrook Manor

MARGERY FISH'S VILLAGE GARDEN, WELL RESTORED AND FULL OF THE PLANTS SHE MADE FAMOUS

For anyone seeking to understand what is meant by a cottage garden East Lambrook Manor is an excellent starting place. Not, of course, that it is a cottage – it is a pretty, Tudor manor house of modest size. But the style of gardening practised here, uninfluenced by any grand theories and enriched by an unpretentious love of plants, encapsulates the essential cottage garden ideal. The garden history of the place starts in 1938 when Margery Fish came to live here with her redoubtable husband, Walter. They found "a poor battered old house . . . and a wilderness instead of a garden". She described their first steps in gardening in a most attractive book, *We Made a Garden* (1956), and their desire to make a garden that was "as much part of the house as possible".

A PRIVATE WORLD

Today, more than thirty years after her death, the house is shrouded in plants and the garden seems keen to embrace it. The site undulates and there are virtually no straight lines – any path that sets off to follow a direct route finds its edges blurred with plants. There is no attempt at contrived formality; one of the few firm structural shapes is an irregular line of pollarded willows that rises in the ditch garden – home to a lovely profusion of essential Margery Fish plants. Here are hellebores (forms of *Helleborus orientalis*), swathes of snowdrops (of which she had over 50 varieties in her day) and her beloved primroses, of which she rescued odd forms spotted in Somerset hedgerows. Throughout the garden Margery Fish grew a bewildering range of plants, with the emphasis, no doubt through lack of space, on herbaceous perennials, paying great attention to siting them so that they had the best conditions in which to flourish.

Although the garden is a small one it gives the impression of much greater size because of the maze-like network of paths, many half-concealed nooks and crannies and no distant views. This is an inward-looking garden that concentrates attention on the abundant planting, creating a microcosm isolated from the surrounding world. The present owners maintain the garden as closely as possible to the tradition that Margery Fish established. A valuable nursery attached to the garden sells a good stock of Fish plants.

The ditch garden at East Lambrook

INFORMATION

Location East Lambrook, South Petherton TA13 5HL, Somerset; 2m N of South Petherton, signed from A303
Tel 01460 240328
Email enquiries@eastlambrook.com
Website www.eastlambrook.com
English Heritage Register Grade I
Owner Mr and Mrs R. Williams
Open daily (closed 25 Dec to 5 Jan) 10–5
Area 1½ acres/0.6 hectares

The Eden Project

A 21ST-CENTURY PHENOMENON – IMMENSE GREENHOUSES AND A COLLECTION OF PLANTS WITH A MESSAGE

The Eden Project opened to the public in 2001 and became an instant success. At its heart are two immense greenhouses – "biomes" designed by Nicholas Grimshaw and Partners as mounded organic shapes – built of numerous hexagonal frames covered in a double film of ETFE (ethyltetrafluoroethylene). The larger of the two is 790ft/240m long, 180ft/55m high and 370ft/110m wide – the biggest greenhouse in the world. The biomes are built against the south-facing cliffs of a former china-clay pit. Two climates are housed – a humid tropical climate and a warm temperate climate, each containing characteristic plants from appropriate regions. Between the visitor centre and the enclosed biomes is an unenclosed biome with lavish mixed plantings of hardy plants clothing the slopes.

THE BIOMES REVEALED

The humid tropical biome has a naturalistic jungle air, with a waterfall plummeting through exotic foliage from a great height, a stream and a pool, all shrouded in dense planting. There are over 1,000 species of tropical plants, both ornamental and useful, many of which have now grown to superb maturity; some, indeed, are touching the ceiling. The atmosphere is hot and humid and paths swoop upwards among unfamiliar vegetation. The warm temperate biome houses plants coming from climates of a Mediterranean kind. Indeed, the spirit of the Mediterranean is evoked with village streets of stucco and tiles, terracotta pots and venerable gnarled olive trees. A vineyard displays different varieties of grapevine and there is a figure of Dionysus in the form of a rampaging bull surrounded by frolicking maenads. Here too are charming and convincing evocations of a kitchen garden and an orchard.

The purpose of the Eden Project goes well beyond the usual motives for making a garden. It was the intention here "to provide a living theatre of plants and people" in the words of Tim Smit (who restored Heligan, *see page 46*), whose idea the Eden Project was and who masterminded its astonishing fruition: "Eden isn't so much a destination as a place in the heart." Its purpose is to divert, instruct and inspire. These are rare aspirations for a garden and indeed it is rare enough that any garden maker has such an explicit programme. Huge numbers of visitors come, over 1,000,000 a year, and plainly have a good time.

The Eden Project biomes

INFORMATION

Location Bodelva, St Austell PL24 2SG, Cornwall; 1½m NE of St Austell signed off A390
Tel 01726 811911
Fax 01726 811912
Website www.edenproject. com
Owner The Eden Trust
Open daily 9–6.30 during Summer Time, 10–4.30 in winter (closed 24 and 25 Dec)
Area 37 acres/15 hectares

Forde Abbey

ROMANTIC HOUSE WITH THE COMPLETE GARDEN – BORDERS, TREES, WATER GARDEN AND SUPERB KITCHEN GARDEN

Forde is an unforgettable place – the remains of a Cistercian abbey started in the 12th century, onto which were grafted in the mid 17th century an elaborate castellated mansion with a dashing Italianate loggia. Built of golden Ham stone it lies low in the valley of the river Axe, pinned down by avenues which follow lines already established in the early 18th century. Although the garden today is almost entirely of the 20th century, largely created by Geoffrey Roper, the present owner's father, it is given depth and richness by features from the past. South-west of the house a canal on an east-west axis, the Long Pond, dates from the early 18th century. Mixed borders along its north side, punctuated by a procession of clipped yew columns, are filled in late summer with an explosion of dahlias. A grassy walk rises among trees to a statue of Diana the Huntress silhouetted against the sky. A modern neo-classical domed rotunda above a cascade marks the head of the Long Pond, whose south bank in February is a tapestry of crocuses and wild daffodils (*Narcissus pseudonarcissus*) which still grow in Dorset meadows.

The Long Pond at Forde Abbey

THE GREAT POND

An avenue of limes and American black walnuts (*Juglans nigra*), following the early 18th-century axis, marches south across the garden into the fields that rise gently above it. A former 18th-century wilderness has a series of pools with much good planting, culminating in the Great Pond which is overlooked by a rare and enchanting pavilion of pleached beech (a perfect hide for bird watchers). A bog garden is rich in Asiatic primulas, *Gunnera manicata*, ferns and the skunk cabbage (*Lysichiton americanum*).

Below the north walls of the abbey lies one of the great glories of Forde – the walled kitchen garden. This is kept up to old country-house standards, nothing flashy and a far cry from the fashionable potager. Great quantities of varied fruit and vegetables are skilfully cultivated and standards of maintenance are impeccable – a thrilling sight. A pair of borders, filled with late summer flowers, perennials and annuals, runs down the central path, and the beautiful old walls of the 13th-century monks' dormitory protect the east side. The garden has a further attraction – a high class nursery of well-chosen plants.

INFORMATION

Location nr Chard TA20 4LU, Somerset; 4m SE of Chard by B3162 and minor roads
Tel 01460 221290
Email info@fordeabbey.co.uk
Website www.fordeabbey.co.uk
English Heritage Register Grade II*
Owner Mark Roper
Open daily 10–4.30
Area 30 acres/12 hectares

The Garden House

REMARKABLE PLANTSMAN'S GARDEN IN AN IDYLLIC SETTING ON DARTMOOR WITH EXCELLENT PLANTING

The garden was the creation of an intrepid retired schoolmaster, Lionel Fortescue, who came here in 1945. The charm of the place comes from its fine setting on the edge of Dartmoor, with its distant prospect of the tower of St Andrew's church rising above blowsy trees, and an atmospheric old walled enclosure built on a slope with terracing. Here are the ruins of an early 16th-century house built for the abbot of Buckland Abbey, a square tower with stone mullioned windows. At 400ft/120m above sea level the climate can be harsh here – the temperature fell to –15˚C/5°F in the winter of 1979/80, killing anything slightly tender in the garden, including every ceanothus. However, the walls do provide protection, and this was enhanced by planting windbreaks.

The South African garden at The Garden House

CAREFUL GROUPINGS

Fortescue's ambition was to unite a sense of design with discerning plantsmanship and his success in doing this may be seen today. Just before his death in 1981 he wrote, "Owing to limited space available, the qualifying test for plants has to be severe. We search for the best forms and pay great attention to our grouping for colour, form and foliage." Before his death he had already recruited as his gardener Keith Wiley, who retired in 2003 and was succeeded by Matt Bishop. Both these head gardeners maintained the tradition of the garden and expanded it with new interests. A ruined cottage is lavishly planted with suitably cottagey planting. A South African garden celebrates that part of the world with brilliant crocosmias, eucomis, kniphofias and many annuals. There is a glade of maples, a wild flower meadow, a mesmerising bulb meadow and a rhododendron walk. The walled garden still forms the garden's spiritual heart and in 2007 was undergoing wholesale refashioning with a bold new layout, enriched soil and radical new planting that honours Fortescue's principles.

Throughout the garden splendid trees and shrubs, especially magnolias and rhododendrons, survive from the past. Eight splendid lime trees were planted in the 18th century by the last vicar to live here, to celebrate the birth of his daughters. Both Keith Wiley and Matt Bishop have immensely increased the diversity of planting throughout the garden, which has an atmosphere of sprightly endeavour wherever you care to look. The garden still maintains an admirable nursery.

INFORMATION

Location Buckland Monachorum, Yelverton PL20 7LQ, Devon; 5m S of Tavistock by A386
Tel 01822 854769
Email office@thegardenhouse.org.uk
Website www.thegardenhouse.org.uk
Owner The Fortescue Garden Trust
Open Mar to Oct, daily 10.30–5
Area 8 acres/3.2 hectares

Glendurgan Garden

EARLY 19TH-CENTURY WOODLAND GARDEN WITH SUPERB TREES AND SHRUBS AND A FINE MAZE

The great gardening family of Fox made the garden at Glendurgan, taking every advantage of the wonderful site – a ravine irrigated by streams that plunges southwards to the fishing village of Durgan. Alfred Fox came here in the 1820s and gradually cleared the ground and planted windbreaks, especially of the maritime pine, *Pinus pinaster*.

ORNAMENTAL EXOTICS

Alfred used part of the gardens as an orchard but gradually he, and his son George who inherited in 1891, began to introduce the ornamental exotics, especially camellias and rhododendrons, for which the garden became famous. An early surviving feature from Alfred's time, supposedly planted in 1833, is the irregular maze of cherry laurel with its winding walks and thick rounded hedges. It looms up dramatically, spread out on its slope, the only piece of topiary in the whole garden. Glendurgan was given to the National Trust in 1962 and the Fox family continues to live in the house.

Streams feed many pools that run along the bottom of the valley, crossed from time to time by decorative bridges. Here, enough space is given to plants for their character to be displayed; on the slopes above, the planting is far more dense though frequently enlivened by the brilliant colour of some flowering shrub. The camellia walk at the head of the valley contains specimens going back to the 19th century; old cultivars such as 'Preston Rose' and 'Ville de Nantes' were probably planted by George Fox. The climate is remarkably benign and many tender plants grow superbly, among them *Michelia doltsopa*, with its waxy cream flowers; a conifer, *Cupressus torulosa* 'Cashmeriana', with wonderfully graceful tumbling cascades of ferny foliage; and the myrtle *Luma apiculata* with its cream and coffee bark.

Like most old gardens in the south-west Glendurgan lost many trees in the storm of 1990. There is little sign of that today, with much replanting among the surviving older specimens, which give the place its rare character. It is rich in the characteristic Cornish flowering shrubs but it has much else, including a stupendous old tulip tree (*Liriodendron tulipifera*) with gnarled and mossy bark and widespread branches.

The ravine at Glendurgan

INFORMATION

Location Helford River, Mawnan Smith, nr Falmouth TR11 5JZ, Cornwall; 4m SW of Falmouth on road to Helford Passage
Infoline 01326 250906 or 01872 862090
Email glendurgan@nationaltrust.org.uk
English Heritage Register Grade II
Owner The National Trust
Open mid Feb to early Nov, Tue to Sat (open Bank Hol Mon; closed Good Fri) 10.30–5.30
Area 25 acres/10 hectares

Gnome Reserve

THE PRIVATE RETREAT OF A COMMUNITY OF GNOMES IN A
WOODLAND SETTING WITH EXCELLENT WILD PLANTING

I realise that gnomes are treated with the greatest contempt by many right-thinking gardeners. Indeed, it is said that the Royal Horticultural Society refuses them admission to the Chelsea Flower Show. However, there is another, pretty numerous, body of gardeners who treasure them, and anyone driving about the country will spy them (gnomes, I mean) occupying positions of greater or lesser importance in many a front garden. Here at the Gnome Reserve – the very name of which suggests a threatened race – they find a happy home where they are not merely tolerated but given pride of place. A community of over 2,000 (as the Guiness Book of Records says) live in bosky comfort here in North Devon, doing their gnomely thing, cushioned in moss or masked by ivy, in the shade of handsome old beeches. They are skilfully displayed to take advantage of all kinds of nooks and crannies. Gravel paths wind through the woods and the visitor may find it easy to succumb to the enchanted

The head gardener
at the Gnome Reserve

atmosphere. Pointed felt hats are issued to make humans seem more congenial to the natives. A gnome museum traces their long history and new gnomes are produced in large quantities on the premises and may be watched as they are given their gleaming sets of clothes. To one side, the 2 acre/0.8 hectare Pixies' Wildflower Garden displays over 250 native plants arranged in naturalistic habitats – a most delightful and unusual sight. Some precious antique gnomes, dating from the first examples of the 19th century, are displayed in the museum here.

PART OF GARDEN HISTORY

I have never been able to make up my mind how seriously the owner takes her subject. The best approach for the visitor is to keep an open mind and enjoy whatever it is that seems enjoyable. For better or for worse gnomes are part of garden history and it is hard to imagine them being more sympathetically displayed than they are here. The founder of the Gnome Reserve, Ann Fawssett Atkin, trained as an artist at Brighton Art College and the Royal Academy Schools and much artistry is seen in her irresistible garden. She came to live at West Putford in 1971 and began to form a collection of gnomes in 1978. Exactly what sparked her interest is uncertain – "Gnomes became very important and I wanted to share them with people." So she did.

INFORMATION

Location West Putford, nr Bradworthy EX22 7XE, Devon; 7½m N of Holsworthy by A388 and minor roads (follow rose sign)
Tel 01409 241435
Email info@gnomereserve.co.uk
Website www.gnomereserve.co.uk
Open end Mar to Oct, daily 10–6
Area 4 acres/1.6 hectares

Greencombe

AN EXCEPTIONAL GARDENER'S WORLD IN AN EXQUISITE SETTING OVERLOOKING PORLOCK BAY

The garden at Greencombe was started in 1946 by Horace Stroud, who terraced the ground about the house and made the lawn that lies at the heart of the formal gardens. He also acquired the ancient woodland west of the garden, which was threatened with destruction, and began to plant distinguished trees and shrubs. In 1966 house and garden were acquired by Joan Loraine who has made it a most remarkable place.

A DRAMATIC SITE

The garden has a curious site on north-facing slopes in a notably balmy part of the country, close to the sea at Porlock. Rainfall is around 40in/100cm per annum, the soil is acid and hard frosts are rare. The site is ancient, with woodland of great antiquity west of the house, with old holly trees, English oaks and coppiced sweet chestnut.

There is an easy flow of movement within the garden but this is, supremely, a place for plants. Everywhere one has the impression of plants flourishing – in the right sites and well cared for. Where sweeping lawns and terraces frame the house, the planting is intricate – mossy stones edge beds of shrubs and trees which are densely underplanted with ferns, hellebores, hostas, primulas and violas. Camellias, of which there is an admirable range, are finely used not as lonely exhibits in a beauty show but woven into the garden.

The woodland parts of the garden have marvellous acers, magnolias and rhododendrons. Several National Collections are held here: of erythroniums (22 species and 24 cultivars); of polystichum ferns (24 species, 100 cultivars) of gaultherias (including pernettyas – 45 species and 7 cultivars) and of vacciniums (44 species,

The woodland garden at Greencombe

7 cultivars). All these exotics consort well with the native wood anemones, bluebells, celandines and scillas that ornament the mossy woods.

Greencombe is a whole world and Miss Loraine gardens in accordance with firmly held beliefs about the environment. She makes tons of compost and leaf-mould. Few gardens are as well gardened as Greencombe and few take advantage of the site to such marvellous effect. For the millennium Miss Loraine commissioned a new building, the Chapel of our Lady of the Secret, at the western extremity of the wood. Circular in shape, it is beautifully built of sweet chestnut wood taken from a tree at Greencombe.

INFORMATION

Location Porlock TA24 8NU, Somerset; ½m W of Porlock by road to Porlock Weir
Tel 01643 862363
Owner Miss Joan Loraine
Open Apr to Jul, Oct to Nov, Sat to Wed 2–6
Area 3½ acres/1.4 hectares

Heligan

NOTABLE 19TH-CENTURY CORNISH PLANTSMAN'S GARDEN
BROUGHT BACK TO LIFE IN AN EPIC FEAT OF RESTORATION

When the restoration of this garden started, and it opened to the public, it was called the Lost Gardens of Heligan. However, since the immense success of the garden as a star of TV and books it is perhaps time to revert to its plainer name – few gardens look less lost. Yet only a cynic would criticise Heligan's success.

The estate belongs to the ancient Tremayne family which had lived at St Martin in Meneage on the Helford River since the 15th century. Sampson Tremayne bought Heligan in 1569 and the first signs of garden activity appeared a hundred years later when a walled garden was built in front of the house. Here, according to a surviving plan, John Tremayne laid out in 1735 an elaborate garden of parterres, distinctly old-fashioned and delightful. All this was removed when the grounds were landscaped in the 1770s. In the early 19th century John Hearle Tremayne started the tradition of plant collecting that earned Heligan its reputation. In 1825 he received seeds of the tender Himalayan dogwood *Cornus capitata* which had been discovered by

Nathaniel Wallich in Nepal in 1821. Some of the trees he raised survive to this day. John's son and grandson continued plant collecting throughout the 19th century, receiving seeds from J.D. Hooker's Himalayan expedition of 1847–50. One of the grandest of all rhododendrons, *R. sinogrande*, discovered by George Forrest in 1912, first flowered in Cornwall at Heligan in 1919. Later in the 20th century things stood still at Heligan until, after World War II, they dramatically declined, and eventually gardening ceased altogether.

GARDEN RESTORATION

In 1991 restoration of the by now totally overgrown garden began, supervised by Tim Smit and his colleagues. The jungle garden with its watery ravine filled with bamboos, tall tree ferns and gigantic specimens of unusual trees – *Cedrela sinensis*, *Pinus thunbergii* and *Podocarpus totara* – has exceptional character and beauty. The rest of the site is flat – very flat as Cornish gardens go – with some good trees and large clumps of cultivars of *R. arboreum*. The most memorable features here are the beautiful kitchen garden and ancillary garden buildings – the wall of bee-skeps, the potting shed, the fully restored and fully working pineapple pit and melon house.

The jungle garden at Heligan

INFORMATION

Location nr Megavissey, St Austell PL26 6EN, Cornwall; 4m S of St Austell by B3273

Tel 01726 845100

Email info@heligan.com

Website www.heligan.com

English Heritage Register Grade II

Owner Heligan Gardens Ltd

Open daily Mar to Oct 10–6, Nov to Feb 10–5

Area 57 acres/23 hectares

Barbara Hepworth Garden

THE PRIVATE AND IDIOSYNCRATIC GARDEN OF A GREAT ARTIST WITH MUCH BOLD AND BRASSY PLANTING

Gardens made by artists often have a special atmosphere. Although not necessarily of any special horticultural interest they are, nonetheless, the products of exceptional visual sensitivity, assuming a special interest in relation to the artist's work. The Trewyn Studio in the heart of St Ives was bought by the sculptor Barbara Hepworth in 1949. She wrote, "Finding Trewyn Studio was a sort of magic." It was part of the estate of Trewyn House and the garden already existed when she took on the studio.

Hepworth had come to Cornwall in 1939, finding the light here especially sympathetic to her art, and she remained connected to Cornwall for the rest of her life. Before her death in 1975 she had made provisions for her executors to explore the possibility "of establishing a permanent exhibition of some of [my] works in Trewyn Studio and its garden". This they have done and the place, diminutive and packed with plants and sculptures, has an extraordinarily powerful character.

A bronze in the Barbara Hepworth Garden

BOLD AND BRASSY

Much of the planting is bold and brassy with special emphasis on foliage – bamboos, cordylines, spires of *Echium pininana* and giant blades of New Zealand flax. Hepworth's sculptures, especially those of organic character, look splendid in this setting, far more beautiful than in the frigid featureless rooms of museums or dealers' galleries. Some of them are at least partly shrouded in planting, only to be discovered by wandering and looking carefully. She believed strongly in the relationship between the organic shapes of her sculptures and the natural world. Thus, the garden was seen as a specially appropriate environment to display her works, although during her life it always remained an emphatically private place.

The studio in which she worked has been left more or less as it was when she died, with her overalls hanging on a peg, chippings of white marble scattered on the floor and tools ready to hand. I should find it hard to believe that anyone could visit this place and come away unmoved. The Tate Gallery has cared for the studio and garden since 1980 and it makes a remarkable adjunct to the exhibits in Tate St Ives. Delightful in themselves, the studio and garden are also richly informative about the influences that inspire artists and the way in which they work.

INFORMATION

Location Barnoon Hill, St Ives TR26 1AD, Cornwall
Tel 01736 796226
Website www.tate.org.uk/stives/hepworth/
English Heritage Register Grade II
Open Mar to Oct, daily 10–5.20; Nov to Feb daily except Mon 10–4.20
Area ¼ acre/0.1 hectare

Hestercombe

A MASTERPIECE BY EDWIN LUTYENS AND GERTRUDE JEKYLL, AND A DELIGHTFUL 18TH-CENTURY LANDSCAPE GARDEN

Hestercombe offers two exceptionally attractive gardens, of completely different kinds yet subtly linked. In 1903 Edwin Lutyens was commissioned by the Hon. E.W.B. Portman to lay out a new garden. Lutyens created a dazzlingly inventive pattern of garden spaces and subtle changes of level, with walls of Ham stone and paving of Morte slate, and delightful architectural detail.

The Great Plat at Hestercombe

The sunken Great Plat is a giant square parterre overlooked by raised terraces and flanked by a pair of terraces with narrow rills cut into the paving. These run from beautifully fashioned niches and curved lily pools towards a rose-enshrouded pergola. Above the Great Plat to the north-east Lutyens designed a circular enclosure with a circular pool – the Rotunda. Beyond lies a magnificent orangery and the Dutch Garden, a deft parterre of lavender, roses, yuccas and lamb's ears.

MASTERPIECES RESTORED

Underlying all this is Gertrude Jekyll's bold and simple planting. Bergenias outline the divisions of the Great Plat; bushes of myrtle guard gateways; terraces are studded with cistus, rosemary, santolina and, everywhere, swags of Mexican daisy (*Erigeron karvinskianus*). It is a brilliant display of what lay at the heart of Miss Jekyll's gardening – "the best plants in the best places". This masterpiece had been almost irretrievably lost when Somerset County Council took it on in 1973 and carried out a pioneer feat of faithful garden restoration.

The other garden at Hestercombe, an astonishing piece of rediscovery, is a miniature 18th-century landscape garden. To the north of Lutyens's Dutch Garden a lake rises in a wooded combe, with temples gleaming among the trees. By 1995, when Philip White first saw it, it was a jungle of saplings and undergrowth but, mesmerised by its beauty, he resolved to bring it back to life. This garden had been created by Coplestone Warre Bampfylde, who inherited Hestercombe in 1750. He was a gifted amateur artist, and his paintings of the garden at Stourhead and of his own park at Hestercombe vividly evoke the great days of the landscape park. At Hestercombe he created a charming landscape – a cascade erupts from rocky crags, ornamental buildings cling to the valley's slopes and a serene pear-shaped lake lies at its foot. Today, once again, it resembles the views depicted in Bampfylde's own watercolours.

INFORMATION

Location Cheddon Fitzpaine, nr Taunton TA2 8LQ, Somerset; 2m NE of Taunton off A361
Tel 01823 413923
Email info@hestercombegardens.com
Website www.hestercombegardens.com
English Heritage Register Grade I
Owner Hestercombe Gardens Trust
Open daily 10–6
Area 50 acres/20 hectares

Killerton

SUPERB TREES AND SHRUBS ADORN A NOBLE 18TH-CENTURY LANDSCAPE, WITH A FINE FLOWER GARDEN

Fine trees are magnificently displayed at Killerton, rising from perfect close-mown turf on the slopes about a late 18th-century mansion. The site is splendid, lying below the volcanic mound of Killerton Clump, with rich, fertile soil and rainfall that averages 36in/90cm per annum. The Acland family had lived in these parts for centuries and the gardens at Killerton were started by Sir Thomas Acland in the 1770s, shortly before he rebuilt the 17th-century family house. He was helped by John Veitch, the founding father of the great dynasty of nurserymen, who started his business at Budlake, quite close to Killerton, and later moved it to Exeter. The connection between the Aclands and the Veitches continued well into the 20th century. The Veitch nursery was one of the first to invest in plant-hunting expeditions, financing people like William Lobb and E.H. Wilson to hunt on their behalf. Many of their discoveries came to Killerton and thus there are large numbers of early specimens of new introductions or uncontaminated species propagated from seed gathered in the wild. Such trees as the cork oak (*Quercus suber*) perform magnificently here, and everywhere are marvellous trees finely displayed: an American horse chestnut (*Aesculus californica*), which first flowered in Veitch's Exeter nursery in 1858; the Japanese *Zelkova serrata*, another Veitch introduction; another exceptional tree from Japan, the walnut *Juglans ailanthifolia*; and, a tree of special local significance, the Lucombe oak (*Quercus* x *lucombeana* 'William Lucombe') – Lucombe was a nurseryman in Exeter. These and many other rare, beautiful and venerable species, and dozens of distinguished flowering shrubs, are seen at their best – given plenty of breathing space and disposed on fine lawns.

ON A SMALLER SCALE

Trees and shrubs in a parkland setting are what make Killerton special, but there are also good ornamental interludes on a smaller scale. Close to the house decorative mixed borders with fine Coade stone urns are all that remains of a garden designed by William Robinson in about 1900. Further from the house a rock garden is rich in camellias, Japanese maples, ferns, primulas and, in late spring, sheets of *Cyclamen repandum*. The Bear's Hut nearby is a rustic summerhouse out of Grimm's fairy tales, with a lavishly decorated interior of wickerwork, rattan and patterns of pine cones.

Spring at Killerton

INFORMATION

Location Broadclyst, Exeter EX5 3LE, Devon; 5m NE of Exeter by B3181 and B3185, Jct 28 of M5
Tel 01392 881345
Email killerton@nationaltrust.org.uk
English Heritage Register Grade II*
Owner The National Trust
Open daily 10.30–7
Area 22 acres/9 hectares

Kingston Lacy

FINE TREES AND MAGNIFICENT ORNAMENTS FOR A GREAT HOUSE, WITH A PRETTY 19TH-CENTURY FERNERY

The house at Kingston Lacy was built in the 1660s for Sir Ralph Bankes and twice altered, most unhappily in the 1830s by Sir Charles Barry. In 1982 the Bankeses gave the estate to the National Trust, which has restored both house and garden. The garden is not a flowery place – it is best seen as a magnificent landscape setting for the house. South of the house a terrace and deep gravel walk are ornamented with pink stone urns supported on bronze tortoises, superb Venetian wellheads (planted with clipped bay) and a pair of bronze lions tussling with snakes. A great sweep of lawn opens out, with its trees and ornaments. This is essentially the work of William John Bankes in the 19th century. It was he who placed here in 1827 a noble obelisk dating from *c.*150 BCE and dedicated to King Ptolemy. It is flanked, at a discreet distance, by two beautiful trees – a fern-leafed beech (*Fagus sylvatica* var. *heterophylla* 'Aspleniifolia') and a holm oak (*Quercus ilex*). Beyond the obelisk a ha-ha forms the boundary of the garden, with field and woodland beyond, and a row of small cannons point out to the countryside.

The parterre at Kingston Lacy

Two further obelisks are visible: one to the south-east commemorates Queen Victoria's diamond jubilee of 1887, and the other, to the south-west, probably dates from the 18th century.

PERFECTLY BALANCED

From the lawn there is just enough ornament to be easy on the eye and not to detract from the beauty of the trees and the orchestrated view of the rural landscape; equally, looking back towards the house, the trees on either side concentrate the attention on the house, giving it a frame of noble simplicity. The grandly simple setting of grass, trees and a few superlative ornaments is all that is needed – not minimalist, but exactly enough on exactly the right scale.

Immediately below the east façade of the house, in a sunken space overlooked by grassy terraces, is a dapper parterre of L-shaped beds filled with pink begonias and egg-shaped topiaries of clipped golden yew, designed by C.E. Ponting and put in place in 1899. Beyond it, running eastwards, is a majestic procession of venerable cedars of Lebanon planted in 1835 – a symphonic blast after the piccolo parterre. Dating from the same period is a rare and charming fernery.

INFORMATION

Location nr Wimborne Minster BH21 4EA, Dorset; 1½m W of Wimborne by B3082
Infoline 01202 880413
Tel 01202 883402
Email kingstonlacy@ nationaltrust.org.uk
English Heritage Register Grade II
Owner The National Trust
Open Apr to Oct, daily 10.30– 6; phone for out of season openings
Area 20 acres/8 hectares

Knightshayes Court

BEAUTIFUL 20TH-CENTURY WOODLAND GARDEN AND A STATELY VICTORIAN SETTING FOR A 19TH-CENTURY HOUSE

Knightshayes Court has two faces, formal and wild, both of which are exceptionally attractive. The house was designed by William Burges for Sir John Heathcoat Amory and built from 1867 onwards. Immediately south of the house the garden designer Edward Kemp laid out formal grass terraces when the house was built. These, with gravel walks, monumental yew topiary and central steps leading down to a fountain pool flanked by stone urns, survive, commanding splendid views over parkland beyond to a distant prospect of the town of Tiverton.

The most important period in the garden's development took place after World War II under Sir John and Lady Heathcoat Amory. They replanted the upper terrace beds with distinguished mixed plantings of shrubs and herbaceous perennials and, most important of all, extended the garden eastwards – adding to the existing formal garden and creating a woodland garden of great beauty. Continuing the axis of the upper terrace with a path passing through a corridor of yew hedges, they also created a brilliantly dramatic enclosure leading off it – a square of fine lawn surrounded by castellated yew hedges with, at its centre, a circular pool edged with stone.

The woodland garden at Knightshayes

"A GARDEN IN A WOOD"

The path continues, up gentle steps, to the woodland garden or what Lady Heathcoat Amory insisted was "a garden in a wood". Underneath high old beeches, Scots pines, larches and oaks are distinguished ornamental trees and shrubs – dogwoods, hydrangeas, magnolias, maples, nothofagus, rhododendrons and the lovely spring-flowering *Stachyurus praecox* with tassels of pale yellow flowers. These are underplanted with naturalised plants – exotics such as cyclamen, erythroniums (including two hybrids, 'Knightshayes' and 'Knightshayes Pink' which have their origins here), ferns, fritillaries, gentians, leucojums, ranunculus and narcissi intermingling happily with native anemones, bluebells, foxgloves, scillas, violets and wild garlic. The effect is unlike that of woodland gardens of the Cornish coast, for the microclimate here is not especially mild and exotics that may be grown at Knightshayes look much less exotic than those found in Cornish gardens. It is as if a piece of wild native English woodland had been transformed into an extraordinary cornucopia of plants, disposed in the most natural fashion.

INFORMATION

Location Bolham, Tiverton EX16 7RQ, Devon 2m N of Tiverton by A396
Tel 01884 254665
Email knightshayes@nationaltrust.org.uk
English Heritage Register Grade II*
Owner The National Trust
Open early Mar, Fri to Mon 11–4; early Mar to early Nov, daily 11–5
Area 40 acres/16 hectares

Lanhydrock

SUPERB PARKLAND SETTING FOR A HOUSE WITH A VICTORIAN FORMAL GARDEN AND EXCELLENT SHRUBS

The Robartes family came to live here in 1620 and the estate continued in family ownership until it was given to the National Trust in 1953. The house and garden at Lanhydrock, set in romantic ancient parkland, form a rare and beautiful ensemble, yoking together elements of very different periods and giving the place great character. Linking landscape and house is a long double avenue of beech, originally planted in the 17th century with sycamore, of which a few original trees survive. The castellated stone house, U-shaped about a courtyard, is a mixture of the 17th and 19th centuries. A 17th-century granite gatehouse with battlements guards the entrance to the house. In 1857 George Gilbert Scott built battlemented walls to enclose the court between gatehouse and house.

The courtyard garden at Lanhydrock

FORMAL GARDENS

New formal gardens were laid out within the walls: six lawns, on gently terraced slopes, are each marked with four Irish yews enclosing a shaped bed planted with a block of a single variety of bedding roses – 'Bright Smile' (yellow), 'The Fairy', 'Else Poulsen', and 'Escapade' (all pink). The beautiful bronze urns that decorate the garden are copies of those made for Louis XIV's Versailles by the goldsmith Claude Ballin. On the north side of the house a parterre in an intricate pattern of shaped beds is cut out of grass and edged with box, and planted with spring and summer bedding schemes.

Behind the house informality reigns except for the herbaceous circle, a pattern of four quadrants encircled with yew hedges and filled with herbaceous perennials – in particular crocosmias, of which Lanhydrock has a National Collection (about 60 cultivars)· Paths wind through woodland, from time to time animated by some special planting. At Borlase's Stream is a wonderful collection of magnolias, started in the 1930s and continued in more recent times. The stream itself, tumbling down a cascade, is fringed with mossy rocks, ferns and, in April, drifts of rich purple Himalayan primulas. The wooded slopes above are studded with fine trees and shrubs – camellias, cherries, dogwoods, hydrangeas, magnolias, rhododendrons and Himalayan rowans. At the top a delicious view awaits you: look back eastwards over the house, formal gardens and avenue to distant glimpses of Bodmin Moor – a lovely mixture of domestic order in a wild setting.

INFORMATION

Location Bodmin PL30 5AD, Cornwall; 2½m SE of Bodmin by A38 or B3268
Tel 01208 265950
Email lanhydrock@nationaltrust.org.uk
English Heritage Register Grade II*
Owner The National Trust
Open daily 10–6
Area 25 acres/10 hectares

Lytes Cary Manor

DELIGHTFUL MEDIEVAL HOUSE WITH TOPIARY, BORDERS, ORCHARD AND A CHARMING ATMOSPHERE

The house is a late medieval hall-house, which despite a certain amount of subsequent fiddling preserves its essential delightful character. The Lyte family lived in these parts from the 13th to the 18th century. In the 16th century the lord of the manor, Sir Henry Lyte, translated into English a famous Flemish book about herbs, Rembert Dodoens's *Cruÿdeboeck*, which appeared in English in 1578 as *Nievve Herball*. Lyte added his own observations on plants, recording, for example, that bluebells grew "not far from my poore house at Lytescarie". Nothing is known of gardens at Lytes Cary until the estate was bought in 1907 by Sir Walter Jenner, the son of Sir Edward Jenner, the inventor of vaccination. It was Walter Jenner who was responsible for making the delightful formal gardens close to the house.

The entrance forecourt has an avenue of yew topiary – curious dumpy pudding shapes surmounted by a flattened cone, vaguely echoing the shape of an old dovecote seen across a field, on which the avenue is precisely aligned. To the side of the house a flagged path runs between a mixed border and a yew hedge that breaks out from time to time in buttresses capped with finely wrought topknots. A raised grass walk with a row of Irish yews overlooks a formal orchard planted with rows of crab-apples, medlars, pears, quinces and walnuts with, at each corner, an arbour formed of a weeping ash. In spring the grass in the orchard is brilliant with cowslips, snake's head fritillaries and narcissi.

NOBLE YEW HEDGES

Running along the southern boundary of the garden a long broad path of turf is flanked by noble hedges of yew. There is no ornament save for a curvaceous bench at one end and topknots of yew topiary at the other end. Here, screens of yew partly conceal a circular pool with a fine fountain in the form of a lead statue of Triton spouting water. An enticing tunnel of hornbeam leads through to an enclosed glade lightened by walls of *Weigela* 'Florida Variegata', creating a mysterious effect. The unostentatiously attractive gardens at Lytes Cary, with occasional idiosyncrasies, precisely suit the character of the house. The estate also offers walks through the agricultural grounds with promises of "ancient hedges and rare arable weeds".

The forecourt garden at Lytes Cary

INFORMATION

Location Charlton Mackrell, Somerton TA11 7HU, Somerset; 4m SE of Somerton off B3151

Tel 01458 224471

Email lytescarymanor@nationaltrust.org.uk

English Heritage Register Grade II

Owner The National Trust

Open end Mar to Oct, Wed and Fri to Sun 11–5 (open Bank Hol Mon)

Area 3 acres/1.2 hectares

Mapperton House Gardens

LOVELY AND MYSTERIOUS FORMAL GARDENS FOR A BEAUTIFUL
HOUSE IN A SECRET VALLEY IN MARVELLOUS COUNTRY

Mapperton is a memorable place – a completely unspoilt rural setting, a beautiful house of the 16th and 17th centuries, equally attractive outhouses, and an astonishing garden that suddenly reveals itself, like a burst of sunshine, in the valley behind the house. There had been formal gardens here in the 17th century, of which traces survive today, but the formal valley garden dates almost entirely from the late 1920s when the house was owned by Mrs Labouchère. Parts of the valley garden look much older – the crisply shaped grass terraces on the western side have an early 18th-century look. But what Mrs Labouchère made, almost certainly with the help of a local architect, Charles William Pike, was an Italianate pastiche – a feast of decorative exuberance executed with panache. None of this is visible as you first enter.

The entrance courtyard has shapes of clipped bay, a majestic *Magnolia delavayi* and other decorative plants. This is followed by a large empty lawned space enclosed by the house, walls and a yew hedge. Camellias are planted between the windows of the house and a *Garrya elliptica* and *M. undulata* against a wall.

A SPLENDID REVELATION

Walk through an opening in the yew hedge and the valley garden is suddenly displayed below – a splendid revelation. The upper part of the garden, the Fountain Court, is arranged in a series of paved terraces following the line of the valley, with a pool at the centre and, facing each other at each end of a cross axis, grotto-like summerhouses built into the valley slope. Lavish ornament animates the scene – composition stone or lead figures; benches and urns interspersed with monumental yew topiary. The unexpected and delightful ebullience of the formal garden makes plants seem almost superfluous. Christopher Lloyd described it as "the best unplanty garden I know".

At the southern end of the Fountain Court a slightly muddled pergola leads to a high-roofed 17th-century summerhouse, and at a lower level a long canal is edged with tall, rounded cones of clipped yew. But the garden does not stop here, for the valley is planted with good trees and shrubs as it falls away towards the sea.

The canal garden at Mapperton House

INFORMATION

Location nr Beaminster DT8 3NR, Dorset;
2m SE of Beaminster by B3163
Tel 01308 862645
Email office@mapperton.com
Website www.mapperton.com
English Heritage Register
Grade II*
Owner The Earl and Countess of Sandwich
Open Mar to Oct, daily except Sat 11–5
Area 12 acres/5 hectares

Marwood Hill Gardens

PLANTSMAN'S GARDEN FILLED WITH RARE AND LOVELY THINGS IN A CHARMING SETTING

Dr Jimmy Smart, who made this garden, thought of gardening as "a disease, at times infectious, and certainly, as far as I am concerned, quite incurable". Dr Smart himself became infected when he bought Marwood Hill in 1949. With land sloping down to a stream, it was an admirable site for a garden but Smart got off to a bad start – the only plant of much note in the garden was a very fine *Rhododendron nobleanum*, which died of honey fungus the year after he arrived. His aim, however, was to "make trees and shrubs grow happily" and in this he was very successful, clothing both sides of the valley with birches, cherries, dogwoods, firs, magnolias, maples, oaks, pines and the occasional jolt of eucalyptus, and taking advantage of the well-drained south-facing positions in the valleys to plant many of the less hardy shrubs – abutilons, *Acca sellowiana*, cistus, olearias and phygelius. The far bank (which has acid soil) has a memorable grove of camellias.

The valley garden at Marwood

NATIONAL COLLECTIONS

The banks of the stream are planted with relatively chaste astilbes, hostas, lysichitons and primulas, but in late summer there is an explosion of the showiest crocosmias and lobelias. At the head of the stream a life-size bronze statue of Jimmy Smart, erected by his family to celebrate the millennium, gazes quizzically down the valley as if itching to do a spot of planting. A National Collection of *Iris ensata* cultivars is kept here, over 200 of them, many of them gathered about a pool in the valley – a flamboyant sight in the Devon countryside. A quite different National Collection also finds a home here – of tulbaghias (15 species), those elegant South African bulbs with a savoury scent and daintily nodding flowers, which are planted high up in well-drained soil in a sunny position.

In a walled garden a good nursery sells all sorts of plants, many of them hard to come by elsewhere, propagated from those in the garden. The walls also provide protection for some more tender plants – callistemons, ceanothus, *Carpenteria californica* and leptospermums. Marwood Hill is an excellent example of the garden of an ardent collector who does not give a fig for fashion. Dr Smart knew what he liked and you may well like it too.

INFORMATION

Location nr Barnstaple EX31 4EB, Devon; 4m NW of Barnstaple signed off A361
Tel 01271 342528
Owner Mrs J.A. Smart
Open daily 9.30–5
Area 20 acres/8 hectares

Minterne

A WOODLAND AND WATER GARDEN OF 18TH-CENTURY ORIGINS WITH BEAUTIFUL 20TH-CENTURY PLANTINGS

The house at Minterne was an Edwardian replacement, designed by Leonard Stokes, for a 17th-century house. Pevsner finds "verve and freshness" in its design; others may be struck by its blockish disconnection from its site. At all events, although you pass the house to enter the garden, it scarcely impinges on the character of the garden, whose chief part lies in the densely wooded valley below.

The Digby family came here in the mid 18th century when Admiral the Hon. Robert Digby bought the estate from the Churchill family. Digby took much interest in the garden and embarked on an immense programme of tree planting on what was then bare downland. He also saw the picturesque possibilities of the river Cerne in the valley below, where he built bridges and created several dams and cascades. An entry in his diary in 1768 reads, "Spent the day at my favourite ploy, cascading."

The woodland garden at Minterne

Early in the 20th century the west side of the valley, below the house, was enriched with many new exotics introduced by Reginald Farrer, Frank Kingdon Ward and E.H. Wilson. Some of these are now substantial trees, such as a *Davidia involucrata* (one of several in the garden) planted in 1909; Wilson had introduced the tree to Europe only six years previously, sending seed to Veitch's nursery. Superlative Japanese maples and beautiful specimens of *Cercidiphyllum japonicum* also decorate the slopes. A handsome *Metasequoia glyptostroboides* was planted in 1949, only two years after seeds of this newly discovered Chinese tree had been collected. A Monterey cypress (*Cupressus macrocarpa*), planted in 1938, must be among the oldest in the country.

CLEVERLY PLANNED PATHS

In April and May the wooded valley and the banks of the pools at the valley bottom glow with rhododendrons, and waves of candelabra primulas brilliantly colonise the damp ground. The walks along the river, crossed by bridges from time to time and fringed with ferns and irises, are delightful. On the far bank sheep graze among the oaks and limes of fine old parkland. The paths that link the various parts of the garden are cleverly planned. Shifting prospects as you descend or climb the valley provide differing views of the garden, especially of individual trees and shrubs.

INFORMATION

Location Minterne Magna, nr Dorchester DT2 7AU, Dorset; 9m N of Dorchester by A352
Tel 01300 341370
Email enquiries@minterne.co.uk
English Heritage Register Grade II
Owner The Hon Mr and Mrs Henry Digby
Open Mar to Oct, daily 10–6
Area 21 acres/8.5 hectares

Montacute House

A GREAT TUDOR HOUSE WITH MAGNIFICENT GARDENS REPLANTED IN THE 20TH CENTURY

When the great golden house at Montacute rose majestically from the ground in the late 16th century it must have astonished the villagers, few of whom could ever have seen a building of such size and splendour. It was built for a prosperous lawyer and Member of Parliament, Sir Edward Phelips, who had become an influential courtier to Queen Elizabeth. A suitably splendid garden was made – as early as 1630 a visitor described "large and spacious Courtes, gardens, orchards, a parke". The "Courtes" were walled enclosures, several of which survive today. The essential garden layout survived the 18th-century craze for landscaping and remains, albeit with later additions and modern planting, one of the best preserved and most attractive surviving formal gardens of its period.

The East Court garden at Montacute House

A HOUSE OF SPLENDOUR

The East Court, formerly the entrance courtyard to the house, is enclosed in balustraded walls with coping decorated with narrow obelisks and openwork stone lanterns. The outer corners of the court are triumphantly closed by enchanting ogee-roofed gazebos. In the 19th century exuberant borders were made to line the walls here. (G.S. Elgood's watercolour of 1886 shows veils of pale colours fizzing from time to time with eruptions of scarlet zinnias or sunflowers.) In the 1950s these borders were redesigned by Phyllis Reiss who lived nearby at Tintinhull House (*see page 69*) and a version of her scheme, tweaked by the National Trust, survives today. The North Garden is at a lower level, with terrace walks. Rows of Irish yews, clipped into rounded cones, and thorns (*Crataegus* x *lavallei*) frame the garden, which has a galleried pool at its centre. An excellent border of species and shrub roses runs along the south wall, laid out in the late 1940s by Vita Sackville-West and Graham Thomas – pioneers in the rediscovery of old roses. The Cedar Lawn, which is enclosed on two sides by huge and memorably baggy ancient yew hedges, has two spectacular trees of *Cupressus arizonica* – the largest specimens in England – and a beautiful sweet chestnut. Throughout the garden there is planting and architecture to be relished, but at its heart, dominating the atmosphere of the place, is the great house, a garden ornament of irresistible splendour. This is especially apparent in winter when there is little distraction afforded by plants except for some superb trees.

INFORMATION

Location Montacute, nr Yeovil TA15 6XP, Somerset; 4m W of Yeovil by A3088
Tel 01935 823289
Email montacute@nationaltrust.org.uk
English Heritage Register Grade I
Owner The National Trust
Open end Mar to Oct, daily except Tue 11–6; Nov to end Mar, Wed to Sun 11–4
Area 12 acres/4.8 hectares

Mount Edgcumbe

GREAT CORNISH GARDEN WITH CLIFFTOP WALKS, FINE
FORMAL GARDENS AND EXCELLENT PLANTING

Celia Fiennes came here in 1698 and wrote, "its scituation makes it esteemed by me the finest seat I have seen." She was by no means the first to be bowled over by the site of Mount Edgcumbe – a dramatic sloping headland, bursting out into cliffs, overlooking Plymouth Sound. If it is not true that Admiral Medina Sidonia had already earmarked the estate for himself when his Armada had conquered England, it would be easy to understand his covetousness. Sir Piers Edgcumbe (of Cotehele, *see page 33*) had a royal licence to make a deer park here in 1539 and a house was built a little

later. When Celia Fiennes visited the garden she saw "a hill all bedeck'd with woods which are divided into severall rowes of trees in walks". Badeslade's engraving of 1737 shows the house with a double avenue and formal walks, straight or winding, cut through woods. A grand triple avenue of oaks and limes, of 20th-century planting, gives a similar effect today, sweeping down the hill in front of the house.

A CLASSICAL LOOK

In the 18th century the Edgcumbes embarked on improvements to the landscape: zig-zag walks leading along the edge of the cliffs south-east of the house; a ruinous ivy-clad folly placed on

The French Garden at Mount Edgcumbe

grassy slopes leading to the sea; Milton's Temple, in the Ionic style with a dome and pillars, below an amphitheatre close to the sea; and Thomson's Seat, an open Doric Pavilion in a grove of holm oaks with a quotation from "The Seasons" by the Scottish poet James Thomson, reading, "On either hand/ Like a long wintry forest, groves of masts/Shot up their spires; the bellying sheets between/ Possessed the breezy wind." More surprisingly, from the mid 18th to early 19th century, the Lords Mount Edgcumbe laid out a new series of formal gardens. The Italian garden has a conservatory (now a restaurant), a grand double staircase with a statue of Apollo, a bust of Ariosto and other figures, a fountain supported by a double-tailed mermaid standing in a twelve-sided pool and surrounded by citrus plants in pots, and box topiary clipped into spirals. The French Garden has an elaborate box parterre filled with bedding plants and a shell fountain in an octagonal pool at its centre, the whole overlooked by an orangery. In the English Garden an early 18th-century pedimented garden house overlooks a flower garden and some magnificent old cork oaks (*Quercus suber*).

CAMELLIAS AND WALKS

A more recent development, in 1976, some considerable distance away, is the remarkable National Collection of camellias with 1,000 species and cultivars – arranged in a combe, well south of the house near Picklecombe Point. The climate is mild here and the camellias burst into flower very early, making one of the most magnificent winter flowering sights you could imagine. Special conducted camellia walks are organised.

Another modern development is the Earl's Garden immediately alongside the house, which was completely rebuilt after being destroyed in World War II. Pleasant enough, it is of only modest interest compared to the multi-layered splendours of the park. If you are energetic the best way to enjoy this is to take a long walk, starting in the Kingsand car park and walking all round the coast until you come to the formal gardens north of the house. Best of all, take a picnic and make a day of it. The wooded walks along the cliffs, with views of the sea and occasional ornamental buildings, are marvellous. For the less energetic there is a car park at Cremyll Lodge, at the northern tip of the park, alongside the formal gardens.

INFORMATION

Location Cremyll, Torpoint PL10 1HZ, Cornwall; 2½m SE of Torpoint
Tel 01752 822236
Email mt.edgcumbe@plymouth.gov.uk
Website www.mountedgcumbe.gov.uk
English Heritage Register Grade I
Owner Plymouth City Council and Cornwall County Council
Open daily 8–dusk; Earl's Garden (entrance by house) Apr to Sept, Sun to Thurs 11–4.30 (groups by appointment in Mar and Oct)
Area 865 acres/350 hectares

Overbeck's Garden

GARDEN OF CHARACTER ON THE SALCOMBE ESTUARY, FILLED WITH TENDER EXOTIC PLANTS

Otto Overbeck was a scientist and inventor who lived here from 1928 to 1937; he left both house and garden to The National Trust. Part of his house is now a youth hostel and part a museum of antique maritime artefacts, early photographs of the area, shells, stuffed animals and other miscellaneous magpie glories. The museum also tells the tale of Overbeck's Electrical Rejuvenator (patented in 1924) and his non-alcoholic beer. Before Overbeck's time two owners, Edric Hopkins and G. N. Vereker, had introduced all manner of tender exotic plants.

A WHIFF OF THE RIVIERA

The site, with dreamy views over the Salcombe estuary, has a strong flavour of the corniche of the Côte d'Azur. The house, too, has a pronounced whiff of the Riviera, perhaps Italian rather than French. The garden is terraced, 200ft/60m above the water, and is well protected to the north and east. With around 40in/100cm of rain a year, plenty of sun, neutral gravelly soil and sharp drainage, the site is the closest on the British mainland to that of Tresco Abbey. Many tender plants flourish here, some of them becoming naturalised, such as the brilliant yellow *Calceolaria mexicana*. The very tender camphor tree (*Cinnamomum camphora*), groves of self-sown *Echium pininana*, March-flowering mimosa (*Acacia dealbata*), and marvellous ramparts of *Drimys winteri* jostle together in exotic profusion. A superlative old *Magnolia campbellii* flaunts its noble pink, cupped flowers in early spring. By no means a rare tree in the south-west, this example is exceptionally beautiful. Bulbous plants, many from South Africa, sparkle like jewels among the foliage. In truth there is not much design in the garden at Overbeck's apart from a pretty box parterre with gravels of different colours and the Statue Garden with its symmetrical herbaceous beds and a bronze statue, First Flight, by Albert Bruce-Joy. The pleasures of the garden come from the atmosphere of leafy, tropical abundance, the brilliant colours and curious shapes of exotic flowers and, from the top of the garden, the view on a fine day of an improbably blue sea with a jungle of Chusan palms in the foreground. Spring is the best season here but in summer holidaymakers bring a festive feeling.

Soaring echiums in the borders at Overbecks

INFORMATION

Location Sharpitor, Salcombe TQ8 8LW, Devon; 1½m SW of Salcombe by minor roads
Tel 01548 842893
Email overbecks@ nationaltrust.org.uk
English Heritage Register Grade II
Owner The National Trust
Open Mar to Oct, daily except Sat 10–5.30; Nov to Feb daily except Sat 11–4
Area 7 acres/2.75 hectares

Penjerrick

UNSPOILT JUNGLE-LIKE WOODLAND GARDEN, FILLED WITH RARE TREASURES SPLENDIDLY DISPLAYED

Cornish woodland gardens all draw on a similar repertory of plants but vary strongly in character. Penjerrick is unusual in preserving a powerful atmosphere of wildness – paths are narrow and vistas vague, giving a strong feeling of penetrating some thrilling Himalayan forest. Robert Were Fox made the garden at Penjerrick in the 1840s while his brothers Alfred (at Glendurgan, *see page 43*) and Charles (at Trebah, *see page 70*) were making their gardens. Taking advantage of the mild climate and protected position, he introduced immense numbers of appropriate plants. His elder daughter, Anna Maria, also took an interest in the garden, creating the Wilderness, a sort of idealised jungle in which cockatoos and monkeys played in a grove of tree ferns (*Dicksonia antarctica*), some of which survive today – one of the best old groups of these plants in the country.

Deep in the jungle at Penjerrick

SECRETIVE CHARACTER

Later in the 19th century, during the time that Samuel Smith was head gardener, there was much hybridising of rhododendrons – the famous Cornish crosses between *R. griffithianum* and *R. thomsonii*. Penjerrick became a famous garden in this period. In 1874 *The Gardener's Chronicle*, comparing Penjerrick with other gardens, wrote, "I doubt if there is [anywhere] which can compete with Penjerrick in a certain indescribable effect – the effect of landscape gardening carried out with the most exquisitely cultivated taste." Today the great charm of Penjerrick is that it preserves a secretive, densely planted character. Marvellous examples of common trees (like copper beeches) provide a background for splendid specimens of rarities such as *Eucryphia moorei, Laurelia sempervirens, Amomyrtus*

luma and many others. Some plants are exceptional specimens, such as a magnificent *Davidia involucrata* and a gigantic *Podocarpus salignus* well over 50ft/15m high. Everything grows exceptionally vigorously here, partly because of the wet warm climate but also because of the springs that irrigate the garden. Early in the season a walk among the densely planted groves, suffused with heady whiffs of the scented rhododendron 'Lady Alice Fitzwilliam', is one of the finest pleasures that Cornish gardens can offer. Visitors should be warned that paths can be muddy and precipitous, and although the garden is not huge, it is remarkably easy to lose one's way. Happily, Penjerrick is still privately owned, by a member of the Fox family.

INFORMATION

Location Budock, nr Falmouth TR11 5ED, Cornwall; 3m SW of Falmouth by minor roads
Tel 01872 870105
Website www.penjerrickgarden.co.uk
English Heritage Register Grade II
Owner Mrs R. Morin
Open Mar to Sept, Wed, Fri and Sun 1.30–4.30
Area 15 acres/6 hectares

Pine Lodge Gardens

LATE 20TH-CENTURY GARDENS WITH A REMARKABLY RICH COLLECTION OF RARE AND BEAUTIFULLY GROWN PLANTS

As you walk from the car park at Pine Lodge you pass a delightful Cornish dry-stone wall capped with turf and planted with ferns and navelwort; there is also a very urban street lamp of the slightly old-fashioned kind often seen in suburban gardens. The garden too reflects a certain clash of styles, but the plants, and the standards of practical horticulture, are superb. Much of the detailing is marvellous, too – granite slabs of lovely quality are used for paving paths or for making steps. The steps that lead down to the arboretum, for example, becoming deeper as they descend, are magnificent. Occasionally there are attractive but simple ornaments – a fine terracotta pot-bellied pot placed alongside *Viburnum plicatum* 'Mariesii', for example – but elsewhere in the garden poor quality statues or fiddly interludes of paving are unworthy of the quality of the plants. Having said that, anyone who loves plants and prefers to see them bursting with vigour will have a marvellous time here.

Fine planting at Pine Lodge Gardens

AN EXPANDING GARDEN

The Clemos have been building up their garden since 1976, starting with 2 acres/0.8 hectares and expanding to 30 acres/12 hectares. Much of the garden consists of intricate planting and winding paths surrounding the house, but west of the house there are handsome open areas with an arboretum, a lake (ornamented with black swans) and a pinetum (planted in 1993 – who else has planted a private pinetum in the last fifty years?). Everything is impeccably labelled and over 6,000 different species and cultivars are grown. A National Collection of the Australian genus *Grevillea* (15 species and cultivars) is kept

here. Nothing seems to stop the Clemos and a new 4-acre/1.6-hectare Winter Garden was started in January 2006 and the planting completed at the end of 2007. The Clemos also run a nursery at Pine Lodge for which they propagate more than 1,000 different species from the garden, many of them hard to come by. No plants are bought in – all are raised from seed, some of which is gathered in the wild on the Clemos' behalf. Thirty garden benches are distributed throughout the garden, encouraging visitors to sit and admire the views. Altogether this is a place that is most pleasurable to visit, where one may also learn about unfamiliar plants in fine surroundings.

INFORMATION

Location Holmbush, St Austell PL25 3RQ, Cornwall; on the E edge of St Austell signed on the A390
Tel 01726 73500
Email gardens@pine-lodge.co.uk
Website www.pine-lodge.co.uk
Owner Shirley and Ray Clemo
Open daily (except 24–26 Dec) 10–6
Area 30 acres/12 hectares

Prior Park Landscape Garden

EXQUISITE 18TH-CENTURY LANDSCAPE GARDEN IN A RARE AND MEMORABLE POSITION WITH VIEWS OVER BATH

By comparison with other 18th-century landscape parks Prior Park is delightful chamber music rather than formidable symphony. The site is very beautiful – a shallow wooded valley scooping down to the north, with Elysian views of Bath. The Palladian mansion (now a school) was built in 1735–48 to the designs of John Wood the Elder for Ralph Allen, an entrepreneur and quarry owner who supplied stone for the building of Georgian Bath.

ARCADIAN LANDSCAPE

The park was laid out from 1734 onwards, probably by Allen himself, with help from Richard Jones and the poet Alexander Pope who corresponded with Allen and made several visits. Jones, Allen's clerk of works, also acted as an architect, and it was he who, in 1756, designed the key garden building here – the lovely Palladian bridge which spans the neck of an ornamental lake at the foot of the valley. There are three lakes here, with the woods pressing in about them on three sides. To the west are the foundations of an ornamental 18th-century thatched cottage and an ice-house of the same period.

Capability Brown was consulted about Prior Park in about 1764 and although there is no evidence that he worked here, the garden certainly changed from the intricate semi-formality of Pope's ideas to the Arcadian landscape of shorn turf, placid water, brisk descents and distant prospects the visitor sees today.

The National Trust was given the garden in 1993 and restoration has moved slowly. By 2007, with support from the Heritage Lottery Fund, work was underway to restore the remarkable Wilderness at the top of the hill near the house. This consists of a serpentine lake, into which tumbles a dramatic cascade built of rustic stone overlooked by the Cabinet, a planted clearing from which visitors would admire the tumbling water. A poem written by Mary Chandler in 1734 describes it: "From thence the foaming waves fall rapid down, in bold cascades, and lash the rugged stone." To the east of the lake were the ruins of the ornamental stone sham bridge which has been finely restored. On the garden's western edge is The Rock Gate, a wooden gate of 18th-century design flanked by rustic stonework rising in narrow cones.

The Palladian Bridge at Prior Park

INFORMATION

Location Ralph Allen Drive, Bath BA2 5AH, Somerset; on Combe Down, 1m S of the centre of Bath

Infoline 09001 335242

Tel 01225 833422

Email priorpark@nationaltrust.org.uk

English Heritage Register Grade I

Owner The National Trust

Open Mar to Oct, daily except Tue 11–5.30; Nov to Feb, Sat and Sun 11–dusk.

NB No parking at the garden; phone or consult NT website for details of access

Area 28 acres/11 hectares

Rosemoor Garden

THE PRIVATE GARDEN OF A NOTED PLANTSWOMAN TRANSFORMED BY THE RHS INTO A FINE DISPLAY GARDEN

Colonel J.E. and Lady Anne Palmer had come here in 1959 and started to make a garden on a west-facing slope running southwards from the house. The garden was essentially informal, with a large range of trees and shrubs of the kind that flourish in acid soil. Lady Anne became a friend of "Cherry" Ingram from whom many distinguished flowering trees and shrubs found their way to Rosemoor. The garden had in addition notable collections of primulas and of the smaller decorative bulbous plants.

A NEW DISPLAY GARDEN

In 1988 Lady Anne Berry (as she had become) gave the estate to the Royal Horticultural Society. The garden has since been greatly extended to form a display garden, and has a visitor centre built at a discreet distance from the house. Lady Anne's garden survives, with some of its original character, and the new garden, separated by the A3124, does not impinge on it but is craftily connected by a tunnel under the road. The two gardens, one busy with plants and information, the other serenely reticent, serve very different purposes. The chief part of the new garden, spread out below the visitor centre, displays different garden styles. These gardens are either thematic (Potager, Herb and Cottage Gardens) or devoted to particular groups of plants (Modern Roses and Shrub Roses) or are model gardens for particular sites or seasons (a Shade Garden, a Winter Garden, a Terrace Garden). The Plantsman's Garden has the attractive idea of gathering together many of the exotics that were introduced by the great local firm of Veitch & Son of Exeter. A Foliage Garden skilfully deploys ornamental grasses, shapely plants like euphorbias and New Zealand flax (*Phormium* cultivars), trees and shrubs with decorative foliage (*Eucalyptus* and *Pittosporum*) and a curious screen of clipped *Sorbus thibetica* 'John Mitchell' with very large rounded leaves, underplanted with ferns.

At a little distance is a lake and bog garden and an outstanding decorative kitchen garden enclosed in split chestnut paling. Although prettily ornamental, with swags of runner beans, espaliered fruit and edgings of Welsh onion, this is an efficient working garden seen in full productive action. Throughout Rosemoor emphasis is placed on plants that are suitable for the relatively wet, relatively warm climate of the south-west, making it an admirable resource for local gardeners.

The Foliage Garden at Rosemoor

INFORMATION

Location Great Torrington EX38 8PH, Devon; 1m SE of Great Torrington by A3124
Tel 01805 624067
Email rosemooradmin@rhs.org.uk
Website www.rhs.org.uk
Owner The Royal Horticultural Society
Open Apr to Sept, daily 10–6; Oct to Mar, daily (except 26 Dec) 10–5
Area 40 acres/16 hectares

Saltram House

AN 18TH-CENTURY HOUSE IN HANDSOME PARKLAND WITH A CONTEMPORARY ORANGERY AND GOOD TREES AND SHRUBS

There has been a house at Saltram since at least the 16th century but the present house is 18th-century, of various periods, with grand interiors designed by Robert Adam for the Parker family between 1768 and 1772. The grounds were laid out at this time too, and much of the informal and picturesque character of the period survives today. The house is set in beautiful parkland although it is uncomfortably close to busy roads. The garden spreads west from the house with a lawn overlooked by an 18th-century pedimented orangery with giant sash windows; it is agreeable, and rare, to see an orangery still used for oranges. Nearby is a magnificent old sweet chestnut. Walks among trees and shrubs beyond the orangery show many fine plants – a huge bush of *Euphorbia mellifera*, *Albizzia julibrissin* and *Cornus* 'Norman Hadden'. Hidden away is "the Castle", an octagonal Gothic summerhouse with a pretty blue and white interior and a fireplace in the style of William Kent. A flag was flown from a flagpole on the Castle when the family was at home. Close to the Castle is a splendid Lucombe oak (*Quercus* x *hispanica* 'Lucombeana'), an essential tree for great Devon gardens of this period for it was the discovery, in the 1760s, of an Exeter nurseryman, William Lucombe.

The lime avenue at Saltram

"FANNY'S BOWER"

An avenue of limes leads back towards the house, underplanted in spring with pale narcissi and beautiful later in the season with immense drifts of cow parsley. The avenue runs along the garden's boundary with lovely views southwards over old parkland. At a little distance from the house in the woods below the orangery is "Fanny's Bower",

a Palladian temple celebrating a visit by Fanny Burney, keeper of Robes to Queen Charlotte, who accompanied the royal family when they visited in 1789 – a grand firework display took place in the garden. Although there are many fine trees and flowering shrubs at Saltram the planting is restrained – it provides a gentlemanly setting for a gentlemanly house, and is perfect in its understated way. In 1957 the estate was acquired by the National Trust, which has carried out much work in the gardens. This work has included the construction of a ha-ha to prevent parkland deer from grazing up to the windows of the house, which in the past they had been able to do.

INFORMATION

Location Plympton, Plymouth PL7 3UH, Devon; 3m E of Plymouth by A38
Tel 01752 333500
Email saltram@nationaltrust.org.uk
English Heritage Register Grade II*
Owner The National Trust
Open (Garden) Mar to Oct, daily except Fri (open Good Fri) 11–4.30; Nov to Feb, daily except Fri 11–4; (Park) daily dawn–dusk
Area 21 acres/8.5 hectares

Shute House

A MAGICAL 20TH-CENTURY GARDEN – SIR GEOFFREY JELLICOE'S MASTERPIECE OF WATER, TREES AND TURF

There was no notable garden here before Michael and Lady Anne Tree bought the handsome 18th-century house. The garden they commissioned from Sir Geoffrey Jellicoe was laid out from 1968. The most important ingredient at Shute is water, and this dominated Jellicoe's ideas. The centrepiece of his design is a long, stepped, formal rill on the gentle slope of a lawn, its upper part masked by dense and informal planting. At the head of the rill, paths on each side lead down through arbours of wisteria with lavish plantings of honeysuckle, Japanese anemones and shrub roses. The lower part of the cascade, now a narrower rill, flows across an uneven open lawn, dropping into pools that are octagonal, hexagonal or square in shape, with a bubbling jet at the centre of each. Finally, the water falls into a fern-lined rill and is carried away to other watery parts of the garden.

The rill at Shute House

From the head of the rill a secretive passage leads between hedges of yew and beech to show water used in an entirely different way. Here, 17th-century busts of Achilles, Neptune and Zeus, standing in niches cut into a beech hedge, look over a low amphitheatre of box down a long, still, rectangular pool. Clumps of arum lilies are planted regularly down one side of the pool, and on the other side are viewing platforms set in a grove of ilexes. A mown path leads down into the woods where the source of Shute's water, a pool with bubbling springs, gleams in the shade.

INTREPID ECLECTICISM

The Lewises came to Shute in 1993 and have finely restored the existing garden, adding excellent ideas of their own, especially around the house. In front of the pedimented east façade they have completed the enclosure of a forecourt with high yew hedges, put in place a magnificent pair of wrought-iron gates, and added clematis and climbing roses to the walls of the house. In the hidden lower part of the garden, near Jellicoe's rustic temple of ivy, they have continued the theme, introducing a sinister planting of dark and poisonous plants round a bust of Pan. Set comfortably within rural surroundings, garden and landscape have become a seamless garment and provide a perfect setting for the house.

INFORMATION

Location Donhead St Mary, Shaftesbury SP7 9DG, Dorset; in Donhead St Mary village, 3m E of Shaftesbury by A30 and minor roads
Tel 01747 828866
Owner Mr and Mrs John Lewis
Open only to groups of between 20 and 40 by written appointment
Area 7 acres/2.8 hectares

Sticky Wicket

A LATE 20TH-CENTURY GARDEN WHERE THE ENVIRONMENT IS AS IMPORTANT AS THE DELIGHTFUL COLOUR HARMONIES

From 1987 Pam Lewis made a garden "designed to show different planting styles and colour themes", with the additional aim of "attracting bees, butterflies and birds". The ornamental qualities of the garden remain, with ecological principles coming to the fore. The formal parts of the garden are gathered together about the house. The Frog Garden has swerving mixed borders round a lawn and a pool. Blue and yellow dominate the colour scheme, with shrubs such as *Cytisus battandieri*, *Euphorbia mellifera* and *Rosa* 'Maigold' underplanted with crocosmias, daylilies and geraniums, and grasses such as *Millium effusum* 'Aureum'. A pergola and terrace continue the theme with *Coreopsis verticillata* and *Lonicera periclymenum* 'Graham Thomas'. The Bird Garden has a more sprightly colour scheme of deep reds, purples and pinks. A circular gravel bed has a sea of the Mexican daisy (*Erigeron karvinskianus*), trailing silver-pink *Convolvulus althaeoides* and the native sea thrift, *Armeria maritima*.

The Round Garden at Sticky Wicket

CIRCLES AND MEADOWS

On ground sloping up from the house to the south, the Round Garden is a series of concentric circles in which the planting ebbs and flows from pastels to rich red, magenta or purple. Grasses, especially festuca, pennisetums and the delicate little *Agrostis nebulosa*, provide crisp shapes or blurred texture. The site is open and sunny, making it attractive to bees and butterflies. Farther away, the White Garden, largely of trees and shrubs, extends the theme to white doves in a dovecote and the geese in an adjacent poultry run. A ½-acre/0.2 hectare hay meadow has been recreated by removing the excessively fertile topsoil and sowing the subsoil with seed gathered from a nearby meadow – a splendid sight, with bird's-foot trefoil, corky-fruited dropwort, orchids, ragged robin, yellow rattle and much else. A smaller garden version following the same principle includes non-native plants such as campanulas and geraniums and also makes use of bulbs such as narcissi and snowdrops. A little copse of birch provides habitats for many creatures (as many as 229 fauna will thrive among birch); piles of logs or dry-stone walls also give habitats.

Many beautiful gardens pay little attention to the demands of nature's fauna. A garden such as Sticky Wicket, where provision for such creatures is a guiding principle, may arrive at a different kind of beauty, not a visual aesthetic but a moral one.

INFORMATION

Location Buckland Newton DT2 7BY, Dorset; Buckland Newton village, between the church, the school and the Gaggle of Geese pub, 10m N of Dorchester by B3143
Tel 01300 345476
Website www. stickywicketgarden.co.uk
Owner Pam Lewis
Open Jun to Sept, Thurs 10.30–8
Area 2 acres/0.8 hectares

Tapeley Park

MAGNIFICENT EDWARDIAN TERRACED GARDEN FOR AN 18TH-CENTURY HOUSE IN A BEAUTIFUL POSITION

The house at Tapeley occupies a wonderful position high up on wooded slopes above the Torridge estuary, with broad views south-west. Commodore William Clevland, who built the house in about 1700, was a naval officer, so this was an appropriate place to live. Between 1898 and 1916 the exterior of the house was completely rebuilt for Augustus and Lady Rosamond Christie under the supervision of John Belcher, whom they also asked to make a new garden.

NOBLE TERRACES

On the slopes below the southern façade of the house Belcher made three Italianate terraces linked by brick steps and decorated with statues. To descend the terraces you squeeze between a pair of old Irish yews, with thickets of fuchsia and lavender and on either side. Many distinguished tender plants flourish in the protection of the terraces, including the showiest of all buddleias, *Buddleja colvilei*, with its dazzling red flowers, *Callistemon citrinus*, *Crinodendron hookerianum* and

Drimys winteri. Below each retaining wall is a deep mixed border designed in 1999 by Mary Keen. A sundial sits at the centre of the middle terrace and a row of Irish yews guards the lowest terrace. On the other side a long flight of steps, made from surplus World War I gravestones and watched over by a pair of putti, climbs a slope. Nearby is a pretty brick summerhouse – a former tool house – with statues in niches and a sweeping gable of Dutch character. At the top of the hill are a so-called grotto, in fact a shell-house, and an ice-house, which must both date from the 18th century. Beyond lies a large walled kitchen garden where a huge greenhouse with an unusual curved roof runs the whole length of the south-facing wall. North-east of the entrance shop, paths lead down through woodland planted with camellias and rhododendrons. At the bottom of the valley is a long narrow lake with ducks. In woods west of the terraced garden is a new Permaculture Garden in which productive and ornamental plants live in harmony in irregularly shaped beds roughly edged with wood or stone – a pretty sight. However, it is the breathtaking position of the house, the noble terraces and the older garden buildings that give Tapeley Park its distinction.

Tapeley Park's summerhouse

INFORMATION

Location Instow EX39 4NT, Devon; 2m N of Bideford by A39
Tel 01271 860897
Website www.tapeleypark. com
English Heritage Register Grade II*
Owner Tapeley Park Trust
Open end Mar to Oct, daily except Sat 10–5
Area 10 acres/4 hectares

Tintinhull House

A MASTERLY GARDEN OF HARMONIOUS COMPARTMENTS WITH DISTINGUISHED PLANTING AND WONDERFUL CHARACTER

Tintinhull is among the most rewarding of English gardens. It is in essence like a miniature Hidcote or Sissinghurst in the way in which a harmonious sequence of spaces, often with strong architectural features, is embellished with carefully thought-out planting. The house is a very pretty 17th-century Ham stone village house, with a fine early 18th-century façade facing west over the garden. The garden is chiefly the creation of a remarkable woman, Phyllis Reiss, who came here in 1933, though she inherited some strong formal features made by her predecessor, Dr Price.

The Eagle Court at Tintinhull House

A SEQUENCE OF SPACES

An exact rectangle, almost entirely walled in stone, spreads out west and north of the house. The garden's great beauty comes from the easy and logical flow of events leading from enclosure to enclosure. From the garden door of the house a long axial vista is marked by a paved path running between rows of clipped box mounds. The first enclosure, the Eagle Court, has stone eagles rising on piers and mixed borders under the walls. In the Middle Garden the box mounds continue but the planting on either side of the lawns is more free-flowing, with a woodland character. Finally, the Fountain Garden, hidden away behind walls of yew, has a more intimate atmosphere, with a circular lily pool and corner beds rich in white-flowered and variegated foliage plants. This sequence of gardens runs parallel to three others, all intercommunicating – an ornamental kitchen garden, the Pool Garden with borders and a summerhouse, and the Cedar Court with magnolias planted in a lawn and a fortissimo purple and gold border backed by a yew hedge.

In 1980 Penelope Hobhouse came to live at Tintinhull with her husband, Professor John Malins, and transformed the quality of the detailed planting. Recognising the brilliant skills of Phyllis Reiss – whom she describes as "one of the great gardeners of the 20th century" – she sensitively revitalised the garden, adding much of her own but always respecting Phyllis Reiss's original intentions. Since Penelope Hobhouse left Tintinhull in 1993 the garden lost much of its magic. It nevertheless remains one of the best designed and worthwhile gardens in the country – eminently approachable because of its modest size and a source of continuing inspiration for all gardeners.

INFORMATION

Location Tintinhull, nr Yeovil BA22 8PZ, Somerset; 5m S of Yeovil, signed from A303
Tel 01935 823289
Email tintinhull@nationaltrust.org.uk
English Heritage Register Grade II
Owner The National Trust
Open mid Mar to Oct, Wed to Sun 11–5
Area ¾ acre/0.3 hectare

Trebah

EXCEPTIONAL CORNISH PLANTSMAN'S GARDEN IN A RAVINE SITE OF OUTSTANDING BEAUTY

In 1904 when the garden was in its maturity, S.W. Fitzherbert wrote: "For the natural beauty of its grounds . . . none can excel Trebah." A house had existed here from the mid 18th century and the estate was later acquired by Robert Were Fox I, of the great dynasty of Cornish garden makers. His son, Charles, took over in 1842 and embarked on a new garden. In the valley immediately adjacent, his brother, Alfred Fox, had already been hard at work on his garden at Glendurgan since 1821 (*see page 43*). On Charles's death in 1868 the Trebah estate was left to his son-in-law, Edmund Backhouse, but throughout the 20th century it changed hands repeatedly and the garden became increasingly neglected.

The ravine garden at Trebah

A DRAMATIC SITE

In 1981 Trebah was bought by Major Tony Hibbert and his wife, Eira, who have together carried out a remarkable feat of privately funded restoration. The site is one of the best, with a vertiginous ravine plunging southwards towards Polgwiddon Cove on the Helford estuary. The view from the top of the ravine, with distant glimpses of water, is very beautiful. The upper slopes of each side of the valley are clothed with dark trees, giving the ravine a greater sense of drama than any other Cornish garden. The upper banks of the valley are threaded with paths offering wide views across a jungle of astonishing vegetation. It is best to walk down the valley on one side, zigzagging up and down when something draws the eye, and then return in the same way on the other side. The tallest specimens of Chusan palm (*Trachycarpus fortunei*) in England rise from the valley floor and a group of

giant tree rhododendrons with blood-red flowers, *R.* 'Trebah Gem', erupts from the side of the ravine. At the foot of the valley a stream links pools whose banks are planted with a grove of *Gunnera manicata* and immense thickets of hydrangea. There are admirable specimens of camellias, tender *Cornus capitata*, magnolias, *Podocarpus totara*, a superlative wide-spreading *Davidia involucrata* var. *vilmoriniana* over a path, rhododendrons, and tree ferns which are thoroughly naturalised here. It is the profusion of exotic flowers and foliage, cultivated in naturalistic informality in a dramatic and lovely site, that gives Trebah such beauty.

INFORMATION

Location Mawnan Smith, nr Falmouth TR11 5JZ, Cornwall; 4m SW of Falmouth, signed from A394 and A39 approaches to Falmouth
Tel 01326 252200
Email mail@trebah-garden.co.uk
Website www.trebah-garden.co.uk
English Heritage Register Grade II
Owner The Trebah Garden Trust
Open daily 10.30–5 (winter openings may vary)
Area 25 acres/10 hectares

Trengwainton Garden

TENDER PLANTS, OUTSTANDING OLD FLOWERING SHRUBS,
AND WONDERFUL VIEWS OF ST MICHAEL'S MOUNT

The estate of Trengwainton is an ancient one, inhabited at least by the 16th century. Its garden fame, however, belongs to a much later period. In 1814 the estate was bought by Rose Price who made the drive, planted the woods that flank it and built the walled gardens at the end of the drive. The estate changed hands again in 1867 when it was bought by a banker from an old Cornish family, Thomas Simon Bolitho. It was inherited in 1925 by his great-nephew, Lieutenant Colonel Sir Edward Bolitho, who gave the garden its present distinction with the help of his exceptional head gardener, A.Creek, a skilful propagator. Colonel Bolitho also had valuable acquaintances in the world of plants and gardens, among them J.C.Williams of Caerhays (*see page 26*), George Johnstone of Trewithen and Lawrence Johnston of Hidcote (*see page 173*). From such people he received plants and they also put him in touch with plant collectors like Frank Kingdon Ward.

Trengwainton's site is especially favoured − close to the tip of the

An old magnolia at Trengwainton

Cornish peninsula on slopes that face south-east, protected by old woodland to the north and west. This, together with a fairly high rainfall and the benign effect of the North Atlantic Drift, makes it a wonderful place to grow plants. The most protected part of the garden is on the northern edge of the drive, close to the visitors' entrance, and it is here that there is the greatest concentration of plant excitement.

EXCEPTIONAL MAGNOLIAS

In a series of walled gardens are exceptional magnolias, many of which date back to Colonel Bolitho's first plantings. Everywhere there are excellent specimens of shrubs and ornamental trees, while tender herbaceous plants such as *Echium pininana* and *Geranium palmatum* seed themselves profusely. Beside the far side of the drive the margins of a stream are densely planted with *Darmera peltata*, Himalayan primulas, ligularia, lysichiton and meconopsis, and woods flanking the drive are rich in camellias and rhododendrons. In front of the house a lawn opens out and reveals the first views of the open countryside − with the breathtaking distant prospect of St Michael's Mount. Trengwainton has a wonderful collection of plants but it also possesses a bewitching atmosphere, enfolded in its exotic woodland with a secretive air.

INFORMATION

Location Madron, nr Penzance TR20 8RZ, Cornwall; 2m NW of Penzance by B3312
Infoline 01736 363148,
Email trengwainton@nationaltrust.org.uk
English Heritage Register Grade II
Owner The National Trust
Open mid Feb to early Nov, Sun to Thur (open Good Fri) 10−5
Area 15 acres/6 hectares

Tresco Abbey Gardens

A DAZZLING TERRACED JUNGLE OF RARE AND TENDER PLANTS IN A CLIMATE UNIQUE IN BRITAIN

In gardens where plants reign supreme the climate is the key to the spirit of the place. Tresco has much sunshine, little frost and moderate rainfall of 30in/75cm per annum; violent, salt-laden winds and poor soil are normally the only enemies to gardening here. The garden was started in 1834 by Augustus Smith who built a new house above the ruins of a Benedictine priory on a south-facing slope. He chose Tresco for his house and garden because it had a good water supply and was protected by the other islands. Around the ruins of the priory he built new walls and made a small garden which is still one of the most

The subtropical jungle of Tresco

atmospheric parts of the garden. He greatly extended the scope of the garden by terracing the steep south-facing slopes above the priory and by planting windbreaks of Monterey pine (*Pinus radiata*) and Monterey cypress (*Cupressus macrocarpa*). As he began to collect plants, many specimens came from Lord Ilchester's garden at Abbotsbury (*see page 16*) and from Kew (*see page 142*), where Smith made contact with Sir William Hooker.

A REMARKABLE SAGA

Tender species from the southern hemisphere flourish here and Augustus Smith and his descendants eventually built up one of the greatest collections of subtropical plants in Europe.

However, although the climate here is usually remarkably benign, in 1987 and 1990 nature showed her claws as never before in these parts, and devastated the gardens. In January 1987 heavy snow fell, breaking the branches of many trees and shrubs. The snow was immediately followed by frost, with the temperature falling to –8°C/17°F for two weeks. This was made even worse by a fierce easterly wind, and huge numbers of plants were destroyed. A rescue operation was mounted and plants brought back to Tresco from countless different sources. Then, in January 1990, a hurricane tore through the old windbreaks, destroying 90 per cent of the trees planted by Augustus Smith (800 mature trees) and many of the newly planted replacements of those lost in the great frost. The work of clearing the debris and restoring the planting is a remarkable saga, eloquently described in a book by the garden

curator, Mike Nelhams: *Tresco Abbey Garden: a personal and pictorial history* (2000).

An astonishing recovery has been made from these setbacks, and the gardens once again present a scene of extraordinarily exotic abundance. Agaves from the Mexican desert, proteas and silver-leafed leucadendrons from South Africa, banksias from Australia, olearias from New Zealand and spectacular echiums from the Canary Islands now clothe the slopes. Many exotics seed themselves here – clouds of purple-flowered *Geranium maderense*, *Euphorbia mellifera* giving off its honey-scented perfume – while *Agapanthus praecox* subsp. *orientalis* has escaped out of the gardens to scatter its rich blue flowers in the countryside.

A UNIQUE CLIMATE

The paths that run along the terraces give marvellous views over the gardens, and exhilarating cross vistas are opened by paths or steps that cut vertically up the slopes. There are subtle differences in the microclimates between the upper terraces and the lowest point of the garden. Plants that like it hot and dry flourish at the highest point and those, like tree ferns, that need shade and humidity enjoy air humidified by the close proximity of the sea at the foot of the slopes. The range of plants grown at Tresco makes it unique in the British Isles. Distinguished collections of plants do not necessarily make satisfying landscapes. However, quite early in the history of the garden Augustus Smith contrived a design that made the best of the site and created a wonderful setting for these subtropical exotics.

INFORMATION

Location Tresco, Isles of Scilly TR24 0QQ, Cornwall; 31m off the SW coast of Cornwall, access by helicopter or ferry from Penzance
Tel 01720 424105
Email mikenelhams@tresco.co.uk
English Heritage Register Grade I
Owner R. Dorrien Smith
Open daily 10–4
Area 16 acres/6 hectares

SOUTH-CENTRAL ENGLAND

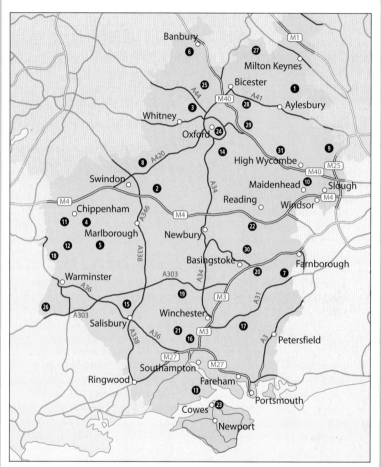

GARDENS TO VISIT

Image *West Green House Garden*

Ascott

A ROTHSCHILD GARDEN WITH SUMPTUOUS TOPIARY AND ORNAMENT, GRAND BORDERS AND DELICIOUS VIEWS

The house, originally a farmhouse built in the early 17th century, was acquired by Baron Mayer de Rothschild in 1873 as part of the neighbouring Mentmore estate. His nephew, Leopold de Rothschild, in a succession of alterations, transformed it into the "palace-like cottage" it is today. In 1949 the estate was given to the National Trust by Anthony de Rothschild.

The Venus fountain at Ascott

The site is a splendid one, with fine views of the Vale of Aylesbury. Much of the architectural work on the house was done by George Devey who also made a design for the gardens in collaboration with Leopold de Rothschild and Sir Harry Veitch and his nursery, Veitch & Son.

VICTORIAN CHARACTER

The garden, with its exuberant sense of decoration, still keeps much of its original high Victorian character. The Victorian garden, at a little distance from the house, is separated from it by magnificent trees which provide a park-like setting. On the slope below the trees is a rare topiary sundial; the now rather lumpy gnomon is of yew, the figures of box, and a motto is made of clipped golden box – "Light and shade by turn but love always".

At the heart of the Victorian garden the Madeira Walk leads between mixed borders, backed by a hedge of golden yew on one side and a terrace wall on the other, capped with a hedge of gold variegated holly. The colour scheme is restricted to purple, lilac and pink, with much repeated planting of alliums, bergenias, caryopteris, delphiniums,

lavender and penstemons. The beds are punctuated by the bold foliage of artichokes and by stone urns brimming with pink pelargoniums. Spring and summer bedding plants are put into place to maintain the momentum and fill gaps. At the centre of a circular pool enclosed in hedges of golden yew is a sumptuous bronze statue of Venus, by Thomas Waldo Story, of around 1890.

In 2006 a superb new formal garden, the Lin garden, designed by Jacques and Peter Wirtz, was put into place at a little distance from the house. Here, concealed behind a looping walk of beech hedges, are swirling patterns of hedges and ornamental grasses with pools, a mount and fine trees.

INFORMATION

Location Wing, nr Leighton Buzzard LU7 0PS, Buckinghamshire; 2m SW of Leighton Buzzard by A418
Tel 01296 688242
Email info@ascottestate.co.uk
English Heritage Register Grade II*
Owner The National Trust
Open Apr, and Aug to mid Sept, daily except Mon 2–6 (open Bank Hol Mon); May to Jul, Tue, Wed and Thur 2–6
Area 39 acres/16 hectares

Ashdown House

THE REMOTE AND BEAUTIFUL LANDSCAPE OF A 17TH-CENTURY HUNTING LODGE, HIGH UP ON THE BERKSHIRE DOWNS

The Berkshire Downs (as they are still known, despite the county boundary change of 1974) are surprisingly wild and unspoilt. This is an ancient site, already settled in Iron Age times and with a pattern of Roman fields. Owned by the Abbey of Glastonbury in the middle ages, the site contained a deer park, and a herd of wild fallow deer has been reintroduced. Fields are scattered with sarsen stones among which shaggy highland cattle graze. This is the kind of memorable landscape that makes gardening seem almost superfluous.

BUILT OF "CLUNCH"

On high, intermittently wooded land, Ashdown House appears at once mysterious and dramatic, sharpened by the ghostly pale "clunch" (in effect, chalk) of which it is built. Built as a hunting lodge in the 1660s for the 1st Earl of Craven, it was possibly designed by William Winde who had worked on other houses for Lord Craven. A Kip engraving of 1707 shows it standing at the centre of a square courtyard with four rides shooting out through dense woods enclosing the house, and in the heathland beyond, huntsmen, a pack of hounds and a fox. There is a romantic story that Lord Craven also proposed the house as a refuge from the plague for King Charles I's sister, Elizabeth of Bohemia, the "Winter Queen", who died in 1662 before the house was complete. The estate now belongs to The National Trust, who have planted avenues of limes following some of the original rides and laid out a double parterre of box scrolls.

The house is crowned with a lantern and gallery from which there are magnificent views over Ashdown Forest and the downs, and surrounding woodland makes a marvellous place for walks, punctuated by sudden revelations of the immensely elegant house. With minimal means Ashdown possesses a powerful sense of place.

INFORMATION

Location Lambourn, nr Newbury RG17 8RE, Oxfordshire
Tel 01488 72584
Email ashdownhouse@nationalrrust.org.uk
English Heritage Register Grade II*
Owner The National Trust
Open (House and grounds) Apr to Oct, Wed and Sat 2–5 (guided tours of house only at 2.15, 3.15 and 4.15); (Woodland) daily except Fri dawn–dusk
Area 346 acres/140 hectares

The parterre
at Ashdown House

Blenheim Palace

AN EARLY 18TH-CENTURY PALACE, WITH GRAND FORMAL
GARDENS AND A LANDSCAPE PARK BY CAPABILITY BROWN

There is nothing cosy about Blenheim. The monumental palace was built in the early 18th century to honour the victor of a great battle and the surrounding landscape is in scale with it. But long before all this, in the 12th century, Henry II made a garden, Rosamund's Bower, at Woodstock Palace, quite close to modern Blenheim, of which only a spring seems, tantalisingly, to survive. Woodstock Palace survived in a more or less ruinous state until Sir John Vanbrugh arrived in 1704 to build the new palace, in collaboration with Nicholas Hawksmoor, for the Duke of Marlborough. Vanbrugh loved the ruins and urged the duchess to preserve them as a picturesque adornment of the landscape – "one of the most agreeable objects that the best of landscape-painters can invent", as he wrote. She refused, and the building was finally demolished in 1723.

In 1705 a new garden for Blenheim was started as the palace was being built. To the south of the palace

The Italian Garden fountain

Vanbrugh and the royal gardener, Henry Wise, devised a formal garden of formidable elaboration, guarded by eight 150ft/45m bastions of suitably military aspect.

SUPERB WATER

This vast garden was short-lived for Capability Brown came in 1764 to introduce a new kind of landscape. The traveller Colonel John Byng wrote after his visit in 1782: "Here Lancelot Brown (the great planner of land) will be immortalised in his management of the ground about the house and the formation of the superb water; at which, when finish'd, he exclaimed with his usual pompous drollery, 'Thames, Thames, you will never forgive me.' "

Brown is often accused of destroying earlier formal landscapes with ruthless insensitivity. However, at Blenheim there is much evidence of his appreciation of the existing genius of the place. He preserved Vanbrugh's splendid bridge over the river Glyme and above all he maintained the northern vista from the palace, over the bridge, to the giant Column of Victory and beyond, up the hill, to Vanbrugh and Wise's Grand Avenue (originally of elms but now of limes). Brown's great coup was to dam the river and create a wasp-waisted lake spanned by Vanbrugh's bridge. The view of all this from the Triumphal Gate in Woodstock village is one of the most unforgettable of any English landscape.

The last great episode in the story of the garden at Blenheim is the creation by Achille Duchêne of the Italian Garden and the Water Terraces flanking the palace, which have a sprightly, festive character that contrasts admirably with the more solemn Baroque spirit of the palace. Duchêne

The Italian Garden at Blenheim

was a French garden designer whose speciality, usually in collaboration with his father, Henri, was reinstating the great 17th-century gardens of France, in particular those of André Le Nôtre. The Italian Garden (completed in 1910) is a parterre with hedges of golden yew, swooping arabesques of box, and a fountain by Thomas Waldo Story of a naked nymph holding a ducal coronet aloft while standing in a pool supported by mermaids and dolphins. The Water Terraces, completed in 1930, are in two parts. The upper level has elaborately scalloped pools, each with a fountain, and parterres *de broderie* of box. The lower level is much calmer, with two rectangular pools, one of which has a small-scale version of Bernini's superb river gods fountain of 1651 in the Piazza Navona in Rome. The Water Terraces, magnificently enlivened with splendid statuary, have skilfully orchestrated changes of level which multiply the viewpoints and add to the decorative exuberance. From the lower terrace an Arcadian view of the wooded lake and its tree-shrouded banks opens out.

The route by which visitors leave runs across parkland with superlative old oaks. The great 8-acre/3.2-hectare kitchen garden, completed in about 1712 with high walls and rounded bastions, houses various modern amusements – a herb garden, a butterfly house, an adventure playground and a maze. Blenheim is run as a tourist attraction but it is skilfully managed so that the beauties of the palace, park and gardens remain intact.

INFORMATION

Location Woodstock OX20 1PX, Oxfordshire; in Woodstock, 8m N of Oxford by A44
Tel 01993 811325
Email operations@blenheimpalace.com
Website www.blenheimpalace.com
English Heritage Register Grade I
Owner The Duke of Marlborough
Open (Formal gardens) mid Mar to Oct, daily 10.30–4.45; (Park) daily 9–4.45
Area 2,000 acres/810 hectares

Bowood

A ROBERT ADAM HOUSE WITH VICTORIAN GARDENS, PINETUM, RHODODENDRON WOOD AND AN ARCADIAN LANDSCAPE

Few places are better than Bowood for displaying the peculiar genius of Capability Brown. Brown devised an idealised view of rural scenery, so unostentatious and so widely influential on the English countryside that it is easy to think of it as the norm from which other kinds of landscapes are an unfortunate aberration.

At Bowood Brown started work on the new park in 1761. A stream was dammed, which required demolition of a hamlet, and a long serpentine lake formed which, when a wind ruffles its surface, resembles from certain viewpoints a flowing river. At the north end of the lake is a spectacular naturalistic cascade, designed in about 1785 by the Hon. Charles Hamilton of Painshill (*see page 136*). You hear the noise of the tumbling water before the cascade is revealed, gushing down among huge rocks in three tiers and flowing into a peacefully winding stream fringed with ferns. In the cliff to one side are grottoes made by Josiah Lane of Tisbury; on the bank of the lake, Lane also made a hermit's cave decorated with tufa, ammonites and stalactites. Nearby, a grassy isthmus projects from densely planted woodland, ornamented with an early 19th-century Doric temple, which was moved to the site from elsewhere in the garden in 1864.

The cascade at Bowood

BROWN'S WOODLAND

Brown was also involved in the woodland planting that now forms the Rhododendron Walks at some distance from the house. The woodland is the setting for the great mausoleum that was built by Robert Adam in 1761 to celebrate the life of the 1st Earl of Shelburne. The domed building rises on a slight eminence, with a gap in the woods revealing distant views of the house and its larger setting. During the 19th century a rhododendron collection was started in the woods, and this has been much enriched by the present Marquess of Lansdowne.

These are the best parts of the garden at Bowood. Immediately south of the house, however, are two ornamental terraces, of 1818 and 1851, with clipped Irish yews and rose beds. A particularly coarse figure of a sprawling nude woman is an exceptionally unhappy late 20th-century addition. The terraces, decorative as they are for the most part, are minor pleasures compared with the uncontrived grandeur and simplicity of Capability Brown's work.

INFORMATION

Location Calne SN11 0LZ, Wiltshire; ½m W of Calne by A4
Tel 01249 812102
Website www.bowood-house.co.uk
English Heritage Register Grade I
Owner The Marquis of Lansdowne
Open Apr to Oct, daily 11–6 (the separate Rhododendron Walks usually open from Apr to early Jun depending on flowering; phone for times)
Area 100 acres/40 hectares

Broadleas Gardens

A 20TH-CENTURY WOODLAND GARDEN OF MESMERISING CHARM CREATED BY AN ACCOMPLISHED PLANTSWOMAN

The approach to Broadleas is as unexpected as could be. To arrive at the head of the drive you have to pass through a large modern housing estate. Lady Anne Cowdray came here in 1946 and, having exhausted the delights of hunting and shooting, began to make a garden. In this otherwise rather flat part of the country the site at Broadleas is unusually hilly. In addition to the charms of the land the place is especially attractive to a gardener for the soil here is excellent greensand.

A CHARMING DELL

When Lady Anne came the only ornamental plants were thickets of *Rhododendron ponticum* and bamboo but there was the protection of some good old trees. She seized upon this to make an intimate woodland garden, the Dell, in an occasionally precipitous valley now planted with an outstanding collection of trees and shrubs. The lower part of the Dell is protected from the south-westerly winds by a tall

The Dell at Broadleas

serpentine hedge of Leyland cypress. A southern beech (*Nothofagus* x *procera*), with a dramatically gnarled trunk, shoots up to a great height, far taller than would be expected in a tree that is less than fifty years old. The acid soil has allowed the cultivation of admirable ericaceous plants – species rhododendrons, and beautiful camellias, enkianthus and stewartias. A fine collection of magnolias is one of the greatest beauties. Throughout the Dell herbaceous underplanting adds to the attractions of the place – erythroniums, ferns, hostas and primulas – and occasionally more unusual plants like the giant lily *Cardiocrinum giganteum*, and the beautiful *Tulipa sprengeri*. Such exotic planting gives way from time to time to pretty groups of wild flowers such as bluebells, buttercups, red campion and stitchwort. The planting is for the most part naturalistic with the occasional touch of something more contrived, such as a *Catalpa* x *erubescens* 'Purpurea' standing at the centre of a close-mown glade. Paths run along each side of the glade, sometimes striking out in a stiff zig-zag up the slope.

Formal gardens cluster about the house. A sunken garden has old roses, a secret garden is veiled by a beautiful spreading *Liquidambar styraciflua*, and a grey border running along a wall is full of salvias, elaeagnus, olearias and rosemarys. These are pretty, but it is the Dell that catches the heart.

INFORMATION

Location Devizes SN10 5JQ, Wiltshire; 1m S of Devizes W of A360, signed from centre of Devizes
Tel 01380 722035
Email broadleasgardens@btinternet.com
Owner Broadleas Gardens Charitable Trust
Open Apr to Oct, Sun, Wed and Thur 2–6
Area 9 acres/3.6 hectares

Broughton Castle

A MOATED LATE-MEDIEVAL FORTIFIED MANOR HOUSE WITH A VICTORIAN FORMAL GARDEN AND 20TH-CENTURY BORDERS

Broughton Castle is a marvellous house in an exceptional setting. Built of toffee-coloured stone it dates from the 14th century with much rebuilding in the 16th century. It overlooks a moat and is set in serene parkland. A *Country Life* article in 1898 describes the garden as having "the all-pervading influence of dainty and cultivated taste". Photographs show a rather busy garden of which only a single, delightful feature survives today: The Lady's Garden.

Since the 1960s the garden has been raised to a standard of high excellence. Lanning Roper was consulted in 1969, and he designed a virtuoso mixed border, 200 yards long, following a west-facing wall between the castle and the moat. In his notes on the garden he wrote: "Treat area simply and play up the beauty of the buildings, walls and landscape" – the admirable response of an unusually sensitive and subtle designer. The border is given harmony and balance by a carefully arranged colour scheme, with predominantly reds and blues at the north end, and pink, purple, white and silver at the south, spiked with the occasional note of blue to connect with the other half.

THE LADY'S GARDEN

Lying immediately below the castle walls is the Lady's Garden. This walled enclosure retains its 19th-century design, laid out as a kind of parterre, with a pattern of box-edged beds in shapes of *fleurs-de-lys*. A central circular bed is edged in stone with an inscription from "The Rubáiyát of Omar Khayyám": 'I sometimes think that never blows so red/The rose as where some buried Caesar bled." The ornamental planting in the box-edged beds is modern, with pink roses ('Gruss an Aachen' and 'Lavender Pinocchio') and rich purple roses ('De Rescht') underplanted with annuals varying from year to year. Mixed borders line the walls, with shrub roses underplanted with lavish waves of herbaceous perennials in pink, purple, blue or white – alliums, aquilegias, foxgloves, penstemons, poppies, sages and verbascums. The area is small but the crisply shaped *fleur-de-lys* shapes give clarity at the centre, and the borders, exuberant as they are, have a deftly harmonious colour scheme. This garden, and Lanning Roper's border, strike just the right note of celebratory gaiety but allow the rare character of the castle and its ancient setting the prominence they deserve.

The Lady's Garden at Broughton

INFORMATION

Location Broughton, nr Banbury OX15 5EB, Oxfordshire; 2m SW of Banbury by B4035
Tel 01295 262624 **Fax** 01295 272694
Website www.broughtoncastle.demon.co.uk
English Heritage Register Grade II
Owner Lord Saye and Sele
Open May to mid Sept, Wed, Sun and Bank Hol Mon 2–5 (Jul and Aug, also open Thur 2–5)
Area 3 acres/1.2 hectares

Bury Court

OLD FARM BUILDINGS AS THE PICTURESQUE BACKGROUND TO TWO OUTSTANDING MODERN GARDENS

John Coke, formerly of the admirable nursery Green Farm Plants, left the nursery business and created a garden, on a new site, that bristles with excitement. An old farmhouse of brick and stone and fine outhouses form a beautiful framework. In fact, there are two, quite different, gardens. The first, behind the house, was started in 1995 and designed in collaboration with the Dutch garden designer and nurseryman Piet Oudolf. The space is divided by paths of paving stone or cobbles, straight or curved, but no overwhelming axes. A gravel bed is planted with clipped hummocks of sage and santolina. A circular arbour of weeping pear (*Pyrus salicifolia* 'Pendula') has a millstone at its centre and a wheel pattern of bricks and cobbles. Grasses are repeatedly used both as structural thickets and as ingredients in borders.

Below the stone wall of a barn is a raised pool edged with brick and stone, two of its corners marked emphatically by the unusual fastigiate form of *Koelreuteria paniculata*. A parterre of box with criss-cross patterns of hedging has yew-filled compartments. A curved screen of yew and a mound of clipped box lend firm shape amid profuse planting. A path between densely planted borders is so narrow that in late summer soft grasses brush your face as you pass. The garden is dominated by contrasts of hard and soft – of sharp edges and the cloudy insubstantial form of grasses.

A GRID PATTERN GARDEN

At the entrance to the house a new garden was designed by Christopher Bradley-Hole in 2001. The ground,

Piet Oudolf's garden at Bury Court

rising very slightly as it extends from the house, is subtly terraced and disposed in a grid of metal-edged square enclosures. Most of these are planted but some are occupied by a pool; in one there is an oak tea-house. Coffee-coloured gravel is used for the paths that flow between the squares. These enclosures are not of exactly the same width on each side, a subtle variation that gives movement to the rigidity of the grid. The planted squares are, for the most part, filled with herbaceous perennials, and frequent use is made of grasses with the occasional brilliant kniphofia or lobelia.

The two gardens at Bury Court, quite different in style, suit the vernacular farm buildings equally well. They show very vividly how successful modern design can be in an old setting.

INFORMATION

Location nr Bentley GU10 5LZ, Hampshire; 1m N of Bentley off the Crondall road
Tel 01420 520351 **Fax** 01420 22382
Owner John Coke
Open Apr to Sept, last Wed of each month 10.30–3.30; groups by appointment only
Area ½ acre/0.2 hectare

Buscot Park

A MASTERLY EARLY 20TH-CENTURY GARDEN WITH A DAZZLING
WATER GARDEN AND DECORATIVE NEW PLANTING

The house at Faringdon, by an unknown architect, was built in the late 18th century and there are indications of contemporary landscaping east of the house, of which the surviving lake must have formed part. Apart from this the gardens are entirely 20th century, dominated by a mesmerising water garden that links house and lake, designed by Harold Peto in 1904 for Alexander Henderson, later the 1st Lord Faringdon.

Peto's water garden at Buscot Park

On ground that slopes gently downhill through woods, Peto created a stepped canal which opens out from time to time – now a scalloped circular pool with a dolphin fountain, now a plain rectangle – and is traversed by bridges of different kinds. The water channel itself narrows and widens, with water cascading down at changes in level. It is edged in mown grass and enclosed in box hedges which follow the shape of the canal, with statues ornamenting the larger compartments and occasional exclamation marks of Irish yews or fastigiate juniper (*Juniperus communis* 'Fastigiata'). When you make the leisurely descent, you find yourself crossing back and forth, the scene varying with your viewpoint. As you descend you see on the far side of the lake a domed, pillared temple exactly aligned with the canal. The woods press in all about and the filtered light and flickering shade add to the charm.

AVENUES OF TREES

Buscot offers other pretty things. There is a pattern of avenues of various trees (one, of Lombardy poplars, opens with a pair of Egyptian figures), and some of the trees are unusual avenue species (for example, the fastigiate English oak, *Quercus robur* 'Fastigiata'). The avenues are ingeniously planned, with two long avenues radiating out from the house to form a three-part *patte d'oie* with the water garden. Cross-vistas link subsidiary avenues with the water garden, and urns and other ornaments decorate junctions.

The walled kitchen garden is now partly turned over to beautifully maintained ornamental gardens. Here are swashbuckling borders by Peter Coats in blue and yellow, which almost redeem that overplanted and bilious tree *Robinia pseudoacacia* 'Frisia'. The very attractive formal plantings in the garden are designed by Tim Rees, with an alley of pleached hop hornbeam (*Ostrya carpinifolia*) underplanted with daylilies and a tunnel of Judas trees (*Cercis siliquastrum*).

INFORMATION

Location Faringdon SN7 8BU, Oxfordshire; 3m NW of Faringdon on A417
Infoline 0845 3453387
Tel 01367 240786
Email estbuscot@aol.com
Website www.buscot-park.com
English Heritage Register Grade II*
Owner The National Trust
Open Apr to Sept, Mon and Tue (closed Bank Hol Mon) 2–6 and various other days in this period (consult infoline/website)
Area 20 acres/8 hectares

Chenies Manor

A MEDIEVAL AND TUDOR MANOR HOUSE WITH AN ARTS AND CRAFTS GARDEN ENLIVENED BY MODERN FLOWER PLANTING

The manor house at Chenies was built in the 15th and 16th centuries by the Cheyne family and later owned by the Russells, who became Dukes of Bedford. Built of beautiful slender bricks and bristling with ornament – crow-stepped gables, barley-sugar twisted chimneys and battlemented bay windows – it has a dashingly decorative air. In front of the house a sunken garden has possible Tudor origins but today has more of the character of the Arts and Crafts movement. Behind a screen of clipped ivy and a row of lollipops of clipped yew, it is divided into four with paths of stone flags.

TULIPS GALORE

Lawns fill each of the four quarters and a circular pool in the middle is surrounded by domed drums of clipped box. The entrance and exit are flanked by dumpy rounded cones of clipped box while narrow beds run round the garden's retaining brick walls. These beds are in May the scene of a rare and wonderful sight. Every year Elizabeth MacLeod Matthews beds out thousands of tulips from the bulb specialist Walter Blom & Son, planting them in groups of a single kind and accompanying them with forget-me-nots and pansies in different colours. It is rare to see tulips used with such prodigal abandon in a private garden, and here their lavish use brilliantly decorates the splendid historic setting.

The celebratory cheerfulness of this classic combination of plants seems appropriate to the Tudor setting. In late May the tulips are whipped out and replaced with a summer scheme of yellow, blue and white which is gradually changed to the pink, white and reds of argyranthemums, cosmos, dahlias and salvias among others. In all about 1,000 plants are bedded out each year in this part of the garden.

There is much else to admire at Chenies – a white garden (which also makes use of tulips); a physic garden of both medicinal and useful plants evoking the Tudor past; a walk under arches covered in *Clematis armandii*; and a turf maze (replacing in a different site one that had been at Chenies in the 17th century). The whole garden is finely maintained and always a pleasure to see. But at tulip time in early May the pleasure takes on an altogether more thrilling quality.

The sunken garden at Chenies Manor

INFORMATION

Location Chenies, Rickmansworth WD3 6ER, Buckinghamshire; 4m E of Amersham on A404
Tel 01494 762888
Email macleodmatthews@btinternet.com
Website www.cheniesmanorhouse.co.uk
Owner Lt Col and Mrs MacLeod Matthews
Open Apr to Oct, Wed, Thur and Bank Hol Mon 2–5
Area 5 acres/2 hectares

Cliveden

A GREAT THAMES-SIDE HOUSE WITH RICHLY VARIED GARDENS RANGING FROM THE 17TH CENTURY TO THE 20TH CENTURY

Cliveden is one of the most attractive, and varied, gardens in the country. The house – now a grand hotel – was built in the 17th century to William Winde's designs for the Duke of Buckingham but completely refashioned for the 2nd Duke of Sutherland by Sir Charles Barry in the mid 19th century. The position is one of breathtaking beauty on the brow of wooded slopes high above the Thames whose waters curve gently away to the west.

The estate was bought in 1893 by William Waldorf Astor (later the 1st Viscount Astor) whose descendants gave it to the National Trust in 1942.

ITALIAN INFLUENCES

A view of the garden must start with the terraces south of the house where William Winde built a long retaining wall with blind arches. The lower terrace has a beautiful 17th-century balustrade made for the Villa Borghese in Rome, which, like so many of the wonderful architectural fragments and classical antiquities in the garden, was brought to Cliveden by William Waldorf Astor. These terraces overlook a long apron of lawn pointing away from the house, with a parterre of beds edged in box, each compartment filled with blocks of santolina or *Brachyglottis* Dunedin Group 'Sunshine', and pyramids of clipped yew. At the far end is a bronze statue of the Rape of Proserpine by Vincenzo de Rossi. To the west wooded ground slopes down to the Thames. Here is an early 18th-century turf amphitheatre by Charles Bridgeman and the pretty Octagon Temple, designed by Giacomo Leoni in 1735. From here a walk of venerable yews descends to the river and a palatial half-timbered boathouse built for Lord Astor.

In the forecourt to the north of the house is a pair of virtuoso herbaceous borders – warm colours on one side, cooler on the other – laid out in 1969 by Graham Stuart Thomas. An avenue of limes leads to Thomas Waldo Story's late 19th-century Fountain of Love with cavorting nymphs and a giant cockleshell. Close by is the enigmatic and attractive Long Garden with snaking hedges of box, whimsical yew topiary and Lord Astor's wonderful 18th-century Venetian characters from the Commedia dell'Arte. At this northern end of the garden a water garden has an irregular lake overlooked by a ravishing little Chinese pavilion.

The lake at Cliveden

INFORMATION

Location Taplow, Maidenhead SL6 0JA, Buckinghamshire; 2m N of Taplow on B476, jct 7 of M4 and Jct 4 of M40

Infoline 01494 755562

Tel 01628 605069

Email cliveden@nationaltrust.org.uk

English Heritage Register Grade I

Owner The National Trust

Open mid Mar to 23 Dec, daily 11–6 (11– 4 Nov and Dec)

Area 375 acres/152 hectares

Corsham Court

AN ELIZABETHAN HOUSE WITH PLEASURE GROUNDS BY CAPABILITY BROWN AND 20TH-CENTURY PLANTING

Corsham Court was built in 1582 for Thomas Smythe but much altered in the 18th century. Capability Brown was asked by Paul Methuen in 1761 to alter the house and grounds. Behind the house he designed a richly decorative Bath House with a castellated parapet and finials bristling with crockets – this was further gothicised by John Nash c.1800. It is connected to the adjacent walled garden by a tunnel, originally decorated with patterns of pine cones. The Bath House stands close to the southern end of the North Walk which Brown laid out between the pleasure grounds and the park, separated by a ha-ha immediately to the east.

AN IMMENSELY TALL TREE

A remarkable tree is a startlingly expansive oriental plane (*Platanus orientalis*), some of whose limbs sprawl dramatically sideways, giving it the appearance of a grove of trees rather than a single tree. Now well over 90ft/28m high, it is one of the two or three tallest in the country and could date from Brown's time. Brown planted other fine trees here, of which a very handsome cedar of Lebanon and two Turkey oaks (*Quercus cerris*) are other possible survivors. Brown also planted shelter belts to the north and east, where he proposed a lake which was not executed until Humphry Repton came to work here in 1797.

Formal gardens close to the house present a largely 19th-century air. The flower garden has long narrow beds edged in box and animated by topiary of box and yew. The planting here, chiefly roses in the past, is rather scrappy but is to be restored. To the north, a walk of hornbeam runs along the side of the walled garden where a central path is flanked by trees of

The Bath House at Corsham Court

Catalpa bignonioides which curve round at the head of the garden to embrace a circular pool ringed with ironwork adorned with climbing roses. In a border on one side is a superlative large *Paeonia suffruticosa* subsp. *rockii*, one of several examples in the garden of this most beautiful of flowering shrubs.

Corsham, happily untouched by any recent passing fashions, is not as well known as it deserves. With some exceptional plants, finely designed landscape and all the atmosphere of an old estate it has memorable character.

INFORMATION

Location Corsham SN13 0BZ, Wiltshire; in Corsham town, 4m W of Chippenham by A4
Tel 01249 701610
Website www.corsham-court.co.uk
English Heritage Register Grade II*
Owner James Methuen-Campbell
Open mid Mar to Sept, Tues to Thurs, Sat and Sun (open Bank Hol Mon) 2–5.30; Oct to mid Mar (closed Dec), Sat and Sun 2–4.30
Area 360 acres/146 hectares

The Courts Garden

A GEORGIAN VILLAGE HOUSE WITH A GARDEN OF DAZZLING
INVENTIVENESS – TOPIARY, MAGNIFICENT HEDGES AND WATER

The house is early 18th-century but the garden is wholly 20th-century, made when Sir George Hastings lived here between 1900 and 1910, and it retains much of its original Arts and Crafts atmosphere with much topiary. You are immediately confronted, below the entrance façade of the house, with four clipped shapes of box resembling moulded blancmanges starting to melt in a hot sun. A beautifully wrought yew hedge directs the eye along to a dapper summerhouse in the form of a pillared temple. This hedge, breaking out from time to time into ornament, encloses the chief part of the formal gardens. On the far side of the hedge the garden changes gear. Here an arboretum with a fine collection of trees and many spring bulbs curves about the formal garden. There is topiary here, too: a wriggling hedge of holly shaped into a series of giant cottage loaves.

The water garden at The Courts

A FEAST OF TOPIARY

In the south-western part of the formal garden a feast of cunningly deployed topiary is partly hidden behind a procession of clipped Irish yews rising above a border of euphorbias, fritillaries, geraniums, lamb's lugs, *Thalictrum aquilegiifolium* and white tulips. Here a gentle step in a lawn forms a stage-like area, backed by the curving boundary hedge of yew with piers of clipped yew on each side. The opening of the stage is flanked by elaborately tiered shapes of box and mushrooms of silver pear (*Pyrus salicifolia*) underplanted with irises. This splendid set-piece by no means exhausts the use of topiary, which crops up throughout the garden, appearing to delight in its own virtuosity.

Behind castellations of yew close to the house a water garden forms the eastern boundary of the garden. A long stepped runnel, breaking out at its far end in a fit of curves, opens into a sweeping pool shaded by a swamp cypress (*Taxodium distichum*) and a wide-spreading yew, with drifts of shuttlecock ferns on its shady bank. A rectangular lily pool is associated with excellent ornamental trees, and mixed borders run along on each side. The Courts, with much good planting and an irrepressible decorative character, has been gently restored in recent years and is beautifully cared for.

INFORMATION

Location Holt, nr Bradford-on-Avon BA14 6RR, Wiltshire; in Holt village, 3m SW of Melksham by B3107
Tel 01225 782875
Email courtsgarden@nationaltrust.org.uk
English Heritage Register Grade II
Owner The National Trust
Open mid Mar to Oct, daily except Wed 11–5.30 (out of season open by appointment only)
Area 7 acres/2.8 hectares

Exbury Gardens

A SUPERB COLLECTION OF RHODODENDRONS SET AGAINST A BACKGROUND OF MAGNIFICENT TREES

The estate at Exbury was bought in 1918 by Lionel de Rothschild whom someone described as "a banker by hobby but a gardener by profession". The site is a beautiful one, on the east bank of the estuary of the Beaulieu river, looking south across the Solent. The acid soil and the benign climate make it a wonderful place for growing rhododendrons and other ericaceous plants. Lionel de Rothschild embarked on the garden with meticulous fervour.

Rothschild set out to plant every woody plant that could be cultivated on such a site. His particular interests were rhododendrons, of which he bred countless successful hybrids, and orchids for which he built an enormous glasshouse. He died in 1942 and after the war his son, Edmund, took over, having inherited whatever genes determine a passion for gardening. New plants continue to be added and the garden, now regularly open to the public, is magnificently cared for.

The site at Exbury is mostly flat, with occasional gentle hollows and hillocks. Native Scots pines and oaks, with some superb cedars of Lebanon which must have been planted when the house was built in the 18th century, make a fine background to the exotics that now fill the garden. Two streams, at the northern and southern ends of the garden, provide water for pools in which rhododendrons are at times magnificently reflected. The landscape intermingles open spaces of grass, frequently ornamented with specimen trees, and intimate woodland laced with paths and airy glades. The paths are more often than not densely lined with rhododendrons, of which Exbury probably has the largest collection in the British Isles. Also lavishly represented are fine examples of camellias and magnolias.

A GREAT ROCK GARDEN

Lionel de Rothschild made a great rock garden, completed in 1930 with an area of 2 acres/0.8 hectare – probably the largest in Europe. The rocks are treated ornamentally rather than as a monotonous background, rising up among the plantings of conifers (many of them fastigiate), azaleas (many of them blue) and heathers.

As a place to learn about trees and shrubs, and to enjoy a remarkable landscape, Exbury has few equals. You may relish, too, the miniature railway from which to view some of the best features, including the rock garden.

The ponds at Exbury

INFORMATION

Location Exbury, nr Southampton SO45 1AZ, Hampshire; in Exbury village, 11m from Totton (W of Southampton) by A326 and B3054
Tel 023 8089 1203 **Fax** 023 8089 9940
Website www.exbury.co.uk
English Heritage Register Grade II*
Owner Edmund de Rothschild
Open mid Mar to early Nov, daily 10–5.30 (or sunset if earlier)
Area 200 acres/81 hectares

Harcourt Arboretum

THE WOODLAND GARDEN AND ARBORETUM OF THE OXFORD BOTANIC GARDEN WITH A SUPERB 10-ACRE BLUEBELL WOOD

Originally part of the Nuneham Courtenay estate, the arboretum has been in the care of the University of Oxford Botanic Garden since 1962. It dates from 1835 when W.S. Gilpin, who was a protégé of the 3rd Earl Harcourt, was asked to lay out a picturesque pinetum on land newly acquired, running along the Oxford road. A chief ingredient of Gilpin's design was a pattern of serpentine walks and the Main Ride, a broad grassy walk lined with ramparts of *Rhododendron ponticum* and backed by trees, in particular conifers. This survives today, with some magnificent old specimens of such trees as Corsican pines (*Pinus nigra* var. *maritima*), of which a dramatic trio confronts you as you enter the garden. There are also fine specimens of Wellingtonias and several of the incense cedar (*Calocederus decurrens*) whose emphatic upright form punctuates the arboretum.

From the Oxford Botanic Garden's point of view the Harcourt Arboretum formed the perfect country department for its activities. Apart from providing much more room and a fine existing collection it has, unlike the Botanic Garden, acid soil which greatly extends the range of plants that they can grow.

DECORATIVE CHARM

Complementing the precious backdrop of old conifers and native silver birch and oaks, many trees and shrubs have been added – among them azaleas, Japanese maples, such beautiful flowering shrubs as witch hazels (*Hamamelis* species), the exquisite *Halesia monticola* (including its rarely seen pink form) and rhododendrons. A superb 10-acre/4-hectare bluebell wood and a 37-acre/15-hectare meadow of wild flowers add to its decorative charms. The garden also has a National Collection of bamboos.

The arboretum has a strongly educational remit. An excellent timber trail with placards spells out the precise uses of the wood of 15 different trees grown in the arboretum, with an admirable accompanying leaflet. However, for many visitors it will be the beauty of the plants, triumphantly animating an otherwise featureless site, that will be the chief attraction.

The bluebell wood at Harcourt Arboretum

INFORMATION

Location Nuneham Courtenay OX44 9PX, Oxfordshire; 6m S of Oxford by A4074

Tel 01865 343501

Fax 01865 341828

Email postmaster@botanic-garden.ox.ac.uk

Website www.botanic-garden.ox.ac.uk

English Heritage Register Grade I

Owner University of Oxford

Open Apr to Nov, daily 10–5; Dec to Mar, Mon to Fri 10–4.30 (closed 22 Dec to 3 Jan)

Area 55 acres/22 hectares

Heale Garden

A 17TH-CENTURY RIVERSIDE HOUSE WITH A FORMAL GARDEN BY HAROLD PETO AND A RAVISHING KITCHEN GARDEN

Some exceptionally attractive gardens ignore fashion, ruled by a love of gardening rather than by the rise and fall of horticultural hemlines. Heale is the perfect country house garden, memorable for the beauty of the setting, the excellence of the design, fine plants and irresistible charm. On low-lying ground by the river Avon the house, built in rosy pink bricks with stone dressings, is 17th-century with thoroughly convincing late 19th-century additions designed by Detmar Blow.

The kitchen garden at Heale

The garden designer Harold Peto came here in 1906 to advise the new owner, the Hon. Louis Greville, and made new formal gardens which take their cue from the house. A terrace below the western façade has scalloped lily pools from which a gentle terraced slope descends, with stone balustrades marking the changes in level. The planting of the deep mixed borders at the top was done by Lady Anne Rasch who lived and gardened at Heale from 1959 to 1998. She simplified Peto's herbaceous borders and introduced mixed plantings, with many shrub roses and shrubs all richly underplanted with herbaceous perennials.

THE KITCHEN GARDEN

It was she, too, who was responsible for the exceptional ornamental kitchen garden south of the house. Walled on three sides its long south side has an open pergola garlanded with the purple-leafed grapevine *Vitis vinifera* 'Purpurea', and roses. The garden is divided into four, its centre marked by a rectangular lily pool and eight giant domes of clipped box. A tunnel of espaliered fruit trees – apples and pears – runs down the length of the garden, with the pool at its centre. Mixed borders line the walls and within the garden there is a delightful mixture of productive orderliness and unpretentious ornament.

South of the kitchen garden is a Japanese garden, made in 1901, with a graceful orange-red bridge spanning a stream, a teahouse (with the stream flowing under it) and stone snow lanterns among ferns and Japanese maples. This startling piece of orientalism seems remarkably at home. This, and Harold Peto's formal gardens, are vital ingredients in the character of Heale, but it is Lady Anne Rasch's detailed planting throughout the garden, and the exquisite kitchen garden, that make Heale exceptional. Visitors may take some of it home by buying plants in the excellent nursery here.

INFORMATION

Location Middle Woodford, nr Salisbury SP4 6NT, Wiltshire; in the Woodford valley, 4m NW of Salisbury by minor roads, signed from A345 and A360
Tel 01722 782504
Email info@healegarden.co.uk
Website www.healegarden.co.uk
English Heritage Register Grade II*
Owner Guy Rasch
Open Feb to Oct, Wed to Sun (open Bank Hol Mon) 10–5
Area 8 acres/3.2 hectares

The Sir Harold Hillier Gardens

ONE OF THE BEST COLLECTIONS OF TREES AND SHRUBS IN THE COUNTRY – A MEMORIAL TO A NURSERYMAN AND COLLECTOR

The Hillier dynasty of nurserymen who took over the Farthing Nursery in Winchester in 1864 made it in the 20th century one of the finest nurseries for trees and shrubs in the world. It reached its zenith under Sir Harold Hillier (1905–85) who himself collected many seeds in the wild to propagate for the nursery. In his day the firm's catalogue, *Hillier's Manual of Trees and Shrubs*, not only offered 7,000 species of woody plants for sale but also provided a detailed guide to woody plants worth growing in the garden, and much valuable information about their cultivation.

The magnolia avenue at the Hillier Gardens

WOODY PLANTS

Sir Harold lived at Jermyn's House and his garden and private arboretum now form a large part of the Sir Harold Hillier Gardens and Arboretum which is owned by Hampshire County Council. With 12,500 different woody plants, it is one of the finest collections of hardy trees and shrubs in the world. The soil is acid, the rainfall around 30in/75cm and the climate fairly mild. Several National Collections of plants are held here; of major interest to gardeners are the collections of cotoneaster, dogwoods, oaks, pines and witch hazels, although there are also more specialist collections of hazels, hornbeam, lithocarpus, photinia and privet. But every genus of woody plants hardy in the British Isles is well represented. The nursery, with various branches, including one on the premises here, still exists and still sells excellent plants, but not in the range available in the 1960s and 1970s.

This is primarily a plant collection and this concern overrides any notion of the aesthetics of the landscape. However, close to the house there are areas that are finely designed. The magnolia avenue, which runs up to the front door is, with its attractive underplanting, a dazzling sight. The heather garden nearby and the long Centenary Border west of the house also have their charms. But it is the plant collections that are the overwhelming attraction. These are arranged by genus (such as Acer Valley or Oak Field) or by habitat (such as Peat Garden or Bog Garden). A resource like this, apart from the delight of seeing so many fine plants displaying their beauties in different seasons, is of precious value to gardeners.

INFORMATION

Location Jermyns Lane, Ampfield, nr Romsey SO51 0QA, Hampshire; 3m NE of Romsey by A31
Tel 01794 369318
Email info@hilliergardens.org.uk
Website www.hillier.hants.gov.uk
English Heritage Register Grade II
Owner Hampshire County Council
Open daily 10–6 (or dusk if earlier); closed 25 and 26 Dec
Area 180 acres/73 hectares

Hinton Ampner Garden

A 20TH-CENTURY GARDEN OF TERRACES, TOPIARY, BORDERS AND TREES WITH GLIMPSES OF ARCADIAN LANDSCAPE

Ralph Dutton, the 8th and last Lord Sherborne, inherited the estate at Hinton Ampner in 1935. His ancestors had lived here for many generations but the gloomy house that he inherited had been heavily Victorianised and was not to his taste. He rebuilt it, revealing its late Georgian core, and created a gentlemanly Georgian-style house. He rebuilt it again in 1960, when it was almost destroyed by fire.

The garden takes its cue from the house, south of which the land falls away giving open prospects of fields and parkland. Dutton terraced the slopes and to each level gave a distinctive character. The first terrace has a lily pool at its eastern end. At the next a very large lawn is hedged in yew on its far side, with a statue of a nymph at one end and a little formal garden with hexagonal raised beds filled in spring with tulips and in summer with bold plantings of dahlias. The lowest terrace is a dramatic flourish of splendid panache. Here is a sundial and rows of yews clipped into rounded

cones backed with shrub roses. The central part has more yew topiary and long narrow beds with tulips in spring and pale pink dahlias ('Park Princess') in summer. Below the supporting wall of the upper terrace, taking advantage of a protected south-facing exposure, are mixed borders on each side of linking steps. To the east, a grass path passes between beds densely planted with shrubs, among which is suddenly glimpsed a pedimented summerhouse.

A FORMAL ORCHARD

On the north side of the house is a formal orchard, made on the site of the house that existed here in Tudor times. Divided into four by box hedges, and with tall cones of clipped yew, the grassy compartments are planted with apples, cherries, crab-apples and quinces underplanted with bulbs – anemones and narcissi in spring; autumn-flowering crocus (*C. speciosus*) in September and October.

With its strong sense of design, unfussy sense of ornament and excellent planting, the garden at Hinton Ampner is exceptionally attractive. For reasons inexplicable to me, it is not a well-known garden. Yet it is one of the finest English gardens of its period and worthy of comparison with both Hidcote and Sissinghurst – two other 20th-century gardens made by amateurs of genius.

The lowest terrace at Hinton Ampner

INFORMATION

Location Bramdean, nr Alresford SO24 0LA, Hampshire; 1m W of Bramdean village by A272
Tel 01962 771305
Email hintonampner@nationaltrust.org.uk
Website www.nationaltrust.org.uk/southern
Owner The National Trust
Open mid Mar to Oct, Sat to Wed 11–5
Area 8 acres/3.2 hectares

Iford Manor

HAROLD PETO'S OWN GARDEN – ITALIANATE TERRACES LAID OUT IN THE HEART OF THE WILTSHIRE COUNTRYSIDE

The architect and garden designer Harold Peto came to live here in 1899 and made a marvellous garden, the most eloquent expression of the English love affair with Italy. The site is very beautiful, on the south-west facing wooded slopes of the valley of the river Frome. The Elizabethan house was rebuilt in the 1720s with a fine classical front of Bath stone.

The garden to one side and behind the house had been terraced at some time in the past and Peto seized upon this as the essential ingredient of his garden. At its entrance a fine wrought-iron gate in a stone wall leads through to a paved enclosure where an Italianate loggia juts out from the house, garlanded with grapevines and wisteria, and facing a semicircular pool. A mound of clipped *Choisya ternata* glistens in the sunshine. A flight of stone steps rises steeply to the terraces to the north, quite narrow with tall stone piers capped with splendid lead urns or stone figures. Tufts of *Campanula poscharskyana* and *Erigeron karvinskianus* have established themselves in the steps.

ITALIANATE TERRACES

The first terrace is quite small, leading up to a conservatory against the wall of the house. The steps pass under the spreading limbs of an old yew into which a *Vitis coignetiae* has grown, soaring to the top and in autumn splashing the dark green with its brilliant red leaves. The next terrace, of mown grass, has at its centre a fountain and an oval pool fringed with wisterias. Trees ornament the lawn, among them, to the west, a perfect old specimen of *Cercidiphyllum japonicum*, surely planted by Peto himself. Beyond the pool double steps, flanked

with bold clumps of bergenia, pass under a peristyle to the top, grandest terrace. Surfaced with immaculately raked gravel (sometimes twice a day) the terrace is broad and calm. Italian cypresses (*Cupressus sempervirens*) run along on either side with wonderful

The terrace steps at Iford

statuary – stone dogs, sarcophagi, a Byzantine wellhead, stone seats and columns. One end of the terrace is marked by an early 18th-century octagonal pavilion with pilasters and crisply ornamented cornice below the steeply pitched roof. The other end has a semicircular seat jutting out beyond the perimeter of the formal garden, with views west over a simple orchard. This end of the terrace is embellished by colonnades on either side. Past bronze figures of Romulus and Remus, a path leads up to yew topiaries of the Chigi crest – six money-bags surmounted by a star – in memory of Mrs Cartwright Hignett's Chigi grandmother. North of the terrace the colonnade screens a little hidden garden (a true *giardino segreto*), with superb tightly clipped shapes of *Phillyrea latifolia*, a loggia, parterres of box and magnificent Tuscan pots.

ALI BABA POTS

The slopes above the top terrace are densely wooded but the uphill axis, established by the first flights of steps, continues deep into the woods. From a semicircular paved area guarded by giant Ali Baba terracotta pots and flowering cherries, with a majestic London plane on one side, rustic steps climb upwards, flanked from time to time by old staddle stones clothed in ivy. Almost immediately on your left as you climb is a convincing Japanese garden overlooked by a rustic summerhouse. An irregular pool fringed with mossy rocks and ferns is overarched by a Japanese maple with a thicket of bamboo rearing up on one side; snow lanterns and an airy stone pagoda stand among tall old box trees with pale stems.

As you walk downhill again you look past the columns of the peristyle, out over the formal garden, and across the river to the rural landscape. In Tuscany the Renaissance maker of a garden of this sort would have delighted in drawing the eye beyond the garden to olive groves and vineyards spread out on the slopes. Here in Wiltshire Peto evoked exactly the same spirit, revealing views of cattle grazing in pastures edged with hedgerows thick as bolsters.

INFORMATION

Location Iford, nr Bradford-on-Avon BA15 2BA, Wiltshire; 7m SE of Bath by A36, 2m SW of Bradford-on-Avon by B3109 and Westwood
Tel 01225 863146 **Fax** 01225 862364
English Heritage Register Grade I
Owner Mrs Cartwright Hignett
Open Apr and Oct, Sun (also Easter Mon) 2–5; May to Sept, Sat, Sun and Tues to Thurs 2–5
Area 2½ acres/1 hectare

Longstock Water Gardens

A LABYRINTH OF POOLS AND STREAMS LAID OUT TO FORM A MESMERISING AND RICHLY PLANTED NATURALISTIC GARDEN

The gardens here have their origins in the 19th century when a large lake was dredged by Alfred and Arthur East. The beauty of the site was understood by the early 20th century under the ownership of Reginald Beddington. It was John Spedan Lewis, however, who from 1946 gave the gardens their modern character. The gardens today are maintained for the delectation of the staff (or "partners") of the John Lewis Partnership, but nothing could be less institutional than this rare water garden. Close to the river Test, with its famously gin-clear water, here is a miniature archipelago of grassy islands about which flows a bewildering network of streams which from time to time open out into pools. The islands, linked by simple board bridges, are meticulously mown and their banks are lavishly planted with bold, naturalistic clumps of appropriate herbaceous plants – geraniums, hostas, irises, ligularias, lysichitons and primulas. Ornamental grasses are often skilfully deployed, running in long swathes along the island banks and curving over towards the water. A rustic thatched pavilion sits in the middle of one of the islands, embellished in early summer with clumps of yellow flag irises. Fine trees and substantial shrubs form a backdrop to the maze of planted islands: a beautiful cut-leaf alder (*Alnus glutinosa* 'Laciniata'), a swamp cypress (*Taxodium distichum*) relishing a notably swampy position, Himalayan birches and *Liquidambar styraciflua*. The occasional brilliantly flowered rhododendron provides a surprise among the sombre woodland planting.

ALL IMPORTANT WATER

In many gardens water is one ingredient among many. At Longstock it is the essence of the garden, not only providing the essential moist conditions for many plants but also a reflective surface in which the shapes and colours of herbaceous plants and the distant foliage of trees are mirrored. Although some of the ingredients, and the setting, are those appropriate to a Robinsonian wild garden there is nothing wild here. The garden is exceptionally well cared for, with wonderfully pampered herbaceous plants, and there is a perfection about it that creates an atmosphere of dream-like intensity. In spring the racemes of a white wisteria hang in veils over the water and ribbons of crimson Asiatic primulas or piercing blue-purple irises along the banks are reflected in the crystalline water.

Naturalistic planting at Longstock

INFORMATION

Location Longstock, Stockbridge SO20 6EH, Hampshire; 1½ m NE of Longstock village
Tel and Fax 01264 810904
Owner The John Lewis Partnership
Open Apr to Sept, 1st and 3rd Sun in each month 2–5
Area 8 acres/3 hectares

The Manor House

AN ARTS AND CRAFTS VILLAGE HOUSE SET IN GERTRUDE JEKYLL GARDENS BROUGHT BACK TO LIFE BY PRIVATE OWNERS

When Rosamund and John Wallinger came here in 1984 they did not know that Gertrude Jekyll had designed the garden. Its restoration is a tribute to their perseverance, dedication to detail and sheer hard slog.

The garden presents two completely different aspects, vividly showing the range and character of Gertrude Jekyll's skills. Below the southern façade of the house the garden is terraced, with a central axis strongly linking the parts. Dry stone walls support the terraces and are lavishly planted with aubrieta, cerastium, fumitory, phlox, poppies and sedums.

The wild garden at Manor House

BOISTEROUS PLANTING

The top terrace is divided by a pergola of roses and *Aristolochia macrophylla*. Immediately below is a lawn with a pattern of formal beds lavishly planted with double pink peonies (*Paeonia* 'Sarah Bernhardt'), *Lilium regale* and the sumptuous pink rose 'Caroline Testout'. The geometry of the beds is all but blurred by the boisterous planting. The next terrace, a rectangular bowling green, is flanked by billowing hummocks of rosemary – a characteristic Jekyll emphasis. The final terrace, a grass tennis court, is enclosed on three sides by impeccably tailored yew hedges and overlooked by an arbour of roses. The upper terraces are flanked by terraced walks edged by herbaceous borders whose planting moves from cool blues through warmer colours to blazing reds. The sequence of events in the formal garden resembles the contrasts of a well planned meal. Lavish planting is held in check by the crisp pattern of spaces. Sumptuous effects are contrasted with cool open lawns.

The far side of the house now displays a rare example of a Jekyll wild garden. Paths sweep across meadows sparkling with buttercups, daffodils, meadowsweet, oxslips, speedwell and wood anemones. Here are thickets of roses of wild character (some of which are English natives like *Rosa arvensis*) as well as trees – crab-apples, a grove of walnuts, silver birch and weeping ash (*Fraxinus excelsior* 'Pendula'). A stream tumbles down a cascade to feed a pool that is prettily edged in campanulas, ferns, geraniums, irises and willows.

The Manor House at Upton Grey displays the full repertory of Gertrude Jekyll's art and is maintained to the same high standards that she would have demanded. But it does more than provide a horticultural history lesson; it is an exceptionally enjoyable garden, wholly delightful to be in.

INFORMATION

Location Upton Grey, nr Basingstoke RG25 2RD, Hampshire; in centre of Upton Grey village, 6m SE of Basingstoke by minor roads, Jct 5 of M3
Tel 01256 862827
Email wallmoll@lineone.net
Website www.gertrudejekyllgarden.co.uk
English Heritage Register Grade II*
Owner Mr and Mrs John Wallinger
Open Apr to Oct, Mon to Fri by appointment only
Area 5 acres/2 hectares

Mottisfont Abbey Garden

MEDIEVAL MONASTIC BUILDINGS SET IN WOODED GROUNDS, WITH FORMAL GARDENS AND A COLLECTION OF OLD ROSES

The abbey at Mottisfont was an Augustinian foundation, some of whose 13th-century buildings survive, with a suave brick house of the 1740s grafted onto them. In 1930 Sir Geoffrey Jellicoe designed a fine pleached lime walk underplanted with sheets of blue chionodoxa. At about the same time Norah Lindsay laid out a box parterre planted with spring and summer bedding schemes. These formal features are well done and associate harmoniously with the character of the house.

To rose lovers, and gardeners in general, Mottisfont is famous for its great collection of roses. It has a National Collection of over 300 old shrub roses, but includes the best of 20th-century roses, too. Disposed in the former walled kitchen garden, they celebrate a remarkable man, Graham Stuart Thomas, who rediscovered many old roses and was a pioneer in their revaluation as the marvellous garden plants we cherish today. As gardens adviser to the National Trust from 1955 to 1974, Thomas took a special interest in the making of this garden.

COMPANION PLANTING

The first roses were planted in the winter of 1972–73, and the charm of the garden lies in the way in which they are deployed, not merely presented as exhibits in a museum. The walled garden is divided, as all old kitchen gardens were, into four parts, with four clipped Irish yews making emphatic shapes about a circular pool at its centre. Each quarter has a lawn surrounded by beds of roses. and box-edged beds run under the walls on which climbing roses are trained. The occasional old apple tree was preserved with, as often as not, some appropriate rose scrambling through its branches.

Plant associations at Mottisfont

Furthermore, excellent use was made of companion plants – an important consideration, for most old shrub roses flower once only and need a supporting cast to enliven other seasons. The range of companion planting is wide but many perfectly ordinary plants are used with panache. Thickets of ferns, aquilegias in many colours, white foxgloves or Jacob's ladder, spreading cushions of scented pinks and veils of artemisia or meadow sage create exactly the right atmosphere, effective yet not pretentious. In late June the exuberance of flower, colour and scent provides one of the most memorable experiences of any garden in the country.

INFORMATION

Location Mottisfont, nr Romsey SO51 0LP, Hampshire; 4½ m N of Romsey signed off A3057
Infoline 01794 340757 **Tel** 01794 341220
Email mottisfontabbey@nationaltrust.org.uk
English Heritage Register Grade II
Owner The National Trust
Open Jun, daily 11–8.30; Jul to Aug, daily except Fri 11–5 (phone infoline for other openings)
Area 21 acres/8.5 hectares

The Old Rectory

A PRIVATE GARDEN WITH OUTSTANDING BORDERS, MANY UNUSUAL PLANTS AND IDIOSYNCRATIC ORNAMENT

Ralph and Esther Merton came here in 1950 and started a garden shortly after. Esther Merton, who died in 1995, was of a distinctive breed of English gardeners – independent-minded, strong-willed, enterprising and intrepid. Although she had an original and highly developed taste in plants, the layout of her garden follows classical principles. The house is a handsome pedimented rectory and the gardens take their cue from it.

HERBACEOUS BORDERS

Immediately behind the house a large lawn is ornamented with a splendid old cedar of Lebanon (*Cedrus libani*) and a free-standing *Magnolia grandiflora* 'Exmouth'. Ornaments as fine as these are always best in such a simple context. Leading the eye away from the house is a pair of herbaceous borders backed by yew hedges. Pure herbaceous borders, with no help from woody plants and always requiring meticulous and skilled maintenance, are a rare thing these days. Here, there is much repetition of

Antinous in the pond at the Old Rectory

plants and the use of bold foliage – acanthus, cardoons, fennel, geraniums, iris, thalictrum and tradescantia. The path between the borders points towards a statue of Antinous standing in a pond whose banks are densely planted with ferns, irises, Japanese maples, rhododendrons and rodgersias. To one side, lurking inconspicuously in woodland, is a stone carving of a rhinoceros which in winter stands hoof-deep in snowdrops and in summer seems to graze peacefully among martagon lilies. A former kitchen garden, enclosed in yew hedges on three sides, is now an ornamental swimming pool garden. A pedimented pavilion stands with its back to a wall, overlooking the pool. Climbing plants clothe the wall –*Actinidia kolomikta*, clematis, roses and wisteria. Borders on each side of the pavilion are planted with *Aralia elata* 'Variegata', cistus, hoheria, shrub roses and yucca.

The garden has a powerful and simple layout enlivened everywhere by the unusual plants gathered by Mrs Merton, often in her travels to exotic places, planted in troughs by the house or tucked away in countless appropriate corners of the garden. Such well-judged idiosyncrasies as the stone rhinoceros, and additional statues of a great bull in the swimming pool garden and a grand elephant close to the house, add strongly to the exotic flavour of the place.

INFORMATION

Location Burghfield, nr Reading RG3 3TH, Berkshire; in Burghfield village, 5m SW of Reading
Tel 0118 983 2206
English Heritage Register Grade I
Owner Mr A.R. Merton
Open on several days for the NGS and by appointment
Area 4½ acres/1.8 hectares

Osborne House

MID 19TH-CENTURY GARDENS OF THE HOLIDAY PALACE OF QUEEN VICTORIA NOW BRILLIANTLY BROUGHT BACK TO LIFE

In 1845 Queen Victoria and Prince Albert acquired Osborne and built a new house, made a new garden, and contrived a life as private as was possible. In recent years house and grounds have been magnificently restored by English Heritage. The garden is probably the best surviving example of an early Victorian formal layout in the country, and the house gives a brilliant and delightful glimpse of Victoria and Albert, and their family, at home.

To the north of the house terraced gardens bristle with ornament. A gravel terrace has a pattern of shaped lawns and formal bedding schemes in the Victorian style that is changed from year to year, and a grand triple-tiered fountain pool surmounted by a kneeling figure of Venus has a pink marble basin supported on dolphins' tails. To one side an ornate pattern of shaped beds is filled with bedding plants, with statues of women holding flaming torches representing the four seasons; at its centre winged sphinxes support a giant basin planted with an agave. At a lower level a figure of Venus stands at the centre of a circular sunken pool. Four flights of steps lead down to the pool, each guarded by a pair of seahorses. Shaped beds filled with bedding plants are cut into turf and a wall is covered in neatly clipped *Magnolia grandiflora*. A very grand pergola is covered in grapevines, wisteria and roses.

To the south of the house, across lawns of beautiful evergreen trees, cedars and holm oaks, is the 19th-century walled kitchen garden. This has been redesigned by the garden designer Rupert Golby to present a dazzling scene of ornament and productivity.

THE SWISS COTTAGE

About a mile from the house is an enchanting pair of buildings. In 1850 a Swiss cottage was brought from Switzerland for the children, in front of which is a pretty pattern of rectangular beds in which Prince Albert encouraged his children to cultivate vegetables which he would buy from them at the current market rate. A thatched summerhouse displays the small garden tools and wheelbarrows used by the children. A separate Swiss-style building houses the children's museum, filled with stuffed birds, eggs, geological specimens and all sorts of ethnographic curiosities displayed in beautiful cabinets.

The terraced gardens at Osborne

INFORMATION

Location East Cowes PO32 6JY, Isle of Wight; 1½m SE of East Cowes by A3021
Tel 01893 200022 **Fax** 01983 281380
Website www.englishheritage.org.uk
English Heritage Register Grade II*
Owner English Heritage
Open Apr to Sept, daily 10–6; Oct, daily 10–4; Nov to Mar, Wed to Sun 10–4 (closed 24–26 Dec and 1 Jan)
Area 50 acres/20 hectares

Oxford Botanic Garden

FOUNDED IN THE EARLY 17TH CENTURY AND MARVELLOUSLY PLANTED FOR BOTH BOTANISTS AND GARDENERS

This is the first botanic garden in Britain, founded in 1621 as a "phiseck garden", and its chief purpose remains to provide plants for the teaching of botany and biology. In recent years, however, it has gone out of its way to make the garden attractive to gardening members of the public.

The garden is still largely enclosed in splendid 17th-century walls and its layout corresponds to its appearance at that time as seen in the print by Loggan published in *Oxonia Illustrata* (1675).

The old bog garden at Oxford Botanic Garden

FINE COLLECTIONS

Most of the walled garden is still given over to the order beds. These, devoted essentially to botanical purposes, are nevertheless frequently dazzlingly ornamental. A group of "economic beds" contains plants used for culinary purposes, for dyeing, for medicine and for their fibres. The walled garden also contains collections of ornamental garden plants, among them a National Collection of euphorbias (well over 100 species and around 30 cultivars), a collection of old cultivars of bearded irises, and collections of ferns and bamboos. Several excellent trees provide striking ornament – a magnificent Austrian pine (*Pinus nigra* subsp. *nigra*) planted in 1800, a yew planted in 1645 by Jacob Bobart, the first director of the garden, and an especially fine collection of rowans.

A particularly attractive part of the garden is given over to "geographical borders", with plants from a particular region. The South African collection, for example, is rich in agapanthus, amaryllis, kniphofias and phygelius, and there is a collection of species pelargoniums which are given winter protection in the conservatory. There are also collections of plants from North America, the Mediterranean countries and Australasia.

South-west of the walled garden an admirable deep herbaceous border runs along the outside wall. There is also a rock garden with many alpine plants and bulbs and a collection of winter-flowering plants. Flowing borders of cardoons, *Melianthus major*, *Elaeagnus* 'Quicksilver' are underplanted with carmint, Californian poppies and ornamental grasses. The former water garden has been replanted with moisture-loving plants and given a small pool. On the banks of the Cherwell, against the east-facing outside wall, a range of glasshouses contain alpine plants, tender ferns and lilies, orchids, palms and succulents. The botanic garden is exceptional for its historic setting, the charm of its layout and the rare interest of its plant collection.

INFORMATION

Location Rose Lane, Oxford OX1 4AZ, Oxfordshire; in the centre of Oxford, near Magdalen bridge
Tel 01865 286690
Email postmaster@obg.ox.ac.uk
Website www.botanic-garden.ox.ac.uk
English Heritage Register Grade I
Owner Oxford University
Open Nov to Feb, daily 9–4.30; Mar, Apr, Sept and Oct, daily 9–5; May to August, daily 9–6
Area 4½ acres/1.8 hectares

Rousham House

WILLIAM KENT'S MASTERPIECE, AN EARLY 18TH-CENTURY ARCADIA, STILL PRIVATELY OWNED AND STILL BEAUTIFUL

Rousham, happily, is still in private hands; it has no whiff of the heritage industry about it. There is no tea room, no gift shop and no ticket kiosk. You put your money in a machine and the garden is yours. The garden was made by William Kent between 1737 and 1741 for General James Dormer, a veteran of the battle of Blenheim, who intended the place for his "philosophic retirement".

Below the house, at the far edge of a lawn, beyond a statue by Scheemakers of a lion attacking a horse, the ground falls away, down to the banks of the river Cherwell, with long views of the countryside beyond. An inconspicuous path through woodland leads to the Dying Gladiator (also by Scheemakers), beyond which the river is seen once again. Below is Praeneste, a lovely arcaded building by Kent. On a broad open grassy slope, Venus's Vale, the goddess teeters by a rustic cascade, overlooking a pool, below which is a second cascade. Cupids ride on swans, and lead fauns lurk among the trees. A

The Dying Gladiator at Rousham

rill winds through the woodland shade to a pool and a simple grotto. The rill continues until you see a fine cedar of Lebanon with the Temple of Echo (Kent, *c.*1740) standing at the head of a grassy slope with the river far below. A distant view is revealed of the 13th-century Heyford Bridge, a pretty piece of borrowed landscape.

SHIFTING SCENES

Walks follow the curving river bank and soon Venus's Vale is displayed from a new angle. From this point, too, there is a splendid view of Praeneste on the wooded slopes to one side. Continuing along the river you come to the shadowy remains of Charles Bridgeman's turf amphitheatre, now a semicircular glade, with lead figures of Ceres, Mercury and Bacchus. Passing the foot of the slope below the bowling green you come to a pyramid-roofed pavilion by William Kent facing out over the river.

Throughout the garden the ingredients seem only lightly sketched in, forming shifting scenes. Above the river, statues gaze outwards over fields and farms. Framed views are directed, too, by the arched openings of Praeneste. Within the building were finely made seats, designed by Kent, so that visitors could sit and relish these views.

INFORMATION

Location Steeple Aston OX25 4QX, Oxfordshire; 12m N of Oxford by A4260 and B4030
Tel 01869 347110
English Heritage Register Grade I
Owner C. Cottrell-Dormer
Open daily 10–4.30
Area 30 acres/12 hectares

Stourhead

AN 18TH-CENTURY LANDSCAPE GARDEN WITH ORNAMENTAL BUILDINGS AND WOODLAND PLANTING ABOUT A LAKE

The garden is the work of Henry Hoare II who, shortly after inheriting the estate in 1741, transformed the valley of the river Stour into an arcadian landscape. He dammed the river to form a lake, about which he planted trees and placed ornamental buildings in carefully chosen positions. These buildings are mostly of classical inspiration, of the sort that an English gentleman would have admired on the Grand Tour. The pillared and pedimented Temple of Flora (1744) on the eastern bank of the lake has an inscription from Virgil's *Aeneid*: "*Procul, o procul este, profani*" ("Be gone, be gone you who are uninitiated") – the warning that Aeneas encountered at the entrance to the underworld.

The lake and Pantheon at Stourhead

MANY MOODS

The lake is girdled by a path, with offshoots making occasional deviations to such buildings as the Temple of Apollo which stands high among trees on the southern edge of the lake. In this way the garden composes itself into different views, with water, shorn turf, ornamental building, and trees and shrubs playing varied roles. Different atmospheres evoke different emotions – the Temple of Apollo rising triumphantly on its lofty crag on the sunny side of the garden fills the heart with elation. On the western bank, where the path leads down into a shivery grotto, the mood of gloomy introspection is broken by an exhilarating view through an aperture pierced in the grotto wall – with distant prospects of the Temple of Flora on the lake's eastern bank. The suave classical Pantheon standing on a grassy promontory is visible from many parts of the garden. Near it, veiled by trees, is Watch Cottage, a little Gothic building of striking contrast. (The Gothic style was associated with ancient liberties.)

Stourhead possesses a remarkable collection of trees. Planting had been started by Henry Hoare II but it was his son, Richard Colt Hoare, who began recording all tree plantings from 1791. Many trees survive from his time, and some are the largest examples of their species in the country, such as a Japanese white pine (*Pinus parviflora*) and a tulip tree (*Liriodendron tulipifera*). Subsequent generations of the Hoare family have added to the planting. In 1946 Sir Henry Hoare gave the estate to the National Trust.

INFORMATION

Location Stourton, Warminster BA5 12 6QH, Wiltshire; in Stourton village, 3m NW of Mere by A303 and B3092
Tel 01747 841152
Email stourhead@nationalrust.org.uk
English Heritage Register Grade I
Owner The National Trust
Open daily 9–7
Area 40 acres/16 hectares

Stowe Garden

SUPERB LANDSCAPE GARDEN DESIGNED BY THE BEST GARDEN
DESIGNERS AND ARCHITECTS OF THE 18TH CENTURY

Like other gardens great in size and historical importance, Stowe may be enjoyed in different ways. As a garden for a long walk punctuated by beautiful trees, marvellous works of architecture and thrilling vistas, it is enchanting. As a piece of landscape design enriched with buildings and ornaments of the finest quality, it is certainly among the most absorbing in the country. For anyone interested in garden history, and in particular the early development of the English landscape park, it is a living document. Having said all that, I had better admit that I find the garden lacks unity – it presents a sequence of often marvellous and occasionally disparate delights that

never seem quite to coalesce. The fact that it has a golf course in its midst is unfortunate – brilliantly coloured anoraks do not suit well the spirit of the 18th-century landscape park.

WEAVING MAGIC

Charles Bridgeman, William Kent and the youthful Capability Brown, who became head gardener here at the age of twenty-five, each wove their magic at Stowe in different periods. Among the architects who worked on garden buildings and the house in the 18th century were Sir John Vanbrugh, James Gibbs and Robert Adam. Perhaps the only other garden in Europe that employed the talents of so many exceptional artists to such resounding effect was the Versailles of Louis XIV.

Stowe's Palladian bridge

The Temple family, later Viscounts Cobham, had owned the estate in the 17th century. It was Sir Richard Temple who recruited Charles Bridgeman in 1713 and set in motion the creation of the new garden.

William Kent came here in the 1720s and by 1735 he had created the Elysian Fields. This was a famous moment in English garden history when, in Horace Walpole's words, "Kent first leapt the fence and saw that all nature was a garden". Here, often masked by trees, a winding stream separates Kent's Temple of British Worthies (1735) and his Temple of Ancient Virtue (1736). The first is a curiously decorative curved screen of golden stone with niches that contain busts of Lord Cobham's special heroes, among them Bacon, Milton, Shakespeare and Pope. The second, domed and pillared and rising on an eminence on the far side of the stream, originally contained statues by Peter Scheemakers of the greatest poet (Homer), philosopher (Socrates), general (Epaminondas) and lawyer (Lycurgus) of the ancient world. These figures, and many other precious garden ornaments, were sold at auction in 1921.

TREES, TURF AND STREAM

North-east of the Elysian Fields is Brown's unemphatic Grecian Valley, decorated with no buildings or ornaments but already deploying his characteristic vocabulary of subtly undulating belts of trees and shorn turf as smooth as a fitted carpet. The stream that flows through the Elysian Fields emerges in the Octagon Lake with the Eleven-Acre Lake to one side. The first is the site of Bridgeman's formal octagonal pool which formed a punctuation mark at the end of his long vista. Its easterly neck is spanned by the Palladian Bridge (1738). With cattle grazing in the meadows on either side, it has the treasured English atmosphere of rural life coupled with classical harmony. On the far side of the bridge, tucked away in a glade, is the painted Chinese House (1738), possibly by Kent.

There are many other buildings and ornaments at Stowe – all have their charms and all play their part in the atmosphere of the place. But too great a concentration on individual buildings, marvellous as they are, detracts from one of the park's essential beauties. The buildings are reference points in the landscape, deftly fitted into glades, eminences and walks. They form part of a network of vistas, spanning great distances and rising and falling with the lie of the land. This large-scale animation of the landscape is Stowe's most thrilling and memorable quality.

INFORMATION

Location Buckingham MK18 5EH, Buckinghamshire; 3m NW of Buckingham on A422
Infoline 01494 7555568 **Tel** 01280 822850
Email stowegarden@nationaltrust.org.uk
English Heritage Register Grade I
Owner The National Trust
Open Mar to early Nov, Wed to Sun 10.30–5.30; early Nov to Feb, Sat and Sun 10.30–4
Area 250 acres/101 hectares

Waddesdon Manor

THE EPITOME OF ROTHSCHILD TASTE – A LOIRE CHATEAU IN WOODED GROUNDS WITH 19TH-CENTURY FORMAL BEDS

The house at Waddesdon, a dazzling pastiche of a renaissance Loire château, was completed in 1889 for Baron Ferdinand de Rothschild to the designs of Hippolyte Destailleur. It sits on the top of a knoll with beautiful views across well-wooded grounds to the Vale of Aylesbury. The site was landscaped between 1874 and 1881 by Elie Lainé who clothed the slopes in mature trees and devised an ingenious pattern of looping drives and walks that girdle the hill. Lainé was responsible only for the larger scheme of things and it was Ferdinand de Rothschild himself who looked after the detail. He recorded in his privately published *Red Book* (1897): "The pleasure grounds and gardens were laid out by my bailiff and gardener according to my notions and under my superintendence." The result is a beguiling mixture of formality and informality enriched with a lively decorative sense.

From the *rondpoint* of the North Fountain – an 18th-century sculpture of Triton and frolicking nereids by Giuliano Mozani – an avenue of oaks runs up to the north façade of the house. On the south side of the house the terrace and its parterre is the scene of spectacular high Victorian decorative exuberance. Here, thousands of bedding plants are deployed in patterns known as raised ribbon bedding, which creates a padded effect like a well-filled eiderdown. At the centre of the parterre is a fountain with Pluto and Proserpine, also by Mozani.

THE AVIARY GARDEN

To the north-west of the house is another piece of ornamental formality: the aviary garden. A splendid Rococo ironwork aviary with sweeping wings houses a collection of exotic birds. It overlooks a garden designed by Lanning Roper in the 1960s – with hedges of hornbeam and box, clipped lollipops of bay, beds of 'Iceberg' roses and 18th-century marble lions – a satisfying exercise in restrained simplicity. Further from the house, with a backdrop of trees and hedges, many fine statues are skilfully placed to enliven the scene.

No visitor to the Waddesdon gardens should fail also to visit the house, which has beautiful interiors filled with the finest furniture, pictures and china. House and garden are all of a piece, springing from the same desire to make something of the highest quality.

The terrace parterre at Waddesdon

INFORMATION

Location nr Aylesbury HP18 0JH, Buckinghamshire; 6m NW of Aylesbury by A41
Infoline 01296 653211
Email waddesdonmanor@ nationaltrust.org.uk
Website www.waddesdon.org. uk
English Heritage Register Grade I
Owner The National Trust
Open Jan to mid Mar, Sat and Sun 10–5; mid Mar to 23 Dec, Wed–Sun 10–5)
Area 160 acres/65 hectares

Waterperry Gardens

EXCELLENT PLANTS, AN INVENTIVE WALLED GARDEN AND THE SPLENDID STOCK BEDS OF A BUSY NURSERY

Waterperry was founded in 1932 by a remarkable woman, Beatrix Havergal, in order to educate women in all branches of horticulture. It still has that purpose, in the form of a multitude of garden courses, but it also has a large nursery and garden centre as well as an attractive and diverse garden.

The flat site, with many good trees, lies by the river Thame and and has rich, slightly alkaline, loam soil. The entrance leads along a deep herbaceous border, past a fine statue (Meditation by Nathan David) standing in a thicket of *Maccleaya x cordata*. Other sculptures adorn the garden and temporary exhibitions are mounted (such as an interesting collection of works by the Shona people of Zimbabwe). Apart from the Long Walk which links various of the garden's parts, there is no strong layout; it is a place for ambling in. The most strongly designed part is the Formal Garden, designed by Bernard Saunders and Mary Spiller. Enclosed in yew hedges and bristling with decorative ideas skilfully executed, it has a swirling knot garden of box and purple berberis compartments filled with summer bedding. There are lavish herbaceous borders, a tunnel of white wisteria, columns of clipped hornbeam, a vine arbour and shady sitting places. At its centre is a slightly sugary statue of a young girl, The Lamp of Wisdom.

The Formal Garden at Waterperry

south-facing herbaceous border runs along the outer wall (18th-century, of very pretty silvery brick) of the area that now houses the garden centre. Honeysuckle, *Solanum crispum* 'Album', *Vitis coignetiae* and wisteria clothe the wall, and the bed is planted with bold groups of delphiniums, *Eupatorium purpureum*, geraniums, Michaelmas daisies, mulleins and phlox. A collection of dwarf conifers and of heathers shows what varieties can be cultivated in alkaline soil. A charming riverside walk is planted with aconites, snake's head fritillaries, narcissi and snowdrops. Of special interest to alpinists is the National Collection of *Kabschia* saxifrages – a staggering range of over 300 species and cultivars.

NURSERY BEDS

One of the best sights, at the garden's heart, is the great array of nursery beds of herbaceous perennials that provide propagation material for the nursery. A rose garden nearby, enclosed in yew hedges and decorated with a charmingly wonky arbour of oak, includes shrub and species roses and modern bedding varieties. A long

INFORMATION

Location Waterperry, nr Wheatley OX33 1JZ, Oxfordshire; 9m E of Oxford by A40, near Jct 8 of M40
Tel 01844 339254
Email office@waterperrygardens.fsnet.co.uk
Website www.waterperrygardens.co.uk
Owner The School of Economic Science
Open Apr to Oct, daily 9–5.30; Nov to Mar, daily 9–5
Area 83 acres/34 hectares

West Green House Garden

A LOVELY 18TH-CENTURY HOUSE WITH WALLED GARDENS
SUPERBLY PLANTED BY A MODERN PLANTSWOMAN

In 1975 Alistair McAlpine (later Lord McAlpine) took a tenancy of West Green House which had been owned by the National Trust since 1957. He restored the garden and commissioned a series of monuments from the architect Quinlan Terry. An ornate Baroque nymphaeum with trick perspective forms an eyecatcher at the end of a vista from the kitchen garden. Perhaps the most memorable among the monuments from this time is the one erected to McAlpine's gardener, Thomas Mann, who died in 1986. An obelisk soars up from the bank of a pool with a splendid sculpture of Mr Mann, elbow cocked on the obelisk's plinth, a jaunty grin on his face and a spade at the ready in his hand.

McAlpine's gardening idyll came to an unhappy end in 1990 when an IRA bomb severely damaged the house. The second stage in the development of the garden started in 1993 when Marylyn Abbott restored house and garden and introduced refined new flower plantings.

The nymphaeum at West Green House

The formal gardens are clustered about the house. To its west, the theatre lawn is a brilliant exercise in creating drama out of restraint. A long rectangle of lawn, enclosed in yew hedges and gently terraced, extends away from the house – devoid of ornament except for a pair of urns and one or two benches.

AN EYE FOR COLOUR

The walled former kitchen garden is the scene of Marylyn Abbott's most detailed attentions. Part of it has been retained as a true kitchen garden, with ornamental fruit-cages with Chinoiserie roofs designed by Oliver Ford. Neat rows of vegetables, with lively associated flower plantings, radiate outwards from the fruit-cages, and paths are decorated with lollipops of standard *Weigela florida* and *Viburnum* x *burkwoodii*.

The other half of the walled garden is divided into four lawns planted with fruit trees. Running along its south-facing wall, borders are filled with shrub roses, peonies, philadelphus and lilacs underplanted with geraniums, irises and violas. Marylyn Abbott has a brilliant eye for colour and texture and is constantly experimenting with new plantings. The Quinlan Terry and other monuments are skilfully integrated into the pattern of the garden. The house overlooks no flower garden and the explosion of floriferousness that meets the eye in the walled garden is all the more effective for being hidden away.

INFORMATION

Location Thackhams Lane, West Green, nr Hartley Wintney RG27 8JB, Hampshire; 2¼m NE of Jct 5 of M3
Tel and Fax 01252 844611
Owner Marylyn Abbott/The National Trust
Open May to Aug, Wed to Fri and Bank Hol Mon 11–4
Area 6 acres/2.4 hectares

West Wycombe Park

A MYSTERIOUS BUT CHARMING 18TH-CENTURY LANDSCAPE PARK WITH A LAKE AND FINE ORNAMENTAL BUILDINGS

The garden at West Wycombe dates from the 18th century. The house was built for Sir Francis Dashwood shortly after 1707 and his son, another Sir Francis, was the chief maker of the garden, but is probably more famous as the instigator of the so-called Hell Fire Club which had its meetings at Medmenham Abbey where hanky-panky of various kinds took place.

The landscape today presents a delightful scene. The house faces down a long grassy slope towards the lake with the river Wye flowing into it. A wooded island has a beautiful Music Temple designed by Nicholas Revett between 1778 and 1780. The lake itself is supposed to represent a swan, and the stream to the west does resemble a slender serpentine neck. A cascade, guarded by two recumbent nymphs, links the river to the lake and below it is a new bridge designed by Quinlan Terry (1985). The Gothic boathouse on an isthmus jutting out from the southern bank of the lake is also a modern re-creation, by Patrick Crawford in 1983, based on an 18th-century design.

The Music Temple at West Wycombe

SEDUCTIVE VIEWS

West of the lake the Broad Walk has a tall column surmounted with a figure of Britannia, put up in 1987 to celebrate the Queen's sixtieth birthday. Nearby is Quinlan Terry's domed Temple of Venus (1982) above an 18th-century mound and cavern. The stream winds peacefully across meadowland and the pillared house to the south is partly veiled in trees which continue in belts and clumps on the land that rises above it. All the ingredients of the park are harmoniously related and form a series of shifting and seductive views.

In the distance, on the far side of the A40, are the wooded slopes of West Wycombe Hill which also forms part of the Dashwoods' 18th-century landscape. The medieval church of St Lawrence, which stands at the top of the hill, was remodelled in the 1750s when a new tower was built, surmounted by a giant golden sphere, making a striking eyecatcher from the park. More extraordinary than this church is an immense mausoleum which Pevsner suggests may be the largest mausoleum built in Europe since Antiquity. A hexagonal, roofless enclosure of soaring flint walls whose parapet is busy with urns, it houses several Dashwood memorials.

INFORMATION

Location West Wycombe HP14 3AJ, Buckinghamshire; at the W end of West Wycombe, S of the A40
Infoline 01494 755571 **Tel** 01494 513569
Email westwycombe@nationaltrust.org.uk
English Heritage Register Grade I
Owner The National Trust
Open Apr to Aug, Sun to Thurs 2–6
Area 46 acres/19 hectares

SOUTH-EAST ENGLAND

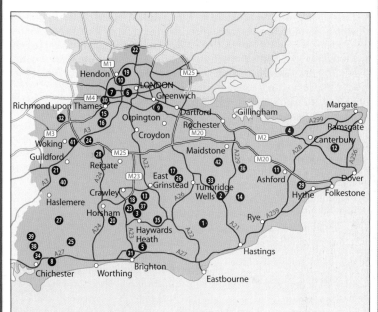

GARDENS TO VISIT

1. Bateman's
2. Bedgebury National Pinetum
3. Borde Hill Garden
4. Brogdale Horticultural Trust
5. Charleston
6. Chelsea Physic Garden
7. Chiswick House
8. Denmans
9. Eltham Palace
10. Fenton House
11. Godinton House
12. Goodnestone Park
13. Gravetye Manor
14. Great Dixter
15. Ham House
16. Hampton Court Palace
17. Hever Castle
18. The High Beeches
19. Kenwood House
20. Leonardslee Gardens
21. Loseley Park
22. Myddelton House Gardens
23. Nymans Garden
24. Painshill Landscape Park
25. Parham House
26. Penshurst Place
27. Petworth House
28. Polesden Lacey
29. Port Lympne Gardens
30. Royal Botanic Gardens
31. The Royal Pavilion
32. Savill and Valley Gardens
33. Scotney Castle Garden
34. Sculpture at Goodwood
35. Sheffield Park Garden
36. Sissinghurst Castle Garden
37. Wakehurst Place
38. Weald and Downland Museum
39. West Dean Gardens
40. Winkworth Arboretum
41. Wisley Garden
42. Yalding Organic Gardens

Image *Polesden Lacey*

Bateman's

RUDYARD KIPLING'S DELIGHTFUL GARDEN, REDOLENT OF THE EDWARDIAN AGE AND IMPECCABLY MAINTAINED

Rudyard Kipling lived at Bateman's from 1902 until his death in 1936. The house is an early 17th-century stone ironmaster's house which bears the date 1634 carved on the entrance porch. It contains much Kiplingiana: the study remains as it was when Kipling died, and his Rolls Royce is preserved in the garage – a 1928 Phantom I Limousine with special fittings (total cost £1,880, the equivalent of £54,294 today). When Kipling first saw the house he wrote, "We entered and felt her Spirit – her Feng Shui – to be good." He later recorded, "Sooner or later, all sorts of men cast up at our house", and Bateman's became a literary meeting place. As a literary shrine, Bateman's is by no means overdone but Kipling is nevertheless the powerful presiding spirit of the place.

The attractive garden, in which he took much interest and delight, has been kept largely as it was in his time; a painting by Sir Edward Poynter of the house and garden, painted before 1919 and still hanging in the hall at Bateman's, shows it much as it is today. Kipling loved the house and revelled in the surrounding countryside – the hill that inspired *Puck of Pook's Hill* (1906) may be seen from the house.

LILY POOL AND PEARS

The garden, to the south and west of the house, has an Arts and Crafts formality, with screens of pleached lime and a rectangular lily pool. The north side of the pool is marked by a yew hedge which embraces a curved bench and has clipped piers rising high on either side. At the end of the pool there is a rose garden with flagged paths, and to one side of the house Kipling made a tunnel of late-season pears ('Conference', 'Doyenné de Comice' and 'Winter Nelis'); trained over a broad metal framework, the ripening fruit makes a splendid sight in autumn. A brick path runs along the tunnel, with beds on each side filled with herbaceous perennials suitable for the shady position – bergenias, comfrey, hardy geraniums, Corsican hellebores and pulmonaria. Down the side of the house a yew hedge has occasional windows cut in it, framing views of the rural scenery beyond. Bateman's has a strongly nostalgic air, redolent of the Edwardian period – the kind of garden dreamed of by homesick men in Poona.

The lily pool at Bateman's

INFORMATION

Location Burwash, Etchingham TN19 7DS, East Sussex; ½m S of Burwash by A265
Tel 01435 882302
Email batemans@nationaltrust.org.uk
English Heritage Register Grade II
Owner The National Trust
Open mid Mar to Oct, Sat to Wed 11–5.30; phone for out of season openings
Area 10 acres/4 hectare

Bedgebury National Pinetum

A FOREST OF MAGNIFICENT CONIFERS FORMS A BEGUILING LANDSCAPE FULL OF RARE AND NOBLE TREES

Bedgebury was founded as the National Conifer Collection in 1925. The site is a hilly one with two valleys and lakes. This in itself makes an attractive piece of landscape but the planting is not obviously dominated by aesthetic considerations: its chief aim is to build up a reference collection of conifers that will grow in a temperate climate. It now contains 61 per cent of all such conifers, with 488 species and over 1,600 cultivars. Some are grouped by genus, others regionally – the Japanese Glade, American Glade and Chinese Glade. It is the intention to increase the collection so that it contains every conifer hardy in the south of England. All this is obviously of great scientific value and irresistible to conifer enthusiasts, but is it of interest to the rest of us?

Bedgebury National Pinetum

PLEASURES OF CONIFERS

The problem about conifers is that they seem at first so obvious. They stay green (or, much worse, glaucous or yellow) all the year round; many of them grow with bewildering speed, forming huge cones like perpetual Christmas trees; they produce no pretty flowers. However, an open-minded visit to Bedgebury, and a close look at the trees, shows how wrong these assumptions are. Many conifers change colour with beguiling subtlety. They are also immensely varied in habit: some of them (like the podocarps) produce long leaves which sway gracefully in the wind; others, like the startlingly prostrate forms, an affront to the vertical ambitions of many of their tribe, are merely of curiosity value. Conifers do not, indeed, have pretty flowers but they do sometimes have the most beautiful cones, intricately shaped and at times startling in colour, ranging

from crimson (*Picea orientalis*) to a sumptuous blue (*Abies koreana*). A walk among conifers on a hot summer's day is a delicious pleasure. Their scent is strangely invigorating, their shade seems far denser than that of deciduous trees, and their sheer size is a thrilling sight. No deciduous tree is anywhere near as tall as the biggest conifer, and whereas the dwarf conifer can be seen as a ghastly aberration of nature or a blatant vulgarity of the nurseryman, real conifers are something else. Bedgebury is one of the finest collections in the world of these astonishing trees, and it is worthy of the interest of anyone who likes trees.

INFORMATION

Location nr Goudhurst, Cranbrook TN17 2SL, Kent; 4½m S of Goudhurst by B2079
Tel 01580 879820
Email bedgebury@forestry.gsi.gov.uk
Website www.forestry.gov.uk/england
English Heritage Register Grade II*
Owner Forestry Commission
Open daily 8–dusk (closes at 8 in summer)
Area 320 acres/217 hectares

Borde Hill Garden

A GREAT COLLECTION OF FLOWERING SHRUBS AND TREES IN AN EXCEPTIONALLY ATTRACTIVE SETTING

Borde Hill is in the heart of a part of Sussex famous for woodland gardens, especially those associated with the Loder family. All benefit from the acidic loam of the Hastings Beds which is shown on the Ordnance Survey geological map as an alluring expanse of tawny gold running from Horsham in the west to Dungeness in the east, and from Tonbridge in the north to Bexhill in the south. The position here, on the Sussex high weald, is exceptionally attractive. The distinction of the garden at Borde Hill is due to Colonel Stephenson Clarke who bought the estate in 1892 and became a sponsor of some of the great plant-collecting expeditions of the 20th century. He built up a very large collection of trees and shrubs, with a particular interest in camellias, magnolias and rhododendrons. Colonel Clarke was also a gifted hybridiser and among his most successful crosses was *Camellia x williamsii* 'Donation'.

The formal garden at Borde Hill

A VAST RANGE OF PLANTS

The charm of Borde Hill comes from the beauty of the groups and individual specimens of these plants, many of which are very large, set in a fine, gently undulating landscape. With 200 acres/81 hectares and a vast range of plants, there is much to explore and marvel at. Many of the best plants are close to the house, but you should walk to Warren Wood, spectacular in May with brilliant rhododendrons in the native woodland. There are also excellent conifers here, with some very large specimens such as the Formosan cypress (*Chamaecyparis formosensis*), propagated from the first seed brought to England in 1910. A little further on is Little Bentley Wood with particularly good, and often rare, deciduous trees which will give even knowledgeable tree-spotters some delightful headaches.

Closer to the house, gardens of a formal character are attractively done. Here are a Mediterranean Garden, an Italian Garden, a Garden of Allah, a Rose Garden and excellent herbaceous borders. Some of these give much flowery pleasure in the summer when the woodland gardens with their remarkable collections are not at their best. The Garden of Allah has an especially distinguished collection of rhododendrons, many of them species raised from seed collected in the wild. It is the rare shrubs and superb trees that give Borde Hill its distinction.

INFORMATION

Location Haywards Heath RH16 1XP, West Sussex; 1½m N of Haywards Heath by minor roads
Tel 01444 450326
Email info@bordehill.co.uk
Website www.bordehill.co.uk
English Heritage Register Grade II*
Owner Borde Hill Gardens Ltd
Open daily 10–6
Area 200 acres/81 hectares

Brogdale Horticultural Trust

A GIANT ORCHARD OF HISTORIC FRUIT PLANTS IN THE GARDEN OF ENGLAND – A MOUTH-WATERING SIGHT

Brogdale is the home of the National Fruit Collection, one of the greatest collections of its kind in the world. Its chief aim is conservation – to preserve from extinction the vast range of fruit varieties and their genes. The site is superficially as unpropitious as you could imagine: flat and windswept, horribly close to the permanent roar of the M2. The contents, however, are absolutely wonderful. This corner of England is a sacred spot for fruit growing. Kent is, of course, the orchard of England, and one of the first large-scale orchards was planted at Teynham, quite near Brogdale, by Henry VIII's fruiterer, Richard Harris.

The collection at Brogdale has over 2,300 varieties of apple, 550 of pears, 350 of plums, 220 of cherries, 320 of bush fruit (gooseberries, blackcurrants, etc) and many varieties of nut (over 40 hazelnuts) and grapevines. The National Collection consists of rows of plants grouped by variety and is not open to unsupervised visits. Tours of the collection are organised from March to November four times a day and are extraordinarily interesting. Your guide will be deeply knowledgeable and what he or she has to tell of the history of these fruit is gripping. Many of the fruit you will see will be unfamiliar and often beautiful. Many of the fields are protected by high hedges which are themselves frequently ornamental. One of the plants most used for hedges is the native alder (*Alnus glutinosa*) whose glossy leaves shimmer attractively in the wind. Another beautiful hedge is planted of alternate hazelnut and dog rose which scrambles high up through the trees.

BROGDALE EVENTS

Some parts of the garden at Brogdale are open to unsupervised visits. A plant centre sells many ornamentals as well as hundreds of different fruit plants. In addition there is a Plum Weekend in July, a Cider Festival in September and an Apple Festival in October. Day courses, workshops and demonstrations cover practical fruit-growing, pruning and grafting, preserving and planning an orchard. Advisory services are also available. The explosion of spring blossom and the dazzling profusion of autumn fruits are the most exciting events at Brogdale. A walk through the collection at these times is one of the finest garden pleasures. The work of the Trust is important, and there is no other organisation undertaking it.

'Early Strawberry' apples at Brogdale

INFORMATION

Location Brogdale Road, Faversham ME13 8XZ, Kent; 1m SW of Faversham, Jct 6 of M2
Tel 01795 535286/535462
Email info@brogdale.org.uk
Website www.brogdale.org.uk
Owner Brogdale Horticultural Trust
Open daily 10–5 (10.00–4.30 in winter)
Area 150 acres/61 hectares

Charleston

THE IDIOSYNCRATIC AND CHARMING COUNTRY GARDEN OF THE BLOOMSBURY SET, PRESERVING ITS ORIGINAL FLAVOUR

On a visit to Charleston in 1929 Frances Partridge wrote, vividly evoking the character of the place: "The garden here is a rampant jungle of sunflowers and hollyhocks, and the apple-trees are bowed down with scarlet apples; pears hanging bobbing at one's head." The garden of the rural retreat of the Bloomsburys is no great work of horticultural art but it is nonetheless delightful and imbued with a most distinctive atmosphere.

The 17th-century farmhouse was discovered by Virginia and Leonard Woolf in 1916 when Virginia's sister, Vanessa Bell, was looking for a house in the area. Vanessa Bell came to live here with the painter Duncan Grant and the

writer David Garnett, and Charleston established itself as a great meeting place for the Bloomsbury Group. The interior was decorated with abandon – swirling patterns on the walls, frescoed fireplaces, tumbling acrobats or vases of flowers on the panels of doors, and eruptions of angels in unexpected places, a feast of surprises.

DECORATIVE EXPLOSIONS

The character of the house spills over into the walled garden behind the house. It was laid out in the 1920s by Roger Fry with a firm framework of paths and lawn to which the detailed planting could be added. Here are gravel paths, sitting places, old apple trees and borders abundantly filled with flowers, and here the Bloomsbury *furor*

The walled garden at Charleston

decorandi is given full rein. The garden seems more like a series of decorative explosions than anything more sedate. A truncated pottery torso (female) filled with a pink hydrangea, flanked by troughs of nasturtiums, sits on concrete slabs (not entirely horizontal) mounted on brick piers. A patio is surfaced in sprightly patterns of broken flower pots and shards of pottery or porcelain (much of it of fine quality, some of it rubbish). A pottery mask peers over a pool between the upright leaves of an iris. Box hedges are clipped into rolling curvaceous mounds, as plump as a fine South Down sheep before shearing, and among the curves a copy of Giovanni da Bologna's Venus adds her own distinction. Behind a little hedge of santolina a spreading forest of sweet peas nudges thickets of statuesque plants – pink hollyhocks, sweetly scented tobacco plants, yellow mulleins and great grey veils of thistles. Miscellaneous busts crown the top of a garden wall on which a plaque of pottery tiles, prettily decorated with a painted trellis of vines with purple grapes, reads, "Two of the above heads were given by friends to celebrate Quentin Bell's 80th birthday and commemorate others that are gone. August 1980".

The east-facing entrance front of the house overlooks a pool with overarching willow trees. The banks of the pool are decorated with sculptures by Quentin Bell – a figure of Pomona, made of concrete, with a basket of prettily glazed apples on her head, a truncated Venus, a bust of a woman (named Spink) made of finely carved brick, and a mysterious horizontal figure, Levitating Lady, rising in the grass.

"INTELLECTUAL LARKING"

One of the great attractions of the Bloomsbury attitude to life was that much was taken seriously but much was not; they were never afraid of what Henry James called "intellectual larking". High art coexisted with junk

Quentin Bell's Spink

and profound ideas with frivolity – juxtapositions designed to sharpen the judgement. Charleston – both house and garden – most vividly evokes the Bloomsbury world and epitomises the paradoxes within it. Even the austere economist J.M. Keynes was known to work in the garden; Vanessa Bell wrote to Roger Fry, "One would often find Maynard on the gravel path at the front of the house kneeling like a muslim on his prayer mat and, with enormous thoroughness, weeding a small patch of pathways with a penknife."

A visit to the house is essential to understanding the garden: views from the windows show house and garden to be all of a piece – the decorative exuberance forming a continuum. Few gardens possess such a strong flavour of the people who made them and such a strong sense of place. Charleston shows Bloomsbury at its best.

INFORMATION

Location nr Firle, Lewes BN8 6LL, East Sussex; 6m E of Lewes by A27
Infoline 01323 811265
Tel 01323 811626 (administration)
Email info@charleston.org.uk
Website www.charleston.org.uk
Owner The Charleston Trust
Open Apr to Oct, Wed to Sun (open Bank Hol Mon) 2–6 (Jul and Aug, Wed to Sat 11.30–6, Sun and Bank Hol Mon 2–6)
Area 1 acre/0.4 hectare

Chelsea Physic Garden

A 17TH-CENTURY WALLED PHYSIC GARDEN: AN URBAN OASIS FILLED WITH FINE PLANTS AND GREAT CHARACTER

John Evelyn visited the Chelsea Physic Garden in August 1685: "I went to see Mr Wats, keeper of the Apothecaries Garden of Simples at Chelsea, where there is a collection of innumerable rarities of that sort particularly." He also noted "the tree bearing jesuits bark, which had don such wonders in quartan agues". This, the Peruvian *Cinchona officinalis*, the source of quinine which had dramatically transformed the treatment of malaria ("quartan ague"), was grown at Chelsea in a conservatory with an ingenious source of "subterranean heate" which Evelyn much admired.

The garden had been founded in 1673, making it the second botanic garden to be founded in England; only Oxford is older. It entered its period of greatest fame with the appointment as curator in 1722 of the remarkable Philip Miller whose *Gardeners Dictionary* (1731) was one of the best and most successful gardening books published in the 18th century. The garden continued to flourish after Miller's death in 1770 but in the later 19th century entered a period of decline, to recover splendidly

in the 20th century. A delightful place of great character, the finely kept garden is today a lively centre of botany and horticulture.

AN ALLURING GARDEN

The Physic Garden presents an alluring aspect to those outside: hidden behind brick walls, its fine trees flaunt their crowns enticingly above. The gardens do not disappoint. A grand central walk runs down the centre of the garden, with a pause in the middle marked by a splendid statue of Sir Hans Sloane, a great benefactor of the garden. About one third of the whole area is given over to traditional order beds in which plants are grouped under genera disposed in correct scientific order, and everywhere the garden is animated by old trees – among them a beautiful olive which in a good year produces a fine crop. There are also collections of South African plants (especially agapanthus and kniphofias), of Australasian plants, and of culinary and medicinal herbs. The garden holds a National Collection of cistus (with over 80 species and cultivars), a study collection of hypericums and a beautiful collection of snowdrops for which there are special visits in February. As botanic gardens go, Chelsea is very small but it is unusually packed with interest and charm.

Statue of Sir Hans Sloane
in the Chelsea Physic Garden

INFORMATION

Location 66 Royal Hospital Road, London SW3 4HS; in central London, Sloane Square tube
Tel 020 7352 5646
Email enquiries@chelseaphysicgarden.co.uk
Website www.chelseaphysicgarden.co.uk
English Heritage Register Grade I
Owner Chelsea Physic Garden Company
Open Apr to Oct, Wed 12–dusk, Thur and Fri 12–5, Sun and Bank Hol Mon 12–6 (also winter openings; phone for details)
Area 4 acres/1.6 hectares

Chiswick House

A PALLADIAN PLEASURE DOME IN A NOTABLE EARLY 18TH-CENTURY GARDEN WITH LIVELY VICTORIAN PLANTING

In 1732 Alexander Pope wrote, "I assure you Chiswick has been to me the finest thing this glorious sun has shined on." Richard Boyle, the 3rd Earl of Burlington, had built his Palladian pleasure dome in 1725 and laid out, with the help of William Kent in the 1730s, a garden of extraordinary enchantment. At first the garden had been formal but under Kent's influence the straight lines were softened and such romantic

The Italian Garden at Chiswick House

features as a grotto cascade at the head of a lake were added. The complicated evolution of the gardens is one of the best documented of its time, most valuably in paintings by Peter Andreas Rysbrack and drawings by Jacques Rigaud – all executed between the years of 1728 and 1734.

Much of this survives: the house has been superbly restored and the garden preserves many of its original features, among them marvellous statuary and garden buildings. As a monument to the taste of a great and influential connoisseur, Chiswick is wonderful. However, there is today a scruffiness about much of the grounds that is quite alien to the spirit of such a place. A visit to Chiswick is essential to anyone who wants to know about one of the most attractive ensembles of house and garden in the country, but with the present condition of the garden, delight can swiftly turn to deepest gloom. In 2007 the gardens were on the verge of restoration with the assistance of a Heritage Lottery Fund grant.

Lord Burlington died in 1753, leaving as his heiress his daughter Charlotte who had married the Marquess of Hartington, heir to the dukedom of Devonshire. When he inherited, the 6th Duke bought the neighbouring estate of Moreton Hall in 1812 and linked the two estates.

CAMELLIA CONSERVATORY

To the north-east of Chiswick House the Duke built a magnificent conservatory, designed by Samuel Ware, which he filled with camellias. In its day this was the longest conservatory ever built in England. It still houses camellias, some of which, it is believed, date from 1812. In front of the conservatory, the Italian Garden, a semicircular parterre, was laid out by Lewis Kennedy. This today is finely kept, with Coadestone urns and mop-headed acacias rising among brilliant bedding schemes.

INFORMATION

Location Burlington Lane, Chiswick, London W4 2RP; 4m SW of central London by A4 and A316
Tel 020 8742 1978
Owner English Heritage; gardens in the management of London Borough of Hounslow
English Heritage Register Grade I
Open 8.30–dusk
Area 62 acres/25 hectares

Denmans

THE SECLUDED PRIVATE GARDEN OF THE GARDEN DESIGNER JOHN BROOKES, BRISTLING WITH INSPIRATION

It is fascinating to see what professional garden designers get up to in the privacy of their own gardens. The garden at Denmans was started in 1946 by Joyce Robinson who said of her gardening principles, "The emphasis is on the shape, colour and texture of the whole growing picture, rather than on the plants." John Brookes has continued in this tradition, adding much else that is emphatically his own.

Although the garden is close to the very busy A27 it is remarkably secluded; if you raise your eyes to the skyline you will see an encircling panorama of trees of all kinds. The atmosphere is unconstrained – in the garden there are no dictatorial routes, scarcely a straight line, and varying approaches encourage wandering and contemplation.

MEANDERING PATHS

The entrance leads to a walled garden where a gravel path meanders, its outline blurred by plants. In summer the boundaries here are almost invisible, such is the luxuriance of the planting, but the profusion is tempered both by skilful grouping and repetition of plants. Large mounds of clipped box make shapely reference points or form part of carefully arranged groups of plants acting as interludes punctuating the garden walks. There is also much contrast of foliage and plant shape: the feathery fronds of a sumach (*Rhus typhina*) spread alongside a weeping beech and the stately toothed foliage of *Melianthus major* rises among double white dahlias and the bronze stems and explosive scarlet flowers of *Lobelia* 'Queen Victoria'.

The chief part of the garden lies beyond the walled garden. Here are sweeping shapes of turf and gravel and decisively effective groups of plants.

The walled garden at Denmans

The grass is close mown along its periphery, where it follows a bed, and left slightly longer towards the centre where a single specimen tree, or a group of trees, make emphatic statements. Gravel beds flow like a river through the garden, ending up at one point at a pool fringed with bulrushes and irises, its surface decorated with waterlilies.

Denmans runs counter to the mainstream of English 20th-century garden fashion: its effects are painterly and organic, with no tyrannical vistas, no contrived borders and no exquisitely artificial colour harmonies; it is full of good plants deployed without fuss, and underlying the design is a rhythmic shapeliness that is deeply satisfying.

INFORMATION

Location Denmans Lane, Fontwell, nr Arundel BN18 0SU, West Sussex; 6m E of Chichester by A27
Tel 01243 542808
Email denmans@denmans-garden.co.uk
Website www.denmans-garden.co.uk
Owner John Brookes MBE and Michael Neve
Open daily (except 25 and 26 Dec, and 1 Jan) 9–5 (or dusk if earlier)
Area 3½ acres/1.4 hectares

Eltham Palace

A RARE MEDIEVAL ROYAL PALACE WITH SPRIGHTLY 20TH-CENTURY GARDENS AND GREAT ATMOSPHERE

Eltham Palace has a long history of royal connections from the 11th century to the 17th century, when the palace was far larger than Hampton Court. Charles I was the last king to use it. By the 20th century only the medieval great hall survived when, in the 1930s, it was restored and a spectacular new house grafted onto it for Sir Stephen Courtauld. In 1995 English Heritage took over the estate and have restored what remained of palace and gardens.

Little is known of early gardens here, and when the Courtaulds arrived there was nothing except the splendour of the site and the now mainly waterless moat with its splendid medieval stone bridge. The garden they laid out, essentially a thoroughly traditional Arts and Crafts garden of compartments, strikingly contrasts with the extraordinary Art Deco interiors they commissioned for the new house. Parts of the moat were excavated and once again filled with water; a sunken rose garden was made, edged with lavender and mounds of clipped box; and a shady shrub garden has tall columns of holly and plantings of Japanese anemones, ferns,

hydrangeas and pulmonaria. Beyond it the reflooded part of the moat curves round the palace ramparts, turning into a grass walk under the medieval bridge. On the far side of the moat, a great rock garden also dates from the Courtaulds' time. Japanese maples and a sprawling old juniper are underplanted with *Alchemilla mollis*, ferns, geraniums, hostas and rheums.

SPRIGHTLY NEW GARDENS

On the south side of the palace, where the moat remains dry, are sprightly new borders by Isabelle van Groeningen, rich in brilliant yellows and reds. On the grass terrace above them, flamboyant bedding schemes of apricot and scarlet dahlias, cannas and tobacco plants lie below the medieval hall. On the north-east corner of the palace, in an awkward triangular site, English Heritage has laid out a brilliant little parterre of diamond-shaped beds filled with purple sage, creeping thyme or autumn-flowering kniphofia.

Eltham Palace presents an unusual mixture of ingredients. The palace ramparts are a patchwork of early Tudor brick and medieval stone. The palace itself lurches from romantically medieval to crisply neo-Georgian. The gardens, newly restored, and finely kept, show similar diversity with appropriately bold effects and much good detail.

The rock garden at Eltham Palace

INFORMATION

Location Eltham, London SE9 5QE; 11m SE of central London by A20, signed from Eltham High St
Tel 020 8294 2548
Website www.english-heritage.org.uk/eltham
English Heritage Register Grade II*
Owner English Heritage
Open Apr to Oct, Sun to Wed 10–5; Nov to 23 Dec and Feb to Mar, Sun to Wed 11–4
Area 10 acres/2.4 hectares

Fenton House

A BEAUTIFULLY DESIGNED, CHEERFUL COUNTRY GARDEN FOR A HANDSOME 18TH-CENTURY HAMPSTEAD HOUSE

Fenton House was built in 1693 – the date is scratched on one of the chimneys. In 1703 it was bought by a silk merchant, Joshua Gee, and in 1793 by another merchant, Philip Fenton. It is one of the prettiest and least spoilt houses of its date surviving in Hampstead and, together with its garden, gives a delightful idea of the sort of gentlemanly life led in the past in one of London's outlying villages. The house was given to the National Trust in 1952.

CHEERFUL FORMALITY

The approach to the house has a village feel. Narrow streets lead to a beautiful set of wrought-iron gates which date from Joshua Gee's time and bear the initials J. A. G. A short drive, with an avenue of *Robinia pseudoacacia*, leads to the front door. The garden lies almost entirely to the north of the house and its layout is a model for a garden of this

sort. Of rectangular plan, enclosed in old brick walls, it is edged on its eastern and northern boundaries by a raised gravel terrace. This, in all likelihood, would have been the garden's original layout: a raised walk to give views over a neatly formal garden spread out below. Box-edged beds line the walls which are clothed in clematis, grapevine, passion flower and roses. Large tubs of blue agapanthus and clipped Portugal laurel follow the edge of the terrace. At the lower level is a sequence of small gardens enclosed in yew hedges occasionally embellished with topiary. Immediately below the north wall of the house a lawn has rows of lollipops of holly and cones of variegated holly; a sunken garden has rose borders; and the smallest of the enclosures has miniature herbaceous borders. The largest area is given to a splendid orchard, lovely in spring with anemones, narcissi and snake's head fritillaries in the grass. At its far end is a vegetable garden.

Containing all the ingredients one could wish for in a garden, everything is on exactly the right scale, and the garden's cheerful formality precisely echoes that of the house. When Fenton House was built it was in a small village in a rural setting. Today, engulfed in later development, it nonetheless preserves a delightful country air.

The walled garden at Fenton

INFORMATION

Location Windmill Hill, Hampstead, London NW3 6RT; 5m NW of central London in Hampstead village, Hampstead tube
Infoline 01494 755563 **Tel** 020 7435 3471
Email fentonhouse@nationaltrust.org.uk
Owner The National Trust
Open Mar, Sat and Sun 2–5; Apr to Oct, Wed to Fri 2–5, Sat and Sun 11–5 (open Bank Hol Mon and Good Fri 11–5)
Area 1 acre/0.4 hectare

Godinton House

OUTSTANDING FORMAL GARDENS AND ANCIENT PARKLAND FOR AN ENCHANTING 17TH-CENTURY HOUSE

Godinton is set in marvellous old parkland studded with ancient Spanish chestnuts and English oaks. The brick gabled house, of a lovely silver-russet colour, is essentially early 17th-century. The garden is a sequence of architectural hedges and other enclosures designed by Sir Reginald Blomfield for G. Ashley-Dod in 1898 – one of his grandest surviving gardens.

New borders and parkland at Godington

East and south of the house high yew hedges have curved gables echoing those of the house. Behind them further divisions are marked by substantial hedges of box, often decorated with architectural features. Within the hedges is a sequence of gardens of different moods. Pan's Garden is a maze-like parterre of monumental shapes of box whose tops are clipped into sturdy pyramids; a statue of Pan rises among them. A sunken garden has a long narrow pool with a scalloped end overlooked by a statue of Venus. Below the south wall of the house is a rose garden with mixed plantings and good statues. At Godinton, Blomfield brilliantly linked the garden's various ingredients in a flowing progression. From the mysterious drama of Pan's Garden an unadorned lawn leads towards a pair of weeping silver pears and a figure of Ceres. Behind her are a pair of excellent herbaceous borders. The path between them leads down to the sunken pool garden.

ITALIAN WALLED GARDEN

South-west of the house is a little walled garden half-concealed behind a colonnade entwined with wisteria. This, the Italian Garden, was designed by Blomfield but not put into place until between the wars. Fine statues of the four continents stand between the columns. Putti frolic with a dolphin at the centre of a lily pool and raised borders on each side are filled with repeated plantings of eryngiums, lavender, *Perovskia atriplicifolia* and sweetly scented *Pittosporum tobira*. The whole is overlooked at the far end by a semicircular terrace shaded by a pergola of grapevines and roses. A summerhouse built into the wall on one side of the garden leads through to a very large walled kitchen garden.

The gardens at Godinton were excellently restored with advice from Hal Moggridge. In a county that contains many outstanding gardens, Godinton is easily one of the finest.

INFORMATION

Location Ashford TN23 3BW, Kent; 1½m W of Ashford at Potter's Corner on A20
Tel 01233 620773 **Fax** 01233 647351
Website www.godinton-house-gardens.co.uk
English Heritage Register Grade I
Owner Godinton House Preservation Trust
Open April to Oct, Thurs to Mon 2–5.30 (groups of 12 or more by appointment only)
Area 12 acres/5 hectares

Goodnestone Park

A GRAND VILLAGE HOUSE WITH GOOD TREES, A PARTERRE AND DELIGHTFUL WALLED FLOWER GARDENS

Goodnestone was built in the very early 18th century. It is unusual to find a grand house and old park of this kind so close to the village. Despite the splendours of the house and its parkland setting, Goodnestone has a domestic charm, as if drawn into the life of the village.

Below the façade of the house the garden has been simplified. Fussy borders were replaced by a boldly simple terraced parterre designed by Charlotte Molesworth to celebrate the millennium. Box-hedged compartments are filled with gravel or with blocks of a single variety of lavender. A central sundial is encircled with the tender and very attractive *Lavandula canariensis*.

On the far side of the house an avenue of limes rises gently up a slope, with a stone urn as an eyecatcher. Nearby, paths lead among some remarkable trees, including the spectacular remains of an ancient cedar of Lebanon and a superlative sweet chestnut. A youthful arboretum is rich in dogwoods (*Cornus* species), eucryphias, magnolias and *Parrotia persica*. Hidden away in the only part of the garden with acid soil is a rockery garden with a pool and rhododendrons – made in the 1920s by Lady Emily FitzWalter.

DEFT COLOUR

A great walled garden is enclosed in 18th-century brick with openings forming a vista that is aligned on the tower of the village church. Here are frequent deft colour combinations but nothing too showily calculating: rusty orange *Helenium* 'Moerheim Beauty' is seen through a veil of the powdery violet-blue flowers of *Perovskia atriplicifolia*; dahlias (rich red 'Bishop of Llandaff' and deepest blood-red 'Arabian Night') jostle with inky purple

The walled garden at Goodnestone

aconitum; and pale pink-apricot kniphofias erupt from a thicket of crimson fuchsia. A path leads through arbours of roses where swaying *Dierama pulcherrimum* arches over many different penstemons with repeated columns of clematis or of Irish yews. Large parts of the walled garden are given over to vegetables and fruit but there are ornamental episodes here too – a rampart of sweet peas and buttresses of *Clematis* 'Etoile Violette'.

Jane Austen was a visitor here; her brother Edward had married a daughter of the house. Goodnestone has an air of old-fashioned permanence, with no trace of ossification but a healthy wariness of fleeting fashion. It is skilfully gardened and the result is delightful.

INFORMATION

Location nr Wingham, Canterbury CT3 1PL, Kent; 7m E of Canterbury by A257 and minor roads, or A2 and B2046, signed from Wingham
Tel 01304 840107
Email fitzwalter@btinternet.com
Website www.goodnestoneparkgardens.co.uk
English Heritage Register Grade II*
Owner Margaret, Lady FitzWalter
Open Apr to Oct, Mon, Wed to Fri 11–5, Sun 12–6
Area 6 acres/2.4 hectares

Gravetye Manor

THE SPLENDID GARDEN OF WILLIAM ROBINSON, THE PROPHET OF WILD GARDENING AND PIONEER GARDEN WRITER

Gravetye is a holy place in garden history: William Robinson, the most influential garden writer of his time, lived here from 1885 until his death in 1935. Gravetye was both Robinson's home and a kind of horticultural laboratory where he could experiment with his gardening ideas.

When Peter Herbert bought Gravetye Manor in 1957 the garden had long been neglected. He converted the house into a hotel and restaurant and restored the gardens in keeping with Robinson's ideas. Visitors may get a good idea of the spirit of the place by following the perimeter walk, which shows Robinson's taste for naturalistic planting on the grand scale. Woodland to the north of the gabled 16th-century manor house includes Corsican pines (*Pinus nigra* subsp. *laricio*), Scots pine and silver birch. To the south a steeply sloping south-facing meadow is spangled in spring with anemones, wild daffodils, fritillaries and scillas. The meadow grass is left uncut until the late summer to allow plants to seed.

Robinson is best known for his naturalistic arrangements but it is a myth that he disapproved of formal gardening. He considered a formal pattern of beds close to the house entirely appropriate, the best way of linking the architecture of the house with wilder surrounding landscape, exactly as here. However, you may inspect these beds only as a customer of the hotel or restaurant.

ROBINSONIAN PLANTING

To the south and west of the house beds are filled with plants that Robinson loved. In the Flower Garden to the west are mixed plantings of old shrub roses underplanted with pinks, sedums, violas and, a Robinson favourite, *Silybum marianum*, "bright glistening with broad white veins", as he wrote. The little walled South Garden retains its original pattern of small beds and paved paths. This too is full of plants about which Robinson wrote, such as *Carpenteria californica*, *Cynara cardunculus* (cardoon), *Melianthus major* and *Perovskia atriplicifolia*.

Robinson had an extraordinarily perceptive eye for good garden plants and the plant directory section of his *English Flower Garden* (1883) constitutes in effect a list of the essential English garden plants of the 20th century. Gravetye honours a great man, but it is far from being a solemn place of worship. Under its current owner, Andrew Russell, it still palpitates with the excitement of plants and gardening.

Spring at Gravetye Manor

INFORMATION

Location nr East Grinstead RH19 4LJ, West Sussex; 4m SW of East Grinstead by B2110
Tel 01342 810567
Fax 01342 810080
English Heritage Register Grade II*
Owner Andrew Russell
Open (Perimeter walk only) Tue and Fri 10–5; entry to Robinson's flower gardens is restricted to hotel and restaurant customers only
Area 30 acres/12 hectares

Great Dixter

CHRISTOPHER LLOYD'S ICONIC GARDEN DISPLAYS HIS GREAT DELIGHT IN GARDENING – A MONUMENT AND MASTER CLASS

Great Dixter was made famous by Christopher Lloyd, who died in 2006. He was both one of the most remarkable gardeners of his day as well as a brilliant garden writer whose books and articles profoundly influenced a generation of gardeners. He was raised at Great Dixter where his parents had made a good garden before he was born. His father, Nathaniel Lloyd, bought the estate in 1910 and with the help of the architect Sir Edwin Lutyens laid out a new garden in the Arts and Crafts spirit.

After training and lecturing in horticulture at Wye College, Christopher Lloyd returned to Great Dixter in 1954. He began to assert himself in the garden, which became a perpetually evolving test-bed for new plants and new arrangements. His Long Border, 15ft/4.5m deep by 200ft/60m long, is an exuberant, constantly changing array of plants, with foliage of different kinds, and a very long season of interest, at least from April to October.

One of the great charms of Great Dixter is the mixture of formality and informality. There are several meadow-like areas – including those that flank the garden's entrance path – in which countless plants have been naturalised with crocus, erythroniums, snake's head fritillaries (*Fritillaria meleagris*), narcissus, orchids, primroses, quamash (*Camassia quamash*) and much else. This new style of planting, new in its day, was begun by Christopher Lloyd's mother and he continued it with relish.

A DAZZLING DEPARTURE

Lloyd respected good ideas from the past but liked to look to the future. Bored with Lutyens' enclosed formal rose garden, he replaced it with an explosive "tropical" mixture of cannas, brilliant dahlias, tender hedychiums and bananas, and New Zealand flax (*Phormium tenax*), all revealed through diaphanous veils of tall *Verbena bonariensis*. This dazzling departure in the 1990s pioneered a "new" taste for the dramatic and brilliant instead of the soporific pastels and greys of genteel "good-taste" gardening. In fact, it was not new; it was a timely resuscitation of William Robinson's "sub-tropical" planting, using exactly the plants he recommended. It was not Lloyd's fault that it has been so imitated as to become a cliché of modern gardening. Lloyd recruited an exceptional head gardener, Fergus Garrett, who remains in that post and maintains the garden in the spirit it possessed under Lloyd.

In the Long Border at Great Dixter

INFORMATION

Location Northiam, Rye TN31 6PH, East Sussex; 11m N of Hastings off A28

Tel 01797 252878

Email office@greatdixter.co.uk

Website www.greatdixter.co.uk

English Heritage Register Grade I

Owner The Great Dixter Charitable Trust

Open April to Oct, daily except Mon (open Bank Hol Mon) 11–5

Area 5 acres/2 hectares

Ham House

GRAND 17TH-CENTURY THAMES-SIDE VILLA ADORNED BY LIVELY RECREATED PERIOD GARDENS

The banks of the river at Richmond were in the 17th and 18th centuries favourite places on which to build great houses and gardens. Ham House is one of the finest, and best preserved, of these grand riverside villas. Started in 1610 for Sir Thomas Vavasour, it was altered in 1672–74 for the Duke of Lauderdale and his wife.

By 1948, when the National Trust acquired Ham, the house had survived remarkably unchanged but the old garden had long disappeared. Since 1976 it has been most attractively reinstated, so that once again house and garden form a harmonious ensemble of 17th-century splendour.

In the entrance forecourt the visitor is greeted by a grand Coadestone figure of a river god. Drums of clipped bay line the enclosing walls which are decorated with lead busts set into ovals let into the walls. To one side of the house the East Court is now an immense parterre with a lozenge pattern of low hedges of dwarf box, each compartment filled with alternate blocks of santolina and Dutch lavender (*Lavandula angustifolia* 'Vera'). The parterre is flanked by tunnels of pleached hornbeam and at its centre is a statue of Bacchus.

The parterre at Ham House

LIVELY FORMALITY

Behind the house a deep gravel terrace is decorated with pots filled with juniper, laurustinus, myrtle and yellow broom. The terrace overlooks squares of turf arranged in rows and separated by gravel paths with obelisks of clipped yew in Versailles boxes. Beyond, the Wilderness has hedges of hornbeam, and a central walk opens out into a circle from which six hedged paths radiate outwards. Within the enclosed areas are elegant little white pavilions,

each topped with a gleaming golden finial, and in the long grass of some of the compartments wild plants are naturalised – anemones, campions, cowslips, ox-eye daisies and primroses. It is an attractive mixture of rather austere formality and a lively ornamental sense, with the pavilions and long grass like a scene from some rural midsummer festival.

To the west of all this, where a kitchen garden had been in the 17th century, is a very early orangery, dating from before 1677. The walls of the kitchen garden survive, the orangery is now a tea room, and some vegetable beds have been reinstated. It is attractive, but more Beatrix Potter than Duchess of Lauderdale.

INFORMATION

Location Ham, Richmond, London TW10 7RS;
9m SW of central London off A307 at Petersham
Tel 020 8940 1950
Email hamhouse@nationaltrust.org.uk
Website www.nationaltrust.org.uk/southern
English Heritage Register Grade II*
Owner The National Trust
Open Sun to Wed 11–6
Area 18 acres/7 hectares

Hampton Court Palace

GREAT TUDOR AND 17TH-CENTURY PALACE WITH RESTORED PRIVY GARDEN AND LOVELY TRACES OF THE PAST

The most famous picture of Hampton Court Palace in its heyday is Leonard Knyff's giant bird's-eye view painted in 1702 and hanging at the palace – one of the grandest of all garden paintings. It is a scene of breathtaking splendour, showing the huge palace with its labyrinthine Tudor and late 17th-century buildings, and gardens spreading out on three sides. In the foreground, east of the palace, three double avenues and a central canal radiate outwards from a semicircle of trees which encloses a brilliant pattern of ornate parterres with pools and water jets. The avenues were created by André Mollet for King Charles II in 1661–62 and the parterres were designed a little later by the Huguenot Daniel Marot. On the left of the painting, below the south windows of Sir Christopher Wren's new buildings, is the Privy Garden, with four parterres *de broderie* and circular pools designed by Henry Wise *c.*1689. At the southern tip of the garden, by the banks of the Thames, is a curved screen of intricately worked

wrought iron by another Huguenot, Jean Tijoux. Beyond the Privy Garden a group of small enclosures, the Pond Garden and the Knot Garden, are overlooked by Sir Christopher Wren's banqueting house, where Henry VIII had first made a garden after 1525. To the right of the painting, north of the palace, is the astonishing sight of the Wilderness: a maze of clipped hedges designed by George London and Henry Wise in the late 17th century.

REMAINING SPLENDOUR

In its day Hampton Court was one of the greatest gardens in Europe and even today visitors can see enough of its splendour to appreciate what a spectacle it must have been. In 1995 the Privy Garden was superbly restored and now precisely resembles what is seen in the Knyff painting. Henry VIII's gardens below the banqueting house are brilliant with bedding schemes but no water flows in Marot's water parterre and parterres *de broderie* are now bedding schemes. Mollet's avenues, and the central canal, are still in place, but of the Wilderness only a trace remains. The palace has been much restored and is one of the most attractive and interesting of all the royal palaces.

The Privy Garden at Hampton Court

INFORMATION

Location East Molesey KT8 9AU, Surrey; 6m SW of central London at Hampton Wick
Tel 020 8781 9500
Fax 020 8781 9509
Website www.hrp.org.uk
English Heritage Register Grade I
Owner Historic Royal Palaces
Open April to Oct, daily 10–6; Nov to Mar, daily (except 24–26 Dec) 10–4.30
Area 60 acres/24 hectares

Hever Castle

A 14TH-CENTURY MOATED CASTLE WITH WALLED GARDENS FILLED WITH ORNAMENT, AND A SERENE LAKE

The moated castle is 14th-century, built for Sir John Cobham and sold to Sir Geoffrey Bullen or Boleyn (Henry VIII's Queen Anne was a descendant) in the 15th century. The garden, however, is all of the 20th century, created after the estate was bought by William Waldorf Astor (later 1st Viscount Astor) in 1903. He engaged the architect Frank Pearson and the nurserymen Joseph Cheal & Son to lay out elaborate formal gardens in keeping with the castle spirit. Astor had built up a large and distinguished collection of classical antiquities and other fine objects which, as in his other garden at Cliveden (*see page 86*), he proposed to display in the garden.

The lake at Hever Castle

On the edge of the moat east of the castle is an evocation of "an old English garden" with whimsical yew topiary and a yew maze. Anne Boleyn's Garden has a herb garden, beds of modern roses and a set of chess pieces of clipped yew. Lord Astor's treasures are already to be seen, among them a grand early 18th-century astrolabe on a carved plinth and a Roman wellhead with a frieze of frolicking maenads.

ASTOR'S ITALIAN GARDEN

The real excitement here, however, starts with the Italian Garden on the mainland south-east of the maze. This walled enclosure opens with a flourish – a vast semicircular pool backed by a sweep of yew hedging, against which a Roman figure of Venus is poised. Within the enclosure the Pompeian Wall runs along the long north wall, divided into bays by stone buttresses housing busts, carved capitals, urns and sarcophagi against a background of shrubs and herbaceous perennials with spring and summer bedding. On the opposite side, facing north, a pergola has stone columns planted with honeysuckle, roses, vines and wisteria. Camellias are trained against the wall, flowering well before the deciduous climbers are in leaf. Here, too, is a series of mossy grotto-like niches with the occasional cascade, planted with ferns, hostas, polygonums, primulas and Welsh poppies. At the far end of the garden, where it overlooks a lake, a double flight of steps sweeps down to the water, curving about a scalloped pool with a cascading fountain and a pair of white marble nymphs, giving the appearance of a grand Roman piazza.

INFORMATION

Location nr Edenbridge TN8 7NG, Kent; 3m SE of Edenbridge by minor roads
Infoline 01732 865224
Email mail@hevercastle.co.uk
English Heritage Register Grade I
Owner Broadland Properties Ltd
Open Apr to Sept, daily 11–6; Mar and Nov, daily 11–4
Area 50 acres/20 hectares

The High Beeches

A PRIVATE WOODLAND GARDEN OF ENCHANTMENT; MARVELLOUS SHRUBS AND TREES IN A LANDSCAPE TO SUIT

The High Beeches is a kind of minimalist wild garden whose charms are subtle and insidious but once you have succumbed to them impossible to forget. Formerly a property of the gardening Loders, it now belongs to a member of another gardening dynasty, Edward Boscawen. I call the garden minimalist because, although there are great exotics here, the landscape has such a natural air, and so much care has been taken to preserve the character of the place, that it is hard to tell where artifice ends and nature starts. In the woodland garden, for example, the grass is cut only when the enormous range of wildflowers has had a chance to seed. Some parts of the garden have probably never been cultivated: Front Meadow, for example, with its 15 species of grasses and lavish spread of the orchid *Dactylorhiza fuchsii* in high summer (not a rare plant but seldom seen in such beautiful circumstances). In many parts of the garden bulbous plants or perennials have become naturalised to resounding effect – *Cyclamen hederifolium*, the English native daffodil (*Narcissus pseudonarcissus*) and its Mediterranean cousin *N. bulbocodium*, and astonishing drifts of willow gentian (*Gentiana asclepiadea*) in early autumn pouring like rich blue water over the land.

The valley garden at the High Beeches

ROOM TO ADMIRE

The triumph of the High Beeches is that, unlike many woodland gardens, most of the trees and shrubs have plenty of space so that their whole beauty may be admired. In late April or early May, when the new foliage of the Japanese maples is at its best, the many old English oaks, not yet fully in leaf, present a bold pattern of shapes. Although many trees were lost in the 1987 storm there are some wonderful survivors, including a handkerchief tree (*Davidia involucrata*) propagated from seed gathered in China by E.H. Wilson in 1904. The soil is acid and the garden is rich in rhododendrons planted by Colonel Loder in the early part of the 20th century, some of them hybrids of his own devising.

The garden has many unfamiliar trees and shrubs but it is their arrangement, with each other and within their landscape, that is exciting, rather than the mere flaunting of rarities. After all, anyone can plant something rare, but who could make another High Beeches?

INFORMATION

Location Handcross RH17 6HQ, West Sussex; 1m E of Handcross off B2110
Tel 01444 400589
Email gardens@highbeeches.com
Website www.highbeeches.com
English Heritage Register Grade II*
Owner High Beeches Gardens Conservation Trust
Open Apr to Oct, daily except Wed 1–5
Area 25 acres/10 hectares

Kenwood House

THE LANDSCAPE PARK OF AN 18TH-CENTURY HOUSE, WITH SCULPTURES BY BARBARA HEPWORTH AND HENRY MOORE

Kenwood was acquired by John, 3rd Earl of Bute in the early 18th century. Rocque's map of 1745 shows formal gardens, and the terrace formed here at this time has remained an important feature of the landscape. In 1754 the estate was sold to the 2nd Earl of Mansfield and the landscape was refashioned in a more informal style at this time. A sham bridge was built at the east end of the lake; a more recent version may still be seen today, painted white and standing out against the dark trees. In 1793 the 3rd Earl of Mansfield, when he inherited, called in Humphry Repton who produced a Red Book the same year. Repton recommended doing away with the sham bridge – "an object beneath the dignity of Kenwood". He wanted to open up views to the south so that a splendid panorama of London would be revealed, dominated by the dome of St Paul's. Not many of Repton's suggestions were adopted and even the grand view of London had been concealed by new growth when J.C. Loudon saw it in 1838.

The character of the landscape at Kenwood today is very much that of an 18th-century landscape park. The view from the south terrace shows lawns with groups and scattered individual trees sweeping down to the lake whose far banks are densely planted. On the far side of the lake is an open-air auditorium much used for summer musical events. A brick bridge crosses the water and paths lead through the woods – ash, beech, holly, beautiful English oaks and rowans –to emerge eventually on Hampstead Heath. Immediately west of the house is a large open lawn (an extension of the terrace) with a lime walk running along its south side. A border with shrubs forms the lawn's north boundary and paths lead through shrubberies with many rhododendrons to the west. Sculptures by Barbara Hepworth and Henry Moore are not displayed to their best.

VIEWS OF THE PARK

Kenwood House and grounds are open free and thus immensely popular. The atmosphere, especially at weekends, is lively and the park, busy with visitors having a good time, seems to come into its own. The house has some of the finest 18th-century interiors in London, with superlative paintings. The view of the park from any of the rooms on the south side of the house is delightful.

Kenwood House from the lake

INFORMATION

Location Hampstead Lane, London NW3 7JR; 5m NW of central London between Hampstead and Highgate
Tel 0208 348 1286
Website www.english-heritage.org.uk
English Heritage Register Grade II*
Owner English Heritage
Open Apr to Oct, daily 11–6; Nov to mid Mar, daily 11–4 (closed 24–26 Dec and 1 Jan); Park usually remains open later throughout the year
Area 112 acres/45 hectares

Leonardslee Gardens

IN A WOODED VALLEY, ONE OF THE FINEST RHODODENDRON GARDENS, CREATED BY THE LODER FAMILY

Sir Edmund Loder acquired Leonardslee in 1889. The site is not only beautiful– a wooded valley of acid loam which descends to a sequence of lakes – but also perfect for the kind of gardening he wanted to do. Sir Edmund was a rhododendron enthusiast whose hybridising activities produced the highly scented and glamorous *Loderi* hybrids which became favourites for country house gardens during the rhododendron craze that lasted until World War II.

The slopes of the valley are densely planted, opening out into occasional glades, with paths snaking along the contours. There is a vast collection of shrubs – with the great trio of camellias, magnolias and rhododendrons leading the way. Although most of the rhododendrons are cultivars the species are also well represented: *R. arboreum, R. campylocarpum, R. williamsianum* and *R. thomsonii* among them. In addition there are many other shrubs: enkianthus, fothergilla, gaultheria, pieris, and the unusual *Symplocos paniculata* (with dazzling turquoise fruit). Excellent deciduous trees are seen everywhere – maples (especially *Acer*

japonicum and its cultivars), oaks, including the lovely Hungarian oak (*Quercus frainetto*), Chinese tulip trees (*Liriodendron chinense*), hickories such as the American pignut (*Carya glabra*), liquidambars and so on. Leonardslee was hit by the 1987 storm but one of its effects was to clear congested old plantings of large trees, permitting light through to shrubs previously in the shade of the tree canopy; as a result old shrubs flower as never before.

FASCINATING WALKS

Leonardslee is a fascinating place for a long garden walk. In May you will be one of thousands, when the gaudier rhododendrons are doing their stuff. The enclosed rock garden, laid out *c.*1900 by Pulham & Company, has a large collection of the most brilliantly coloured *Kurume* azaleas intermingled with many dwarf conifers. Some garden lovers find them too raucous for complete comfort, but there are so many outstanding plants elsewhere, and the lie of the land is so exceptionally attractive, that the garden always has plenty of other pleasures to offer. To my eye it is at least as beautiful in seasons when the rhododendrons are less visible. Sir Edmund Loder also ornamented his estate with exotic animals; of these only charming wallabies remain, hopping agreeably about and looking completely at home.

View to the ponds at Leonardslee

INFORMATION

Location Lower Beeding, nr Horsham RH13 6PP, West Sussex; 4m SW of Handcross, bottom of M23 by B2110 (signposted Cowfold)
Tel 01403 891212 **Fax** 01403 891305
Website www.leonardslee.com
English Heritage Register Grade I
Owner The Loder Family
Open Apr to Oct, 9.30–6
Area 200 acres/81 hectares

Loseley Park

FINELY REPLANTED GREAT WALLED FLOWER GARDEN FOR A GRAND ELIZABETHAN HOUSE

The house at Loseley was built in 1562 for Sir William More. Nothing is known of the early garden history at Loseley except that Gertrude Jekyll supplied plants early in the 20th century. The garden in place today, in the walled former kitchen garden, was started as recently as 1993. Here, a long axial path links different enclosures. Bushes of *Viburnum plicatum* 'Mariesii' mark the entrance to the Fountain Garden, partly concealed behind clipped columns of yew. A rectangular pool has a burbling fountain surrounded by gravel paths and L-shaped beds with almost symmetrical plantings of plants with white flowers. Overlooking the pool is a sea of white or cream chrysanthemums, white hydrangeas, plumes of *Macleaya cordata* and white verbascum. All this, without following any precisely Jekyllian scheme (she disapproved of totally monochrome planting), has a strongly Edwardian flavour.

On the other side of the central path a palissade of crab-apples encloses beds with a high summer planting of crocosmias, dahlias, daylilies, heleniums, potentillas and ornamental grasses. A giant herb parterre has a pattern of triangular beds filled with culinary, dyeing, medicinal or ornamental herbs. Tall bushes of bay, spheres of box and trees of mopheaded acacia (*Robinia pseudoacacia* 'Umbraculifera') punctuate the meeting places of paths.

The walled garden at Loseley

ROSES AND A TUNNEL

In a garden of old roses beds are edged in box and decorated with great cubes or hemispheres of clipped box, mounds of santolina or columns of holly. At the centre is a metal rose arbour on a raised brick plinth with a huge terracotta pot. Along the wall nearby is a tunnel of clematis and purple grapevines, where each metal upright emerges from a pillow of *Hebe rakaiensis*. Between the tunnel and the wall a bed is filled with shrub roses – on a hot summer's day the shady tunnel is suffused with their scent. The wall, at right angles to the main entrance to the garden, is almost entirely covered in an old wisteria underplanted with hundreds of irises.

The walled garden at Loseley is not of startling originality but it is skilfully planted and excellently maintained. Who knows what sort of ornamental garden, if any, was here in Tudor times? But this decorative garden with strong underlying formality is close to the spirit of 16th-century English gardening.

INFORMATION

Location nr Guildford GU3 1HS, Surrey; 3m SW of Guildford by A3 and B3000
Tel 01483 304440
Email enquiries@loseley-park.com
Website www.loseley-park.com
Owner Mr Michael More-Molyneux
Open May to Sept, daily except Mon (open Bank Hol Mon) 11–5
Area 6½ acres/2.6 hectares

Myddelton House Gardens

THE FINE ESTATE OF A NOTABLE GARDENER AND WRITER, E.A. BOWLES, UNDERGOING SPLENDID RESTORATION

Edwin Augustus Bowles (1865–1954), one of the most attractive of plantsmen, gardeners and authors, lived at Myddelton House. Bowles started to garden here as a child and continued until his death. He built up a remarkable collection of plants, several of them new cultivars bearing his name and still much-loved today – such as *Erysimum* 'Bowles' Mauve', *Pulmonaria officinalis* 'Bowles' Blue' and *Viola* 'Bowles Black'. After his death the estate was sold. In 1969 the Lee Valley Regional Park Authority bought it, and restoration began in 1984.

The terrace garden at Myddelton House

A STRONG PRESENCE

Bowles's presence is strongly felt in the garden today. The house overlooks a terrace on the edge of a small lake and tender plants stand on the terrace steps as they did in the past. Many plants survive from Bowles's time. A group of *Viburnum farreri* still fills the garden with winter scent – propagated from seed brought from China by Bowles's great friend, Reginald Farrer. An incredible old yew, which is said to survive from Elizabethan times, remains – but only because Bowles opposed the rerouting of the New River, which would have meant its destruction. Bowles planted the gigantic wisteria which grows through it. A small rose garden – "pretty to look at and useful to cut from but nothing to boast of", as Bowles wrote – has a pattern of box-edged beds with shrub roses and at its centre a splendid ornament, the old Enfield market cross, made in 1826 and busily Gothic. The beautiful *Rosa bracteata*, the kind of plant Bowles loved, is trained against it. The rock garden Bowles made, although almost submerged in overgrowth, is still full of the bulbs, especially snowdrops, in which he took such delight. Naturalised communities of other bulbs – aconites, colchicums, crocus, cyclamen and daffodils – also flourish. A National Collection of award-winning bearded irises is kept here.

What has been achieved in restoring the garden at Myddelton House is admirable but much remains to be done and it is a noble task. Bowles was an excellent gardener, rare plantsman and great writer. His books still delight and inform gardeners and his plant cultivars continue to give pleasure. To restore the whole garden, and grow every plant that he cultivated would be more than an act of piety; it would inspire new generations of gardeners.

INFORMATION

Location Bulls Cross, Enfield EN2 9HG, Middlesex; off the A10 14m N of central London, Jct 25 of M5
Tel 01992 702200
Email info@leevalleypark.org.uk
Website www.leevalleypark.com
English Heritage Register Grade II
Owner Lee Valley Regional Park Authority
Open Apr to Sept, Mon to Fri 10–4.30, Sun and Bank Hol Mon 12–4; Oct to Mar, Mon to Fri 10–3, Sun and Bank Hol Mon 12–4
Area 6 acres/2.5 hectares

Nymans Garden

AN OUTSTANDING PLANT COLLECTION, WITH DAZZLING SUMMER BORDERS IN A WALLED GARDEN

The garden at Nymans was started in 1890 by Ludwig Messel but it was his son, Lieut-Col Leonard Messel, and his great head gardener, James Comber, who made the decisive contribution to Nymans. Under Colonel Messel (who died in 1953) Nymans saw an immense influx of new plants, many from the plant-hunting expeditions of the 1930s. There was also much hybridising of plants and selection of cultivars – *Magnolia* 'Leonard Messel', *Eucryphia nymansensis* 'Nymansay', Rhododendron 'Anne Messel' and several others.

DAZZLING DISPLAYS

The Wall Garden expresses most clearly the essence of the place. This former orchard encloses a large area of irregular shape, roughly that of a stirrup. Two paths meet at right angles in the middle, and subsidiary paths amble away from them. Where the two main paths meet is a fine pink marble Italian fountain and pool and monumental yew topiary. The central path is flanked by the Summer Borders. These are quite narrow and planting is almost entirely herbaceous – both perennials and tender bedding – with the occasional large shrub, such as *Buddleja davidii*, at the back. Substantial veils of such herbaceous perennials as *Eupatorium purpureum*, *Echinops ritro* or *Veronicastrum virginicum* form a backdrop to dazzling crimson or yellow dahlias, blushing cannas and a froth of pink cleomes, with a scattering of bedding pelargoniums, petunias and antirrhinums along the front. The path between them is narrow (just room for two abreast) so that in high summer you have the experience of walking through a flowery ravine.

The rest of the Wall Garden has a much more sober but no less delightful planting of ornamental shrubs and small trees grown in grass filled with daffodils, wood anemones and lady's smock. Here, eucryphias, magnolias, the lovely *Styrax hemsleyanus*, the richly scented late summer-flowering *Clerodendrum trichotomum* and the Asiatic *Cornus kousa* form a miniature woodland garden.

The 1987 storm destroyed the Pinetum here, and throughout the garden eighty per cent of the trees were lost, including 20 out of 28 champion specimens. But the National Trust acted quickly to replant and many vigorous adolescent trees have taken their place. A spectacular pergola was another casualty; this too has been reinstated and is once again entwined with wisteria.

Spring in the Wall Garden at Nymans

INFORMATION

Location Handcross, nr Haywards Heath RH17 6EB, West Sussex; 7m NW of Haywards Heath by A272 and B2114

Tel 01444 405250

Email nymans@nationaltrust.org.uk

Website www.nationaltrust.org.uk/southern

English Heritage Register Grade II*

Owner The National Trust

Open Mar to 23 Dec, Wed to Sun (open Bank Hol Mon) 11–6; early Jan to mid Feb, Sat and Sun 11–4

Area 30 acres/12 hectares

Painshill Landscape Garden

A GREAT 18TH-CENTURY LANDSCAPE PARK BROUGHT BRILLIANTLY BACK TO LIFE IN A SUPERB RESTORATION

Few gardens were more deserving of salvation than this Elysian park in the heart of Surrey commuter land. The garden was made by the Hon. Charles Hamilton in 1738–73, when he sold up and moved to Bath. Gardens of this sort decay quickly but the estate was well maintained until after World War II when it swiftly declined. In 1981 the Painshill Park Trust embarked on a – triumphantly successful – quest to restore it to its 18th-century state.

VISUAL INCIDENTS

At the heart of the park is the river Mole winding through a valley and, running parallel to the river, a long narrow serpentine lake studded with islands. The slopes and the banks of both river and lake are animated with ornamental buildings. Painshill was conceived as a sequence of visual incidents, the buildings ornamenting the landscape and also marking vantage points from which to admire the scene. The Gothic Temple has a special vantage point, on the slopes above the lake, but also looks west along the valley. This airy open "umbrello" has Gothic openings and is crowned with battlements and soaring finials. On the bank of the lake the Ruined Abbey is built of brick rendered to resemble stone and to have the appearance of a crumbling ecclesiastical ruin. An elegant Chinese bridge of white-painted wood links Grotto Island to the shore. Hamilton created a labyrinthine grotto with openings onto water and gleaming crystalline walls, kept wet by concealed pipes. Rising on the grassy slopes above it, with superb views back towards the lake and the Gothic Temple, is the Turkish Tent – blue and white, with golden plumes on its domed roof. Far to the south-west the Gothic Tower rises high among trees, giving huge views across the land. Hamilton's Hermitage really was inhabited by a hermit, "But," as J.T. Smith wrote in 1845, "as the hermit had all the hardship, and Hamilton all the sentiment, the arrangement broke down."

Hamilton, unusually among 18th-century landscapers, was a knowledgeable connoisseur of plants, taking a special interest in exotics from North America, which he obtained through Peter Collinson. Many of these have been replanted. Other gardens have been restored with impeccable historical accuracy but the miraculous charm of Painshill is that the result should so bristle with excitement.

The Ruined Abbey at Painshill

INFORMATION

Location Portsmouth Road, Cobham KT11 1JE, Surrey; 1m W of Cobham by A245
Infoline 01932 584286
Tel 01932 868113
Email info@painshill.co.uk
Website www.painshill.co.uk
English Heritage Register Grade I
Owner Painshill Park Trust
Open Mar to Oct, daily 10.30–6; Nov to Feb, daily (except 25 and 26 Dec) 10.30–4.00 (or dusk if earlier)
Area 158 acres/64 hectares

Parham House

DELIGHTFUL WALLED GARDENS FILLED WITH FLOWERS IN A HISTORIC SETTING WITH TREMENDOUS CHARM

Parham House was built in 1577. The entrance drive crosses the 17th-century park and many beautiful old oaks are to be seen. The garden we see today, however, was made almost entirely in the 20th century, after the estate was bought by the Hon. Clive Pearson in 1922.

The decorative heart of the garden is a very large walled garden north of the house, enclosed in brick and stone before 1778. Formerly a kitchen garden, it is now largely given over to ornamental purposes. Lanning Roper designed a white border along the west wall and in 1982 Peter Coats worked on borders that form the east–west central division of the garden – predominantly blue at one end and gold at the other. A herb garden behind yew hedges has a pool and a fountain of a boy with a dolphin. A rectangular garden has mixed borders edged in small-leafed myrtle (*Myrtus communis* subsp. *tarentina*). One of the most attractive parts of the walled garden is the north-west quarter in which vegetables are beautifully grown in box-hedged rectilinear beds to reveal their ornamental character. Lively combinations of plants include rhubarb underplanted with strawberries. Outside the west wall of the kitchen garden a mixed border has substantial bushes of buddleia and shrub roses underplanted with ferns, geraniums, hellebores, hostas, Solomon's seal and thalictrums. Against the centre of the wall is a magnificent lead figure of a river god reclining on a grand rusticated plinth fringed with ferns, hostas and superb clumps of *Cimicifuga racemosa*. Nearby is a maze of brick paths set into a lawn with an elaborately interlocking pattern designed by Minotaur Designs in 1991. The lawn, with good beeches, English oaks and a large London plane, sweeps

Colour-themed borders at Parham

down towards a balustrade at the head of the Pleasure Pond. On the bank is Cannock House, an elegant stone 18th-century summerhouse from whose large windows are views south across the water to a cricket pitch and its pavilion.

A FRIENDLY PLACE

The gabled house at Parham is imposing and its setting is on a generous scale. In its detail, however, it gives an attractive feeling of domestic intimacy. The charming little Wendy House built into the north-west corner of the walled garden by Clive Pearson for his three daughters in 1928 is typical of the friendliness of the place.

INFORMATION

Location Pulborough RH20 4HS, West Sussex; 4m S of Pulborough by A283
Tel 01903 744888
Email enquiries@parhaminsussex.co.uk
Website www.parhaminsussex.co.uk
English Heritage Register Grade II*
Owner Parham Park Trust
Open Apr to Oct, Wed, Thur, Sun and Bank Hol Mon 12–6
Area 11 acres/4 hectares

Penshurst Place

SUPERB WALLED FORMAL GARDENS WITH GOOD 20TH-CENTURY PLANTING FOR A GREAT MEDIEVAL HOUSE

House, garden and parkland setting at Penshurst form a rare group, the battlemented medieval stone house overlooking one of the largest walled gardens in the country. The essential layout of the gardens has not changed since Kip's engraving in John Harris's *History of Kent* (1719) and was probably established well before that. The parkland, to the north of the walled garden, is even more ancient, having its origins in a medieval deer park. The Sidney Oak, close to a lake in the park, is thought to date from the middle ages.

Rose borders at Petworth Place

During the 18th century the walled garden was neglected; it was thoroughly restored by the architect George Devey in the 1850s. Although two late 20th-century garden designers, Lanning Roper and John Codrington, executed planting plans for the firm old structure of paths and enclosures, the garden's atmosphere is resolutely untouched by the least hint of modishness. In fact, in this area of 10 acres/4 hectares, an astonishing range of garden styles is happily linked together. This includes a vast parterre of the union jack, picked out in brilliantly coloured roses and lavender – not a scheme for those lacking in confidence.

A GRAND PARTERRE

Immediately south of the house is the Italian Garden, a grand parterre of regal simplicity. Enclosed in yew hedges with rounded castellations, the area is sunken and divided into four parts about a central pool with a statue and water jets. Shapes of lawn, box-edged beds of pink roses and blocks of clipped box surround it. The whole is overlooked on two sides by a raised terrace. To the east, double mixed borders, designed by Lanning Roper with easy charm, include purple-leafed *Cotinus coggygria* and roses underplanted with *Alchemilla mollis* and lamb's lugs. Another pair of borders forms a cross-axis, and beyond it John Codrington designed an enclosure of magnolias. Then comes a change of mood and one of the best parts of the garden: an orchard of apples, planted in long grass in neat rows and with close-mown paths through the grass; and a nut garden of different varieties of Kentish cobs. The east-west axis starts beside the nut garden. It is formed by a path of shaven grass between regularly spaced mounds of clipped golden yew against hedges of plain yew.

INFORMATION

Location Penshurst, nr Tonbridge TN11 8DG, Kent; in Penshurst village, 5m W of Tonbridge by B2176
Tel 01892 870307
Email penshurst@pavilion.co.uk
English Heritage Register Grade I
Owner Viscount De L'Isle
Open Mar, Sat and Sun 11–6; Apr to Oct, daily 11–6
Area 10 acres/4 hectares

Petworth House

CAPABILITY BROWN'S MOST BEAUTIFUL PARK, WITH A LAKE AND EXCEPTIONAL TREES, MARVELLOUSLY DISPLAYED

The estate of Petworth is very ancient – there has been a house here since at least 1309 when the Percy family was granted a licence to crenellate an existing manor house. The present house was built in 1682. The beautiful park is the work of Capability Brown in the 1750s. From the house, suave undulations and scatterings of groups of trees decorate the land as it dips down to a lake, shaped like an enormous swollen foot. On the far side the park continues, with distant prospects of the downs beyond.

Although the pleasure grounds near the house are attractive, it is the park that is the truly exceptional thing at Petworth. To enjoy this fully, go to the car park on the edge of the town that gives direct access to the park. From here, walk towards the Lower Pond, a secondary lake near the park's boundary. As the ground slopes upwards you see stupendous old sweet chestnuts or English oaks. From the hillock on top, crowned with ancient sweet chestnuts, is one of the loveliest landscape views you will ever see: the house to your left with an immense lawn running down to Brown's great lake, the Upper Pond, whose far banks are veiled in trees. Walk round the lake to see the endlessly varied prospects conjured out of simple ingredients: trees, grass, the lie of the land, water and the shifting horizon.

PLEASURE GROUNDS

Brown also worked on the Elizabethan pleasure grounds north of the house, which he made much less formal. Here, he made many straight walks, built a ha-ha on the western edge overlooking the park and planted a wide range of ornamental shrubs. The pleasure grounds survive today in much reduced form but two temples built by Brown, one Ionic, one Doric, remain.

The house itself is very beautiful and full of treasures. Turner came to paint at Petworth and a room of his paintings includes two views of the lake bathed in the fiery light of sunset. From the great Marble Hall in the house you may also enjoy magnificent views of the beautiful park from the windows.

INFORMATION

Location Petworth GU28 0AE, West Sussex; in Petworth village, 16m E of Petersfield by A272
Infoline 01798 343929 **Tel** 01798 342207
Email petworth@nationaltrust.org.uk
Website www.nationaltrust.org.uk/southern
English Heritage Register Grade I
Owner The National Trust
Open (Pleasure grounds) Apr to Oct, Sat to Wed 11–6 (phone infoline for out of season openings); (Park) daily 8–sunset
Area 700 acres/283 hectares

Capability Brown's lake at Petworth

Polesden Lacey

SMART REGENCY HOUSE IN AN EXQUISITE POSITION WITH DELIGHTFUL WALLED GARDENS FILLED WITH FLOWERS

The owner of Polesden Lacey in its Edwardian heyday was a noted political hostess, Mrs Ronald Greville. The estate occupies a fine hilly position, with a stately avenue of limes leading up towards the house. The gardens were almost entirely created for Mrs Greville after she came here in 1906. She turned part of the walled former kitchen garden west of the house into a rose garden. The roses today are almost entirely Hybrid Teas, Hybrid Musks and Floribundas. They are disposed in box-edged beds or trained on a wooden pergola and fill the garden with their delicious scent throughout the summer. Some of the roses ('Hugh Dickson', 'Dorothy Perkins', 'Excelsa') are varieties that Mrs Greville could have known, and impart an authentic Edwardian luxuriance.

The walled garden at Polesden Lacey

IRISES AND LAVENDER

Beyond the rose garden is a series of yew-hedged enclosures with a parterre containing an especially attractive collection of irises. Mrs Greville was keen on irises and the National Trust inherited her collection of old cultivars of bearded irises which they have propagated and added to, making a splendid display. Here, too, is an arrangement of beds containing different cultivars of lavender, one with an astrolabe at its centre, another with three bronze mice mysteriously poking their noses above the foliage. The south wall here is especially attractive, its brick and flint richly encrusted with lichen and moss, and the occasional circular window giving views out.

On the south side of the walls that enclose the former kitchen garden is an admirable herbaceous border which runs its whole length – over 400ft/ 120m long. Punctuated by statuesque

clumps of *Yucca gloriosa*, it is full of border favourites – asters, echinops, geraniums, helianthemums, rudbeckia, sages, sidalcea and verbascums. These are enlivened by less common plants such as the tender *Hedychium densiflorum*, *Amsonia orientalis* (with star-shaped pale violet flowers), the lovely ghostly *Galtonia candicans*, and several excellent cultivars of crocosmia and penstemon.

South of the house a terrace with a griffon and urns overlooks a vast lawn which swoops downwards to a low yew hedge. Beyond it the ground falls away precipitously with, on the far side of the valley, pasture, parkland trees and dense woodland – a panorama of wonderful beauty. The rose garden is pretty but this grand view is breathtaking.

INFORMATION

Location nr Dorking RH5 6BD, Surrey; 5m NW of Dorking by A246
Infoline 01372 458203 **Tel** 01372 452048
Email polesdenlacey@nationaltrust.org.uk
Website www.nationaltrust.org.uk/southern
English Heritage Register Grade II*
Owner The National Trust
Open Mar to Oct, daily 11–5; Nov to 23 Dec, daily 11–4; 3 Jan to Feb, daily 11–4
Area 30 acres/12 hectares

Port Lympne Gardens

AVANT-GARDE TERRACED GARDENS AND FINE ORNAMENTS FOR AN EDWARDIAN MANSION ON A MAGNIFICENT SITE

Port Lympne is most famous for John Aspinall's collection of animals whose strange barks, cries, whoops, yelps and growls form an essential part of the atmosphere of the place. It is the animals that certainly draw the greatest number of visitors to Port Lympne, but the garden is outstandingly attractive. The house, on a magnificent site looking over Romney Marsh, was built for Sir Philip Sassoon to the designs of Sir Herbert Baker and Ernest Willmott just before World War I. When John Aspinall bought the estate in 1973 he restored the gardens with the help of Russell Page and founded his zoo here.

South of the house the ground slopes down sharply where the architect Philip Tilden laid out terraced gardens for Sassoon. The top terrace, paved in stone and decorated with lead urns, is flanked by stone gazebos with wrought-iron balustrades, shady with clematis, hydrangea and wisteria. A grand triple flight of steps embraces a goldfish pool and is shrouded with callistemons, *Campsis radicans* and wisteria. Below, a large square pool with a water jet stands at the centre of a lawn. It is hedged in castellated yew and behind, on each side, is a remarkable piece of Art Deco garden design, visible only from the

gazebos above: one side has stripes of orange or yellow marigolds edged in electric blue lobelia, and the other has a chequerboard of alternate squares of turf and red or white begonias.

VINES, FIGS AND ROSES

From the centre of the pool lawn steps lead down between terraced gardens of quite different character – a vineyard on one side and a garden of figs on the other. A final double flight of steps sweeps round to embrace at the lower level a shady summerhouse. On this final terrace is a slightly perfunctory rose garden; further gardens which lay on either side have been turfed over.

To understand Port Lympne it is essential also to see the interior of the house where there is a "Moorish patio" designed by Philip Tilden. Of the palest pink stucco, it has a pool, arcades, rills and glazed green roof tiles – another slice of exoticism to add to this most eclectic of gardens.

INFORMATION

Location Lympne, Hythe CR21 4PD, Kent; 3m W of Hythe by A20
Infoline 0891 800 605 **Tel** 01303 264647
Email hpl.estates@dial.pipex.com
English Heritage Register Grade II*
Owner The Aspinall Family
Open daily 10–5
Area 15 acres/6 hectares

Art Deco checkerboard at Port Lympne

Royal Botanic Gardens

A GREAT BOTANIC GARDEN AND ONE OF THE MOST DIVERSELY ATTRACTIVE GARDENS IN THE WORLD

Some botanic gardens are bigger than Kew, several are older, but none combines such beauty of landscape, such a fascinating history and such a profound influence on the plant world.

The royal family was first connected with Kew in the early 17th century when James I had a hunting lodge near the river. In 1718 it was taken by the Prince and Princess of Wales, later George II and Queen Caroline. In 1731 George II's son, Frederick Prince of Wales, leased a house and added to the garden "many curious & forain trees and exotics". The Prince married another passionate gardener, Princess Augusta of Saxe-Gotha, but died young in 1751. His widow continued their garden-making activities, introducing plants and commissioning a series of beautiful garden buildings from William Chambers – an orangery (1757), the Temple of Arethusa (1758), the Temple of Bellona (1760), the Ruined Arch (1759–60) and, most spectacularly, the ravishing Chinoiserie Pagoda (1761).

When Princess Augusta died in 1772, George III took over her house as a rural retreat. Soon there came onto the scene one of the greatest figures associated with Kew, Sir Joseph Banks. From 1773 he started to transform Princess Augusta's magpie collection of plants into one of consequence. Banks became, in effect, the first director of Kew and was responsible for an astonishing series of plant-collecting expeditions – to Australasia, the Azores, the Canary Islands, China, north Africa, South Africa, India and the West Indies.

In 1841 the gardens were transferred from royal ownership to the state and Sir William Hooker was appointed director. Under him and his son Joseph, who succeeded him as director in 1865 (retiring in 1885), the gardens expanded immensely. the role of Kew in the dissemination of plants throughout the world was of great economic importance – rubber plants from Brazil, for example, were brought to Kew and shipped to Malaya, and tea plants taken from China to India. The Palm House was built in 1844–48, designed by Richard Turner and Decimus Burton. Burton, starting in 1859, also built the striking but less elegant Temperate House. In the 20th century many new buildings were added. The Princess of Wales conservatory, with its several different environments, opened in 1987.

EXCEPTIONAL BEAUTY

Kew's role in plant conservation has become central to its activities but it is also now, in the early 21st century, the most diversely attractive botanic garden in the world, as well as one of the most popular, attracting nearly 1,000,000 annual visitors – far more, until the Eden Project, than any other paid-access garden in the British Isles.

Kew as it is today is an exceptionally beautiful landscape. The great buildings – Chambers's enchanting Pagoda and his suave Conservatory, Decimus Burton's sublime Palm House – and the smaller ornamental buildings animate clearings, make alluring eyecatchers or simply create a powerful sense of place.

As somewhere to enjoy plants Kew is immensely satisfying. You can wander in a trance, making the occasional pilgrimage to some superb tree – the mighty chestnut-leafed oak (*Quercus castaneifolia*) near the Waterlily House, for example; planted in 1846, it is now over 100ft/30m high and very beautiful. The alpine house is the best in Britain, with small plants, often bulbous and frequently rare, displayed like precious jewels. The other glasshouses, sheltering a vast range of non-hardy plants, are also a continuous source of pleasure and instruction, while passages of woodland, rich in trees and shrubs, are often underplanted with the loveliest herbaceous plants – erythroniums, lilies and trilliums. But pleasing visitors, which it does superbly, is not the chief purpose of Kew; it remains one of the busiest and most productive institutes of botanical research in the world.

INFORMATION

Location Kew, Richmond TW9 3AB, Surrey; 7m SW of central London, Kew Gardens tube
Infoline 020 8332 5655 **Email** info@kew.org
Website www.kew.org
English Heritage Register Grade I
Owner Trustees of the Royal Botanic Gardens
Open daily (except 24 and 25 Dec) 9.30–4 (summer weekdays 9.30–6.30; Sun and Bank Hol Mon in mid summer 9.30–7.30)
Area 300 acres/121 hectares

The Palm House at Kew

The Royal Pavilion

IRRESISTIBLE REGENCY PLEASURE DOME WITH A RESTORED
PERIOD GARDEN NOW BRISTLING WITH LIFE

Love drew the Prince of Wales to Brighton, not for the town itself but rather for the charms of Mrs Fitzherbert whom he secretly married in 1785 and wanted to establish in a *nid d'amour*. He had a farmhouse rebuilt by Henry Holland and in 1805 asked Humphry Repton to advise on laying out the gardens. The Prince was so taken with Repton's ideas that he also asked him to transform Holland's neatly classical house into an exotic pavilion. In 1806 Repton made suggestions for pavilion and gardens which were not adopted. Instead, Repton's former partner, John Nash, was asked to do the job. Between 1815 and 1822 Nash devised and built the present bizarre and delightful confection of onion domes, minarets and verandahs in styles ranging from Islamic and Indian to Gothic, with a glittering Chinoiserie interior. Nash also laid out the gardens.

In 1982 a programme of complete restoration of the Royal Pavilion started. Nash's garden has been reinstated, following his plans and contemporary

illustrations and using period plants. Here is an informal flowery style of planting, with winding walks, sinuous shrubberies, and specimen trees planted in lawns. The perimeter walk east of the Pavilion shows this in action – a curving walk of such shrubs as bay laurel, box, *Cotinus coggygria*, Guelder rose (*Viburnum opulus*), holly, myrtle and yew is underplanted with asarum, foxgloves and geraniums. North of the Pavilion an open lawn has specimen trees and, to the west, underneath the Prince's private apartment, four curving shrubberies have a similar style of planting but with more seasonal flowers – annuals, bulbs, perennials and biennials such as hollyhocks. Paths are edged with green iron hoop fencing, and copies of Regency street-lights have been installed. The grass of the lawns is cut long to imitate the effect of woodland verges.

A POPULAR PARK

The Royal Pavilion garden, open all the time without charge, is very popular and thronged with young (or would-be young) people sprawling on the grass, reading on benches, eating sandwiches, busking and generally hanging out. This causes much wear and tear and it is a scene more in keeping with a public park than with the garden of a royal house. But passages of the garden, with the irresistible Royal Pavilion rising behind, do evoke its authentic past.

The garden front at Brighton Pavilion

INFORMATION

Location Brighton BN1 1EE, East Sussex; in the centre of Brighton
Tel 01273 290900 **Fax** 01273 292871
Website www.royalpavilion.brighton.co.uk
English Heritage Register Grade II
Owner Brighton and Hove Council
Open daily dawn–dusk
Area 8 acres/3.3 hectares

Savill and Valley Gardens

MAGNIFICENT WOODLAND GARDENS WITH SUPERB TREES AND FLOWERING SHRUBS FINELY DISPLAYED

The gardens lie at the southern end of Windsor Great Park. The Savill Garden was started in 1932 when E.H. (later Sir Eric) Savill who was then Deputy Surveyor at Windsor, began to develop what had been a small estate nursery of ¼ acre/0.1 hectare into a garden. When George V and Queen Mary came to see it in 1934 the Queen said, "It's very nice, Mr Savill, but isn't it rather small?" He was granted more land and began to build up a collection of trees and shrubs in the protection of old beeches and oaks. Between the wars many great estates gave plants, especially rhododendrons – Sir John Ramsden at Bulstrode, the Earl of Stair at Castle Kennedy, Lionel de Rothschild at Exbury, and so on. Savill had a good eye for the arrangement of these treasures which he disposed in glades and used to create long open vistas. He also loved the wilder parts and knew "when to leave well alone" – a skill that was emphasised by Gertrude Jekyll as esssential for successful woodland gardening.

Autumn in the Savill Garden

THE VALLEY GARDEN

After World War II, Savill began to extend the garden into the very much larger Valley Garden (400 acres/162 hectares) to the south, running along the northern bank of Virginia Water. The site is very attractive, slightly undulating and sloping southwards towards the lake. Much clearing had to be done to form glades and rides, and drainage carried out. From the start it was decided to form large collections of particular groups of plants. Some of these have grown into National Collections, among them species rhododendrons (over 600 species), magnolias (over 30 species and over 320 cultivars), mahonias (27 species and 51 cultivars) and ferns (over 130 species and over 150 cultivars). Throughout the gardens there is much underplanting – wood anemones and bluebells but also colchicums, epimediums, ferns, lilies, meconopsis and narcissi and, in moist places, astilbes, gunnera, lysichiton, Asiatic primulas and rheums.

In the Savill Garden there are herbaceous borders and a rose garden but it is the great woodland gardens, with their astonishing collections of plants and subtly beautiful sites, that give the Savill and Valley Gardens their distinction.

INFORMATION

Location Wick Lane, Englefield Green, nr Egham TW20 0HH, Surrey; 3m W of Egham by A30
Tel 01753 743900
Email windsor.tic@rbwm.gov.uk
Website www.windsor.gov.uk
English Heritage Register Grade I
Owner Crown Property
Open Savill Garden, daily (except 25 and 26 Dec) 10–6 (Nov to Feb 10–4.30); Valley Garden, daily sunrise–sunset.
Area 435 acres/176 hectares

Scotney Castle Garden

EARLY 19TH-CENTURY PICTURESQUE VALLEY GARDEN WITH EXCELLENT PLANTS AND DRAMATIC VIEWS

There are two castles at Scotney: Anthony Salvin's Jacobethan pile built between 1837 and 1844 for Edward Hussey, and in the valley below the wildly picturesque remains of the original moated medieval and Tudor fortified manor house. Picturesque is the right word, for the landscape that links the two buildings is a last delightful fling of the Picturesque landscape tradition. Fashionable gardens in Salvin's time were turning to elaborate formal arrangements, but at Scotney something much more original and surprising was made: the garden looked back to the late 18th century but simultaneously anticipated the wild gardening of William Robinson.

With the advice of William Sawrey Gilpin, Hussey positioned his new house on an eminence, with the quarried ground below forming a precipitous slope tumbling down towards the old castle. Below the new house, on the steeply sloping ground, a viewing platform was built from which to admire the carefully orchestrated scene below.

UNUSUAL EYECATCHER

Parts of the 17th-century addition to the old castle were pulled down to enhance its medieval appearance, making it an enchanting eyecatcher; its machicolated tower with witch's hat roof rises splendidly above the boskage. The rocky slopes between the two castles were planted with exotic shrubs and ornamental trees among native beeches, English oaks, Scots pines and yews. Cedars of Lebanon, incense cedars (the handsomely upright American *Cedrus decurrens*) and other exotic conifers provide evergreen presence among the deciduous trees, while magnolias, Japanese maples, rhododendrons (especially azaleas) and *Kalmia latifolia*

The quarry garden at Scotney

form exotic mounds among them. Brilliant with flowers and new foliage in spring, the autumn colouring from maples, *Nyssa sylvatica*, *Parrotia persica* and rhododendrons is a marvellous sight. All this was severely damaged in the 1987 storm but much replanting has been done and the landscape remains dazzlingly attractive.

Near the old castle is a herb garden laid out by Lanning Roper, and the banks of the moat are an ideal home for moisture-loving plants, among them spectacular clumps of the fern *Osmunda regalis*. Tucked away on a little isthmus jutting out into the lake-like extension of the moat is a bronze figure by Henry Moore, quite at home in this wild setting.

INFORMATION

Location Lamberhurst, Tunbridge Wells TN3 8JN, Kent; 1m S of Lamberhurst by A21
Infoline 01892 893820   **Tel** 01892 893868
Email scotneycastle@nationaltrust.org.uk
English Heritage Register Grade I
Owner The National Trust
Open Mar to Oct, Wed to Sun (early Mar, Sat and Sun only) 11–5.30; Nov to mid Dec, Sat and Sun 11–4 (also Bank Hol Mon throughout year)
Area 19 acres/8 hectares

Sculpture at Goodwood

OUTSTANDING WOODED SCULPTURE PARK WITH MARVELLOUS
WORKS BY CONTEMPORARY ARTISTS

There has been a spectacular renaissance over the last ten years in the use of sculptures to ornament the landscape. Sculpture at Goodwood, founded in 1992 by Wilfred Cass, was a pioneer and has set the highest standards. It is in effect an outdoor dealer's gallery – virtually everything is for sale although some pieces remain in place for years. The work of many of the best British artists is shown here – among them, Anthony Caro, Tony Cragg, Andy Goldsworthy, Antony Gormley, Eduardo Paolozzi, William Pye and Bill Woodrow. The work is most skilfully placed – in glades, at the end of rides, under the trees or at the edge of woodland. The sculptures are seen at their best in this setting – with the space they need and a far more sympathetic environment than sterile hard-edged buildings.

The setting of Sculpture at Goodwood is a youthful piece of woodland criss-crossed with rides and punctuated with clearings. The trees are mostly ash, beech, hawthorn, hazelnut and sycamore – planted sufficiently far apart to allow tantalising glimpses of distant sculptures. Furthermore, the long rides allow particularly large sculptures to be displayed as dramatic eyecatchers in the landscape.

A SENSE OF PLACE

The long southern boundary of the garden looks over the open countryside of farms and pasture. Here, clearings in the wood provide beautiful spaces in which to display often huge exhibits, and make a piquant contrast to the domestic scenes of fields, hedgerows and grazing sheep. Sean Henry's Lying Man is a recumbent monumental figure cast in bronze but painted in an eerily naturalistic way. He lies on a catafalque of turf close to the fence that separates the garden from the field. He ignores the view and stares, head on a cushion, up at the sky. Tim Morgan's trio of slender glass and steel blades challenges the soaring trees and glitters in the changing light close to the open space of the field.

Sculpture at Goodwood started with the purpose of displaying works of art, not making a garden. In the event, the setting has been fashioned to create an extraordinary and attractive landscape. The strong sense of place is not derived merely from the exciting presence of the sculptures – their setting has also become an essential part of the exhibit.

Sculpture by Tony Cragg at Goodwood

INFORMATION

Location Goodwood, Chichester PO18 0QP, West Sussex; ½m NE of Chichester by A27 and minor roads, E of Goodwood House
Tel 01243 771114 (recorded directions); 01243 538449 (enquiries)
Fax 01243 531853
Website www.sculpture.org.uk
Owner Wilfred and Jeanette Cass
Open Mar to Nov, daily except Mon (open Bank Hol Mon) 10.30–5
Area 24 acres/9.7 hectares

Sheffield Park Garden

DREAMLIKE AND MEMORABLE LAKESIDE PLANTINGS – TREES, SHRUBS AND SPLENDID HERBACEOUS PERENNIALS

Water is such an important ingredient in the garden at Sheffield Park that it becomes an object of hypnotic fascination. This is in essence a woodland garden with 18th-century landscape antecedents. Both Capability Brown and Humphry Repton worked here for the Holroyd family, who became Earls of Sheffield. Brown produced a plan in 1776 for "the alteration of the place, particularly . . . the water and the ground about it". The water in question was the series of lakes in the valley below the house. Repton's work is even vaguer and it seems that he did not get on well with Lord Sheffield. The way the garden now looks is due to Arthur Gilstrap Soames who bought the estate in 1910 and embarked on a great programme of planting, especially of rhododendrons.

LAKESIDE PLANTING

It is the planting crowding about the banks of the lakes, and the occasional clearings, that provide the most memorable scenes at Sheffield. Virginia Woolf, not generally interested in gardens, wrote in 1937 of the "rhododendrons . . . massed upon the banks and when the wind passes over the real flowers the water flowers shake

and break into each other." Native silver birches, English oaks and Scots pines are intermingled with exotics – *Liquidambar styraciflua*, swamp cypresses (*Taxodium distichum*), Wellingtonias, maidenhair trees (*Gingko biloba*) and many others. They show striking contrasts of habit and foliage, often making dramatic companions for the smaller trees and shrubs for which they form a dazzling backdrop. A soaring swamp cypress, for example, apparently emerges from a billowing clump of rhododendrons or the gracefully sprawling shape of a Japanese maple. In spring and early summer the splashes of colour from rhododendrons glow against sombre coniferous foliage. In autumn the explosion of leaf colour from azaleas, tupelos (*Nyssa sylvatica*), maples and scarlet oaks (*Quercus coccinea*) is a famous sight.

Leading away from the banks of the lakes into the richly planted hinterland are paths often fringed with lovely herbaceous planting – ferns, gentians, lilies, primulas and trilliums among the trees and shrubs. Here the mood is more intimate and the detail finer than in the broad brushstrokes and irrepressible flamboyance of the lakeside plantings. Here you can wander for a long time among the astonishing wealth of plants.

The middle lake at Sheffield Park

INFORMATION

Location Uckfield TN22 3QX, East Sussex; midway between East Grinstead and Lewes off A275
Tel 01825 790231
Email sheffieldpark@nationaltrust.org.uk
English Heritage Register Grade I
Owner The National Trust
Open Mar to Apr and Jun to Sept, daily except Mon 10.30–5.30 (open Bank Hol Mon); May and Oct, daily 10.30–5.30 (phone for winter openings)
Area 100 acres/40 hectares

Sissinghurst Castle Garden

A FAMOUS 20TH-CENTURY GARDEN OF EXCITING CONTRASTS, STILL BEAUTIFULLY GARDENED AND LOVELY TO SEE

The garden at Sissinghurst, famous as it is, has become for many people more an idea, a myth, than reality. Yet a visit to the garden remains a thrilling pleasure. The strength of the design, the beauty of the planting and the standards of practical gardening are all marvellous. Harold Nicolson and Vita Sackville-West bought Sissinghurst in 1930 when it was a decaying if romantic ruin. They were not novices, for they had already made (with the help of Sir Edwin Lutyens) an excellent garden at their previous house, Long Barn, also in Kent. At Sissinghurst they used the scattered buildings and old walls as the framework for a garden of compartments embellished with an ever-growing collection of plants. Vita Sackville-West was an eternal experimenter – rediscovering the beauties of old shrub roses, for example, but also willing to experiment with a cheap packet of mixed annual seeds from Woolworths.

EXCITING CONTRASTS

The excitement of the garden comes from the contrasting character of the planted enclosures separated by hedges or high walls and linked by paths, vistas or passages. The eye is often drawn by an eyecatcher, a distant gate or a fine plant; the strong framework is often blurred by planting, and brilliant colour schemes soothed by an intervening cool corridor of yew. The beauty of the White Garden comes not from its colour scheme (best at night when visitors can't see it) but from the serene pattern of the box hedge parterre which has all the austere and harmonious simplicity of some Islamic patio. The Cottage Garden deploys flamboyant reds, oranges and yellows with aristocratic panache. Here, as

The Cottage Garden at Sissinghurst

almost everywhere in the garden, the planting has been altered since the time of Vita and Harold, but the spirit of the place is nevertheless honoured.

Although Vita Sackville-West died in 1962 and Harold Nicolson in 1968, their garden remains fresh and original. It is this that is perhaps the greatest testimonial to their gardening skills: they devised a style of gardening which allows change while preserving its essence. The admirable team of National Trust gardeners who now care for it so meticulously have added all sorts of plants unknown to Vita but have maintained her zestful spirit.

INFORMATION

Location Sissinghurst, nr Cranbook TN17 2AB, Kent; 2m NE of Cranbrook off A262
Infoline 01580 710701 **Tel** 01580 710700
Email sissinghurst@nationaltrust.org.uk
English Heritage Register Grade I
Owner The National Trust
Open mid Mar to Oct, Fri to Tues 11–6.30 (or dusk if earlier); open from 10 at weekends and Bank Hols
Area 10 acres/4 hectares

Wakehurst Place

THE COUNTRY DEPARTMENT OF THE ROYAL BOTANIC GARDENS AT KEW – MAGNIFICENT TREES AND SHRUBS

The old estate of Wakehurst Place became in 1965 the country department of the Royal Botanic Gardens, Kew. The site is beautiful, on the High Weald of Sussex, with a lively rise and fall of land. The interest lies in the large collection of trees and shrubs displayed in an attractive and varied landscape. The plants have been arranged, in the garden's own words, "into geographical areas with the concept of a walk through the temperate woodlands of the world". Plants are grouped in different ways: by genus, for example the collection of birch (*Betula*) species, or by broader classification (conifers); by region (a collection of trees from the American North Pacific Coast); by topography (the Himalayan Glade); by habitat (wetlands); or by season (the Winter Garden). The garden holds four comprehensive National Collections of woody plants – birches, hypericums, nothofagus and skimmias. Apart from the trees, there are huge numbers of bulbs, meconopsis, orchids, witch hazels, viburnums and much else. But the main meal at Wakehurst, and the overwhelming reason for visiting it, is the tree collection. A long walk, on any day of the year, is a pleasure and is also the best way to learn about trees.

A VALUABLE SEED BANK

A recent development at Wakehurst is the Millennium Seed Bank, housed in a distinguished vaulted building, The Wellcome Trust Millennium Building, designed by the architects Stanton Williams. Raised beds in front of the building contain groups of plants from different British habitats, and the slopes round about have been planted with trees and shrubs of the High Weald and traditional meadow plants. A sculpture by Peter Randall-Page shows three seed-like stone spheres whose surfaces are incised with swirling patterns.

Inside the building an exhibition explains how the seed bank works, and visitors may look into the laboratories, with white-coated scientists going about their work. The seeds are prepared for freezing and stored in underground vaults – by 2010 it is expected that 24,000 species will be stored here. All this reflects a fundamental change in the purpose of botanic gardens. In the past they were seen, to use a Victorian phrase, as "repositories of nature's marvels" and sources of information about plants; today they have the much more urgent task of conservation.

Mansion Pond at Wakehurst

INFORMATION

Location nr Ardingly, Haywards Heath RH17 6TN; West Sussex 1½m NW of Ardingly on B2028
Infoline 01444 894066 **Tel** 01444 894000
Email wakehurst@kew.org
Website www.kew.org
English Heritage Register Grade II*
Owner The National Trust
Open Mar to Oct, daily 10–6; Nov to Feb, daily 10–4.30 (closed 24 and 25 Dec)
Area 170 acres/69 hectares

Weald and Downland Museum

AN OPEN AIR MUSEUM WHERE MANY OF THE VERNACULAR HOUSES HAVE CHARMING PERIOD GARDENS TO SUIT

It is usually only relatively grand gardens that survive from the past. In this enchanting open air museum historic vernacular buildings have been assembled in the fine setting of a wooded valley. All come from the Weald and Downland area of Hampshire, Kent, Surrey and Sussex, painstakingly transported and reassembled to form a scattered rural village of great charm. Some are embellished with vernacular gardens of convincing authenticity.

PERIOD GARDENS

Bayleaf Farmhouse, dating from the 15th century, is set in a productive landscape protected by a distinctive Wealden feature, a "shaw", or broad strip of managed woodland used as a field boundary and planted with ash, oak, field maple, hawthorn and hazel. These shaws, common before the 18th century, are believed to be the remains of primeval woodland cleared for fields. Protected by the shaw is an orchard, and in front of the house a kitchen garden, enclosed in a wattle fence, has beans, brassicas, herbs, leeks, onions, peas and salads arranged in separate beds to allow a three-fold rotation of crops. A bed of such ornamental herbs as hyssop, lavender and sage is raised up and neatly edged with wattle.

Walderton Cottage has a garden of fruit, vegetables and herbs that would have been found in a garden of the early 17th century. It shows a greater variety than the earlier Bayleaf garden, and includes cardoons, endives, turnips, parsnips and winter greens. An orchard would have had bee skeps, a ram and possibly geese. Ornamental plants of the time grow alongside the vegetables, among them lilies, marigolds, pinks, primroses and roses.

Poplar Cottage dates from the mid-

Bayleaf Farmhouse Garden

17th century and shows a kitchen garden worked on the three-field rotation system, with one field being left uncultivated for part of the year and enriched with "nightsoil" from the privy. It is gardened as it would have been in the past, seed is preserved from year to year, and manure is added to the surface without cultivation.

The clapboard Toll Cottage of around 1807 has a brick path, picket fence and beds dotted with hollyhocks, bachelor's buttons, lavender and roses in artless and charming profusion.

INFORMATION

Location Singleton, Chichester PO18 0EU, West Sussex; 6½ m N of Chichester by A286
Tel 01243 811348
Email office@wealddown.co.uk
Website www.wealddown.co.uk
Owner Weald and Downland Open Air Museum
Open Apr to Oct, daily 10.30–6; Nov to Dec, daily 10.30–4 (closed 22–25 Dec)
Area 60 acres/24 hectares

West Dean Gardens

A GREAT EDWARDIAN ESTATE WITH SUPERB RESTORED KITCHEN GARDENS AND PERGOLA BY HAROLD PETO

The setting of West Dean, with the South Downs rising serenely north of the house, is marvellously beautiful. William James bought the estate in 1891. Mrs James was a Dodge and the estate was run on the most opulent scale. The architect and garden designer Harold Peto worked on both house and garden. He designed a giant pergola cutting across a lawn to the north of the house. Another distinguished garden designer who worked here was Gertrude Jekyll who made a wild water garden to the west of the house in the shallow valley of the river Lavant. This area, and the adjacent Spring and Wild Gardens, is well cared for today. South of the house, on the far side of the river, superb parkland and fine old trees rise towards the downs. Sheep graze peacefully and in a clearing an arboretum is being replenished with new planting. The old arboretum, started in the 1830s and 1840s, was devastated in the 1987 storm.

In the great establishments of the Victorian and Edwardian periods a large kitchen garden was the engine room of the household, producing fruit, vegetables and cut flowers. The management of such a garden was complex and required great horticultural skills. At West Dean such a garden has been reinstated and is a wonderful sight. The space is divided into two chief enclosures with an area of glasshouses, cold frames, gardeners' bothy and potting sheds between them. The lower enclosure is devoted to fruit trees. A fine double herbaceous border runs across the garden. The glasshouses grow a prodigious range – aubergines, capsicums (including many hot chillies), cucumbers, figs, tomatoes, grapevines and melons. Tender ornamentals are also grown in profusion.

A BLAZE OF BORDERS

The upper part of the kitchen garden is largely devoted to vegetables, but there is also a magnificent double border, planned to be at its peak at the garden's most productive period – a blaze of yellows and oranges in late summer, with crocosmias, dahlias and kniphofias. It has become fashionable to restore old kitchen gardens. The standard established by West Dean is the one to emulate – it is lovely to look at and plainly immensely productive. Jim Buckland and Sarah Wain, and the other gardeners who work here, have revivified a superb garden.

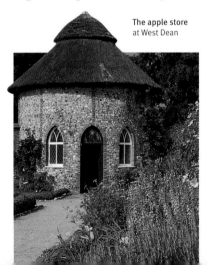

The apple store at West Dean

INFORMATION

Location West Dean, Chichester PO18 0QZ, West Sussex; 6m N of Chichester by A286
Tel 01243 818210
Email gardens@westdean.org.uk
Website www.westdean.org.uk
English Heritage Register Grade II*
Owner The Edward James Foundation
Open Mar to Oct, daily 10.30–5; Nov to Feb, Wed to Sun 10.30–4 (closed over Christmas and the New Year)
Area 90 acres/36 hectares

Winkworth Arboretum

A NOTABLE TREE COLLECTION IN AN EXQUISITE WOODED VALLEY WITH LAKES AND LONG VIEWS

Dr Wilfred Fox bought land here in 1937. What drew him to this place, as he said, was "a valley quite unspoiled, of pastoral and wooded character, patterned with hedgerows and abounding with wild flowers". The site is exceptionally handsome, with two lakes, Phillimore Lake and Rowe's Flash Lake, running along the bottom of the valley. There is a minimal amount of design at Winkworth, except for one or two set pieces such as Azalea Steps with great spreads of Kurume azaleas tumbling down a steep slope on either side of wooden steps. This, made in 1939, was originally called "The Adolf Hitler Glade" because it was constructed with the help of evacuees.

The valley at Winkworth in Autumn

The chief pleasure at Winkworth is to be gained by walking in the woods and discovering all sorts of delights for yourself – for example the beautiful glade of Japanese maples among oaks half way along the west bank of Phillimore Lake. The view from a path that runs along the top of the steep slope above Rowe's Flash Lake distils the essence of the place. You look down over a cascade of exotic trees and shrubs, with the water glittering below, and on the far side of the valley are panoramic views of unspoilt North Downs countryside – copses, rolling pasture and lavish hedgerows.

The background woodland planting is chiefly of ash, beech, holly, oak and sweet chestnut, with prodigious waves of bracken. Most of the planting is on the often steep slopes which run down to the west banks of the lakes, while meadows cover the slopes on the far side. Paths loop along the contours, with the occasional descent cutting straight across them. The banks of Rowe's Flash Lake are relatively unencumbered with planting, giving it more presence in the landscape. The banks of Phillimore Lake are much more densely planted, so that water is merely glimpsed among trunks and foliage. A walk along the banks will be enlivened by the squawks, scrambles and splashes of water fowl.

BALANCED PLANTING

Dr Fox was especially interested in rowans, and a National Collection is held here. Azaleas, eucryphias, hollies, magnolias, maples, rhododendrons and stewartias are also well represented. He hoped to strike a balance between merely collecting, and ornamenting the landscape, and in this he was strikingly successful. He chose many plants for their autumn colour and made plantings for specific colour associations.

INFORMATION

Location Hascombe Road, Godalming GU8 4AD, Surrey; 2m SE of Godalming by B2130
Tel 01483 208477
Email winkwortharboretum@nationaltrust.org.uk
Owner The National Trust
Open daily, dawn–dusk
Area 113 acres/46 hectares

Wisley Garden

CONSTANTLY IMPROVING SHOW GARDEN, WHERE THE ROYAL HORTICULTURAL SOCIETY SHOWS THE PUBLIC HOW TO DO IT

The garden at Wisley was given to the Royal Horticultural Society in 1903 by Sir Thomas Hanbury as "an Experimental Garden" for "the Encouragement and the Improvement of Scientific and Practical Horticulture in all its branches". Today it is one of the country's most popular gardens and a precious resource for gardeners.

The chief building is the Laboratory, a picturesque Arts and Crafts design. The formal gardens here were laid out by Sir Geoffrey Jellicoe and Lanning Roper in the 1960s. A large rectangular pool has a collection of waterlilies and, at its far end, a handsome Arts and Crafts open loggia with two walled gardens behind it. A second chief axis starts to the south with a double mixed border – one of the splendours of Wisley. The borders gently climb a hill, on the far side of which is Portsmouth Field where trial beds test different plants, ornamental and edible (sometimes both).

West of the double borders is a "Country Garden" laid out in 1999 to Penelope Hobhouse's design, with a virtuoso use of plants allied to a crisply classical design – a model small garden. Here too is a rose garden of Edwardian flavour – swagged ropes between pillars garlanded with climbing roses and many standard roses. A pair of monocot borders, filled with agapanthus, daylilies, kniphofias, phormiums and yuccas looks splendid in high summer. At a little distance from all this is a pair of borders designed in 2000 by Piet Oudolf, the doyen of ornamental naturalistic design. They are filled with swathes of alliums, echinaceas, eryngiums, liatris, monarda and sedums with occasional airy puffs of ornamental grasses that lighten the glowing colours. A great rock garden lies behind the

The Country Garden at Wisley

Jellicoe formal gardens, and nearby is the Wild Garden. With trees and shrubs, and much lovely naturalistic planting, especially of bulbs, it is one of the most attractive parts of the garden.

EDUCATIONAL ASPECT

Quite apart from what the visitor sees, much else goes on at Wisley. There is a strong educational aspect: full-time professional courses in horticulture; amateur courses; an advisory service; practical demonstrations; and an excellent library which all visitors may use. A plant centre sells a wide range of high quality plants and the shop carries, among other things, the largest range of gardening books of any shop in Britain.

INFORMATION

Location nr Ripley, Woking GU23 6QB, Surrey; 6m NE of Guildford by A3, Jct 10 of M25
Tel 0845 260 9000
Website www.rhs.org.uk
English Heritage Register Grade II*
Owner The Royal Horticultural Society
Open Mon to Fri 10–6, Sat and Sun 9–6 (NB Sun for RHS members and their guests only)
Area 240 acres/97 hectares

Yalding Organic Gardens

THE PRINCIPLES AND PRACTICE OF ORGANIC GARDENING DISPLAYED IN A LIVELY GARDEN

Yalding is the Kentish outpost of Garden Organic, formerly The Henry Doubleday Research Association, which promotes organic gardening. The site is as flat as a pancake and whatever charms it possesses come from the design of the garden. At the centre of the garden, like a mandala, is a circular lawn surrounded by segmental beds; this is surrounded in turn by a circular pergola clothed in clematis, roses and wisteria and edged with hedges of golden euonymus. The rest of the garden is disposed harmoniously about this strong shape at the heart of the layout.

The underlying theme is, of course, organic gardening. but in addition there is a sequence of historic set pieces which range from a 13th-century apothecary's garden to an allotment of the kind that was encouraged by the Ministry of Agriculture's "Dig for Victory" campaign in World War II. These give some notion of the periods they represent but vary considerably in quality. An Edwardian border "based on designs by Gertrude Jekyll", for example, requires much more detailed attention than is evident here. No doubt Gertrude Jekyll was sympathetic to the principles of organic gardening (there was not much of an alternative in her day), but her style of gardening was labour-intensive and depended on highly skilled labour at that. She also had an artist's eye for every detail of gardening and would certainly not have tolerated motor-car tyres as an aid to cultivating courgettes.

PRACTICAL DISPLAYS

The most rewarding part of the garden is the range of displays showing organic gardening in action, which are excellently done. The control of pests and diseases, the making of compost, the cultivation of the soil and the management of the kitchen garden are all displayed informatively. Apart from the vigour of the plants grown, especially the vegetables, one of the most beautiful plantings I have seen when visiting Yalding was a field of spelt (a primitive form of wheat) with all the wildflowers associated with arable crops – corncockles, cornflowers, corn chamomile, corn marigold and field poppies – a delightful thing to see.

All gardeners, I suspect, would prefer to garden organically. Places like Yalding are valuable because they not only vividly impart the knowledge but also display the results.

The circular lawn at Yalding

INFORMATION

Location Benover Road, Yalding, nr Maidstone ME18 6EX, Kent; S of the village of Yalding, 6m SW of Maidstone on B2162

Tel 01622 814650

Website www.gardenorganic. org.uk/garden/yalding

Owner Garden Organic

Open Apr to Oct, Wed to Sun 10–5 (open Bank Hol Mon and Easter)

Area 10 acres/4 hectares

WALES & WEST of ENGLAND

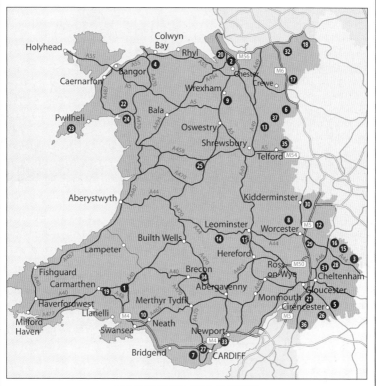

GARDENS TO VISIT

1. Aberglasney Gardens
2. Arley Hall
3. Batsford Arboretum
4. Bodnant Garden
5. Cirencester Park
6. The Dorothy Clive Garden
7. Dyffryn Gardens
8. Eastgrove Cottage Garden
9. Erdigg
10. The Gnoll Estate
11. Hampton Court
12. Hanbury Hall
13. Hawkstone Park
14. Hergest Croft Gardens
15. Hidcote Manor Garden
16. Kiftsgate Court
17. Little Moreton Hall
18. Lyme Park
19. National Botanic Garden of Wales
20. Ness Botanic Gardens
21. Painswick Rococo Garden
22. Plas Brondanw Gardens
23. Plas-yn-Rhiw
24. Portmeirion
25. Powis Castle
26. Rodmarton Manor
27. St Fagans Castle
28. Snowshill Manor
29. Spetchley Park
30. Stone House Cottage
31. Sudeley Castle
32. Tatton Park
33. Tredegar House
34. Tretower Court and Castle
35. Weston Park
36. Westonbirt Arboretum
37. Wollerton Old Hall

Image *Westonbirt Arboretum*

Aberglasney Gardens

DELIGHTFUL AND MYSTERIOUS HISTORIC GARDEN RETURNED TO BRILLIANT LIFE IN AN EPIC FEAT OF RESTORATION

The garden has ancient origins – Aberglasney's "nine green gardens" were celebrated in the 15th century by the bard Lewis Glyn Cothi. In the mid 17th century a new house was built here by the Rudd family who also made a new garden. It later passed to the Dyer family, one of whom was the 18th-century poet John Dyer. (Dyer's poem celebrating the beauties of Grongar Hill – which is visible from Aberglasney – was scorned by Dr Johnson but loved by William Wordsworth who wrote a sonnet to the poet.) The estate changed hands a number of times until 1955 when it was divided and the house left uninhabited. In 1995 The Aberglasney Restoration Trust bought the house and the remains of the estate and embarked on its restoration.

The walled garden at Aberglasney

THE CLOISTER GARDENS

The gardens at Aberglasney present a sequence of formal enclosures to the west and south of the house; to the east, informal planting in woodland gives exquisite views of the countryside – including the famous Grongar Hill. Immediately below the house is the Cloister Garden – a series of arched openings round three sides of a courtyard, with a terrace walk above. This enclosure, which dates from the early 17th century, is now laid out as a handsome formal garden of cut turf shapes and topiary. The terrace walk provides splendid views of this, and of the other formal gardens that have been restored and planted.

A large rectangular pool beyond the Cloister Garden is also probably of Jacobean origin. In each corner and in the middle of each side is a stone-edged rill fed by an underground watercourse. The high stone wall at its northern end, where once there was a lean-to glasshouse, today provides protection for a boisterous mixed border. South of the Cloister Garden, and best seen from above, is a slightly irregular walled garden, planted to a design by Penelope Hobhouse, in which concentric box-edged curved beds, mainly of herbaceous perennials, frame a central oval of lawn. An opening in the wall leads to a walled kitchen and nursery garden with lollipops of clipped bay and a west-facing mixed border. Bishop Rudd's Walk leads east from the house, following a shallow valley and a stream through woods. In the shade of ash, holly and yew are lovely woodland plants of the kind that flourish in a moist climate in acid soil – cypripediums, ferns, meconopsis, primulas and trilliums.

INFORMATION

Location Llangathen SA32 8QH, Carmarthenshire; 2m W of Llandeilo by A40
Tel and fax 01558 668998
Email info@aberglasney.org.uk
Website www.aberglasney.org.uk
Cadw/ICOMOS Register Grade II*
Owner Aberglasney Restoration Trust
Open Apr to Sept, daily 10–6; Oct to Mar, daily 10.30–4
Area 10 acres/4 hectares

Arley Hall

SUPERB 19TH-CENTURY BORDERS AND FINE WALLED GARDENS FOR AN ANCIENT ESTATE STILL PRIVATELY OWNED

The estate at Arley belonged to the Warburton family in the 12th century and has passed by descent ever since. Sir Piers Warburton built a house here in the mid 15th century. The house was Georgianised in the 18th century and survived until the 1830s, at which time the present house was built in neo-Jacobean style.

LAVISH PLANTING

The great feature at Arley is a pair of beautiful borders planted between 1851 and 1852 and probably one of the first known borders to use exclusively herbaceous perennials. They are backed on one side by yew hedges ornamented with architectural topiary and on the other by a brick wall. At the head of the borders stands the surviving 18th-century summerhouse, the Alcove, built in 1791. Each end of the broad grass walk between the borders is marked by a scalloped yew hedge finished with a topiary "dumb waiter" of yew, while buttresses of yew in the borders provide strongly defined shapes among the luxuriant planting, and divide what could be an uncomfortably long expanse of border. The planting has, of course, changed over the years but the brilliant colours of modern planting are kept well under control by the yew, and there is much repetition, especially of strong shapes of foliage. Here are big, bold plants such as *Macleaya cordata*, the giant thistle *Onopordum acanthium* and *Cephalaria gigantea*, as well as smaller plants which have strong shapes – globe-shaped flowers of *Echinops ritro*, bladelike foliage of crocosmias and crisp spires of *Lysimachia ephemerum*. Against this framework is a striking display of orange crocosmias and alstroemerias, brilliant red phlox, magenta *Lychnis coronaria* and yellow anthemis and helenium.

To one side of the borders is a mysterious avenue of ornamental drums of clipped holm oak leading across a lawn to a pair of urns and a small sunken garden. A large part of the old kitchen garden has been turned over to decorative purposes, with a scalloped pool surrounded by heraldic figures, tall columns of clipped beech and mixed borders lining the walls. A walk of rugosa roses is underplanted with *Cyclamen hederifolium*, a seat stands in an arbour of crab-apples, and borders of artichokes and mounds of hebe lead to a domed metal arbour. Arley wears its history lightly and remains a garden of immense charm.

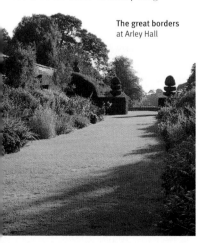

The great borders at Arley Hall

INFORMATION

Location Arley, nr Northwich CW9 6NA, Cheshire; 5m W of Knutsford by minor roads
Tel 01565 777353
Email enquiries@arleyhallandgardens.com
Website www.arleyhallandgardens.com
English Heritage Register Grade II*
Owner Viscount Ashbrook
Open Apr to Sept, daily except Mon (open Bank Hol Mon) 12–5
Area 12 acres/4.8 hectares

Batsford Arboretum

MAGNIFICENT TREE COLLECTIONS AND FLOWERING SHRUBS, AND A CHARMING JAPANESE GARDEN

The house was built between 1887 and 1893 by Sir Ernest George & Harold Peto for A.B. Freeman Mitford (later 1st Earl Redesdale of the second creation). As a diplomat in Japan, Freeman Mitford was bitten deeply by the oriental bug and this strongly influenced his gardening activities. He became an expert on bamboos, of which there is a good collection here; wrote *The Bamboo Garden* in 1896; and laid out a Japanese garden here from 1890. The estate was sold in 1920 to the 1st Lord Dulverton whose son, after 1956, built up a large collection of trees, adding to existing old plantings, some of which go back to the 18th century.

The site, with undulating ground sloping to the south and a winding stream, is attractive. But it is almost 800ft/240m here and winters can be very cold. The arboretum, west and north of the house, contains examples of a very wide range of hardy trees, deciduous and coniferous, though deciduous trees form the bulk of the collection. There are especially good acers (180 species and cultivars),

birches, cherries (especially Japanese flowering cherries, a National Collection), magnolias (97 species), oaks (over 60 species) and rowans. There are also good collections of cedars, junipers, pines and spruce. Batsford boasts three champion trees – the white ash (*Fraxinus americana*), the Syrian juniper (*Juniperus drupacea*) and the California nutmeg (*Torreya californica*). All the trees are impeccably labelled and are disposed about winding walks.

A JAPANESE GARDEN

Lord Redesdale's Japanese garden, west of the house, has a Japanese resthouse crowned with a dragon to ward off evil spirits. It is shaded by a splendid tree of heaven (*Ailanthus altissima*), and, nearby, a bronze Buddha under an English oak overlooks a clearing among bamboos, magnolias and Japanese maples. An old Japanese maple (*Acer palmatum*) spreads over a rocky pool overlooked by a Foo Dog – a fierce bronze dog with its front paws resting on a multicoloured cloisonné sphere. A more recent addition, quite close to the Japanese garden, is the late 20th-century carved stone statue by Simon Verity of Daphne with flying robes and hair turning into wild branches. Batsford is a delightful place to explore in any season and for the ardent tree lover it is a place of quite particular interest.

Batsford Arboretum

INFORMATION

Location Moreton-in-Marsh GL56 9QB, Gloucestershire; 1m NW of Moreton-in-Marsh by A44
Tel 01386 701441
Email arboretum@batsfordfoundation.co.uk
Website www.batsarb.co.uk
English Heritage Register Grade I
Owner The Batsford Foundation
Open daily 10–5 (closed Wed in Dec and Jan, 25 Dec and 1 Jan)
Area 55 acres/22 hectares

Bodnant Garden

AN OUTSTANDING GARDEN OF FORMAL WELL-PLANTED TERRACES AND A GRAND RAVINE OF FLOWERING SHRUBS

Bodnant is a garden of many flavours, most of them delicious, and the prevailing atmosphere is one of plutocratic splendour. The estate was bought in 1874 by a Salford chemical manufacturer, Henry David Pochin. The setting is extraordinarily beautiful, overlooking the Conwy valley with mesmerising views of Snowdonia. Henry Pochin saw the gardening possibilities at Bodnant from early on and began planting trees in the precipitous valley of the river Hiraethlyn which flows through the grounds. He commissioned the landscape architect Edward Milner to make sweeping lawns west of the house, high above the valley, and in around 1882 he built the famous laburnum tunnel – an astonishing sight in May with its cascades of flowers and pink azaleas glimpsed below on either side.

The Pin Mill at Bodnant

LIVELY VARIETY

However, it was Henry Pochin's grandson, the 2nd Lord Aberconway, who introduced the lively variety of garden styles that flow harmoniously one after the other and give the garden the character and charm that it possesses today. Terraces now descend the west-facing slope below the house where Milner's lawns had been, each revealing something remarkable or beautiful: the battered but beautiful *Arbutus* x *andrachnoides* on the top terrace was planted in 1906 and is a tree of rare character; on the Lily Terrace below, a scalloped lily pool is flanked by two veteran trees (both planted by Henry Pochin), a blue Atlantic cedar and a cedar of Lebanon; the steps down are enclosed in a superb trelliswork pergola with ceanothus, roses and *Solanum crispum*; and the lowest terrace has a long narrow canal with a scattering of waterlilies at either end. At one end the canal is overlooked by an elegant arcaded building, the Pin Mill – an early 18th-century garden pavilion. At the other end is the Stage – a platform of turf with a bench designed by William Kent and a splendid Monterey pine (*Pinus radiata*).

A path to one side of the Pin Mill descends into the Hiraethlyn valley where the Dell is rich in exotic conifers, seen among native Scots pines, English oaks and sycamores. Early in the year the Dell explodes with camellias, magnolias and rhododendrons, followed later by the calmer presence of hydrangeas and drifts of astilbes. Paths high up above the stream give delicious views through the planted profusion.

INFORMATION

Location Tal-y-Cafn, Colwyn Bay LL28 5RE, Clwyd; 8m S of Llandudno by A470, signposted from A55
Tel 01492 650460
Email bodnantgarden@nationaltrust.org.uk
Website www.oxalis.co.uk/bodnant.htm
Cadw/ICOMOS Register Grade I
Owner The National Trust
Open mid Mar to early Nov, daily 10–5
Area 80 acres/32 hectares

Cirencester Park

MAGNIFICENT EARLY 18TH-CENTURY LANDSCAPE PARK WITH THE LONGEST AVENUE IN ENGLAND

The house was built in the early 18th century for the 1st Earl Bathurst. In front of the house, where it faces the town, a yew hedge planted shortly after it was built survives today – a giant curved bolster of green along the road, a well-loved landmark to many who have passed through Cirencester.

The enormous park, one of the most astonishing designed landscapes in the country, was the result of an extended collaboration between Lord Bathurst and his friend Alexander Pope. It is one of the few large-scale schemes of this character to survive from the early 18th century. In 1714 Stephen Switzer coined the term "extensive or forest gardening" for this style; still retaining formal avenues and rides, it was a precursor of the informal landscape park. Bathurst, who had also bought the neighbouring estate of Sapperton, clothed the land behind his house with trees, combining forestry and landscaping, commerce and aesthetics on a heroic scale.

THE LONGEST AVENUE

Bold rides and avenues running through woodland form the structure of the park. The Broad Avenue, of horse chestnuts and beech, aligned with the church tower of St John the Baptist in Cirencester, runs westwards all the way to Sapperton village 5 miles away. Ornamental buildings punctuate the avenue – a hexagon with cupola (c.1736), stone piers, Pope's Seat (c.1736), the Horse Guards (a pair of arched Ionic alcoves, c.1800). Just beyond the latter, the avenue joins a *rond-point* linking ten rides. In Oakley Wood Alfred's Hall is a very early Gothick castellated building, completed by 1732. At the centre of Home Park is the Doric Queen Anne's Column (1741).

Lord Bathurst died aged ninety-one in 1775, having lived through one of the most turbulent periods in garden history. His park was a pioneer when he started work on it and, gently embracing informality, naturalism and commerce, remained an idiosyncratic achievement, beyond fashion, as it is today. The entrance gates bear this legend: "You are welcome on foot or on horseback by permission of the Lord Bathurst." I know of no other garden in England that offers such a friendly welcome.

INFORMATION

Location Cirencester GL7 2BU, Gloucestershire; in the centre of the town of Cirencester
Tel 01285 653135
Email enquire@cirencesterpark.co.uk
Website www.cirencesterpark.co.uk
English Heritage Register Grade I
Owner Lord Bathurst
Open daily 8–5
Area 2,400 acres/971 hectares

The Broad Avenue at Cirencester Park

The Dorothy Clive Garden

A WOODED DELL ALIVE WITH EXCELLENT PLANTING AND INVENTIVE MIXED BORDERS FULL OF INTEREST

Some of the best gardens succeed by exploiting some oddity of the landscape. At Willoughbridge, Colonel Harry Clive saw the possibilities of an old gravel quarry and started to make a garden here in 1940. It was designed as a place of recreation for his wife, Dorothy, whose failing health restricted her activities. The quarry is on a slope that faces south. It has acid soil, is well watered and

The cascade in the Quarry Garden

benefits from old oaks and beech which give protection for the rhododendrons that Colonel Clive wanted to plant. He built up an excellent collection, both of the familiar brilliantly coloured hybrid azaleas and also of the beautiful species. In 1990, in order to celebrate the half centenary of the garden, a multi-tiered waterfall was made, whose edges today are planted with astilbes, ferns, hostas, irises, ligularias and rodgersias. On either side of the waterfall, distinguished trees and shrubs crowd in – *Embothrium coccineum*, magnolias, Japanese maples, pieris and rhododendrons. The high canopy of oaks gives protection but also filters the light which illuminates the brilliant flowers of the shrubs below.

THE SCREE GARDEN

At the entrance to the garden, where John Codrington advised on borders and other features in the 1960s, is a completely different style of gardening. Here is an example of that desperately unfashionable garden feature, the scree garden. The best reason for making a scree garden is to provide particular conditions for, say, alpine plants; here, plants from very different environments are unhappily jumbled together: a sea of gravel flows down a gentle slope about dwarf conifers (some with golden foliage), cistus, daphnes, hebes and mounded Japanese maples, while an informal lily pool is edged with bulrushes, *Gunnera manicata*, hostas, pampas grass and persicaria. Some of the planting, however, is more effective. A trio of slender Himalayan birches (*Betula utilis* var. *jacquemontii*) stands against the horizontal, tiered shape of *Viburnum plicatum* 'Mariesii', and the pale silvery foliage of *Cornus argentea* froths among thickets of *Crocosmia* 'Lucifer'.

On the slopes above the scree garden are swooping lawns, mixed borders and specimen trees. Some of the trees are planted in grass, some rise among the lavishly planted borders which are full of excellent and sometimes unusual plants beautifully cared for. However, to my taste, it is the Quarry Garden that is the overwhelmingly distinguished attraction in the Dorothy Clive Garden.

INFORMATION

Location Willoughbridge, nr Market Drayton TF9 4EU, Shropshire; 9m SE of Nantwich by A51
Tel 01630 647237
Email info@dorothyclivegarden.co.uk
Website www.dorothyclivegarden.co.uk
Owner Willoughbridge Garden Trust
Open Mar to Oct, daily 10–5.30
Area 8 acres/3.2 hectares

Dyffryn Gardens

A GREAT EDWARDIAN GARDEN OF FORMAL DESIGN, FINELY
RESTORED WITH DISTINGUISHED PLANTING

This was the estate of a coal and shipping tycoon, Sir John Cory, who started to make a garden shortly after the house was built and in 1906 employed the garden designer Thomas H. Mawson to make a formal garden. John Cory's son, Reginald, a distinguished plantsman, collaborated with Mawson, who wrote: "The credit of the success achieved in these gardens largely belongs to him." After much excellent restoration starting in 1997, with finance from the Heritage Lottery Fund, the garden is probably the best surviving example of a Mawson garden designed for a private client.

The garden starts with bold axes near the house, becoming more intimate and more attractively jumbly to the west of the chief vista. Running along the south façade of the house, a balustraded terrace bristles with urns and vases filled with tender plants. Immediately below, a croquet lawn is edged with Irish yews, many leaning away from the west wind. A long narrow cross-shaped lily pool runs south across another lawn with, at its centre, a great bronze vase with a dragon entwined about it. This is one of various Chinese objects presented to

the garden in the 1950s; among them is a fine figure of the philosopher Lao-tse on a grassy eminence close to the house. The dragon vase is aligned with a sketchy westwards axis leading to a sequence of garden enclosures, many with beautifully fashioned yew hedges. An area of sweeping lawns and trees and shrubs is outstandingly attractive, and contains a large Chinese wingnut (*Pterocarya stenoptera*) and fine Japanese maples planted by Reginald Cory.

THEMED GARDENS

In the enclosed areas, as Mawson wrote, "We felt at liberty to indulge in every phase of garden design which the site and my client's catholic views suggested." Here are deep herbaceous borders, a Mediterranean Garden, a Pompeian Garden (largely built out of concrete), a Rose Garden, a fernery, a Bathing Pool Garden (now containing a very beautiful *Acer griseum*) and much else. The Theatre Garden, with a raised stage, was used to display Reginald Cory's collection of bonsai. At Dyffryn the beautiful yew hedging, the maze-like sequence of rooms and the frequently distinguished planting give great pleasure. In 2007 restoration was continuing in this admirable garden.

The statue of Lao-tse at Dyffryn

INFORMATION

Location St Nicholas, Cardiff CF5 6SU, Glamorgan; 7m SW of Cardiff, Jct 33 of M4, A4232, A48 and minor roads
Tel 039 20593328
Fax 029 20591966
Website www.dyffryngardens. org.uk
Cadw/ICOMOS Register Grade I
Owner The Vale of Glamorgan Council
Open Apr to Oct, daily 10–dusk; Nov to Mar, daily 10–5
Area 55 acres/22 hectares

Eastgrove Cottage Garden

THE DEFINITIVE AND IRRESISTIBLE COTTAGE GARDEN, A CHARMING PLACE FILLED WITH GOOD PLANTS

Eastgrove Cottage is a half-timbered 17th-century house in a rural setting. Carol and Malcolm Skinner came to live here in 1975 and set about making a garden to suit the house. This is a cottage garden but it was made by people exceptionally knowledgeable about plants. Here are *Alchemilla mollis*, aquilegias, Japanese anemones, astrantias, feverfew, geraniums, irises, lavender, pulmonarias, rue, sage and perennial wallflowers.

Eastgrove Cottage Garden

What, then, is a cottage garden? The most important characteristic is the vernacular style of the place, in which a general irregularity prevails. Paths amble in the most convenient way, straight lines are a rarity, plants jostle each other in abundant profusion. It is a garden devised for the pleasure of the owners and their friends rather than to impress the neighbours and keep up with the Joneses. There are touches of formality – a flawless waist-high hedge of *Lonicera nitida* with a voluptuously pillowed top zigzags amidst the profusion and suddenly metamorphoses into a beech hedge.

"THE GLADE"

The Skinners also fashioned a mini-arboretum (they call it "the Glade" and it serves the purpose of mediating gently between the garden and the surrounding rural landscape). The trees in the glade are exotic, even aristocratic – *Acer griseum*, *Betula utilis* var. *jacquemontii* and *Prunus serrula* among them – but there is also a compost-making area in one corner. More recently the Glade has been extended, with the planting of many more trees to form an arboretum that is by no means mini and now covers two acres. The Ride keeps vistas open and a grass labyrinth is a charming feature. "The Thinking Stool", made

from a Nepalese cart wheel, provides a peaceful place to sit and cogitate.

The cottage garden was not merely an aesthetic choice; it originally implied a way of life, and the Skinners have largely embraced this too. The garden is thoroughly productive, with an orchard and a chicken house, and it also has a pair of brick privies – the cottage was once divided in two – that rise up with all the aplomb of elegant gazebos. Nevertheless, plants loom large in their lives. The Skinners also run a nursery of plants propagated on the premises, available only to visitors; they are mostly herbaceous perennials and many are rare. They include tremendous lists of dianthus, geranium and viola cultivars among much else.

INFORMATION

Location Sankyns Green, Little Witley WR6 6LQ, Worcestershire; 8m NW of Worcester on road between Shrawley (B4196) and Great Witley (A443)
Tel 01299 896389
Website www.eastgrove.co.uk
Owner Malcolm and Carol Skinner
Open late Apr to mid Jul and Sept to mid Oct, Thur, Fri and Sat 2–5 (also open Bank Hol Sun and Mon in May)
Area 3 acres/1.2 hectares

Erdigg

DELIGHTFUL 18TH-CENTURY FORMAL WALLED GARDENS WITH
VICTORIAN AND EDWARDIAN TOUCHES

Erddig is a gawky house, rather pompous on the entrance front and too relentlessly long and low on the garden side. For all that, the place has devastating charm, chiefly because of the house's wonderful interiors and contents, its working outbuildings, and the delightful old-fashioned – very old-fashioned – garden which the National Trust has put back since 1973. The house dates from the 1680s but was substantially altered twice: widened in the 1720s, and given a new entrance front, encased in stone, by James Wyatt in the 1770s. The estate was bought in a bankruptcy sale in 1716 by John Meller who left it on his death in 1733 to his nephew, Simon Yorke. The Yorkes remained here until 1973 when the last of the line, Philip Yorke, gave the estate to the National Trust.

John Meller made what was even then an old-fashioned formal garden east of the house, and the essential shape of this garden remains in place today. From the 1760s onwards the landscape designer William Emes made repeated visits to Erddig and did much planting in the park on the west side of the house, but the Yorkes, in defiance of

The Edwardian parterre at Erdigg

fashion, preserved the formal garden. The estate decayed, the park was scarred by mining and the house threatened by subsidence. When the National Trust's representative, Merlin Waterson, saw it in 1971, he reported: "Inside the park the road disintegrated into a ridge of mud flanked by almost continuous potholes . . . Most of the shutters were closed, many of the windows broken and whole sashes were missing. It was the death mask of a house which faced two huge slag heaps in the park."

PRETTY FORMAL GARDENS

The formal gardens today present as pretty a picture as you may see. A central walk, lined with tubs of clipped Portugal laurel (*Prunus lusitanicus*), leads to a canal flanked by double avenues of limes (*Tilia* x *europaea*) surviving from the 18th century. The vista is triumphantly

closed by a pair of beautiful wrought-iron gates made for Erddig in the 1720s by the local blacksmith, Robert Davies. This strong axis unites the various parts of the formal garden. It starts, just below the windows of the saloon of the house, with an anachronistic surprise – a light-hearted Edwardian parterre with domes of clipped box and L-shaped beds filled with tulips and forget-me-nots in spring and with snapdragons, plumbago and verbena in summer. Ornamental walls with eccentrically bulgy Dutch gables made to resemble the façades of pavilions flank the parterre. On either side of the Portugal laurel walk, behind screens of pleached lime (*Tilia* x *euchlora*), are formal orchards. Here the National Trust has established a large collection of 18th- and 19th-century apple cultivars; they are planted in long grass with close-mown paths between the rows – a delightful effect.

On the long brick walls (made of beautiful 1740s bricks) on each side of the garden are espaliered fruit trees underplanted in many cases with rare cultivars of daffodils. The walls are also used for the huge collection of ivies – a National Collection of 170 species and cultivars. Along the south wall is the curious Dutch garden where an avenue of clipped Irish yews, flanked with a low box hedge arranged in a key pattern, leads to a formal garden of Edwardian flavour with shaped pools and beds of roses and clematis. Beyond it the vista continues into woods where a Moss Walk, a sombre place full of holly, laurel and yew, provides a suitably melancholy place for an introspective saunter.

INFORMATION

Location nr Wrexham LL13 0YT, Clwyd; 2m S of Wrexham by A525
Infoline 01978 315151 **Tel** 01978 355314
Email erddig@nationaltrust.org.uk
Cadw/ICOMOS Register Grade I
Owner The National Trust
Open Apr to Oct, Sat to Wed (open Good Friday; July and Aug, also open Thur) 11–5 (closes 4 in Oct); Nov to mid Dec, Sat and Sun 11–4
Area 13 acres/5 hectares

The Gnoll Estate

A PUBLIC PARK WITH WOODLAND GARDEN, A LAKE, STREAMS AND MAGNIFICENT CASCADES – A LITTLE-KNOWN GEM

Sir Humphry Mackworth, an Englishman who married a Welsh heiress, came to the town of Neath and started copper and lead smelting in the 1690s, making use of the abundant water supply. He also built a great house, Gnoll, on a prominent hill overlooking Neath and close to his industrial premises. The house was destroyed in 1957 but garden features survived and since the 1980s have been triumphantly reinstated, revealing a rare early 18th-century layout. The Mackworths used the same water from the hills both as an essential part of their industrial activities and as the chief ingredient of their landscaping.

MAGNIFICENT CASCADES

Between 1724 and 1727 Thomas Greening laid out formal gardens for Sir Humphry, the chief feature of which was a formal cascade and pool to the east of the house. The pool was subsequently changed and now has the appearance of a naturalistic lake, but the cascade has been restored – and an astonishing sight it is. It descends a stately slope, now planted with fine beeches on either side, in a series of pools and shallow falls. In some places the flow of water is concentrated in a narrow passage, with an upright flat stone below it creating a plume of water. The cascade is fed from an open reservoir that originally provided some of the power for Mackworth's factory.

At the highest point of the Gnoll estate is a cascade of a very different character. The walk, uphill all the way, leads through woods of beeches, larch, oaks and pines, and streams lace the land. On the way you pass Half House, a battlemented 18th-century stone alcove, and eventually arrive at a large stretch of water – Mosshouse Wood

The great cascade at The Gnoll

Reservoir – with an inlet and a cascade erupting from rocks. If you cross the inlet and follow a path through Mosshouse Woods (named for a long-lost ornamental house of moss) you come to a swampy clearing. Here is an astonishing cascade, falling from a height of 180ft/55m and owing its beauty to the fact that it is broken into a long series of falls as it curves through the woods. It dates from the 1740s and is a remarkably early man-made cascade. At the head of the cascade is the remains of a grotto, sadly shorn of its tumbling stalactites.

INFORMATION

Location Neath, Glamorgan; on the eastern edge of Neath off Gnoll Park Road, B4434
Tel 01639 635808
Cadw/ICOMOS Register Grade II*
Owner Neath Port Talbot County Borough Council
Open daily 8–5
Area 200 acres/81 hectares

Hampton Court

BRILLIANTLY DESIGNED, FLOWER-FILLED NEW GARDENS FOR AN OLD ESTATE, CARRIED OUT WITH PANACHE

Hampton Court has a complicated history. A 15th-century castle owned by the Lenthall family was completely rebuilt towards the end of the 17th century for Lord Coningsby, and in the early 19th century the estate was bought by R. Arkwright (of the "spinning jenny" family) who called in Sir Jeffry Wyattville to restore more of its original castle appearance and add 19th-century comforts. In 1994 the estate was bought by an American, Robert Van Kampen, who restored the house and, in 1996, embarked on the garden, designed by Simon Dorrell, chiefly within the walled enclosures of an early 19th-century kitchen garden.

PICTURESQUE CANALS

The first part of the garden is an ornamental kitchen garden with ranges of glasshouses. The flower garden beyond it is a tour de force which makes references to the past but has a modern feel. Here are walks of pleached lime with two canals, each fed with a stepped cascade. At the centre of each canal, sitting on an island, a beautifully made octagonal gazebo of brick and wood has a pronounced Arts and Crafts

character. The pools are flanked by large beds of lavender and weeping silver pears (*Pyrus salicifolia* 'Pendula'). Borders run along the walls with much bold planting – thickets of *Stipa gigantea* and *Eupatorium purpureum* – and much repeat planting, including veils of self-sown *Verbena bonariensis*. In one corner a formal rose garden has box-edged beds of chiefly David Austin English roses.

In the adjacent Dutch Garden a long narrow canal is edged in fine stone paving and rows of pots on each side brim with tufts of the ornamental grass *Hakonechloa macra* 'Aureola'. Behind these, running the whole length of the canal, are beds of standard Portugal laurels (*Prunus lusitanica*) alternating with Irish yews, underplanted with giant swathes of *Verbena bonariensis*.

To one side of the walled gardens a new yew hedge maze has, as its goal, a fine Gothic tower from which you may descend through a tunnel to emerge in a very different kind of garden: the Sunken Garden. This is a romantic pool garden overlooked by a rustic thatched hermitage and fed by a tumbling cascade. Surrounding banks are planted lavishly with shade-loving plants – bergenias, epimediums, ferns, hostas and the lovely *Hydrangea quercifolia*.

The flower garden at Hampton Court

INFORMATION

Location Hope-under-Dinmore, Leominster HR6 0PN, Herefordshire; 5m S of Leominster by A49; close to jct with A417
Tel 01568 797777
Email office@hamptoncourt.org.uk
Website www.hamptoncourt.org.uk
Owner Sola scriptura
Open Apr to Oct, Tue to Thur, Sat and Sun (open Bank Hol Mon) 11–5
Area 20 acres/8 hectares

Hanbury Hall

STATELY PERIOD GARDENS OF FLOWERY FORMALITY FOR A GRAND EARLY 18TH-CENTURY HOUSE

Hanbury is a splendid house, built in 1701 for a lawyer, Thomas Vernon, possibly to the designs of William Talman. Of fine brick, with stone dressings, it is crowned with an airy central cupola – the view of it as you cross the fields that lie on your way is enchanting. A Victorian entrance court is decorated with a pair of gauche but charming pavilions whose roofs start off soberly straight but suddenly wriggle into ogee shapes. Mixed borders line the walls and a pair of tall stone vases are planted with variegated agaves.

FLOWERY FORMALITY

South-west of the house the National Trust has recreated the formal garden which was designed, possibly by the royal gardener George London, when the house was built. A sunken parterre surrounded by a gravel walk is divided into four intricately patterned beds outlined with box; it has a central compartment outlined in golden box with a box topiary shape in the middle. The beds are filled with herbaceous

plants – white alyssum, London pride, marigolds, pasque flowers, snapdragons and thrift. The effect is like a riotously coloured Persian rug but it retains an air of gentlemanly formality.

Alongside it a formal fruit garden has rows of apples and pears planted in grass. Narrow borders along its edge contain shapes of bay or laurustinus underplanted with the same range of flowers as the parterre. A formal "wilderness" nearby has rows of bay, hibiscus, variegated holly, phillyrea, *Rosa gallica* 'Versicolor' and sloes enclosing specimen trees in grass – a Judas tree, flowering cherries or laburnum. The adjoining Grove is a pattern of compartments hedged in hornbeam, radiating from a central oval; each compartment is filled with dogwood, guelder rose, hazels and rowans. A bowling green is overlooked by two very pretty ogee-shaped pavilions topped with gilt knobs. To one side is an 18th-century orangery with agaves and citrus plants in Versailles boxes, and behind it, against the north wall, is a mushroom house in full action (a rare garden sight), with wonderful truffly smells in its dark moist interior.

The reinstated formal garden, including its idiosyncrasies, seems to me to be a great success – attractive in itself and providing an elegant but lively setting for the house.

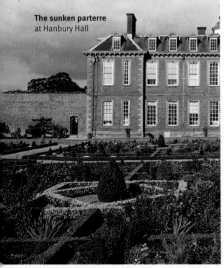

The sunken parterre at Hanbury Hall

INFORMATION

Location Hanbury, Droitwich WR9 7EA, Worcestershire; 4½m E of Droitwich by B4090 and minor roads, Jct 5 of M5
Tel 01527 821214
Email hanburyhall@nationaltrust.org.uk
English Heritage Register Grade II
Owner The National Trust
Open early to mid Mar, Sat and Sun 11–5.30; mid Mar to Jun and Sept to Oct, Sat to Wed 11–5.30; Jul to Aug, daily 11–5.30
Area 15 acres/6 hectares

Hawkstone Park

DRAMATIC 18TH-CENTURY LANDSCAPE PARK WITH GROTTOES, ROCKY RAVINES AND REMARKABLE MONUMENTS

This was the ancient estate of the Hill family. In the latter part of the 18th century two generations of Hills (Sir Rowland and Sir Richard) built an extraordinary landscape park which was strongly influenced by their near neighbour, Richard Payne Knight of Downton Castle. His recommendations for a sublime landscape of precipitous rocks, tumbling waters and a ruined castle are precisely reflected in the scene fashioned by the Hills at Hawkstone.

The Hills took every advantage of the gigantic natural craggy outcrops of red sandstone fringed with trees that erupt from the landscape here. They devised walks which led the visitor on a circuitous and frequently terrifying tour of the park. Paths skirt the crags or cross precipitous bridges, from time to time suddenly revealing vertiginous descents below. A long dark tunnel penetrates the cliffs and emerges in a narrow ravine, almost too narrow to walk along, fringed with ferns and cushioned in moss. Another, almost devoid of light, opens out into an astonishing multi-chambered labyrinthine grotto (the largest room is 80ft/25m across), with windows penetrating the rock sides and an opening leading out onto a cliff – not recommended for visitors with vertigo.

Cliffs at Hawkstone Park

"TERRIFICK GRANDEUR"

There is also a remarkable 100ft/30m column in a grove of monkey puzzles. Climbing the spiral staircase, you emerge on a viewing platform to find yourself standing alongside the giant legs and under the doublet of a 16th-century Sir Rowland Hill, the first Protestant Lord Mayor of London. He scans the horizon, and you do too, for a gigantic panorama of the encircling landscape is revealed.

In the 18th century the park was even bigger and was enriched with more ornamental buildings than survive today; as it is today, it provides one of the least forgettable of all garden visiting experiences. Most historic gardens are impossible to interpret correctly with 21st-century eyes but here at Hawkstone the power of the landscape elicits from the visitor all the feelings of awe and terror – the sublime – that Richard Payne Knight and his followers sought. Dr Johnson visited Hawkstone in 1774 and was moved by the "striking scenes and terrifick grandeur", responding deeply to the "the awfulness of its shades, the horrors of its precipices, the verdure of its hollows and the loftiness of its rocks".

INFORMATION

Location Weston-under-Redcastle, Shrewsbury SY4 5UY, Shropshire; 14m NE of Shrewsbury by A49 or A53 and minor roads
Tel 01939 200611 **Fax** 01939 200311
Website www.hawkstone.co.uk
English Heritage Register Grade I
Owner Hawkstone Estate
Open mid Apr to May, Wed to Sun (open Bank Hol Mon) 10–3.30; June to early Sept, daily 10–4; phone/see website for other openings
Area 300 acres/121 hectares

Hergest Croft Gardens

IDYLLIC PRIVATE WOODLAND GARDENS SET IN A LOVELY LANDSCAPE, WITH SUPERB TREES AND SHRUBS

William Hartland Banks started to build an Arts and Crafts house here in 1896 and began his garden. He was acquiring plants, in particular from Veitch's nursery, at a time when marvellous new introductions were being made, especially by E.H. Wilson in China. Two subsequent generations of the family have built on those foundations, forming an exceptional collection and creating a most seductive landscape. It would be futile to begin to list the plants to be seen here except in the most general terms, but there are three National Collections – maples (excluding *Acer japonicum* and *A. palmatum* cultivars, 129 species and cultivars), birches (59 species and cultivars) and, more recondite but thrilling, zelkova (6 species and cultivars).

Wrought-iron gates at Hergest Croft

The garden falls into two parts: those areas that lie close to the house and those that are arrived at by walking across the Park and Haywood Common to Park Wood. Close to the house are a few passages of relative formality. A croquet lawn is enclosed in yew hedges with clipped spheres along the top, niches and indentations; its entrance has a canopy of golden yew and Gothic benches from which to survey the scene. A fine wrought-iron gate and screen, in lively Arts and Crafts style, leads through to the Azalea Garden where in spring the shrubs glow under a canopy of forest trees. Here, the strong axis of an avenue of conifers rises up a steep hill, with a cross-axis going gently uphill to a beautiful beech. Good trees are all around, including Japanese maples.

MARVELS OF PARK WOOD

The walk across the Park to Park Wood is very beautiful, with excellent parkland trees and wonderful views of the rural landscape. As you enter Park Wood there is little immediate excitement but excitement mounts as you come to a cascade splashing between ferns and rushes into a wooded ravine below. Here, the woodland is more dense, and more exotic, with cypresses, firs, larches, southern beeches (*Nothofagus* species), pines, rowans and spruces. Among them are wonderful rhododendrons. Many of these were among the earliest plantings of their species and have reached great size. Their glowing colours are, to my eye, always best when seen in a densely planted context such as this.

INFORMATION

Location Kington HR5 3EG, Herefordshire; ½m W of Kington off A44
Tel 01544 230160
Email gardens@hergest.co.uk
Website www.hergest.co.uk
English Heritage Register Grade II*
Owner W.L. Banks
Open Mar, Sat and Sun 12–5.30; Apr to early Nov, daily 12–5.30
Area 70 acres/28 hectares

Hidcote Manor Garden

THE MOST INFLUENTIAL ENGLISH GARDEN OF THE 20TH CENTURY – A FEAST OF PLANTS AND DESIGN

Hidcote is the work of an expatriate American, Major Lawrence Johnston, who came here in 1907 and made one of the most influential English gardens of the 20th century. It is, overwhelmingly, a garden of plants, but it is also designed with an artist's eye as can be seen by its changes in mood and the brilliant use of enclosed space.

At the heart of the garden is one of Johnston's earliest schemes: the Red Borders – a pair of deep mixed borders flanking a broad grass path. Rich and brilliant reds of dahlias, fuchsias, lobelias, poppies and roses are soothed down by the sombre foliage of *Cotinus coggygria* 'Royal Purple' and purple-leafed filbert (*Corylus maxima* 'Purpurea'). Rising up in the profusion are gracefully arching fronds of the Chinese grass *Miscanthus sinensis* 'Gracillimus', sharp blades of *Cordyline australis* and the umbrella-like foliage of *Rheum palmatum*. The borders end with a pair of dapper garden pavilions, at a slightly higher level, flanking a wide flight of steps.

Straight ahead is a walk between clipped hornbeam "hedges on stilts", culminating in grand wrought-iron gates and views over the country. This, after the fireworks of the Red Borders, has the effect of a glass of crisp dry white wine.

AN EXHILARATING VIEW

The borders and hornbeam walk, though strikingly different in mood, are similar in scale. But a new and startling view is displayed through the open door of the southern pavilion – on its far side an immensely long grass path, flanked by high walls of hornbeam, swoops down and away towards a distant gate on the garden's boundary. The effect is exhilarating, providing a vast expanse of calm, grand simplicity after the pyrotechnics of the Red Borders.

Closer to the house are several linked compartments – a miniature white garden with yew topiary birds, a box parterre of scillas and fuchsias, the Old Garden with lavish mixed borders, and a circular pool garden of surrealistic proportions, whose pool leaves almost no room for visitors. Quite close to this bustle of gardens is the Theatre Lawn, a huge expanse hedged in yew, with a fine old beech tree raised on a circular platform at its far end. In 2007 the East Court Garden was replanted to its original 1930 scheme.

The box parterre and circular pool garden at Hidcote

INFORMATION

Location Hidcote Bartrim, nr Chipping Camden GL55 6LR, Gloucestershire; 4m NE of Chipping Camden by B4632
Infoline 01684 855370
Tel 01386 438333
Email hidcote@nationaltrust.org.uk
English Heritage Register Grade I
Owner The National Trust
Open late Mar to June and Sept, Sat to Wed 10–6; Jul to Aug, daily except Thur 10–6
Area 10 acres/4 hectares

Kiftsgate Court

AN OUTSTANDING 20TH-CENTURY GARDEN, MAGNIFICENT ROSES AND SPRIGHTLY MODERN IDEAS

The garden was made by Heather Muir from 1920 onwards, with help from her neighbour and friend, Lawrence Johnston of Hidcote (*see page 173*). The gardens have in common a refined taste in plants and the division into compartments of different character. Kiftsgate Court has spectacular open views westwards over the Vale of Evesham towards the Malvern hills. Steep stone steps which lead down the wooded hill are guarded by a grove of Scots pines, sweeps of bergenias and martagon lilies. In the lower garden, with its classical temple and pool, a platform of turf gives giant views to the west of unspoilt landscape.

The formal gardens cluster about the house. Four Squares, divided by paved paths, with a sundial at the centre, has mixed plantings in four beds with a colour scheme of pinks, mauves and purples. A paved sunken garden on the far side of the house has an octagonal pool and fountain at the centre. Terracing surrounds the pool, with plantings of alliums, alstroemerias, eryngiums, geraniums, penstemons and peonies and the occasional clipped dome of box or vertical Irish juniper.

ROSES AND MINIMALISM

Heather Muir loved old shrub roses. In her rose garden a grass path runs between hedges of *Rosa gallica* 'Versicolor', behind which are high ramparts of shrub roses. In one corner a beech tree is shrouded in the famous 'Kiftsgate' rose (*Rosa filipes* 'Kiftsgate'), a staggering sight in June.

Beyond the rose garden a former tennis court, hedged in yew, is now a striking minimalist garden. It was commissioned by Heather Muir's granddaughter and her husband who now look after the garden. A black-

The new pool at Kiftsgate

lined pool is edged in fine Portland stone and has a dazzling fountain by Simon Allison – a row of gently swaying metal stems emerging from the water, each crowned with a bronze cast of the flowerhead of the aroid *Philodendron mamei*, from which water pours back down the stem. Stepping stones of Portland stone, which seem to float on the surface of the inky black water, lead to a rectangular island of turf.

Kiftsgate, now in the third generation of the family that made it, preserves the atmosphere of a family garden – but a family of passionate and discerning gardeners who are not irretrievably buried in the past.

INFORMATION

Location Chipping Camden GL55 6LW, Gloucestershire; 3m NE of Chipping Camden by B4632

Tel and fax 01386 438777

Email info@kiftsgate.aol.com

Website www.kiftsgate.co.uk

Owner Mr and Mrs J.G. Chambers

Open May to July, Sat to Wed 12–6; Apr, Aug and Sept, Sun, Mon and Wed 2–6

Area 6 acres/2.4 hectares

Little Moreton Hall

BRILLIANT LITTLE RECONSTRUCTED PERIOD GARDEN FOR A WONDERFUL TIMBERED TUDOR HOUSE

Cheshire is rich in half-timbered houses and Little Moreton Hall, built in the late 15th and 16th centuries, is one of the best. Famously lopsided, it is described by Pevsner in *The Buildings of England* (in one of his very rare excursions into humour) as "happily reeling, disorderly, but no offence meant – it seems at first unbelievable and then a huge joke". I find the house delightful, with its exquisite timber work (best seen in the wonderful internal roof carpentry), lavishly decorated façades and handsome internal courtyard.

No-one knows in any detail what the gardens of houses of this kind, owned by provincial gentry, were like in the 16th century. The house is moated and on either side of the moat two mounds are conceivably the remains of 16th-century garden mounds. The house was given to the National Trust in 1937 and the garden that exists today, based on what we do know about gardens of the period, was started in 1975.

THE KNOT GARDEN

The design for the knot garden was taken from Leonard Meager's *The English Gardener*, and although this book was published in 1670, the design chosen probably dates from around a hundred years earlier. It lies below the northern façade of the house, not far from one of the mounds, and in the 16th century, mounds of this kind, sometimes topped with a pavilion, were used as viewpoints from which to admire knot gardens such as this. Enclosed in yew hedges, it has an intricate pattern of low hedges of small-leafed box (*Buxus sempervirens* 'Suffruticosa') enclosing compartments of gravel or mown grass, with obelisks of clipped yew rising at the centre of the four chief compartments. On either side is a strip of small box-edged beds with rows of standard gooseberries shaped into lollipops, each underplanted with some herbaceous plant that was used in 16th-century gardens – London pride, strawberries, wall germander, white thrift, woodruff and so on.

Between the garden's hedge and the moat is a narrow walk with plantings of *Darmera peltata*, ferns, geraniums, hostas and periwinkles on the water's edge.

INFORMATION

Location Congleton CW12 4SD, Cheshire; 4m SW of Congleton by A34
Tel 01260 272018
Email littlemoretonhall@nationaltrust.org.uk
Owner The National Trust
Open early to mid Mar, Wed to Sun 11.30–4; mid Mar to Nov, Wed to Sun 11.30–5 (open Bank Hol Mon); phone for other openings
Area 1 acre/0.4 hectare

The knot garden at Little Moreton Hall

Lyme Park

SUPERB ANCIENT PARKLAND AND GRAND 19TH-CENTURY GARDENS FOR A FINE 18TH-CENTURY HOUSE

The Legh family acquired the Lyme Park estate in 1398 and gave it to the National Trust in 1946. The combination of a very grand early 18th-century Palladian house (its south front is fifteen bays wide) with the wild moorland setting on the edge of the Peak District is memorably strange. Visitors are plunged immediately into parkland, with the house on low-lying ground at its centre. The park was established in 1359, originally part of the royal hunting ground of Macclesfield Forest. The herd of red deer which still lives here is thought to be descended from native forest deer; an additional herd of fallow deer was introduced in the 1990s.

LEWIS WYATT

The gardens, on the south side of the house, are chiefly the work of the architect Lewis Wyatt between 1813 and 1820. He laid out a long terrace against the south façade, overlooking a miniature lake. Also seen from this terrace is the Dutch Garden, dating from 1860, a charming piece of kitsch. In the middle is a pool with a water jet surrounded by cherubs. An elaborate pattern of beds edged in tightly clipped ivy or box spreads all around, filled with bedding schemes for spring and summer.

East of the house, Wyatt designed an orangery. Bananas, tender ferns and figs are grown, but most remarkable is an old camellia trained against the wall, said to have been planted when the orangery was completed. In front of the orangery are lawns, Irish yews and two sunken gardens with beds cut out of the turf, planted with seasonal bedding schemes. To one side, behind yew hedges, is an Edwardian rose garden.

On the far side of the lake a wooded valley with a stream is planted with rhododendrons, astilbes, ferns, *Gunnera manicata* and lysichiton. At the head of the ravine is a great stone bridge where you may cross the stream and descend through woods, with wonderful atmospheric views, to emerge on stately lawns east of the house.

The drive across the park, surrounded by great expanses of moorland with the house gradually coming into view, is memorable. The eclectic gardens seem to provide exactly the right note of decorative jollity to make a foil for the sombre grandeur of the house.

The orangery and terraces at Lyme Park

INFORMATION

Location Disley, Stockport SK12 2NX, Cheshire; 6½m SE of Stockport by A6
Infoline 01663 766492
Tel 01663 762023
Email lymepark@ nationaltrust.org.uk
English Heritage Register Grade II*
Owner The National Trust
Open Mar, Sat and Sun 12–3; April to Oct, daily 11–5; Nov to mid Dec, Sat and Sun 12–3
Area (Garden) 17 acres/6.8 hectares; (Park) 1,400 acres/566 hectares

National Botanic Garden of Wales

IN EXQUISITE 18TH-CENTURY PARKLAND, A SUPERB NEW BOTANIC GARDEN WITH A MAGNIFICENT GLASSHOUSE

The Middleton Hall estate dates back to the early 17th century when Henry Middleton built a house here. In the 18th century a landscape park was laid out to the designs of Samuel Lapidge. The setting is exceptionally beautiful – rolling hills, woodland and small fields enclosed by ancient hedgerows. The estate changed hands more than once and the house was gutted by fire in 1931. In the 1990s the importance of the Middleton landscape was recognised and it became the site for the National Botanic Garden which opened in 2000.

The Great Glasshouse

SUSTAINABILITY

In such a setting it would be hard to have no thought for the environment, and from the start the garden embraced notions of sustainability and organic estate management.

The entrance leads past a William Pye water sculpture to the Broad Walk, the chief axis of the garden. This runs gently uphill for much of its way, and has on one side a deep mixed border and on the other collections of rocks showing the geology of Wales, arranged in historical order. At the heart of the garden, and at the head of the Broad Walk, is the beautiful Great Glasshouse, designed by Norman Foster & Partners. This long pod-shaped building seems to emerge from the ground like some organic growth, echoing the gentle curves of the landscape. A ravine 18ft/ 5.5m deep and terraced on each side dominates the interior which was finely landscaped by Kathryn Gustavson of Gustavson Porter. Covering an area of just under 1 acre/0.4 hectare, the glasshouse displays a collection of plants from Mediterranean climates (from several zones) arranged in long curving beds. An interactive exhibition displays the whole life cycle of a plant from germination to reproduction.

All the heating for offices, restaurants and glasshouse is provided by a wood-burning furnace using recycled timber and, increasingly, coppiced timber grown in earth enriched by waste from the waste-recycling unit. Nor is the wider landscape ignored. In the past, a series of lakes formed a vital part of the park but these were drained in the 1930s. One has been reinstated and others will follow, precious for their beauty as well as to provide habitats for many different flora and fauna. There is much to be learned here but also much simply to be enjoyed, not least the exquisite surrounding landscape.

INFORMATION

Location Middleton Hall, Llanarthne SA32 8HG, Carmarthenshire; 8m E of Carmarthen by A48, B4310 and minor roads
Tel 01558 667148/9
Email info@gardenofwales.org.uk
Website www.gardenofwales.org.uk
Cadw/ICOMOS Register Grade II (grounds of Middleton Hall)
Owner The National Botanic Garden of Wales
Open British Summer Time, daily 10–6; British Winter Time, daily 10–4.30 (closed 25 Dec).
Area 586 acres/237 hectares

Ness Botanic Gardens

THE GARDENS OF A GREAT PRIVATE PLANT COLLECTOR
TRANSFORMED INTO AN OUTSTANDING BOTANIC GARDEN

This exceptionally attractive botanic garden started life as the private garden of A.K. Bulley, a prosperous cotton broker who was also a learned plantsman. The site, on the estuary of the river Dee, is windswept, and Bulley, when he came here in 1898, soon saw the need for windbreaks and planted evergreen oaks (*Quercus ilex*) and Scots pines (*Pinus sylvestris*) which today form a distinguished background to the garden. Bulley subscribed to the plant-hunting expeditions of George Forrest and Frank Kingdon Ward and built up a fine collection of their introductions from China, some of which are named after him (such as *Primula bulleyana*). After his death the garden was given to the University of Liverpool in 1948 by Bulley's daughter, who made it a condition of the gift that there should be public access.

The rock garden at Ness

INSTRUCTIVE DISPLAYS

Ness is one of those exceptional botanic gardens that is delightful to all visitors and instructive to gardeners. There are many collections, especially of such smaller ornamental trees as rowans (*Sorbus* species) and birches (*Betula*) that are of particular interest. The large rock garden is a period piece and there is an enchanting collection of plants of an alpine kind, including many of the species Himalayan primulas in which Bulley took a particular interest. Here, too, is an exceptional collection of bulbs, springing into life at the beginning of the year with crocus, irises, scillas and snowdrops in lovely profusion. Later in the season the rock garden displays plants that set the pulse of the true alpinist racing – alpine campanulas, gentians, miniature phlox, roscoeas and saxifrages. A collection of heathers is displayed on a rising slope, and an extended flowering season is ensured by large numbers of all the species and cultivars laid out in huge swathes to form a giant abstract painting – Brobdingnagian carpet-bedding.

The garden also displays a very large collection of shrubs – magnolias, mahonias, pieris, a huge range of rhododendrons (species and cultivars) and witch hazels. Anywhere in the garden you are likely to be stopped in your tracks by the sight of something unfamiliar and beautiful – the vast, languishing flowers of *Magnolia campbellii* subsp. *mollicomata*, thickets of the lovely *Lilium monadelphum* or the ghostly silver stems of *Betula utilis* var. *jacquemontii*.

INFORMATION

Location Ness, Neston, South Wirral L64 4AY, Cheshire; 11m NW of Chester off A540
Tel 01513 530123 **Fax** 01513 531004
English Heritage Register Grade II
Owner The University of Liverpool
Open Feb to Oct, daily 9.30–dusk; Nov to Jan, daily 9.30–4
Area 63 acres/25 hectares

Painswick Rococo Garden

RARE AND CHARMING 18TH-CENTURY LANDSCAPE GARDEN EXQUISITELY RESTORED IN EVERY DETAIL

There is a dreamlike quality about the garden at Painswick – entirely pleasurable but slightly unreal. Until 1984, when restoration started, the garden was invisible, the site choked with saplings and brambles. Its rediscovery is a tribute to the enterprise of its owner and of the garden historians whose advice he sought.

A delightful painting (1748) by Thomas Robins of the garden at Painswick had survived, hanging in Painswick House itself. No-one knew if this painting was pure fantasy, a possible proposal for a garden never made, or a portrait of the garden as it had been. It was known that there had been a garden here, for Bishop Pococke described it in 1757: "The garden is on an hanging ground from the house in a vale, and on rising ground on the other side and at the end; all are cut into walks through woods and adorn'd with water and buildings." In 1982 two architectural historians, Roger White and Tim Mowl, pushed their way through the vegetation and discovered traces of the layout of Robins's garden and even, miraculously, surviving buildings exactly as in the paintings. In 1984 the owner, Lord Dickinson, embarked on a restoration based on Robins's painting, during which many of the painting's details were confirmed by archaeological evidence.

A SECRET WORLD

One of the charms of the garden is that it is quite concealed from the house – a secret world of its own. It is indeed in a wooded valley, with an open area at its lowest point. There are touches of formality – an avenue of beeches, a walk of clipped yew hedges running up to the Gothic Red House (so called because of the colour of its stucco) – but the overall character is that of an intimate landscape garden enlivened by decorative buildings. Paths run through the woods overlooking the garden but there seems to be no deliberately planned walk linking the various beauties of the garden, as there is, for example, at Stourhead (*see page 103*). The elegant Gothic Eagle House, rising on a slope, the ethereal filigree exedra in the valley below, overlooking a formal kitchen garden, and the rusticated temple-like Doric seat are isolated, delightful episodes. They are like props for some light-hearted opera whose plot remains a mystery.

The Red House at Painswick

INFORMATION

Location Painswick, nr Stroud GL6 6TH, Gloucestershire; ½m N of Painswick by B4073
Tel 01452 813204
Email info@rococogarden.org.uk
Website www.rococogarden.org.uk
English Heritage Register Grade II*
Owner Painswick Rococo Garden Trust
Open mid Jan to Oct, daily 11–5
Area 10 acres/4 hectares

Plas Brondanw Gardens

A DELIGHTFUL MASTERPIECE OF FORMAL GARDEN DESIGN IN AN EXCEPTIONAL SNOWDONIA SETTING

Plas Brondanw was bequeathed to the architect Sir Clough Williams-Ellis in 1902 when he was nineteen. The 17th-century house had long been abandoned by his family and he gradually embarked on its restoration and the making of a garden. He was able to finance it only in dribs and drabs: "A cheque for ten pounds would come in and I would order yew hedging to that extent, a cheque for twenty and I would pave a further bit of terrace." The old stone house is attractive, but the greatest beauty of the place is its site in Snowdonia surrounded by some of the grandest scenery in the British Isles. A garden in such a setting needs bold strokes – this is no place for pretty little borders and tinkling effects.

ARCHITECTURE

Williams-Ellis made a formal garden, firmly marked out with yew hedges and enlivened by architectural conceits that link house and garden. A broad, paved terrace runs along the entire west front of the house, and on a grassy slope below, a fine old holm oak rises from a balustraded platform which commands immense westerly views of the mountains, dominated by the peaks of Moel Hebog and Moel Lefn. The

Turquoise and gold at Plas Brondanw

terrace continues far beyond the end of the house to a belvedere with views to the north over pastures and valleys to Mount Snowdon itself.

The other end of the terrace, closer to the house, leads to a series of formal enclosures. In order to focus on the peak of Cnicht to the north-east, Williams-Ellis established a new axis here, not quite parallel to the terrace, whose orientation is determined by the façade of the house. He lined this axis with tall yew hedges which break out from time to time in piers or finials, and in this enclosed area felt free to indulge his relish for ornamental architecture and statuary – an orangery with rounded windows and high-pitched roof, stone piers capped with swagger urns, and a wrought-iron balustrade painted in his distinctive colours of gold and turquoise. A cross-axis has at one end stone niches with statues of Roman emperors and a

figure of Apollo, and at the other end a screen of clipped yew framing a view of Moel Hebog. At the far end of the yew walk steps lead to a circular sitting place with a bench facing back over the garden. From this slightly elevated position there are views through the formal garden and its architectural embellishments, past the holm oak in front of the house, to, in the dead centre of the view, the sharp outline of Cnicht.

RAVINES AND MOUNTAINS

Outside the formal gardens, beyond the entrance drive, Williams-Ellis animated a garden of quite a different kind. Here an avenue of chestnuts leads into pretty woods with ferns and mossy rocks. On the way you pass a pavilion of painted corrugated iron – turquoise and gold on the outside, rich purple inside. You then suddenly come upon an abrupt ravine (the quarry from which the stone for the house was taken) plummeting down to a black pool veiled with trees – dramatic and very sinister. A walk continues uphill through woods which give way to pasture and grazing sheep. From Castel Brondanw, a mock fortress and outlook tower on the hilltop, there is a view over the trees, past the house far below, to a lovely panorama of mountains.

Williams-Ellis had the sensitivity to realise that the surrounding natural landscape was his trump card and he contrived ways of displaying it to its greatest effect, drawing the grand views into the heart of his garden. No garden provides such an eloquent practical example of the virtues of consulting the genius of the place as Plas Brondanw.

INFORMATION

Location Llanfrothen, Penrhyndeudraeth LL48 6SW, Gwynedd; 3m N of Penrhyndeudraeth by A4085
Tel 07880 766741
Website www.portmeirion-village.com
Cadw/ICOMOS Register Grade I
Owner The Trustees of the Second Portmeirion Foundation
Open daily 9–5
Area 4 acres/1.6 hectares

Plas-yn-Rhiw

MAGICAL LITTLE CLIFF-TOP GARDEN CRAMMED WITH PLANTS AND FULL OF CHARACTER IN A BEAUTIFUL SETTING

There are few gardens that have less self-importance and more uncontrived charm than Plas-yn-Rhiw. The estate was given to the National Trust by the Keating sisters whose father had been architect to Boots the chemist in Nottingham. Martin Drury, a former director-general of the National Trust, particularly loved the place, and in a memoir describes going in 1973 to meet Honor and Leonora Keating, who served him "a memorable lunch . . . of sardines on toast and individual pink blancmanges, a speciality of Leonora's".

As children the Keatings had spent summer holidays on the lovely Lleyn peninsula which is how they came to buy Plas yn Rhiw – a medieval stone farmhouse with an 18th-century verandah tacked on. Its position is extraordinary – protected by folds of land and clinging onto a hillside (rhiw is Welsh for slope) with old woods, it faces south with stupendous views of the Atlantic waves crashing against the coast at Hell's Mouth Bay. The little garden lies on the slope in front of the house, with cobbled paths tumbling down, and beds filled with plants and enclosed in blowsy box hedges that

The front garden at Plas-yn-Rhiw

occasionally break out into cheerful fits of topiary. The pillars of a verandah are swathed in roses and fuchsias, and immediately below it a curve of flawless lawn is hedged in small-leafed box. A cottage garden parterre (to admire only, not to be entered) is enclosed in blurred box hedges and filled with agapanthus, azaleas, echinops, lilies, and roses, with occasional weedy but lovely interlopers such as teazels.

TENDER PLANTS

Although blasted by coastal winds, the site is well protected and the climate is mild – bay, fig and myrtle give an unexpectedly Mediterranean air, and such tender plants as the sweet-smelling *Euphorbia mellifera*, *Drimys winteri* and the flamboyant pink climber *Lapageria rosea* and *Rhododendron* 'Fragrantissimum' flourish here. There is nothing obviously calculated about the planting but there are memorable effects – sharply purple aconitums or scarlet *Phygelius capensis* rising from clouds of soft pink *Geranium endressii*, for example.

Plas-yn-Rhiw is a remote place; there is not much to do in these parts except admire the exceptional beauties of the countryside. Fortunately, the remoteness protects the garden, which is so small and of such intimate character that half a small busload of visitors would certainly ruin its atmosphere.

INFORMATION

Location Rhiw, Pwllheli LL53 8AB, Gwynedd; 12m from Pwllheli on S coast road to Aberdaron, signposted from B4413
Tel 01758 780219
Email plasynrhiw@nationaltrust.org.uk
Cadw/ICOMOS Register Grade II
Owner The National Trust
Open Apr, Thurs to Sun 12–5; May to Sep, Thurs to Mon (July and Aug also open Wed) 12–5; Oct, Thurs to Sun 12–4
Area 1 acre/0.4 hectare

Portmeirion

HOLIDAY VILLAGE OF FANTASTICAL ARCHITECTURE WITH A MARVELLOUS OLD WOODLAND GARDEN BY THE SEA

Portmeirion is an extraordinary fantasy village created by the architect Clough Williams-Ellis between 1925 and 1972. Starting with a hotel, he gradually added further buildings, some new and some of them recycling all manner of architectural remnants, many of them of high quality. The architectural style is heterogeneous – Gothico-Moorish, neo-Classical and Baroque (closest to Williams-Ellis's heart, one feels). Here are domes, towers, minarets, gazebos; no peak is without its finial, golden orb or weather vane. Most buildings are faced with stucco washed in different colours – pink, cream, ochre and white. Williams-Ellis's trademark pale turquoise blue is much in evidence on balconies, benches, railings and gates. The planting is heterogeneous, too: Chusan palms, topiary of bay, tall narrow Irish yews resembling Italian cypresses, ramparts of hydrangeas, lapping waves of bedding pelargoniums.

The fantasy roofscape at Portmeirion

EXOTICS IN WOODLAND

Much less known is a great woodland garden which provides a soothing contrast after the slightly overheated hijinks of the village. Clough Williams-Ellis bought the Gwyllt Woodlands in 1941. Here, in natural woodland of birch, sessile oak and rowans, Henry Seymour Westmacott had from the 1850s planted many exotics. Some of the conifers still survive – among them deodars (*Cedrus deodara*), Douglas firs (*Pseudotsuga menziesii*), Monterey pines (*Pinus radiata*) and Wellingtonias. Two later owners, Sir William Fothergill Cooke and Caton Haig, further enriched the planting.

The site is beautiful – south-west of the village on a headland overlooking Tremadog Bay. Although there are a few ornamental buildings – a bridge and pavilion of Chinese character and a domed temple – the character of the woodland is essentially wild (gwyllt is the Welsh for wild). The climate is affected by the North Atlantic Drift so many tender plants flourish: such evergreen rhododendrons as the large-leafed *R. sinograde* and the sweetly scented *R. maddenii* do well, as do many southern hemisphere plants such as the Argentine *Lomatia ferruginea*, the rare New Zealand *Plagianthus regius* and over 40 species of eucalyptus. Because the area is so large and so densely planted, like old native woodland, it is not immediately obvious how astonishingly rich the garden is in exotics. Around 7,000 different species and cultivars are grown here, many rarely seen in gardens.

INFORMATION

Location Penrhyndeudraeth LL48 6ET, Gwynedd; 2m SE of Porthmadog by A487
Tel 01766 770000
Email enquiries@portmeirion-village.com
Website www.portmeirion-village.com
Cadw/ICOMOS Register Grade II*
Owner The Second Portmeirion Foundation
Open daily 9.30–5.30
Area 110 acres/44 hectares

Powis Castle

DRAMATIC 17TH-CENTURY TERRACES WITH EXCELLENT MODERN BORDERS AND A PRETTY WOODLAND GARDEN

Powis Castle dates back to at least the 12th century but the present building is largely 13th century, with much additional 17th-century work. The estate was bought in 1587 by Sir Edward Herbert whose descendant George Herbert (4th Earl of Powis of the second creation) bequeathed the estate to the National Trust in 1952.

The terraces are the dazzling feature at Powis Castle – of a distinctly Italianate character, they are not the only example in Wales of such influence – Llanerch in Clwyd had Italianate terraces of exactly the same date. Facing south-east and descending in stately progression, each 600ft/180m long, the terraces at Powis were built in the 1660s, probably to the designs of the architect William Winde. They bristle with lively architectural ornament: stone balustrades and fine urns, and many charming lead statues from the workshop of John van Nost. Vast and baggy shapes of clipped yew rise above the topmost terrace hard against the ramparts of the castle, and at the extreme eastern end are the extraordinary remains of an ancient yew hedge rising over 50ft/15m high and deformed with age.

All this creates a setting of theatrical splendour which, since the 1980s, has been the scene of much enterprising planting by the National Trust. In the terrace beds colour schemes are skilfully chosen, ranging from the pale and mysterious veils of *Epilobium angustifolium* var. *album* spiked with pale yellow *Kniphofia* 'Sunningdale Yellow' and Miss Willmott's ghost (*Eryngium giganteum*) to the explosive (orange-red *Crocosmia* 'Lucifer', tawny *Alstroemeria aurea* and rich scarlet *Dahlia* 'Bishop of Llandaff'. Bedding is cleverly used: either hardy annuals such as sweet peas (the

Powis Castle terraces from the Wilderness

beautiful blue *Lathyrus* 'Lord Nelson') or tender plants such as the silver-leafed *Plectranthus argentatus* and the intense blue *Salvia cacaliifolia*.

A MINIATURE WOODLAND

On the far side of the Great Lawn at the foot of the terraces is a miniature woodland garden, the 18th-century Wilderness. Here are fine ornamental trees, such as as *Koelreuteria paniculata*, *Quercus* x *lucombeana* 'William Lucombe' and *Davidia involucrata*, underplanted with shrubs (including several species rhododendrons; in spring the delicious scent of *Rhododendron luteum* fills the air). Views back towards the tawny stone castle, rising high above the terraces and framed in leafy branches, are extraordinarily beautiful.

INFORMATION

Location Welshpool SY21 8RF, Powys; 1m S of Welshpool by A483

Infoline 01938 551944 **Tel** 01938 551920

Email powiscastle@nationaltrust.org.uk

Cadw/ICOMOS Register Grade I

Owner The National Trust

Open Apr to Jun, Thurs to Mon 11–6; Jul to Aug, daily except Tue 11–6; also open Mar, Sept and Oct (phone Infoline for times)

Area 24 acres/10 hectares

Rodmarton Manor

OUTSTANDING ARTS AND CRAFTS GARDEN – HEDGES, TOPIARY, STONE PATHS AND BRIMMING BORDERS

Rodmarton is a shrine of Cotswolds Arts and Crafts taste. The house was designed by Ernest Barnsley and built for the Hon. Claud Biddulph between 1909 and 1926. House and garden were conceived as a single entity and the house was built in the vernacular style, down to the last detail.

On the north side, where the entrance is, the house partly embraces a circular drive and lawn. This is enclosed by a curved double lime walk on its far side, giving a very grand and stately effect, as though the circle and lime walk were challenging the higgledy-piggledy nature of the house.

ERNEST BARNSLEY

The gardens, planned at the same time as the house and designed by Ernest Barnsley in collaboration with the head gardener, William Scrubey, are on the south and west side of the house, in a sequence of compartments, walled or hedged. Not linked by any strong axis, they seem to have sprung up about the house like some spontaneous organic growth. On a paved terrace behind the house are yew hedges and topiary birds and other shapes. Two enclosures of yew have tubs of agapanthus or

abutilons, or urns on plinths planted with annuals, and scattered chairs and benches – exterior sitting rooms conveniently close to the house. The Leisure Garden at the west end of the house was originally a rose garden; today it is paved and punctuated with beds containing shrubs – Guelder rose, parsley-leafed elder (*Sambucus nigra* f. *laciniata*), shrub roses and *Viburnum plicatum* 'Mariesii' underplanted with smaller herbaceous plants. Substantial conifers and yews form the background.

The Long Garden, which is quite hidden behind a wall and yew hedges, constitutes the most memorable set piece in the garden. A path of flagstones runs between herbaceous borders filled with asters, astrantia, eryngiums, heleniums, hollyhocks, shrub roses and sedums. Halfway down, the path is interrupted by a circular pool surrounded by monumental shapes of yew, and at the end of the path is a stone summerhouse with a steeply pitched stone tiled roof, the whole veiled by roses.

Houses and gardens such as Rodmarton belong to the end of a tradition. In its heyday Rodmarton had ten gardeners; today it is gardened by the owners and one gardener. However, they are very active and new additions are being made and old features renewed – in 2007 the fine borders were being replanted.

The Long Garden at Rodmarton

INFORMATION

Location Rodmarton, nr Cirencester GL7 6PF, Gloucestershire; in Rodmarton village 6m SW of Cirencester
Tel 01285 841253
Email simon.biddulph1@btinternet.com
Website www.rodmarton-manor.co.uk
English Heritage Register Grade II*
Owner Mr and Mrs Simon Biddulph
Open May to Sept, Wed, Sat and Bank Hol Mon 2–5; groups by appointment
Area 8 acres/3 hectares

St Fagans Castle

CHARMING ANCIENT GARDENS WITH A KNOT GARDEN, FINE BORDERS AND A VICTORIAN ROSE GARDEN

Somewhat confusingly, St Fagans and its fascinating gardens are hidden away in the bosom of the grounds of the Museum of Welsh Life. St Fagans is an Elizabethan house which was built between 1586 and 1596. In 1730 the estate passed by marriage to the 3rd Earl of Plymouth whose family name was Windsor (later Windsor-Clive). In 1946 the 3rd Earl of Plymouth (of the second creation) gave the estate to the nation as a site for the celebration of Welsh craft and culture.

ANCIENT FEATURES

The gabled house, with its symmetrical entrance front, overlooks walled gardens. This pattern of enclosures follows the Tudor arrangement and the garden is a multi-layered accretion of features going back to the middle ages. Although ancient features survive – the fishponds are thought to date from the middle ages – much of the existing garden was made in the 19th century. An avenue of pleached limes runs up to the entrance forecourt, with a circular lead cistern on a plinth at the centre surrounded by clipped box. To one side the house overlooks a box parterre with

Kniphofias and gladioli at St Fagans

shapes of clipped golden yew. The compartments are bedded out with antirrhinums, pelargoniums and silver *Senecio cineraria*, or filled with lavender or santolina. A hornbeam tunnel leads between other formal gardens – a knot garden of box, and a garden of segmental beds surrounding a large clipped yew and circular bench. At the top, a walk has borders of roses or herbaceous perennials, and a fine wrought-iron gate leads to a Victorian rose garden. A section of the herbaceous border is planted with red hot pokers and white, pink, purple and yellow gladioli – as jolly a piece of Victorian exuberance as you could want.

West of the house, overlooking a shallow valley and the ancient fishponds, the Windsor-Clives built a viewing platform and terraces running down to the water, with lead figures on the parapets. Is this an evocation of the much grander terraces at Powis Castle (*see page 184*) – another Clive house? Walks lead past the pools towards a dovecote and a 16th-century thatched barn. The gardens are still being restored and such features as a rock and water garden made by Pulham & Son and a formal Italian garden now add to the Victorian charms of the place.

INFORMATION

Location St Fagans, Cardiff CF5 6XB, Glamorgan; 4m W of Cardiff; Jct 33 of M4 and A4232 (follow signs to Museum of Welsh Life)

Tel 029 2057 3500

Fax 029 2057 3490

Website www.museumwales. ac.uk

Cadw/ICOMOS Register Grade I

Owner National Museums and Galleries of Wales

Open daily 10–5

Area 18 acres/7 hectares

Snowshill Manor

ARCHETYPAL COTSWOLD MANOR HOUSE GARDEN WITH PROFUSE PLANTING, PRETTY ORNAMENTS AND OLD WALLS

Snowshill Manor is the epitome of Cotswold cosiness, built of that distinctive pale stone, roofed in richly textured stone tiles and given a classical façade in the 18th century. Its entrance looks towards the village street but its garden tumbles, in a thoroughly orderly way, down the slopes west of the house.

Charles Paget Wade, an architect with a love of vernacular architecture, bought the estate in 1919, and his friend, the Arts and Crafts architect and garden designer M.H. Baillie Scott, designed a garden for him in 1920, which Wade adapted in his own way. The site, and Wade's inclinations, demanded a terraced garden and enclosed spaces firmly related to the house. Wade linked the spaces with stone steps and marked a descending axis with an avenue of Irish yews. Handsome architectural ornaments – an armillary sphere on a tall stone column, a gilt figure of St George and the dragon and various sundials – decorate the enclosures.

The lower terrace at Snowshill

EPITOME OF THE STYLE

The final ornamental enclosure at the foot of the slope epitomises the style. A Venetian wellhead stands in the middle, shrouded with roses; an astrological sundial is fixed to the wall above a bench in a ferny niche; ivy and roses garland the walls above borders of acanthus, echinops, Japanese anemones, geraniums and phlox; clipped balls of box echo the stone spheres on gate piers; benches and other joinery are painted "Wade blue" (a greeny-blue of Wade's own devising); and inscriptions above gateways take sentimental whimsy to painful extremes ("Hours fly/Flowers die/New Days/New Ways/Pass by/Love stays"). Finally an opening in the wall leads through an arbour of honeysuckle to a kitchen garden with marigolds and nasturtiums among the lettuces and hazels lining the path.

Wade recruited a gardener in his own idiosyncratic way: "I liked his name, which was Hodge, his hat, which was mauve, and having asked him, I was satisfied that he knew nothing about gardening beyond cabbages and cauliflowers." Hodge was, however, a skilful mason and the walls at Snowshill were ultimately more important than the flowers. Although Snowshill is full of flowers in summer, they are not essential; it is the brio of ornamentation, the flow of enclosures, the changing levels, the intimate nooks and crannies and sudden longer vistas that make Snowshill so enchanting.

INFORMATION

Location Snowshill, nr Broadway WR12 7JU, Gloucestershire; in Snowshill village, 3m S of Broadway by A44 and minor road
Infoline 01684 855376 **Tel** 01386 852410
Email snowshillmanor@nationaltrust.org.uk
English Heritage Register Grade II
Owner The National Trust
Open April to Oct, Wed to Sun 11–5.30
Area 2 acres/0.8 hectare

Spetchley Park

DREAMLIKE WALLED GARDENS FILLED WITH NOTABLE PLANTS, AND PARKLAND WITH FINE TREES

Spetchley Park was bought in 1606 by Rowland Berkeley and has remained in the Berkeley family. A new house was built in the early 19th century – a suave late Georgian mansion with walled kitchen gardens to the east of the house. In 1891 Robert Berkeley married Rose Willmott, the sister of the great gardener Ellen Willmott of Warley Place in Essex, who influenced some of the planting here.

In spite of its size Spetchley Park preserves, by some alchemy that I do not quite understand, an attractive secret garden character. Parts are concealed behind enclosures of labyrinthine complexity – few gardens are easier to get lost in – and other parts offer serene open views of parkland, house and water. From the entrance you are instantly plunged into the world of plants. Deep mixed borders run along the outside walls, often with substantial shrubs or trees, such as magnolias, while climbing plants clothe the walls. The western part of the kitchen garden is enclosed in yew hedges, and a new garden was designed by Veronica Cross

A mixed border at Spetchley Park

to celebrate the millennium; its most unusual feature is a pergola covered in *Cercis canadensis* 'Forest Pansy' with blood-red foliage. A Victorian tiered fountain stands at the centre, surrounded by lavish mixed planting.

THE FOUNTAIN GARDEN

The Fountain Garden to the south of the kitchen garden was probably inspired by Ellen Willmott. Overlooked by a pillared summerhouse and a pair of 18th-century lead statues, the area is divided into four, with a fountain pool at the centre and yew hedges enclosing the major divisions. *Campanula lactiflora* flowers throughout the summer in front of the yew hedges along the central path, and narrow openings lead into hedged compartments divided into rows of long narrow beds, like order beds in a botanical garden. In each bed some noble ornamental tree or shrub (a maple, lespedeza, magnolia, sophora or viburnum) is underplanted with treasures – colchicums, epimediums, hepaticas and species peonies.

The house overlooks a lake, with woodland to one side where a statue of the Apollo Belvedere stands out against marvellous drifts of white and purple *Lilium martagon* in summer. From here, with the house seen across fine lawns, framed with splendid trees, the garden at Spetchley has a more patrician air.

INFORMATION

Location nr Worcester WR5 1RS, Worcestershire 3m E of Worcester by A422
Tel 01453 810303
Email hb@spetchleygardens.co.uk
Website www.spetchleygardens.co.uk
English Heritage Register Grade II*
Owner Spetchley Garden Charitable Trust
Open end Mar to Sept, Wed to Sun (open Bank Hol Mon) 11–6; Oct, Sat and Sun 11–4
Area 25 acres/10 hectares

Stone House Cottage

A DAZZLING SEQUENCE OF HEDGED AND RICHLY PLANTED GARDENS OVERLOOKED BY SPLENDID GAZEBOS

I can never make up my mind whether this is a garden with a nursery attached or the other way round. At all events, this very attractive place is a late 20th-century phenomenon – an excellent specialist nursery together with an admirable garden. The arrangement has the great advantage that the visitor can see many of the nursery's plants in action in the garden.

The site is a brick-walled former kitchen garden which James Arbuthnott, a virtuoso bricklayer, has embellished with series of gazebos, towers, minarets and other architectural *jeux d'esprit*. These also serve to display many of the climbing plants which are one of the specialities of the nursery. The shape of the enclosure is irregular, like a cut-off triangle, and strong shapes are needed to impose some feeling of harmony. A brick path runs as straight as an arrow from the entrance in one corner of the walled garden to the house on its far side. The path is edged with tall yew hedges from which openings lead to other parts of the garden.

A gazebo at Stone House Cottage

DEEP BORDERS

An archway of clipped yew serves as the starting point to a pair of mixed borders backed by a hedge of box on one side and of *Prunus cerasifera* 'Nigra' on the other. A broad turf path runs between the borders, and a sundial on a barley sugar twisted column forms an eyecatcher at the end. The borders are about 12ft/3.6m wide, deep enough for large shrub roses like *Rosa moyesii* or substantial herbaceous perennials such as *Thalictrum rochebruneanum* and *Strobilanthes atropurpureus*. The prunus hedge forms an excellent background to the rich colours and noble plants such as *Mosla dianthera* and *Crambe cordifolia* which dominate this side of the borders.

The walls are garlanded with climbers and tender shrubs – many roses, the twining *Araujia sericofera*, cestrums, jasmines and species honeysuckles. The Arbuthnotts live dangerously: many of the plants they grow in this cold and landlocked place should not survive at all, but many of them do, exemplifying one of the great rules of gardening – that you do not really know what will thrive in your garden until you have tried it. Nor can books be much help, for the author has never gardened in your garden.

INFORMATION

Location Stone, nr Kidderminster DY10 4BG, Worcestershire; 2m SE of Kidderminster by A448
Tel 01562 69902
Email louisa@shcn.co.uk
Website www.shcn.co.uk
Owner J.F. and L.N. Arbuthnott
Open mid Mar to mid Sept, Wed to Sat 10–5 (also by appointment)
Area ¾ acre/0.3 hectare

Sudeley Castle

GARDENS OF A HISTORIC ESTATE, BRILLIANTLY REVITALISED: ROSE GARDEN, TERRACED WALK AND KNOT GARDEN

Sudeley Castle rising among woods and fields as you approach is one of the most beautiful country house views you could hope to see. The present house was built largely in the 15th and 16th centuries; Katherine Parr lived here as Sir Thomas Seymour's wife after King Henry VIII's death in 1547. Much of the castle was destroyed in the Civil War and it remained uninhabitable until the Dent (later Dent-Brocklehurst) family came here in 1837.

The gardens are late 20th-century with a strong 19th-century background. The Queen's Garden south-east of the house was laid out as a parterre in 1859 with advice from W.A. Nesfield. At its centre is an octagonal pool edged with a stone balustrade, in the middle of which a triumphant fountain spouts a grand plume of water. Wonderful tunnels of yew planted in the 1850s line the long sides of the garden. The whole slightly sunken area is enclosed in stone balustrades and terrace walks that give wonderful views over serene parkland. The lawns that encircle it are studded with high domes of clipped yew.

In 1988 the divisions of the parterre were replanted by Jane Fearnley-Whittingstall with old shrub roses –
'Albéric Barbier', 'Laure Davoust', 'New Dawn' and 'François Juranville' – grown as standards in the Victorian fashion and underplanted with smaller roses like *R. gallica* 'Versicolor', and with *Allium christophii*, irises, geraniums, lavender and penstemons. It is said there had been an Elizabethan knot garden on this site, and the present arrangement has all the decorative sparkle and stately formality of Tudor times.

THE CHAPEL GARDEN

The 15th-century St Mary's Chapel stands north of the Queen's Garden, and the Chapel Garden alongside it was redesigned by Rosemary Verey in 1979. This secret garden is long and narrow, with raised beds flanking a strip of grass. The borders have mixed plantings of agapanthus, alliums, clematis, *Kolkwitzia amabilis*, penstemons, philadelphus and roses intermingled with tender bedding plants – arctotis, cherry pie (*Heliotropium arborescens*) and *Plectranthus argentatus*.

On the far side of the castle the ruins of a tithe barn, overlooking a lily pond, are festooned with clematis, roses and wisteria, and substantial shrubs such as *Mahonia lomariifolia* and *Hydrangea villosa* stand out against the old stone.

The rose parterre at Sudeley

INFORMATION

Location Winchcombe, nr Cheltenham GL54 5JD, Gloucestershire; 8m NE of Cheltenham by A46

Tel 01242 602308

Email enquiries@sudeley.org.uk

Website www.sudeleycastle.co.uk

English Heritage Register Grade II*

Owner Lady Ashcombe

Open Apr to Oct, daily 10.30–5 (groups by appointment in winter)

Area 10 acres/4 hectares

Tatton Park

GRAND PARKLAND, WALLED GARDENS, FINE GLASSHOUSES, BORDERS, VICTORIAN PARTERRES AND A JAPANESE GARDEN

Tatton Park is one of the most diverse, interesting and attractive gardens in the country. The Egerton family came here in the 16th century and stayed until 1958 when they gave the estate to the National Trust.

The various parts of the garden today are given a link by the Broad Walk – it runs, lined with beautiful old beeches, from a point west of the house to the south-east boundary which is marked by the columned temple-like Choragic Monument of Lysicrates (1820). The Broad Walk leads across sloping land with excellent trees and glimpses of pools gleaming in woodland to the west. In 1910 a Japanese Garden was made, enclosed in a beautifully made bamboo fence. Here is a pool edged with irises, azaleas and Japanese maples, as well as a teahouse and snow lantern.

The Fernery at Tatton

FORMAL GARDENS

The formal gardens cluster about the house, dominated by the Italian Garden, designed in 1859 by Sir Joseph Paxton, and two exceptional glasshouses. The layout Paxton designed is exuberantly Victorian. Here is a pair of flamboyant parterres with compartments outlined in box or thrift (*Armeria maritima*), with topiary shapes of Irish juniper (*Juniperus communis* 'Hibernica') and of cypress (*Chamaecyparis pisifera* 'Squarrosa') and colourful seasonal bedding schemes. Lewis Wyatt's orangery (1818) has a jungle-like interior, packed with tender plants. Close to it is the Fernery designed by Paxton (*c.*1859) which houses tender ferns, including magnificent tree ferns (*Dicksonia antarctica*), in a naturalistic setting of rocky ramparts, with drifts of *Agapanthus africanus* among smaller ferns on either side of a winding walk.

Formal gardens spread out west of the Fernery – mixed borders, an Edwardian sunken Rose Garden and the Tower Garden with remarkable old yew topiary. Lady Charlotte's Bower – a trelliswork alcove seat flanked by filigree wire columns topped with openwork urns and festooned with the roses 'Paul's Lemon Pillar' and 'New Dawn' – was part of a flower garden designed by Lewis Wyatt in 1814. Paths curve across the lawn, planted with a group of *Malus hupehensis*, magnolias, *Acer rubrum* and *Cornus controversa*. In 2002 the walled gardens to the west of the house, formerly leased to the Tatton Garden Society, were taken back and have since been restored to their original role of vegetable garden and orchard. The rare Pinery/Vinery was completed in 2007.

INFORMATION

Location Knutsford WA16 6QN, Cheshire; 3½m N of Knutsford, signposted from the centre of the town
Infoline 01625 534435 **Tel** 01625 534400
Email tatton@cheshire.gov.uk
Website www.tattonpark.org.uk
English Heritage Register Grade II*
Owner The National Trust
Open April to Sept, daily except Mon (open Bank Hol Mon) 10–6; Oct to Feb, daily except Mon 11–4
Area (Garden) 60 acres/24 hectares; (Park) 2,000 acres/810 hectares

Tredegar House

IMPECCABLE EARLY 18TH-CENTURY FORMAL GARDENS RECONSTRUCTED FOR A MAGNIFICENT HOUSE

Tredegar was built between *c.*1664 and 1672 for the Morgan family; Morgans had lived here since the beginning of the 15th century and remained in the house until 1951 when they were forced out by death duties. It was then bought by Newport Borough Council which started to restore it in 1976. The restored gardens are one of the most attractive examples of an early 18th-century formal garden. South-west of the house a large orangery dates from this time, with brick walls enclosing a garden which has been reinstated to its original appearance. The orangery is flanked by a pair of *Magnolia grandiflora* and in the beds on each side are tender shrubs such as figs. Spread out below the orangery is a parterre fashioned of finely mown turf and intricate strips of raked sand, crushed white seashells and glistening fragments of coal. Fruit trees are espaliered against the walls and the beds below contain alternate cones of box and lollipops of privet, with lavender and roses. A second parterre, on the far side of a path, has a more elaborate scheme. A central scalloped lawn is set within corner-pieces of blade-like shapes of white seashells against red-brown sand and stripes of pale raked sand. Lollipops of holly or bay are planted either in terracotta pots or in the ground in the middle of a circle of seashells. In an adjacent walled enclosure a grand cedar of Lebanon rises in a lawn. East of the house is an open lawn with a lovely old sweet chestnut, a sunken rose garden of

The orangery garden at Tredegar

Edwardian flavour, and a lake which was created when Adam Mickle landscaped the grounds in the 1790s.

A POIGNANT SIGHT

From the courtyard near the orangery can be seen a poignant sight. The yard is enclosed in brick walls with beautiful railings and has a magnificent set of wrought-iron gates, made in 1714–18 by William and Simon Edney of Bristol. These gates form a *claire-voie* aligned on the remains of a lime avenue running up a slope into the distance, but the view is now intersected by the M4 and lorries not limes are the most visible feature.

INFORMATION

Location Newport NP10 8YW, South Wales; 2m SW of Newport by A48, Jct 28 of M4
Tel 01633 815880
Email tredegar.house@newport.gov.uk
Cadw/ICOMOS Register Grade II*
Owner Newport City Council
Open Easter to Sept, daily Wed to Sun (open Bank Hol Mon) 11.00–4; Nov to Mar, groups only by appointment
Area 90 acres/36 hectares

Tretower Court and Castle

ENCHANTING MEDIEVAL GARDEN WITH PERIOD PLANTING FOR A BEAUTIFUL 15TH-CENTURY HOUSE

This is an ancient and richly atmospheric place in the splendid setting of the Usk valley. Here are the remains of a Norman castle which Richard Haslam in his Powys volume in *The Buildings of Wales* describes as "among the best Romanesque domestic work left in Wales". The first house here was built in around 1300, to be succeeded by the present Court (now a well-preserved shell) which was built in the late 15th century for Sir Roger Vaughan. Sir Roger was a Yorkist, a courtier to Edward IV, who moved in cultivated circles. Nothing whatever is known of any garden here but Cadw had the idea of creating a garden of the kind that Sir Roger might have known.

AUTHENTIC PLANTING

"Its layout and planting are", as Elizabeth Whittle of Cadw writes, "as authentic as is practically possible for a garden of a wealthy commoner in the mid fifteenth century." She also makes the point that, despite the lack of evidence of a medieval garden here, "It is reasonably certain that such a leading society figure [as Sir Roger] would have had a pleasure garden for peaceful enjoyment in the quieter moments of his turbulent life."

A chequer-board layout of beds, enclosed in wooden fencing, has a stone fountain at its centre. Only plants known to have been in cultivation in the 15th century are grown here – cowslips and primroses, irises, species peonies such as *Paeonia officinalis* and *P. mascula*, sweet rocket, the wild field rose (*Rosa arvensis*) and violets. An oak tunnel is smothered with the sweetly scented white *Rosa* x *alba* 'Alba Semiplena' and grapevines, underplanted with periwinkle, Solomon's seal, violets and wild strawberries. A turf seat overlooks a herber enclosed in a rose-covered trellis, with a raised bed of culinary and medicinal herbs. Old cultivars of fruit trees have splendid names – apples called 'Catshead', 'Court Pendu Plat',and 'Gennet Moyle' and a pear called 'Jargonelle'. A flowery mead is spangled in season with buttercups, celandines, pansies, scarlet pimpernel, selfheal and speedwell. The garden is charming, and the view of it from the first-floor windows of the south side of the Court in high summer, with the scent of roses wafting up, is enchanting.

The medieval garden at Tretower

INFORMATION

Location Tretower, nr Crickhowell NP8 2RF, Powys; in Tretower village, 3m NW of Crickhowell by A479
Tel 01874 730279
Website www.cadw.wales.gov.uk
Owner In the care of Cadw
Open Mar, daily 10–4; Apr to May, daily 10–5; Jun to Sept, daily 10–6; Oct, daily 10–5
Area 1 acre/0.4 hectare

Weston Park

WONDERFUL WOODED GROUNDS, FINE BUILDINGS AND FINELY PLANTED TERRACES FOR A GREAT HOUSE

The estate at Weston Park belonged to the Mytton family in the 15th century and passed by descent, sometimes through the female line, to the Bridgemans (later Earls of Bradford) who gave it to the Weston Park Foundation in 1986. The brick and stone house was rebuilt in 1671 and, with one or two later alterations, remains much as it was at that time.

There was a deer park here by 1346, on the eastern edge of the modern park, to the south-east of the present house; a moated site here may have had a medieval hunting lodge. In 1765 Sir

Henry Bridgeman (later 1st Lord Bradford) commissioned Capability Brown to work on the landscape. This included building a ha-ha to the south of the house to keep out the deer, and laying out new pleasure grounds east of the house in what is now called Temple Wood, with a series of pools of which the largest is Temple Pool. By the end of 1766 Brown had been paid £1,725 (£112,987 in today's money).

In 1770 the architect James Paine designed a beautiful pavilion, the Temple of Diana, on the southern edge of the pleasure grounds. This rare and delightful building serves different purposes, as its eclectic style suggests.

The terraced garden at Weston Park

The south front is an orangery with a magnificent vaulted interior, elaborate plasterwork and tall arched windows from which there are wonderful views over the ha-ha and parkland to a wooded escarpment, with an eyecatcher, Knoll Tower, built in 1883 on land that was formerly part of the Tong Castle estate. The north part of the Temple, in dashing Palladian style with a dome rising over superimposed pediments, had a tea room and a music room and provided "the habitation of the dairy woman".

WOODS AND TERRACES

Close to the Temple is an alignment of marvellous old sweet chestnuts which may have been planted by Brown (it was a favourite tree of his) but elsewhere in the wood are specimens that must predate him. Some of the paths are edged with rhododendrons, and throughout the woods there are splendid beeches and oaks with the occasional exotic such as a fern-leafed beech (*Fagus sylvatica* var. *heterophylla* 'Aspleniifolia'), a swamp cypress (*Taxodium distichum*), southern beeches (*Nothofagus* species) and a weeping spruce (*Picea smithiana*). Across the eastern neck of Temple Pool Paine also designed a noble bridge which originally carried the main drive (the Lichfield Drive) to the house. At each end of the bridge is a grand stone urn on a high plinth, also probably designed by Paine.

Below the southern façade of the house a terraced garden was laid out in the 19th century, partly by Edward Kemp in 1877. On the top terrace a gravel walk overlooks a lawn with shaped beds planted with summer bedding schemes – gold, silver and white for the Jubilee year of 2002. A lower terrace has a long herbaceous border and a sunken rose garden with box-edged compartments, and at the centre an oval stone basket filled with gypsophila and irises. The final terrace, beyond a yew hedge, is a giant semicircle of lawn edged with a

The parterre at Weston Park

balustrade, from which there are views over parkland with a glimmer of water from Park Pool to the south-west. Immediately west of the house an orangery overlooks an elegant parterre designed by Elizabeth Banks, where a scalloped fountain pool stands at the centre of a pattern of curving box-edged beds filled with red begonias, variegated euonymus and purple sage.

PLEASURE GROUNDS

Capability Brown also laid out the pleasure grounds to the west of the house – a long gravel walk, Shrewsbury Walk, has specimen trees in lawns, which include cedars of Lebanon and sweet chestnuts. On the edge of the walk, shaded by old yews, is an 18th-century hermitage, Pendrill's Cave.

Weston Park is not as well known as it deserves. Paine's Temple of Diana, one of the finest of garden buildings, alone makes it worth a visit. In addition, the parkland, Brown's pleasure grounds and the formal gardens by the house are all outstandingly attractive.

INFORMATION

Location Weston-under-Lizard, nr Shifnal TF11 8LE, Shropshire; 8m E of Telford by A5, Jct 3 of M54
Tel 01952 852100
Email enquiries@weston-park.com
Website www.weston-park.com
English Heritage Register Grade II*
Owner The Weston Park Foundation
Open daily, Easter week; mid April to June, Sat and Sun (also Bank Hol Mon); July to Aug, most days (phone/see website for details) 11–6.30
Area 1,000 acres/404 hectares

Westonbirt Arboretum

ONE OF THE WORLD'S GREATEST COLLECTIONS OF TREES AND SHRUBS – A NATIONAL TREASURE

This is one of the best, and most agreeable, places in the British Isles in which to see trees and shrubs, with over 3,000 species and cultivars arranged in an exhilarating landscape. Robert Holford started the collection in 1829. The soil is rich, fertile greensand varying from the fairly acid to the slightly alkaline, providing ideal conditions for a very wide range of plants. The rainfall is high and the terrain is well irrigated with springs.

Holford started with windbreaks and when he embarked on ornamental planting he planted in bold avenues radiating out from his house (now separately owned). He, and later his son, Sir George, planted for the long term, grouping trees with skill and placing enticing specimens to draw the eye. The greatest of their avenues, Holford's Ride, is a wide walk lined with trees and shrubs: on one side a group of soaring slender incense cedars (*Calocedrus decurrens*) is planted alongside a grove of strongly horizontal *Parrotia persica* whose graceful downward-sweeping branches contrast with the vertical emphasis of the cedars; on the other side are spectacular Sierra redwoods (*Sequoiadendron giganteum*), echoing the cedars but far taller.

The Colour Circle at Westonbirt

BRILLIANT COLOURS

The Holfords also paid attention to colour and atmosphere. Their Colour Circle is a glade of trees chosen for the brilliance of their autumn colouring – acers, *Cercidiphyllum japonicum*, *Liquidambar styraciflua*, *Nyssa sylvatica* and *Parrotia persica*. The greatest number of visitors come here in the autumn, and it is indeed a magnificent sight. However, the collection at Westonbirt is so large, the area so vast, that any day of the year will yield pleasures. Most visitors scarcely stray from the "old" arboretum north of the car park, but south and west, across a field, is Silk Wood, a wilder area where you will often find yourself alone surrounded by superb collections of hickories, limes, maples, oaks, pines, poplars and walnuts.

Apart from trees, there is a huge range of shrubs throughout the arboretum – berberis, enkianthus, eucryphias, fothergilla, rhododendrons (many unfamiliar, many gardenworthy, like the charming small Japanese *R. quinquefolium*), stewartias and magnificent witch hazels. In all there are 18,000 specimens of trees and shrubs here – one of the greatest collections in the world and one of the most delightful to explore.

INFORMATION

Location Westonbirt, nr Tetbury GL8 8QS, Gloucestershire; 3m SW of Tetbury by A433
Tel 01666 880220 **Fax** 01666 880559
Website www.forestry.gov.uk/westonbirt
English Heritage Register Grade I
Owner The Forestry Commission
Open April to Oct, daily 9–8 (or dusk if earlier); Nov to Mar, daily 9–5 (or dusk if earlier)
Area 600 acres/243 hectares

Wollerton Old Hall

MASTERLY MODERN GARDENS, FULL OF DISTINGUISHED PLANTING, FOR A HALF-TIMBERED TUDOR HOUSE

The tradition of Hidcote and Sissinghurst – carefully contrived formal spaces abundantly filled with plants – remains a potent garden style. John and Lesley Jenkins started in 1984 to make a garden that would be as intricate and attractive as their half-timbered Tudor house. The entrance to the garden sets the dominant tone – oak balustrades swathed in clematis lead to a stately formal procession of clipped yew obelisks lavishly underplanted in white and blue.

ALICE'S GARDEN

Alice's Garden, named after a cat, is a small enclosure of tender plants with many salvias. To one side the sunken rill garden forms one of the key axes in the garden. Screened behind yew hedges and a latticework fence with turned finials crowning each upright, it has a strong flavour of Arts and Crafts gardens, with a wide upper rill lined with fastigiate hornbeams whose water

The hot garden at Wollerton Old Hall

flows into a narrow rill in a finely laid York stone terrace. From here, an axis at right-angles has a long, deep, richly floriferous herbaceous border, with drifts of plants arranged in Jekyllesque fashion running along the northern boundary wall. At its end a gateway leads into a cool white and yellow garden, beyond which a path is overarched with roses and, leading off it, a "hot" garden smoulders with crocosmias, purple-leafed ligularias, *Lobelia cardinalis* and salvias.

Interconnections are subtly contrived, new views are opened at every turn, and everywhere there are planting schemes to be admired. Some of these are very simple – waves of purple-leafed viola with *Muscari latifolia* flow about the stems of a lime alley. In the Croft Garden, an informal area beyond the easternmost garden wall, is a remarkable collection of trees and shrubs with a winding walk.

Wollerton Old Hall shows the continuing potency of the traditions from which it freely draws. It is brilliantly gardened and the Jenkinses are constantly experimenting with new plants and new arrangements. In addition to the pleasures of the garden there is an admirable nursery here, from which you can buy the kinds of plants you will have seen in the garden. The tea room is marvellous, too.

INFORMATION

Location Wollerton, Market Drayton TF9 3NA, Shropshire; 14m NE of Shrewsbury, brown-signed off A53 between Hodnet and Market Drayton
Tel 01630 685760
Email info@wollertonoldhallgarden.com
Website www.wollertonoldhallgarden.co.uk
Owner John and Lesley Jenkins
Open Good Friday to end Sept, Fri, Sun and Bank Hol Mon 12–5
Area 4 acres/1.6 hectares

HEART of ENGLAND

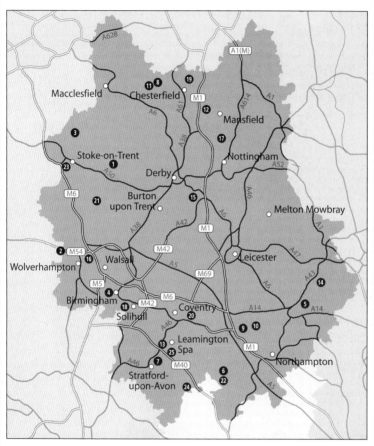

GARDENS TO VISIT

1. Alton Towers
2. David Austin Roses
3. Biddulph Grange Garden
4. Birmingham Botanic Gardens
5. Boughton House Park
6. Cannons Ashby House
7. Charlecote Park
8. Chatsworth
9. Coton Manor Gardens
10. Cottesbrooke Hall
11. Haddon Hall
12. Hardwick Hall
13. Lord Leycester Hospital
14. Lyveden New Bield
15. Melbourne Hall
16. Moseley Old Hall
17. Newstead Abbey
18. Packwood House
19. Renishaw Hall
20. Ryton Organic Gardens
21. Shugborough
22. Sulgrave Manor
23. Trentham Gardens
24. Upton House
25. Warwick Castle

Alton Towers

BEAUTIFUL GARDEN BUILDINGS REMAIN IN THIS EARLY 19TH-CENTURY GARDEN WITH ITS ROCKY WOODLAND DELL

Alton Towers was the creation of the 15th Earl of Shrewsbury who from 1837 onwards built a giant neo-medieval castle, largely to the designs of A.W.N. Pugin, and laid out a prodigious jumble sale of a garden in a rocky wooded dell north of the house. Pugin's house, originally called Alton Abbey, was an extraordinary extravaganza. Even as a gutted shell today it is an awesome sight.

The gardens were laid out chiefly in 1814–27. Lord Shrewsbury formed the habit of asking for advice from many of the leading garden designers of the day without commissioning them to do the work. Among them was J.C. Loudon who visited the new garden in 1831 and recorded, sourly, "Though he consulted almost every artist, ourselves among the rest, he seems only to have done so for the purpose of avoiding whatever an artist might recommend."

Alton Towers owes its survival today to the fact that it has become a family fun park. (The house's pinnacled and gabled silhouette, more like a medieval village than a house, does have a definite touch of Disneyland to it.) Garden visitors of a fastidious disposition may find this regrettable but the Tussauds Group has done a fine job of restoring and maintaining those parts of the garden that survived.

BEAUTIFUL BUILDINGS

The dell garden, shrouded in conifers and Japanese maples, is relatively untouched by fun park amusements and preserves much of its authentic early 19th-century character. The superb conservatory (*c.*1820) by Robert Abraham, running along a terrace on its upper slopes, is crowned by a series of ravishing domes with a delicate tracery of cast-iron glazing bars. The vast central dome is surmounted by a gilt Earl's coronet, and three slightly smaller ones on each side by pineapple finials. Abraham also designed a superlative Chinese pagoda (1827) on the lake at the foot of the dell. Its three storeys of fretwork tracery with pointed Gothic entrances, painted white and scarlet, are each topped with a sweeping roof edged with dangling bells, and the whole is finished with a soaring golden finial. It is extraordinary that a garden inspired by vulgar excess should have ended up with these beautiful buildings.

The dell garden at Alton Towers

INFORMATION

Location Alton ST10 4DB, Staffordshire; 18m E of Stoke-on-Trent

Tel 08705 204060

Website www.altontowers.com

English Heritage Register Grade I

Owner The Tussauds Group

Open mid Mar to early Nov, daily 9.30–6 (closing times vary, check by phone/website)

Area 500 acres/202 hectares

David Austin Roses

IN A CHARMING SETTING, LEARN HOW SOME 700 SPECIES AND
VARIETIES OF ROSES PERFORM THROUGHOUT THE YEAR

David Austin is the rose breeder who created "English Roses", which aim to combine the beautiful flower shapes, and scent, of old roses with the perpetual flowering of modern varieties. He is also a rose nurseryman, stocking an immense range of the best modern roses, old shrub and climbing roses, and species. I include his nursery in this book because of the display gardens. The Plant Centre here has developed over the years and today, in addition to the immense range of roses (both in containers and bare-rooted), sells a fine range of herbaceous perennials, hedge plants, trees and shrubs. It aims to cover every type of plant you could want to create the complete garden.

David Austin's rose 'Gertrude Jekyll'

INSTRUCTIVE DISPLAYS

The gardens lay no claim to the heights of garden art but, with their fine sandy or herringbone brick paths, box-edged beds, lawns, arbours and pergolas, they display the roses to great and extremely pleasurable effect. Here are over 700 species and varieties which demonstrate vividly why roses, despite their various difficulties, have continued to be such treasured plants of British gardens. At the end of June they make a spectacular and instructive sight; few flowering displays combine such unfettered exuberance with such irresistible beauty of flower and scent.

In other seasons the pleasures to be had here are different. You can study the performance of the English Roses and of those old varieties, either early flowering or remontant, which show their charms at other times of the year. For, where most rose specialists tend to concentrate on cultivars of certain periods, David Austin casts his net wider and shows us the great range of this most seductive of genera. The species roses, for example – unequalled in beauty and completely free from the diseases that plague so many of the cultivars – are hard to find. Here, they show their beauty of habit, handsome thorns, and in late summer and autumn the brilliant colouring of often strikingly shaped hips. Their flowering, fleeting though it is, can take the breath away.

The purpose of coming here is not to study design but to learn about roses, and it is one of the most attractive places in which to do it. The other plants, both in the plant centre and the display gardens, give good ideas for association planting.

INFORMATION

Location Bowling Green Lane, Albrighton, Wolverhampton WV7 3HB, West Midlands; 7m NW of Wolverhampton by A41 and A464, Jct 3 of M54
Tel 01902 376300 **Fax** 01902 372142
Email retail@davidaustinroses.com
Website www.davidaustinroses.com
Open daily, Mon to Fri 9–5, Sat, Sun and Bank Hol Mon 10–6 (or dusk in winter)
Area 2 acres/0.8 hectare

Biddulph Grange Garden

A GARDEN RESTORED TO DAZZLING EFFECT, EVOKING THE PASSIONS AND IMAGINATION OF ITS VICTORIAN CREATORS

At Biddulph various interests – plantsmanship, landscaping and a taste for the exotic – have been drawn together to create a dream-like garden of startling originality. It is the creation of James Bateman and his friend Edward Cooke from 1842 onwards, at a time when there was intense interest in garden design of other periods and other cultures, and new plant introductions were flooding into the country in great quantities. Bateman was an orchid lover and his wife, Maria, an assiduous plantswoman; Cooke was

The Chinese pavilion at Biddulph

an artist and garden designer who had married Jane, the daughter of George Loddiges of Hackney, the greatest nurseryman of the day. The garden they made is, to put it mildly, eclectic. Bateman spent a great deal of money on the garden, and the estate was burdened with a mortgage of £35,000 (about £1.5m today) when he passed it on to his son, who was forced to sell in 1871. The sale catalogue described the garden as containing "The Pinetum", "The Glen", "The Stumpery", "The Parterres", "The Arboretum", "The Rose Garden", "The Dahlia Walk" and so on, and on. After the sale, the house

became a hospital and the grounds were cared for but increasingly vandalised. In 1988, after a campaign of fund raising, the estate was taken over by the National Trust which has restored the garden to dazzling effect. What may be seen today is not merely a fascinating glimpse into the byways of Victorian garden taste but also an exceptionally agreeable place to visit.

More remarkable even than the varied contents of the garden at Biddulph is the ingenious way the different parts were linked together, with formality and picturesque informality intermingled with a deft hand. South of the house the land slopes down sharply and the layout of the garden makes inventive use of the changing levels and character. In front of the house the Italian Garden, with terraces and a stepped walk, leads down to a curved

lake whose banks are densely planted with rhododendrons – an adroit passage from crisp formality to naturalism. The decorative building which forms an eyecatcher at the end of the Dahlia Walk also leads sideways to the Stumpery and China.

A TASTE FOR THE EXOTIC

East of the house a long, dead-straight axis passes through formal enclosures close to the house, plunges through woodland and follows a long avenue of deodars (*Cedrus deodara*) and Wellingtonias, culminating in a giant stone vase enclosed in hedges of yew. Winding walks lead through to the most exotic parts of the garden. In China a dark tunnel, lit by flickering candles, suddenly opens out into the gold, scarlet and white of a Chinese pavilion overlooking a pool fringed with Japanese maples and overarched by a scarlet bridge. An alternative route to China follows a shaded path through the Stumpery, a phantasmagorical collection of tree stumps. Egypt is a temple of clipped yew guarded by sphinxes, while immediately behind, forming an extraordinarily contrasting rear entrance, is the Cheshire Cottage, half-timbered and picturesque, with the date 1856 picked out on its façade.

Everywhere there are fine plants to admire, some of which (for example in the Pinetum) survive from the original plantings, and the National Trust has scrupulously replaced countless plants of the period. Few gardens so vividly evoke the passions and excitement of Victorian gardening in its heyday.

INFORMATION

Location Biddulph, nr Stoke-on-Trent ST8 7SD, Staffordshire; 5m SE of Congleton by A527
Tel 01782 517999
Email biddulphgrange@nationaltrust.org.uk
English Heritage Register Grade I
Owner The National Trust
Open mid Mar to Oct, Wed to Sun 11.30–6 (open Bank Hol Mon, closed Good Fri); Nov to mid Dec, Sat and Sun 11–3
Area 15 acres/6 hectares

Birmingham Botanical Gardens

MODEL GARDENS, GLASSHOUSES, A FINE ROCKERY AND A BANDSTAND IN A POPULAR PUBLIC GARDEN

The Birmingham Botanical and Horticultural Society was founded in 1829 and in 1931 leased land on the edge of the city to lay out its gardens. John Claudius Loudon designed a layout of curving paths, which took their cue from the design for an extraordinary circular glasshouse. This visionary masterpiece of *avant-garde* architecture was never built, and more conventional glasshouses were put up. However, some of Loudon's layout was adopted and its pattern of paths is still clearly visible. Alas, his long straight walk to the glasshouse, deprived of its mesmerising eyecatcher, was never made.

The bandstand at Birmingham Botanic Gardens

From the start the gardens embarked on an ambitious programme of plant acquisition, with 9,000 species of plants listed in the catalogue by 1834. At first a private society, the gardens were open initially only to subscribers; from 1844 they were opened to the paying public and assumed the character of a public park – with a bandstand added in 1873.

PLANNED TO PLEASE

Today Birmingham Botanical Gardens are among the most attractive gardens of their kind in the country. The glasshouses contain tropical plants, tender palms, succulents and citrus plants, and alongside is the National Bonsai Collection. Parts of the gardens have been designed to be of specific interest to gardeners and to those with an interest in particular species. A rock garden, built by James Backhouse & Son of York in 1895, sparkles with alpine plants against a background of magnolias, Japanese maples, rhododendrons and such unusual conifers as the beautiful Chinese lace-bark pine (*Pinus bungeana*). Another garden is devoted to the discoveries of one of the greatest of plant-hunters,

E.H. Wilson, who worked here at the age of sixteen. It contains such plants as *Berberis wilsoniae, Hamamelis mollis* and *Lilium regale*. A splendid domed aviary, opened in 1996, overlooks a formal rose garden with statues, topiary and urns. A series of "domestic gardens" show models of different styles – a children's garden, a plantsman's garden, a low-labour garden and so on. Other gardens are devoted to such groups of plants as conifers, herbs, rhododendrons and roses.

There is an attractive atmosphere here of bustling horticultural activity, and a strong flavour of Victorian exuberance may still be seen in the swashbuckling tender bedding schemes.

INFORMATION

Location Westbourne Road, Edgbaston B15 3TR, Birmingham; 2m SW of the city centre
Tel 0121 454 1860
Email admin@birminghambotanicalgardens. org.uk
Website www.birminghambotanicalgardens. org.uk
English Heritage Register Grade II*
Owner Birmingham Botanical and Horticultural Society Ltd
Open daily 9–dusk (opens 10 on Sun; closed 25 Dec)
Area 15 acres/6 hectares

Boughton House Park

A GREAT 17TH- AND 18TH-CENTURY FORMAL GARDEN, BEAUTIFULLY DISHEVELLED, BUT UNDERGOING RESTORATION

The estate goes back at least to the 15th century when a park of 100 acres/40 hectares was enclosed. In 1528 it was bought by Edward Montagu, whose descendants have lived here ever since. The present house was started in the 1680s for Ralph Montagu who had been Ambassador to Louis XIV (he became a duke in 1705). He acquired a taste for French architecture and Boughton House has a decidedly Gallic air – Pevsner describes its north façade as "perhaps the most French-looking C17 building in England".

A formal garden was made to suit the house, to the designs of Leonard van Meulen. John Morton's *The Natural History of Northamptonshire* (1712) gives a vivid picture of it: "Below the Western front of the house . . . three more remarkable Parterres: the Parterre of Statues, the Parterre of Basins, and the Water Parterre . . . On the North side of the Parterre Garden is a small wilderness which is called the 'Wilderness of Apartments', an exceedingly delightful place and nobly adorned with basins, *jets d'eaux*, statues, with platanus, lime trees, beech, bays, etc., all in exquisite form." These gardens, strongly reflecting the kind of garden the Duke must have seen in France, were completed by 1706. Only traces survive but enough to allow the garden archaeologist Dr Christopher Taylor to describe the remains as "the best of their date in England".

MILES OF AVENUES

What does, spectacularly, survive is the noble pattern of avenues laid out by the 2nd Duke in the 1720s and 30s. The remains of what he planted, alignments of common lime (*Tilia x europaea*) to the west and south-west of the house, superbly animate the flat landscape. Here too are the great pools made in the 17th century by diverting the river Ise. By the time he died, the 2nd Duke had planted 21 miles/36km of avenues spread over eight parishes. After his death the estate passed to the Dukes of Buccleuch who had other estates to occupy their attentions.

By 2007 the landscape at Boughton was the subject of an immense programme of restoration, with waterways being cleared and avenues replanted. The work in progress is, in itself, a most interesting feature for visitors. It is, in every way, a thoroughly worthwhile project.

The west front at Boughton House

INFORMATION

Location nr Kettering NN14 1BJ, Northamptonshire; 3m NE of Kettering on A43
Tel 01536 515731
Email llt@boughtonhouse.org.uk
Website www.boughtonhouse.org.uk
English Heritage Register Grade I
Owner The Duke of Buccleuch and Queensberry
Open May to July, daily except Sat 12–5; Aug, daily 12–5
Area 350 acres/141 hectares

Canons Ashby House

FORMAL GARDENS OF GENTLEMANLY DECORATIVENESS MADE FOR THE 18TH-CENTURY DRYDEN FAMILY

The Dryden family lived at Canons Ashby from the 16th century until the estate was given to the National Trust in 1981. The wonderful house, romantic but mysterious, was built in the mid 16th century, of brick with stone dressings, to which Edward Dryden added a fine new south façade of stone in the early 18th century. The garden was refashioned at this time in a style of gentlemanly formality which it preserves today. South of the house the land was shaped into a series of grassy terraces, with a central path descending to a splendid pair of gates with carved lions on the piers. When Harry Inigo Triggs drew a plan of the garden in 1901 for his book *Formal Gardens in England and Scotland* the lower terraces were planted with fruit gardens on either side of the path and four cedars of Lebanon towered above the steps leading from the first to the second terrace. Beyond the lion gates there had been an avenue of elms which extended into the countryside.

The Green Court at Canons Ashby

FAITHFUL REPLANTING

The National Trust has replanted all of this, using limes for the avenue. The top terrace is marked by four youthful cedars of Lebanon and the terraces are ornamented with elaborate shapes of yew topiary, mounds of clipped Portugal laurel and apple trees in long grass; at the foot, the path passes through a wildflower meadow and is edged with different varieties of *Rosa x alba*.

The Green Court, a formal walled garden, lies to the west of the house, with rows of topiary shapes of yew and a lead figure of a piping shepherd and his dog. Old varieties of pear trees are espaliered against the walls and through a gate supported on stone piers are views of open fields. The gate is flanked by clumps of phillyrea and in each corner of the court are clipped bushes of bay. The garden at Canons Ashby is a perfect example of atmosphere that has been achieved by small means. Formality rules and yet the garden does not turn its back on the rural landscape. The garden is a seamless extension of the house and a harmonious link to its larger setting. In 2007 Home Paddock was being made into a fashionable wildflower meadow.

INFORMATION

Location Canons Ashby, Daventry NN11 3SD, Northamptonshire; 11m NE of Daventry by A361, A422 and B4525
Infoline 01327 860044 **Tel** 01327 861900
Email canonsashby@nationaltrust.org.uk
English Heritage Register Grade II*
Owner The National Trust
Open mid Mar to Oct, Sat to Wed 11–5.30 (closes 4.30 in Oct); Nov to mid Dec, Sat and Sun 11–4.
Area 3 acres/1.2 hectares

Charlecote Park

THE ELIZABETHAN ESTATE OF THE ANCIENT LUCY FAMILY,
WITH BEAUTIFUL PARKLAND AND FLOWERY INTERLUDES

The most beautiful thing about Charlecote is the setting of the house in its parkland. The site is flat but it has the priceless advantage of the river Avon (and its tributary the Hele) curving magnificently across the land close by. The house, built for the Lucy family in the mid 16th century, was rebuilt in the mid 19th century. Only parts of the Tudor design survive – in particular a charming gatehouse with tall turrets and a fretwork parapet – yet, despite the disastrous Victorianising of the house, its silhouette preserves an Elizabethan character.

CHANGING LANDSCAPE

In 1760 Capability Brown was called in to widen the Avon and to remodel the river banks to impart a "natural and easy level", and he created a cascade where the Hele flows in. He also planted trees, among them Scots pines and cedars of Lebanon near the house. In the 19th century new formal gardens were made – a pair of elaborate parterres in the entrance forecourt and another on the terrace overlooking the Avon. These were suppressed in the 1950s shortly after the National Trust acquired the estate in 1946.

Today, mixed borders enliven the entrance forecourt; there is a collection of plants mentioned by Shakespeare, who is supposed to have poached on Lucy land as a boy; and trees have been replanted. For the millennium, Victorian parterres were restored, overlooking the Avon. The Victorian scheme, with dwarf box-edged patterns of beds and jolly bedding schemes, certainly suits the Victorian architectural setting with its ponderous balustrade, but it does not make a happy prelude to the idyllic views, across the river, of parkland and avenues. For a more magical experience, follow the wooded walk past the orangery until you come, at the edge of the pleasure grounds, to a curved viewing platform, unadorned except for turf and handsome old mulberries. Here you can enjoy views over the park to the distant church of St Nicholas.

Seen from afar, the house and its setting are still very beautiful; the best way of enjoying this and the ravishing views is to follow the mile-long circuit walk girdling the estate and along the banks of the river.

INFORMATION

Location Wellesbourne, Warwick CV35 9ER, Warwickshire; 5m E of Stratford-upon-Avon by B4086
Tel 01789 470277
Email charlecotepark@nationaltrust.org.uk
English Heritage Register Grade II*
Owner The National Trust
Open late Apr to early Nov, Fri to Tues 11–6
Area 30 acres/12 hectares

Parkland at Charlecote

Chatsworth

SPECTACULAR GARDEN, ON A VAST SCALE, WITH GARDEN STYLES FROM THE 17TH CENTURY TO THE 21ST CENTURY

The dowager Duchess of Devonshire wrote, "Our garden is an inhibiting place to go out in with a trowel. It covers 105 acres . . ." To the visitor, with no need to do any trowel-work, the garden is positively alluring. There are two ways of arranging the visit, each with much to recommend it. The first is simply to wander about, from splendour to splendour, jaw dropping from time to time in amazement or delight. The second is to learn a little about the history of the place, for the garden is a splendid repository of garden styles, layer upon layer, going back to the 17th century.

LAYERS OF GARDEN STYLES

In the early 18th century gardens were designed here by George London and Henry Wise, with splendid waterworks designed by the Frenchman Grillet. In the 1760s the park was landscaped by Capability Brown, and a handsome bridge taking the drive over the river Derwent was designed by James Paine in about 1760.

During the 19th century the gardens were in the charge of one of the great horticultural figures of the time, Sir Joseph Paxton. Under Paxton,

Spring at Chatsworth

glasshouses were built – among them the spectacular Great Conservatory (1836–41), demolished in 1920. The only glasshouses to survive from Paxton's time are the Vinery (near the potting shed) and, most spectacularly, the Conservative Wall running along the north boundary of the garden and facing southwards over it.

Although some historic detail has been lost, much of the essential old pattern of the garden survives, forming a strong framework which holds together later additions. Grillet's spectacular formal cascade tumbles down the slope to the east of the house. The 1st Duke's conservatory of 1698 overlooks a rose garden, enlivened with rows of yews. Concealed in the woods north-east of the house is a superb new yew maze with a vertiginous flight of steps leading to Paxton's pinetum.

The garden is rich in all kinds of pleasures but for some the most beautiful view is that from high up the slopes rising eastwards from the house. From Thomas Archer's cascade house you may look past the garden and the great house, with James Paine's bridge spanning the river, to where the land rises – a lovely rural landscape with cattle or sheep grazing in the pastures.

INFORMATION

Location Bakewell DE45 1PP, Derbyshire; 4m E of Bakewell by A6 or A619 and minor roads

Tel 01246 565300

Email visit@chatsworth.org

Website www.chatsworth.org

English Heritage Register Grade I

Owner Trustees of the Chatsworth Settlement

Open mid Mar to 23 Dec, daily 11–4.30 (park open daily throughout the year)

Area 105 acres/42 hectares

Coton Manor Gardens

FLOWERY TERRACES, A ROSE GARDEN, A WOODLAND GARDEN,
A WILDFLOWER MEADOW AND A BLUEBELL WOOD

The garden at Coton has evolved gradually, south and south-west of the 17th-century stone house. Since 1990, when Ian and Susie Pasley-Tyler inherited the estate, the quality of the garden has leapt ahead. There is no strong overall plan to the garden; the foot, or eye, is led gently from enclosure to enclosure.

Terraced gardens at Coton Manor

Terraces by the house are rich in ornamental plants and walls festooned with climbing plants – clematis, *Fremontodendron californicum*, scented *Trachelospermum jasminoides*, wisteria. Yew and holly hedges protect a circular rose garden divided into four by brick paths. Roses dominate but at the much drier centre are agapanthus, eryngiums, lavender, rosemary and salvias. On the far side of the holly hedge double herbaceous borders are raised above the edge of a large pool with black swans.

A WOODLAND GLADE

A passage leads from the terrace to a woodland glade where cyclamen, epimediums, erythroniums, ferns, hellebores and trilliums flourish in the shade of a tulip tree (*Liriodendron tulipifera*) and a copper beech. A stream descends in gently splashing falls between ferns, hostas, ligularia, pulmonaria and rodgersias, and at the bottom an orchard of apples and pears is decorated with a central stepped rill. A gap in a hedge leads to an open area of grass with specimen trees – *Arbutus unedo*, *Cercidiphyllum japonicum*, a fern-leafed beech (*Fagus sylvatica* var. *heterophylla* 'Aspleniifolia') and mulberries (both black and white). Beyond a meadow of wildflowers and many different grasses is a 5-acre/2-hectare beech wood which in April has an astonishing display of bluebells.

Retracing your steps and taking the most direct route back up the slope towards the house, you pass between borders (including a Mediterranean border taking advantage of a southern exposure and sharp drainage) and a formal herb garden with box-edged beds, espaliered apples and a tunnel of clematis and roses. At the top of the slope a yard is shaded by an American black walnut (*Juglans nigra*).

The varied sites at Coton enable a very wide range of plants to be grown, but the garden's pleasures are displayed with no sense of rush, and contrasting themes – busy borders, open lawns, shady water, woodland glades, enclosing hedges and views over meadows – unfold gently as you walk about it.

INFORMATION

Location nr Guilsborough NN6 8RQ, Northamptonshire; 10m NW of Northampton by A5199 and A428
Tel 01604 740219
Email pasleytyler@cotonmanor.co.uk
Website www.cotonmanor.co.uk
Owner Mr and Mrs Ian Pasley-Tyler
Open Apr to Sept, Tue to Sat and Bank Hol weekends (also Sun, Apr to May) 12–5.30
Area 10 acres/4 hectares

Cottesbrooke Hall

AN ELEGANT 18TH-CENTURY HOUSE COMPLEMENTED BY DECORATIVE 20TH-CENTURY GARDENS

The beautiful house of brick and Ketton stone was built from 1702. It is one of the candidates for the inspiration of Jane Austen's *Mansfield Park* and the house certainly possesses the kind of lively elegance that she might have enjoyed.

The gardens, almost entirely of the 20th century, are of an elegance to match the house. An open lawn with the occasional beech or English oak is the simple setting for the

The Jellicoe garden at Cottesbrooke Hall

entrance front. Two ancient cedars of Lebanon mark the start of a broad paved path leading between deep borders, recently redesigned by James Alexander-Sinclair, planted with grasses, nepetas, salvias, thalictrums and verbascums. Through an opening in a wall is a noble white marble urn and, to the south of it, a sombre yew walk enlivened by statues by Peter Scheemakers. The pool garden is the work of the Arts and Crafts architect Robert Weir Schultz and contains an elegant little pavilion designed by Dame Sylvia Crowe. The entrance to the Pool Garden, also designed by Schulz, is marked by piers crowned with lead eagles garlanded with white wisteria and flanked with shrubs of *Phlomis russeliana* with roses decorating the walls.

DECORATIVE FORMALITY

The original entrance to the house was on the south-east side. If there was once a great formal garden at Cottesbrooke, made when the house was built, this, with its forecourt railings and grand gates, would be the place for it. As it is, in 1937 Sir Geoffrey Jellicoe laid out a pretty arrangement of tall cones of

clipped yew, fine statues of Diana, Eros, Hermes and Venus and beds of creamy white 'Pascali' roses enclosed in L-shapes of yew. With its lead statues and tubs of brilliant blue agapanthus, all this has an appropriate character of decorative formality in keeping with the façade of the house.

Cottesbrooke Hall stands surrounded by parkland. In the early 18th century there were avenues radiating from the north and south sides of the house. Later in the century the landscape was made less formal. On the south-east side of the house the view makes much of the distant prospect of the spire of All Saints, Brixworth, 3 miles/5km away and exactly centred on the old entrance to the house.

INFORMATION

Location nr Northampton NN6 8PF, Northamptonshire; 9m NW of Northampton by A5199
Tel 01604 505808
Email enquiries@cottesbrooke.co.uk
Website www.cottesbrookehall.co.uk
English Heritage Register Grade II
Owner Mr and Mrs A.R. Macdonald-Buchanan
Open May and Jun, Wed and Thur 2–5.30; Jul to Sept, Thur 2–5.30 (open Bank Hol Mon 2–5.30)
Area 12 acres/5 hectares

Haddon Hall

AN IRRESISTIBLY ROMANTIC AND ANCIENT HOUSE, AN EXQUISITE SETTING AND CHARMING TERRACED GARDENS

The house was built from the 12th century onwards, with scarcely anything added after the 17th century. It was built for the Vernons and passed to the Manners family (later Dukes of Rutland) after the romantic elopement of Dorothy Vernon with Sir John Manners in 1563. The approach to Haddon Hall is marvellous, with the grey limestone house rising on wooded heights above the winding river Wye. Despite its castellations it is not in the least aggressive, but has a cosily domestic air. Above you the castle seems to grow out of the ground rather than to be superimposed on it.

ROSE-SHROUDED WALLS

The gardens lie below the south and eastern ramparts, which face the river. In summer you will find the walls shrouded in roses, while borders beneath the windows are filled with delphiniums – purple, pink, white and blue – above drifts of white *Viola cornuta*. Later in the season, Japanese anemones and salvias flourish in these borders, with yellow tropaeolum (*T. peregrinum*) and nasturtiums scrambling through the clematis and roses on the walls. In the Fountain Garden a square pool is ornamented with tufts of lavender and a lawn is punctuated with flowering cherries and crab-apples; bushes of rosemary mark the ends of beds of roses planted in sometimes rather garish blocks of a single colour – yellow, pink or scarlet. A noble 17th-century flight of stone steps, flanked with swathes of richly scented 'Albertine' rose, leads to a terrace with cones of yew, mixed borders and borders of roses. Above it, not accessible to visitors, is Dorothy Vernon's walk, a kind of spacious gallery overlooking the gardens – the supposed route of Dorothy's elopement.

From the terraces you look down over the gardens, across the river (spanned by a fine old stone bridge) to pastures and woods. As far as I know, no noted garden designer ever had anything to do with Haddon Hall. The garden is bereft of unusual plants – most of those you see are of the sort any gardener might have in his or her garden. Yet how easy it is to surrender to its charm and how difficult it would be for a garden designer to weave the same magic. The ensemble of house, garden and exquisite setting is the secret.

INFORMATION

Location nr Bakewell DE4 1LA, Derbyshire; 2m SE of Bakewell by A6, Jct 30 of M1
Tel 01629 812855
Email info@haddonhall.co.uk
English Heritage Register Grade I
Owner Lord Edward Manners
Open Apr to Sept, daily 10.30–5.45; Oct, Mon to Thur 10.30–4.30
Area 6 acres/2.4 hectares

The Fountain Garden at Haddon Hall

Hardwick Hall

THE WALLED GARDENS OF BESS OF HARDWICK'S TUDOR MANSION REVITALISED WITH LATE 20TH-CENTURY PLANTINGS

The house, rising splendidly on its bluff, dominates the garden and the landscape at Hardwick. It was built in the 1590s by Bess of Hardwick after the death of her fourth husband, the 6th Earl of Shrewsbury. The house has an avant-garde quality, its austere stone façade rising through four storeys, each pierced with large unornamented windows, and crowned triumphantly with the initials ES (Elizabeth Shrewsbury) worked in stone.

ELIZABETHAN COURTS

There is no record of work by any notable garden designer at Hardwick, nor is there any early description of the garden. However, one of the great beauties of the place is the surviving Elizabethan courts adjacent to the house. The West Court is the most decorative of these enclosures, with its lively gatehouse, two attractive pavilions flanking it and the parapet decorated with dashing finials. The earliest detailed knowledge of the garden in the West Court dates from the 19th century. Loudon's *Encyclopaedia of Gardening* (1822) has little to say about Hardwick except that "The park abounds in fine old oaks" but we know that in 1832 two cedars of Lebanon were planted in the West Court, of which one remains, and by the middle of the 19th century a parterre in the West Court was tricked out in bedding schemes with the initials ES – a scheme that offended Gertrude Jekyll who described it as "not pretty gardening, nor particularly dignified". The gardens were painted by George Elgood in 1897 and show boisterous borders along the walls in the West Court, with standard red roses among lavish herbaceous planting. In the South Court a new garden was made in the 1870s by Lady Louisa Egerton, daughter of the 7th Duke of Devonshire. Elgood's painting shows grass walks with boldly sculpted yew or hornbeam hedges, which divide the garden into four parts, and statues in niches, looking much as they are today.

The West Court at Hardwick Hall

The estate was given to the National Trust in 1959 and the gardens were revitalised in the last twenty years of the 20th century. In the 1980s the West Court borders were replanted under the supervision of Tony Lord in a thoroughly modern style that also shows a Jekyllian influence, with repeated plantings of arching *Cortaderia fulvida* and the handsome foliage

Yew walk at Hardwick Hall

plant *Aralia elata* 'Aureovariegata'. The colour scheme modulates from hot colours close to the house to cooler ones, with plenty of blue and yellow, further away. The hot colours include *Crocosmia* 'Lucifer', dahlias, dazzling red penstemons, *Rosa moyesii* and salvias. In the yellow and blue sections are agapanthus, buddleia, ceanothus, *Hosta elata* 'Aureomarginata', *Kniphofia* 'Wrexham Butterfly' and St John's wort. Throughout the borders the vibrant colours are soothed down by occasional sombre notes of purple-leafed cotinus and *Rheum palmatum* 'Purpureum'. The richness of the colour schemes and the lively pattern of leaf shapes suits the Elizabethan architecture admirably.

THE SOUTH COURT

In the South Court the hedges of yew or hornbeam, the four-part division with grass paths, and the fine 18th-century statues remain from the garden made by Lady Egerton. In one quarter a boldly conceived herb garden was planted in the 1970s with rows of hops (common and gold-leafed) trained into wigwams and underplanted with waves of culinary herbs and beds of vegetables intermingled with ornamental planting. The herb garden was redesigned for 2007. Other quarters contain specimen trees and magnolias, and two orchards: one with old varieties of fruit trees and the other with a walk of the ornamental *Malus hupehensis* and fruit trees.

The East Court is the plainest enclosure, with a scalloped central pool, yew topiary and a border of shrub roses. The eastern boundary has a low yew hedge beyond which is a ha-ha and pasture with, on its far side, an avenue of limes aligned on the house stretching away into the distance.

The garden at Hardwick Hall makes the best of the existing Elizabethan structures without being excessively, and possibly boringly, purist. The planting is sprightly and the whole effect is of a patterned decorativeness of the sort that Bess of Hardwick, with her love of ornamental embroidery, might well have enjoyed as we do today.

INFORMATION

Location Doe Lea, Chesterfield S44 5QJ, Derbyshire; 6½m NW of Mansfield by A617 and minor roads, Jct 29 of M1
Tel 01246 850430
Email hardwickhall@nationaltrust.org.uk
English Heritage Register Grade I
Owner The National Trust
Open mid Mar to Oct, Wed to Sun 11–5.30
Area 7 acres/2.8 hectares

Lord Leycester Hospital

TWO GARDENS: A DECORATIVE LAYOUT TO CELEBRATE THE MILLENNIUM AND AN OLDER GARDEN OF DIFFERENT PERIODS

The delightful group of buildings that comprise Lord Leycester Hospital range from the 14th to the 19th century. The hospital, for aged or disabled soldiers and their wives, was founded by Robert Dudley, Earl of Leicester, in 1571. Today the hospital is still the home of retired servicemen, who help with its administration. There are two gardens here: one entirely new, made to celebrate the millennium, and the other, the garden of the hospital's Master, much older.

NEW AND OLD GARDENS

The Millennium Garden was designed by Susan Rhodes and Geoffrey Smith and forms, in effect, an entrance courtyard for visitors to the hospital. A tunnel made of green oak leads into the garden where both design and symbolism are firmly rooted in the hospital itself. A statue is based on the Dudley arms – a bear with a ragged staff fashioned of sheet metal and skilfully worked by Rachel Higgins. The bear faces down a brick path flanked by

a pair of knots of Tudor inspiration, which echo the shapes of the half-timbering of the hospital's wall. Compartments are filled with lavender or gravel and eight cones of clipped box symbolise the eight hospitallers. A bench has the date 2000 worked into its back. The garden is lighthearted, decorative and thoroughly welcoming.

The Master's Garden lies below the Master's House which overlooks an open lawn with curvaceous edges and cast-iron urns filled with summer bedding plants. A Norman archway under the canopy of two huge magnolias frames a giant stone urn. Beyond it a herringbone-patterned path runs between borders of *Alchemilla mollis*, bergenias, campanulas, geraniums, phlox and valerian backed by garlands of roses and overlooked by a summerhouse. Behind the roses are a kitchen garden on one side and an open lawn on the other. The edge of the garden has a hidden walk of ancient origin running along the top of the town walls and giving remarkable views over the rooftops of Warwick. In one corner is an Elizabethan gazebo and an early 18th-century pineapple pit. Much is packed into the Master's Garden but cross-vistas and eyecatchers – a bench, an urn in a niche of yew, a sundial – prevent claustrophobia. It is a rare example of an urban garden with a long and interesting history and much charm.

The Master's Garden at the Hospital

INFORMATION

Location High Street, Warwick CV34 4BH, Warwickshire; in the centre of Warwick
Tel 01926 491422
Website www.lordleycester.com
Owner The Board of Governors of Lord Leycester Hospital
Open Easter to Sept, daily except Mon (open Bank Hol Mon) 10–4.30
Area 1 acre/0.4 hectare

Lyveden New Bield

THE POIGNANT REMAINS OF AN ELABORATE ELIZABETHAN GARDEN ABOUT THE SHELL OF AN EXTRAORDINARY HOUSE

Treshams lived at Lyveden from the 15th century. They converted to protestantism and then reverted to the old religion. At Lyveden, from 1596, Sir Thomas Tresham, a catholic at a dangerous time, built a spectacular testimony to his religion. The New Bield (which means new building, as opposed to the Old Bield which was the manor house) was built as a "garden lodge", or banqueting house, on the grandest scale. It was built to a cruciform plan and the seven emblems of the Passion were beautifully carved on a frieze on the exterior. During building, Tresham was under constant persecution – under surveillance, house arrest or actually in prison until his death in 1608. Lyveden New Bield was never completed, the Tresham family fortunes were destroyed by Sir Thomas's persecution, and the family died out in the 17th century. The estate changed hands but the New Bield survived, its beautiful masonry largely intact, until the National Trust acquired the building as well as some of its surrounding land in 1922.

The grass walk and moat at Lyveden

PAST SPLENDOUR

Between the Old Bield and the New Bield there had been an elaborate formal garden. Much of the site was ploughed for arable crops and archaeological evidence of the garden destroyed; however, some land escaped the plough and surviving earthworks and canals give some idea of the splendour of the place. A moat surrounding the New Bield is now dry but immediately to its north, in an area known as the Middle Garden, a level square space has a moat (with water) on two sides, which curves round grassy mounds on two corners. On its far side a raised grass walk, now planted with hawthorns, overlooks the site of Sir Thomas Tresham's orchard, which he planted in 1597 with apples, cherries, pears, plums and walnuts. The orchard has been replanted very recently with "walkes" of cherries and walnuts underplanted with wildflowers of the region, a pretty sight.

Lyveden New Bield stands on an open, windy site with long views. Crows wheel through the rooms of the beautiful pale stone roofless shell. It is a moving experience to walk along the banks of the canal and stand on the raised walk, thinking of the fate of the Treshams. Even without this, the place still possesses a most powerful character.

INFORMATION

Location nr Oundle, Peterborough PE8 5AT, Northamptonshire; 4m SW of Oundle off A427
Tel 01832 205358
Email lyvedennewbield@nationaltrust.org.uk
English Heritage Register Grade II*
Owner The National Trust
Open Mar, Sat and Sun 10.30–4; April to Oct, Wed to Sun 10.30–5 (open daily in Aug); Nov and Feb, Sat and Sun 10.30–4
Area 27 acres/11 hectares

Melbourne Hall

AN ENCHANTING EARLY 18TH-CENTURY FORMAL GARDEN: A HAPHAZARD, INWARD-LOOKING VERSION OF VERSAILLES

The garden at Melbourne is a delightful survival – a formal garden of the early 18th century, untouched by the later fashion for landscaping. The house is an ancient one, substantially rebuilt for Thomas Coke, Vice-Chamberlain to Queen Anne and King George I, by Francis Smith of Warwick in the 1720s. The formal gardens, the work of George London and Henry Wise, were laid out from 1699. Coke asked for a garden "to sort with Versailles".

HAPHAZARD FORMALITY

Below the pedimented east façade of the house great stepped terraces of turf descend a stately slope, past beautiful lead statues by John Van Nost, to a grand shaped pool – the Great Basin. On its far side is one of the loveliest garden buildings in England – Robert Bakewell's wrought iron "birdcage". This airy arbour was made in 1706 and cost £120 – the equivalent of about £8,800 today. Running along each side of the turf descent are magnificently blowsy ancient hedges of yew which must date from the garden's making. These curve about to sweep round the back of the birdcage, and the hedges are interrupted from time to time by niches to enclose more lead figures by Van Nost. South of the Grand Basin is a pattern of radiating lime alleys, rising and falling with the lie of the land and animated by pools, fountains and eyecatchers. At its heart is a vast lead urn, the Four Seasons, made by John Van Nost and presented to Coke by Queen Anne.

Unlike a French garden of this period (never mind Versailles), the lime walks are asymmetrical, shooting off at odd angles in a haphazard fashion. This creates diversity and surprise – vistas

The "Birdcage" at Melbourne Hall

are multiplied kaleidoscopically. Another crucial difference from a garden such as Versailles is that the Melbourne garden is an introspective place with no glimpse of a horizon, giving it a romantically melancholy atmosphere. Versailles was emphatically for impressing your neighbours; Melbourne is for getting lost in. The garden historian and Blenheim archivist David Green described Melbourne as "a mild and tranquil garden, a Wilderness of Sweets . . . It is in fact the perfect compromise, the formal garden grown informal and English: the bob-tailed sheep-dog that was at first taken to be a poodle."

INFORMATION

Location Melbourne DE73 8EN, Derbyshire; 9m S of Derby by A453, Jct 24 of M1
Tel 01332 862502 **Fax** 01332 862263
Website www.melbournehall.com
English Heritage Register Grade I
Owner Lord Ralph Kerr
Open Apr to Sept, Wed, Sat, Sun and Bank Hol Mon 1.30–5.30
Area 16 acres/6.5 hectares

Moseley Old Hall

AN ELABORATE KNOT GARDEN, A TOPIARY, AND PERIOD PLANTS IN A RECONSTRUCTED 17TH-CENTURY GARDEN

Moseley Old Hall is a late Elizabethan house, altered in the 17th century and enclosed in brick in the 19th century. In 1962 it was acquired by the National Trust "although not of great architectural merit". Nothing is known of any early garden here and it was decided to make a garden of 17th-century character.

Below the south-facing windows of the house the Trust laid out a knot garden copied from a design by the Revd Walter Stonehouse in 1640 – a sprightly pattern of lollipops of clipped box at the centre of circles of box hedging. Intricately scalloped compartments fill the spaces between the circles and the whole forms a rectangle. Gravel of different colours is used for the background; small pebbles for the scalloped beds; larger pale grey pebbles for the circular beds; and sandy gravel for the paths. This is a garden to be seen from above so that the pattern may be admired. To one side of the knot is a tunnel of arcaded "carpenter's work" taken from a 16th-century illustration. It is planted with Virgin's Bower clematis (*C. flammula*), *C. viticella*

and purple-leafed grapevine (*Vitis vinifera* 'Purpurea'), with aquilegias, geraniums and lavender planted below the climbers. The tunnel leads to a walk of hazels underplanted with spring bulbs and, on the far side of the knot, a path flanked by medlars, mulberries and quinces.

PERIOD PLANTING

The front garden of the house, where the entrance courtyard used to be, has a cobbled path, lawns and box topiary in the form of cones and spirals. The style of planting here is modern but the plants themselves could all have been found in a 17th-century garden. Here are such old rose cultivars and forms as the Jacobite rose (*Rosa* x *alba* 'Alba Maxima') and *R. gallica* var. *officinalis*; "useful" plants like *Saponaria officinalis*; and natives such as the stinking iris (*I. foetidissima*) and Solomon's seal (*Polygonatum multiflorum*).

The garden at Moseley Old Hall was started in 1963 when faithful reconstructions of old gardens were much less common than they are now. Apart from being delightfully decorative, it gives a vivid idea of the styles of design and the range of plants that were found in 17th-century gardens.

The knot at Moseley Old Hall

INFORMATION

Location Moseley Old Hall Lane, Fordhouses, Wolverhampton WV10 7HY, Staffordshire; 3½m N of Wolverhampton between A460 and A449, S of M54
Tel 01902 782808
Email moseleyoldhall@nationaltrust.org.uk
Owner The National Trust
Open Mar to Oct, Wed, Sat and Sun 12–5 (open Bank Hol Mon and following Tue 11–5); Nov to mid Dec, Sun (guided tours only)
Area 1 acre/0.4 hectare

Newstead Abbey

ENJOYABLE AND FINELY MAINTAINED 16TH TO 20TH CENTURY GARDENS ORNAMENTING LORD BYRON'S FAMILY HOME

An Augustinian priory was founded at Newstead in the 12th century, and this passed to Sir John Byron at the dissolution of the monasteries. The 13th-century west front of the priory church and other monastic remains give the house, with its jumble of later period styles, a wonderfully romantic character. The poet George Gordon, 6th Lord Byron, inherited Newstead from his great-uncle in 1798. He celebrated his inheritance by planting an oak whose dead stump still stands on the lawn south of the abbey, entwined with ivy as Byron had hoped.

From the end of the 17th century the 4th Lord Byron made many improvements to the ancient grounds. From 1749, the 5th Lord enlivened the banks of the Upper Lake, west of the abbey, with castellated forts; these remain but a Gothic sham castle has gone. The large walled garden east of the abbey preserves much of its 18th-century character. With its turf terraces, raised walks running under the walls, and sunken pool, it is a typical formal garden of its period. Lead statues of male and female satyrs, almost certainly by John Van Nost, date from the 4th Lord's time. The lawns are decorated with yew topiary, including virtuoso spirals. A monument to the poet Byron's dog, Boatswain, which died in 1808, is an elegant classical urn on a plinth which celebrates his "Strength without Insolence, Courage without Ferocity, and all the Virtues of Man without his Vices".

THE SPANISH GARDEN

Immediately below the east wall of the abbey is the 20th-century Spanish Garden – a knot of box partitions planted with seasonal bedding. South of the formal walled garden are two further walled enclosures – parts of the 18th-century kitchen garden. One is a very large rose garden, with a pronounced Edwardian flavour, ornamented with L-shaped beds cut into turf and cones of clipped yew. The other, formerly an orchard, has decorative old espaliers and box-edged beds planted with herbs.

On the south bank of the Garden Lake is very different sort of garden. Here is a Japanese garden laid out in the early 20th century, with pools, stepping stones, cascades and snow lanterns of particularly fine quality. *Cercidiphyllum japonicum*, bushes of euonymus, Japanese maples and a mulberry ornament the banks of the pools.

The Japanese garden at Newstead Abbey

INFORMATION

Location Linstead NG15 8NA, Nottinghamshire; 12m N of Nottingham by A60
Tel 01623 455900
Email sally.winfield@nottinghamcity.gov.uk
Website www.newsteadabbey.org.uk
English Heritage Register Grade II*
Owner Nottingham City Council
Open daily 9–6 (closed last Fri in Nov and 25 Dec)
Area 300 acres/121 hectares

Packwood House

A CHARMING AND COLOURFUL WALLED FLOWER GARDEN PROVIDES A CONTRAST TO PACKWOOD'S YEW TOPIARY

The garden at Packwood is famous for a single, astonishing feature but it has other attractions besides. The truly jaw-dropping spectacle is the garden of crowding yew topiary beyond the walled garden south of the house. It falls into two parts. The Sermon on the Mount is built on a rounded hillock with a winding path edged in box. On its summit is the tallest yew – which symbolises Christ – and on the lower slopes are the twelve apostles and the four evangelists – possibly dating from the early 18th century. Bustling about below them are the Multitude – truncated conical shapes of various sizes, with a straight path running across the grass between them to the mount, and dating, in all likelihood, to the 19th century.

The Multitude at Packwood House

THE WALLED GARDEN

The origins of all the gargantuan topiary are shrouded in mystery. There is no early description of them. A mid 18th-century drawing shows the house overlooking a walled garden but the area of the topiary garden, just beyond the outer wall, is not included. Had the yews been in place for thirty years they would certainly have formed striking shapes by that time – so it is odd that the artist did not include them.

The walled garden today closely resembles the drawing and it is finely embellished with 20th-century planting. A series of yew "stalls" run along one wall, with each enclosure planted with a single block of yellow or red floribunda roses – a potentially garish scheme soothed down by the sombre deep green of the yew. A sunken garden with a pool is enclosed by low yew hedges lined with frothy miniature borders pricked out with appropriate annuals. Similar planting runs along a raised walk, with a gazebo at each end, against the southern wall. This wall is pierced by an opening with beautiful brick piers, curving steps and wrought-iron gates that are both lively and delicate. The walled garden, flowery and lighthearted, makes an admirable prelude to the solemn enigma of the yew garden. The entrance courtyard, to the west, has impeccable yew hedges enclosing a grand octagonal lawn with a vertical four-faced sundial on a column at its centre. Views to the west, of a lake and parkland, are idyllic and simple, a delightful contrast.

INFORMATION

Location Lapworth, Solihull B94 6AT, Warwickshire; 11m SE of Birmingham by A34
Tel 01564 783294
Email packwood@nationaltrust.org.uk
English Heritage Register Grade II*
Owner The National Trust
Open Mar to Nov, Wed to Sun (open Bank Hol Mon) 11–5.30 (closes 4.30 Mar, April and Oct)
Area 5 acres/2 hectares

Renishaw Hall

EXQUISITE PLANTING IN SIR GEORGE SITWELL'S REFINED
"ITALIAN RENAISSANCE" GARDEN OF THE 1900'S

The garden at Renishaw was made by Sir George Sitwell who went to Italy repeatedly from the early 1890s to study Renaissance gardens. Inspired by them, he decided to create a garden at Renishaw and put into practice the principles he had observed. The result, impeccably cared for by his grandson, is one of the most beautiful gardens in England and worth going a great distance to see. Rebelling against the 18th-century English park and its claims to imitate nature, Sitwell believed the essential purpose of the garden was to provide a setting for the house and to honour the genius of the place.

At Renishaw he made a gently terraced garden south of the house, hedged in yew and ornamented with fine urns, statues and fountains. The lowermost terrace, in accordance with Renaissance ideas, commands great views of the countryside – not here the olive groves and vineyards of Tuscany but the scarred industrial landscape of Sheffield, but that can't be helped. Cross-vistas, with openings in the yew hedges marked by tall piers of clipped yew, reveal views of the woodland on either side like some Tuscan bosco. The garden is exactly the width of the house; it is entirely in harmony with it and at the same time firmly related to its larger setting. (This is, of course, as all gardens should be.)

SYMPATHETIC PLANTING

Sir George did not regard flowers as an essential ingredient of a garden ("such flowers as might be permitted . . . should not call attention to themselves by hue or scent"). Gradually, however, Sir George's noble enclosures have been sympathetically embellished with flowers, especially shrub roses. The yew hedges provide a fine background and the plantings now seem an essential part of the designer's plan. The lowermost terrace has spectacular mixed borders which in late June explode with the delicious mixed scent of *Buddleja alternifolia*, philadelphus and roses.

There is much else to admire at Renishaw (including a lovely bluebell wood and spectacular tender plants trained on the south façade of the house) but it is Sir George's sublime Renaissance vision that is unforgettable. And Sir George knew when to stop. There is precisely the right degree of austerity in his garden, unadulterated by the later floriferous additions.

The terraces at Renishaw Hall

INFORMATION

Location Renishaw, Sheffield S21 3WB, Derbyshire; between Renishaw and Eckington, 2m WNW of Jct 30 of M1

Tel 01246 432310

Email info2@renishaw-hall.co.uk

Website www.renishaw-hall.co.uk

English Heritage Register Grade II*

Owner Sir Reresby Sitwell Bt.

Open 28 Mar to 28 Oct, Thurs to Sun (open Bank Hol Mon) 10.30–4.30

Area 8 acres/3 hectares

Ryton Organic Gardens

EVERY GARDENER CAN LEARN FROM THE TECHNIQUES AND AESTHETICS OF ORGANIC GARDENING AT RYTON

The organic gardens at Ryton are the best, and most diverse, place in the country to learn about organic gardening. Since 1985 the garden has increased in appeal and value to gardeners all the time. Its purpose is to instruct visitors in the techniques and merits of organic gardening, but there is more emphasis today on aesthetics – in the past the magic came from the muck alone. A border of herbaceous perennials and small shrubs, designed by Brita von Schoenaich and Tim Rees, shows that beauty and organic gardening can live very happily together. Plants are chosen that need no staking and no deadheading – the seedheads are things of beauty. Bold groups of hardy geraniums, lavender, persicaria and *Phlomis russeliana* are enriched with sheaves of low-growing ornamental grasses. This is part of a display that demonstrates diversity in the landscape, with many of the plants chosen for their low maintenance – a far wider range of plants than one would think.

The perennial garden at Ryton

INSPIRATIONAL DISPLAYS

Organic pest, disease and weed control, and compost-making, are the techniques that lie at the heart of organic gardening, and Ryton has eloquent practical demonstrations of all these. Among more specialist displays is a garden planned to thrive on little water – with many drought-resistant plants but also showing how to conserve water. Some of the displays are inspirational: one of the best is the Cook's Garden which, in a small space, provides fruit, vegetables and herbs for the kitchen but is also ornamental. A path curves between beds, an octagonal glasshouse protects tender crops, and in summer an arbour of the rose 'Madame Alfred Carrière' suffuses the garden with scent.

The flat site at Ryton makes little contribution to the beauty of the place and exposes the garden to sweeping winds. Trees and shrubs have now grown sufficiently to offer much protection, and within the garden hedged enclosures create pockets of balmy seclusion. Visitors may come to study organic gardening techniques but are frequently ambushed by beautiful sights – a little avenue of fastigiate hornbeams, good borders, handsome individual trees (such as the outstanding thorn *Crataegus pinnatifida* 'Major') and several attractive display gardens (such as the enclosed garden of unusual vegetables prettily laid out in L-shaped beds).

INFORMATION

Location nr Coventry CV8 3LG, Warwickshire; 5m SE of Coventry by A45 and minor roads
Tel 024 7630 3517 **Fax** 024 7663 9229
Email enquiry@gardenorganic.org.uk
Website www.gardenorganic.org.uk
Owner Garden Organic
Open daily (except Christmas Bank Holidays) 9–5
Area 20 acres/8 hectares

Shugborough

18TH-CENTURY PARK ADORNED BY A FEAST OF GARDEN BUILDINGS, INCLUDING A PIONEER CHINESE HOUSE

The Anson family has lived at Shugborough since the early 17th century. The house, of the same date, was remodelled by Samuel Wyatt between 1790 and 1806. Thomas Anson was the man who made the greatest contribution to the garden. As you approach the house you will see across parkland two monuments that were commissioned by him in the 1760s from the architect James "Athenian" Stuart: the Tower of the Winds, a tall octagonal temple framed in a group of trees; and the Arch of Hadrian, on an eminence further away, erected to commemorate the circumnavigation of the world by Thomas Anson's younger brother, George, who became 1st Lord of the Admiralty in 1747. On a voyage to China, George Anson had taken an interest in Chinese architecture; it is said that his second-in-command, Sir Piercy Brett, had sketched a Chinese house in Canton for him. Thus, by 1748 the garden at Shugborough had one of the first, and supposedly most authentic, Chinese buildings in England – only a handful antedate it. It may still be seen on the bank of a stream which is spanned by a handsome iron bridge painted ox-blood red.

The Chinese house at Shugborough

position in the views from the western windows of the house. This ornament, now much reduced in size, has become that great paradox, a ruin of a ruin, gently veiled in trees. Much later, formal gardens were made close to the house – a bold and brassy Victorian scheme with an avenue of clipped golden yews and a fountain pool, and a gentler rose garden of arbours and walks.

The gardens at Shugborough are like a meal consisting of canapés. The canapés are very appetising, of excellent quality and of many different flavours, but they do not quite have the satisfying effect of a solid plateful of meat and two veg.

"WIZARD OF DURHAM"

Close to the Chinese house is the enigmatic Cat Monument, a charming urn surmounted by a crouching cat, designed by the equally enigmatic "Wizard of Durham", Thomas Wright, who worked here from 1748 to 1749. Wright also designed the Shepherd's Monument with the inscription *Et in Arcadia Ego*, enclosed in rustic stonework. His most effective garden building in terms of its role in the landscape is the Ruin on the bank of the river Sow, commanding a central

INFORMATION

Location Milford, nr Stafford ST17 0XB, Staffordshire; 6m E of Stafford by A513
Tel 01889 881388   **Fax** 01889 881323
Email shugborough.promotions@staffordshire.gov.uk
English Heritage Register Grade I
Owner The National Trust
Open mid Mar to end Oct, daily 11–5
Area 18 acres/7 hectares

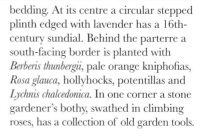

Sulgrave Manor

CHARMING AND BEAUTIFULLY DESIGNED FORMAL GARDEN LAID OUT IN 1921 BY SIR REGINALD BLOMFIELD

This is the only garden in England owned by the Colonial Dames of America and the only English country house I know to fly the Stars and Stripes. The American connection is an important one for Sulgrave Manor was the home of George Washington's ancestors – Lawrence Washington came to live here in 1540.

The house was comprehensively restored by Sir Reginald Blomfield and opened to the public in 1921 with its original 16th-century appearance. He also added a charmingly unpretentious formal garden in the tradition of the architectural gardens in which he specialised – one of his most complete gardens to survive. It takes its cue, as all gardens of this sort must, from the house. To the south, running up to the front door with its gabled porch, a gravel path forms the central axis, uniting spaces of different character. Yew hedges and low stone walls enclose a wide rectangle in front of the house, and plump birds of yew topiary guard the front door. An upper lawn has an old walnut tree and a box knot garden filled with herbs. To the side of the house a box parterre is planted with summer bedding. At its centre a circular stepped plinth edged with lavender has a 16th-century sundial. Behind the parterre a south-facing border is planted with *Berberis thunbergii*, pale orange kniphofias, *Rosa glauca*, hollyhocks, potentillas and *Lychnis chalcedonica*. In one corner a stone gardener's bothy, swathed in climbing roses, has a collection of old garden tools.

CIRCULAR SHAPES

From the forecourt the gravel path leads into a formal orchard whose trees are underplanted with daffodils and scillas. Shrub roses are planted along one side and beehives sit among the trees. This, too, is enclosed in yew hedges, which curve round in a semicircle. The circular shape recurs on the far side of the house where Blomfield devised an elegant car entrance and turnaround. The pattern of yew hedges and stone walls, often ornamented with stone cannon balls, is very attractive and perfectly suits the house. The planting, while intermittently pretty, does not rise to this level of architectural distinction; this could be the framework for an outstanding garden. The Herb Society maintains an admirable herb garden at Sulgrave.

The forecourt at Sulgrave Manor

INFORMATION

Location Sulgrave, nr Banbury OX17 2SD, Northamptonshire; 7m NE of Banbury by B4525, Jct 11 of M40

Tel 01295 760205

Fax 01295 768056

Email enquiries@sulgravemanor.org.uk

Website www.sulgravemanor.org.uk

English Heritage Register Grade II

Owner Colonial Dames of America

Open Apr, Sat and Sun 12–4; May to Oct, Tue to Thur 2–4, Sat and Sun 12–4

Area 2 acres/0.80 hectare

Trentham Gardens

MAGNIFICENT GARDENS FROM THE HEYDAY OF VICTORIAN HORTICULTURE BROUGHT BRILLIANTLY BACK TO LIFE

In 1833 the second Duke of Sutherland had an older house at Trentham rebuilt by Sir Charles Barry as an Italianate palace of astonishing splendour. Barry also supervised the creation of a superb garden. With its parterres, balustraded terraces, statuary, pavilions and pools, it became known as "the Versailles of the Midlands". By the early 20th century the pollution of the river Trent, which flows through the grounds, had become so great as to make the house uninhabitable. After the Sutherland family left, the house decayed and the grounds became a lugubrious municipal park. Now, in a brilliant feat of resuscitation, the grounds have been magnificently brought back to something closely resembling their original splendour.

Between the remains of the house (which is to be rebuilt as a smart hotel) and a handsome lake are magnificent formal gardens. Close to the house, at an upper level, Barry designed a balustraded terrace with flower gardens. Today patterns of box-edged beds have superb bedding displays; a circular pool at the centre has a soaring water jet; and box spheres, standard roses and fastigiate yews enliven the scene. The terrace looks down on the Italian

Garden, a dazzling re-creation designed by Tom Stuart Smith. A lavish pattern of beds, richly planted with herbaceous perennials, has subtle changes of level and is decorated with mop-headed sweet bay trees in Versailles boxes, columns of Iris yews, clumps of golden yew and circular pools with water jets. Tall white fox-tail lilies sway in the breeze with swathes of purple alliums, geraniums, ornamental grasses and pale irises below. Colours are carefully chosen and much repeat planting gives lively harmony. On the southern edge of the garden a splendid bronze statue of Perseus and Medusa faces the garden and behind it a great lake spreads out with woodland pressing in on each side. This was the scene of Capability Brown's activities from 1759.

NEW PLEASURE GARDENS

To the east of the upper flower garden and the Italian garden are the eastern pleasure gardens designed by Piet Oudolf and opened in 2007. Here is a wild grass meadow, swathes of colourful perennials, places for picnics and two viewing mounds from which to survey the splendid scene. This area, close to the river Trent, is prone to partial flooding and Piet Oudolf included in his planting plan many moisture-loving flowering perennials

The Italian garden at Trentham

INFORMATION

Location Stone Road, Trentham, Staffordshire ST4 8AX; 2m S of Stoke-on-Trent by A34

Tel 01782 646 646

Email shamilton@trentham. co.uk

Website www.trentham.co.uk

Owner St Modwen Properties

Open Apr to Sept, daily 10–6; Oct to Mar, daily 10–4

Area 70 acres/28 hectares

Upton House

A LATE 17TH-CENTURY HOUSE WITH A DAZZLING PATCHWORK OF GARDENS THAT PLUMMET DOWN A SLOPE

The house, dating from 1695, was remodelled in neo-Georgian style, and greatly increased in size, after the estate was bought by Walter Samuel, 2nd Viscount Bearsted, in 1927. Lord Bearsted gave the estate to the National Trust on his death in 1948.

Broad paved terraces running along the south façade of the house overlook a great lawn. The terrace is bright with flowers, in particular roses, with underplantings of artemisia, nepeta and pinks. Stately cedars of Lebanon, some going back to the 18th century, fringe the lawn.

A DAZZLING PATCHWORK

Beyond the edge of the lawn the land falls away into a valley and it is here, on the south-facing slopes, that the true garden excitement begins. Formal steps and a balustrade entwined with wisteria lead down to a dazzling patchwork of gardens. The protected slope had in the past been devoted to kitchen gardening, which is still practised with exemplary skill, but much of the area has now been given over to ornamental purposes. A pair of herbaceous borders, designed by Kitty Lloyd Jones, plummet down the slope. The borders are filled with achilleas, campanulas, *Echinops ritro*, geraniums, kniphofias and repeated plantings of *Kolkwitzia amabilis* and of cardoons. At the bottom is a copper beech and views over a pool dappled with waterlilies. The slopes to one side are terraced, with many tender plants thriving in the shelter of the walls – such as *Drimys winteri*, *Campsis radicans*, *Carpenteria californica* and *Hoheria lyallii*. This is not a warm part of the country.

At the foot of the slope, close to the water, is the kitchen garden where many different vegetables and soft fruits are grown. At its west end a border

The borders at Upton

contains a National Collection of Michaelmas daisies (*Aster amellus*, *A. cordifolius* and *A. ericoides* cultivars). Nearby, enclosed in a yew hedge, a paved rose garden of Edwardian flavour has L-shaped beds of bedding roses and, at the centre, a lead figure of Pan happily surrounded by the musk rose 'Felicia'. Edwardian, too, is an elaborate flight of stone steps. Further to the west is a curious sunken garden – a rectangular former pool whose perimeter is planted with cherries. Above it, on terracing supported by walls of brick or stone, are old yews, some of them very old indeed – the remains of a formal garden.

INFORMATION

Location Banbury OX15 6HT, Warwickshire; 7m NW of Banbury by A422
Tel 01295 670266
Email uptonhouse@nationaltrust.org.uk
English Heritage Register Grade II*
Owner The National Trust
Open Mar to Oct, Sat to Wed (open every day in Aug) 11–5; Nov to mid Dec, Mon to Fri 12–4
Area 19 acres/8 hectares

Warwick Castle

AN 11TH-CENTURY CASTLE, A CAPABILITY BROWN LANDSCAPE, A MAGNIFICENT PARTERRE, AND A MAGICAL ROSE GARDEN

On visiting Warwick Castle in 1751 the irrepressible Horace Walpole wrote to his friend Geoerge Montague: "The castle is enchanting; the view pleased me more than I can express; the river Avon tumbles down a cascade at the foot of it. It is well laid out by one Brown . . . One sees what the prevalence of taste does." Most of the surviving building dates from the 14th century and although much has been added subsequently its medieval character remains. Plainly this was a full-blooded fortified castle, occupying as it does a position of strength, with long views, above the river banks. Features dating from the 11th century, such as the mound, may also be seen and Capability Brown's work, so admired by Walpole, may still be relished today.

There were gardens at Warwick Castle certainly by the 16th century. By the early 18th century an elaborate pattern of formal gardens ran along the river to the west of the castle. In the late 1740s Capability Brown laid out new gardens. Today you may stand on the top of the mound and see the results: the river winding among belts of trees, with fine individual trees in pastures on its far bank, and in the distance more belts of trees on the Cotswold hills – one of the grandest views from any city in the country.

MAGNIFICENT PARTERRE

Later in the 18th century a superlative conservatory was built to the design of the Warwick architect William Eboral to display the great Roman Warwick Vase which had been found at Hadrian's Villa. What you see today is a replica; the original is in the Burrell Collection in Glasgow. With its magnificent Gothic tracery windows, beautifully restored, the conservatory houses a collection of tender plants, some of them very unusual. Here are bananas, Arabian jasmine (*Jasminum sambac*), Jamaican cherry (*Ficus citrifolia*) and the giant fronds of *Strelitzia nicolai* – big plants for a big space. It overlooks a deep paved terrace, giving views of a magnificent parterre designed by Robert Marnock in 1868. At its centre a round lily pool and fountain are surrounded by parterre-like segmental beds of clipped yew. In the upper part the hedges are waist high with swathes of floribunda roses filling the compartments. The tops of the hedges are crowned from time to time with a triumphant topiary bird. Real birds play their part, too, for languid peacocks pose

The conservatory and parterre at Warwick

here and there, sometimes sprawling on the top of a hedge with tail spread expansively behind. The lower part of the parterre has lower hedges forming compartments that are filled with a single variety of rose, with white roses in the centre and scarlet pelargoniums in outlying compartments.

HIDDEN ROSE GARDEN

In the 1980s a distinguished feature of the garden was recreated after the discovery in Warwickshire County Record Office of designs made in 1868 by Robert Marnock for a formal rose garden, which had been removed in the 1930s. This, hidden away in woods to the north of the castle, has now been triumphantly reinstated by Paul Edwards. It is arranged like a parterre, with a pattern of beds cut into turf, paths, and roses in box-edged beds, soaring on pillars or tumbling from arbours. Many old roses are used, such as 'Adélaïde d'Orléans' and 'The Garland' but there are also David Austin's English Roses, among them the richly scented pink 'Warwick Rose'.

The crisp geometry of the rose garden's layout contrasted with the lavish abundance of the roses makes it a dazzling success. To one side, of a slightly later date, is a fine rock garden and pool, the work of James Backhouse & Co of York in about 1900.

Warwick Castle and its immediate surroundings were sold by the 7th Earl of Warwick to the Tussauds Group in 1979. In 2007 Tussauds merged with Merlin Entertainments. Its condition today, in particular that of the gardens, which have been finely restored and are impeccably maintained, shows that its transformation into a commercial tourist attraction has had a happy outcome.

INFORMATION

Location Warwick CV34 4QU, Warwickshire; in the centre of Warwick, Jct 15 of M40
Tel 0870 442 2000
Email customer.information@warwick-castle.com
Website www.warwick-castle.com
English Heritage Register Grade I
Owner Merlin Entertainments Group
Open daily 10–6 (closes from 5 Oct to Mar; closed 25 Dec)
Area 60 acres/24 hectares

EAST of ENGLAND

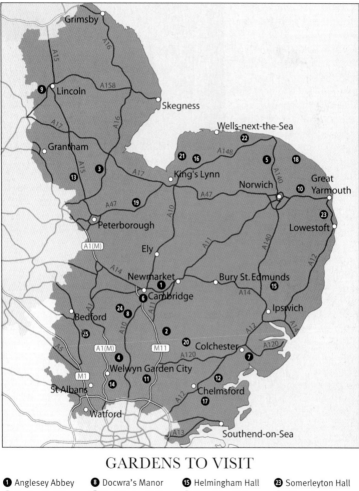

GARDENS TO VISIT

Image *Saling Hall*

Anglesey Abbey

MAGNIFICENT AVENUES, LIVELY BORDERS AND A BEAUTIFUL WINTER GARDEN FOR AN ALL-SEASON GARDEN

The garden at Anglesey Abbey, like many distinguished British gardens, was made by an amateur. The estate was bought in 1926 by Huttleston Broughton, later 1st Lord Fairhaven. He laid out a thoroughly original garden on the scale of a great 18th-century landscape park but using the crisply formal language of an earlier period. It is one of the largest, most ambitious and most original 20th-century private gardens.

The Winter Walk at Anglesey Abbey

BOLD AVENUES

This part of the Cambridgeshire fens is as flat as a pancake. The problem of animating such a large area of featureless, windswept land is not one that many gardeners have to confront. Lord Fairhaven planted bold avenues to divide the land and create vistas, adding distinguished statuary as eyecatchers and decorative interludes. Two great avenues of horse chestnuts form the main axes of the garden: the Coronation Avenue, which runs east and west for half a mile (it was planted to celebrate King George VI's coronation in 1937), and the Cross Avenue which cuts across it. Smaller avenues, of other trees, make lighter brush-strokes in the scene. Ornaments are skilfully woven into this framework – marking the meeting place of two avenues, forming a punctuation mark, or flanking an opening. These, of fine quality, have a superb presence when used in conjunction with the trees. More intimate enclosures are also often enlivened by ornaments – a circle of pale columns on Temple Lawn, a row of white marble urns against a yew hedge on the Rose Garden lawn, and a solemn procession of twelve busts of caesars in the Emperors' Walk.

Close to the house is a notable curved herbaceous border behind a horseshoe of beech hedging and, to one side, another curved beech hedge runs behind a bed filled with different cultivars of dahlia. The beautiful bronze urns here are copies of 17th-century Versailles originals. On the eastern boundary of the garden is the Winter Walk, a winding path with bold groups of winter-flowering bulbs, herbaceous perennials and shrubs, and trees and shrubs with beautiful bark or fine berries. The formal gardens and the Winter Walk, though attractive, have none of the drama of the huge garden of avenues that recalls the great days of garden-making. Will any private individual ever again make a garden on this heroic scale?

INFORMATION

Location Lode, Cambridge CB5 9EJ, Cambridgeshire; in Lode village, 6m NE of Cambridge by B1102
Tel 01223 810080
Email angleseyabbey@nationaltrust.org.uk
English Heritage Register Grade II*
Owner The National Trust
Open late Mar to Oct, Wed to Sun (open Bank Hol Mon in summer) 10.30–4.30; Winter garden also open Nov to Feb, phone for times
Area 100 acres/81 hectare

Audley End House

A CAPABILITY BROWN PARK, A DAZZLING FLOWER PARTERRE AND AN ELYSIAN WATER GARDEN

The present house is essentially Jacobean, built between 1605 and 1614 by Thomas Howard, 1st Earl of Suffolk and Lord Treasurer to James I, and what survives today is only a modest part of it.

From 1763 Capability Brown removed earlier formal gardens and his work dominates the landscape today. He serpentined the course of the river Cam which was spanned by the bridge designed in 1764 by Robert Adam, and planted long belts and bushy clumps of trees. Another beautiful building by Robert Adam survives – the domed and pillared Temple of Victory.

In the 1780s, the intriguing Elysian Garden was designed by Richard Woods and Placido Columbani on the banks of the river north-west of the house. Originally a tunnel of evergreens led to winding walks wandering among beds of sweet-smelling flowers, with a statue of Flora, a Turkish tent and a Coade stone altar. Although much of the detail is missing, the layout of the Elysian Garden is substantially intact.

Water erupts from a rustic cascade on the Cam and the pool below is spanned by a delightful covered bridge – the Palladian Teahouse Bridge, designed by Robert Adam in 1782. Superb London planes stand on either side of the river – the one on the west bank is exceptional, with immense spreading branches.

A DAZZLING PARTERRE

East of the house a new parterre was laid out in around 1831, based on a design from an 18th-century pattern book and with advice from William Sawrey Gilpin. This was reinstated from 1989 with shaped beds cut into the turf, some planted with brilliant annuals and some with herbaceous perennials and roses. From here the ground to the east slopes up to a long gravel walk above a ha-ha. In the old deer park to the north is Lady Portsmouth's Column, designed by Robert Adam in 1774 for Sir John Griffin Griffin who wished to honour his aunt who had bequeathed the Audley End estate to him.

Behind the stable block, the kitchen gardens are enclosed in beautiful brick walls dating from the 18th and 19th centuries. Now well restored, they are cultivated now by the HDRA organic gardening organisation, Garden Organic, and vividly display the character of such a garden in its heyday.

The parterre at Audley End

INFORMATION

Location Audley End, nr Saffron Walden CB11 4JF, Essex; 1m W of Saffron Walden by B1383
English Heritage Register Grade I
Tel 01799 522842 **Fax** 01799 521276
Website www.english-heritage.org.uk/ audleyend
Owner English Heritage
Open Phone or consult website for opening times
Area 99 acres/40 hectares

Ayscoughfee Hall

A CHARMING PUBLIC GARDEN WITH ANCIENT YEW HEDGES, FORMAL ROSE GARDENS AND A FINE LUTYENS WAR MEMORIAL

A house was built here in the 1430s for a wool merchant, Richard Alwyn, and the estate changed hands many times subsequently. In the late 17th century it was acquired by Maurice Johnson who took a great interest in the garden. A map of 1732 shows it occupying the same area as it does today and it was about this time that extraordinary yew walks were planted. John Byng saw them on his visit to Spalding in 1790: "As I enter'd the town, I had observ'd a very ancient house of bay windows, surrounded by yew hedge gardens."

PUBLIC GARDENS

In 1898 Isabella Johnson sold the estate to a group of local citizens and it was subsequently transferred to the Spalding Urban District Council in 1902. The gardens were immediately opened to the public and the house became a museum and art gallery.

With its brilliant bedding schemes, the garden has a municipal flavour – but unexpected pleasures are in store. The ancient yew hedges, now wide and tall and billowing out into bulges and lumps, remain a lovely feature. A long sunken canal with a three-tiered fountain has at its head a noble war memorial designed by Sir Edwin Lutyens in around 1925: its loggia-like pavilion, with Doric columns and arches, pantiled roof and grandly vaulted interior, has a decidedly Italian flavour, while the floor is paved with stone and strips of herringbone brick in typical Lutyens fashion. Nearby is a garden celebrating fifty years of peace (1945–95). It has a pretty pattern of box-edged beds filled with roses and bedding schemes and an obelisk at its centre. To one side of the garden is a tall 19th-century stone drinking fountain.

The garden now fulfills the role of a public park and its attractions include an aviary of exotic birds, tennis courts, a putting green and a superb bowling green below the east façade of the house. The museum is largely devoted to local history and natural history and has a fascinating exhibit about the draining of the fens in South Holland. This began in the 7th century when it was realised that arable farming and grazing were far more lucrative than wildfowling, and, much later, permitted bulb nurseries (especially for tulips) to be established.

The war memorial at Ayscoughfee Hall

INFORMATION

Location Churchgate, Spalding PE11 2RA, Lincolnshire; in the centre of Spalding
Tel 01775 725468
Fax 01775 762715
Website www.sholland.gov.uk
English Heritage Register Grade II
Owner South Holland District Council
Open daily dawn–dusk
Area 7 acres/3 hectares

Benington Lordship

FORMAL FLOWER GARDENS, A ROSE GARDEN AND LIVELY HERBACEOUS BORDERS FOR A HANDSOME HOUSE

This is a delightful, unassuming place whose subtle charms have a cumulative effect. The house is early 18th-century with a neo-Georgian wing added in 1906 to take advantage of the beautiful views facing west over the valley. Next to the house are the remains of a Norman castle and, built onto the 11th-century keep, a startling flight of fancy: a neo-Norman sham ruin of flint and Pulhamite (indeed James Pulham himself seems to have been the clerk-of-works for the building when it was put up in 1832) in the form of a truncated gatehouse. The entrance is enclosed by a Norman arch, there is a statue of Buddha within, and an ancient tombstone with a Greek inscription.

The rose garden at Benington Lordship

A PICTURESQUE SETTING

The garden, taking every advantage of its picturesque setting, has been made almost entirely since Harry and Sarah Bott came here in 1971. The former moat of the castle ("cleared with the help of a goat") is densely planted with snowdrops – for which there are special openings in February or March. These are followed by an astonishing spread of the pale blue East European squill (*Scilla bithynica*), flowering among drifts of daffodils. The south façade of the house overlooks a rose garden with a central sundial surrounded by beds of pale pink roses underplanted with irises and edged in lavender. The plinth of the sundial is edged with bergenias and, in summer, pots of agapanthus. The land begins to fall away below the rose garden, with views over pools and thickets of alders and willows to long views of the rural landscape. At the top of the slope a path leads eastwards. Before you arrive at the entrance to the walled kitchen garden, you are ambushed by a surprise – the path cuts across a pair of lavish herbaceous borders running along the outside wall of the kitchen garden. These existed before the Botts came but had been horribly neglected; now comprehensively replanted, they present a cataract of colour tumbling down the slope. The rare setting, the delight in good plants and the unassuming charm of the place give Benington great character.

INFORMATION

Location Benington, nr Stevenage SG2 7BS, Hertfordshire; 4m E of Stevenage by minor roads, signposted from Watton-at-Stone
Tel 01438 869668 **Fax** 01438 869622
Email garden@beningtonlordship.co.uk
Website www.beningtonlordship.co.uk
English Heritage Register Grade II
Owner R.R.A. Bott
Open Feb or Mar for snowdrops (phone/see website for details); Easter, May and Aug bank hol, Sun 2–5, Mon 12–5
Area 7 acres/3 hectares

Blickling Hall

EXQUISITE JACOBEAN HOUSE WITH A SPLENDID FLOWER PARTERRE AND WOODLAND WALKS

Blickling is marvellously beautiful; however often you see it, its sudden revelation from the road will make you catch your breath. The house, bristling with gables, turrets and chimneys, is framed in ancient, immensely wide yew hedges which were already in place in 1745. The house was built between 1618 and 1629 for Sir Henry Hobart to the designs of Robert Lyminge, the architect of another great house of the period – Hatfield (*see page 244*). With its pink-brown brick and pale stone dressings, Blickling combines decorative exuberance with a peacefully rural air; it has devastating charm.

This was not the first house on the site and there has been parkland here since the 12th century, but nothing is known in detail about the landscape before the 17th century when most of the garden activity was on the east side of the house – as it is today. There are signs of 18th-century landscaping, including a curious formal scheme dating from early in the century, and in the early 19th century John Adey Repton advised on some decorative schemes – a picturesque trelliswork pergola and Hardenberg baskets – drawings of which survive at the house today. In 1856 the Marquess of

The parterre
at Blickling

Lothian, who had inherited the estate, came to live at Blickling and started a long process of renovation. In the 1860s he introduced formal rides, in the form of *pattes d'oie*, in the woodland to the east of the house, harking back to the 18th-century garden.

THE FLOWER PARTERRE

In the 1870s the east garden was redesigned by Matthew Digby Wyatt and Markham Nesfield with terracing, steps and a parterre, much as it is today, and the planting was devised by Lady Lothian herself. The parterre itself, in true renaissance style, is exactly the width of the house and lies handsomely spread out below its long façade. Lady Lothian's planting scheme, however, bore no relation to the character of its setting. It presented a riot of ornament – a fussy pattern of flower beds and topiary spreading around the splendid central 17th-century fountain (bought in the Oxnead Hall sale of 1732).

Christopher Hussey, writing in *Country Life* in 1930, referred despairingly to the "multiplicity of dotted beds". In 1932 Norah Lindsay was asked to simplify the parterre, which she did with great success, and it is her design that survives today. She retained the bold shapes of yew topiary – "grand-pianos" and rounded cones – and divided the area into four square beds with a yew cone at each corner. The beds are edged in strips of roses and catmint and richly planted with mixed woody and herbaceous plants graded in size so that in high summer they form a floriferous brilliantly coloured pyramid. The beds close to the house are chiefly planted in pink, mauve and blue, and those further away in yellow and orange. The strong design and disciplined but luxuriantly decorative planting now form a perfect accompaniment to the house.

THE TEMPLE WALK

The parterre shares an axis with the Temple Walk which Norah Lindsay also advised on. Steps lead up to the walk which pierces woodland and ends in a pedimented temple of *c*.1730. Mrs Lindsay removed the rows of conifers that once lined it, to reveal the handsome woodland trees behind. She also introduced azaleas about the temple and along the subsidiary walks (reinstated in the 19th century) that thread the woods on either side. All this presents a scene of great variety and harmony, in which the formality of the past is combined with lively 20th-century planting. Above all, it holds its own beside the splendour of the house.

INFORMATION

Location Blickling, Norwich NR11 6NF, Norfolk; 15m N of Norwich
Tel 01263 738030
Email blickling@nationaltrust.org.uk
English Heritage Register Grade II*
Owner The National Trust
Open (Garden) mid Mar to Oct, Wed to Sun (open Mon in Aug and Bank Hol Mon) 10.15–5.15; Nov to Feb, Thurs to Sun 11–4; (Park and woods) daily dawn–dusk
Area 46 acres/19 hectares

Cambridge Botanic Garden

AN OUTSTANDING COLLECTION OF PLANTS FINELY DISPLAYED, A BEAUTIFUL WINTER GARDEN, AND A DRY GARDEN

The Cambridge University Botanic Garden was founded in 1760 and moved to its present site in 1846. The site is an attractive one, with a fine lake and water garden near the Trumpington Road entrance, animated by many fine mature trees, some planted at the time of their first introduction – including *Sequoiadendron giganteum* (introduced in 1853, planted in 1855) and *Metasequoia glyptostroboides* (introduced in 1947, planted in 1949). The only part of the garden with a somewhat contrived vista is the main walk which leads straight from the Trumpington Road entrance to a circular pool with a fountain.

FINE PLANT COLLECTIONS

It is the plants that are the chief attraction here – and there is much to delight the gardener. There are several National Collections, of which the most attractive is that of species tulips (56 of them) and their primary hybrids (17). All are beautiful and many make admirable garden plants, in some cases naturalising with abandon. A National Collection of hardy geraniums (over 100 species and over 40 primary hybrids) is also of great interest to gardeners. A

collection of over 70 species of European fritillaries, several garden-worthy, will be an eye-opener to most gardeners, as will the collection of over 90 honeysuckles (*Lonicera* species). The collections of alchemilla, bergenias, ribes, ruscus and European saxifrages are of chiefly botanical interest.

The Winter Garden has an admirable display of what may be achieved in that season. The gleaming yellow stems of *Cornus stolonifera* 'Flaviramea' and the Chinese lacquer red of *Salix alba* subsp. *vitellina* 'Britzensis' enliven the gloomiest day. A collection of heathers forms a glowing eiderdown and the silver-white stems of *Rubus biflorus* sparkle among dwarf conifers. There are spring bedding schemes and herbaceous borders, perfectly nice in a municipal park sort of way, but the real interest of the garden lies in the quality of the plants and the opportunity gardeners have to see large and fascinating collections of particular ones. A very attractively designed little formal garden uses plants especially suitable for the dry Cambridge climate (which has half the national average rainfall). Here euphorbias, fennel, grasses, lavenders and sedums are deployed to good effect. It is so well laid out that it could be the model for many a small private garden.

Cambridge Botanic Garden

INFORMATION

Location Bateman Street, Cambridge CB2 1JF, Cambridgeshire; ¾m S of the city centre by Trumpington Road (A10)

Tel 01223 336265

Email enquiries@botanic.cam.ac.uk

Website www.botanic.cam.ac.uk

English Heritage Register Grade II*

Owner University of Cambridge

Open daily 10–6 (closes 5 in spring and autumn, 4 in winter; closed 25 Dec to 2 Jan)

Area 40 acres/16 hectares

Beth Chatto Gardens

THE SUPERB GARDENS OF A BRILLIANT PLANTSWOMAN, WITH A WONDERFUL NURSERY ATTACHED

Many interests converge in Beth Chatto's gardens – respect for the environment, a desire to plant in a naturalistic way, and an informed interest in the ecology of plants. These things, worthy as they are, do not by themselves make good gardens, but Beth Chatto, apart from being a deeply knowledgeable practical gardener, is also an artist in the use of plants.

Beth Chatto and her late husband, Andrew, started gardening here in 1960 and opened a nursery in 1967. In the 1970s and 80s she exhibited regularly at Royal Horticultural Society shows, winning ten gold medals in a row at Chelsea. With plants beautifully arranged in naturalistic groups according to the conditions they needed, she provided gardeners with lessons in that most important thing of all – the right site for the right plant.

THE RIGHT CONDITIONS

Beth Chatto's first garden here was made along a moist, spring-fed ditch whose banks are fringed with astilbes, ferns, gunneras (*G. tinctoria*), lysichitons and marsh marigold (*Caltha palustris*). These plants come from all over the world, but the fact that they all need the same conditions not only allows them to flourish but also to look *right* together. In 1991 she made a very different garden. Essex is the driest county in England, averaging around 20in/50cm of rain a year, and Beth Chatto capitalised on such conditions, using plants that would flourish with no artificial irrigation. Many of the plants she chose are from the Mediterranean area – cistus, lavender, santolina, spurges and so on. A path leads across gravel, resembling a dry river bed. At the edge of the path and weaving their way through low shrubs are many bulbous plants –

Beth Chatto's dry garden

alliums, alstroemerias, lilies and tulbaghias. Substantial grasses such as *Stipa gigantea*, shrubs like *Atriplex halimus*, or soaring herbaceous plants such as verbascums, give height and drama. There is artistry in their arrangement, with repetition of plants and occasional happy juxtapositions of form or colour, but the triumph of the garden comes from its abundantly natural appearance and the fact that the plants seem to be relishing the same extreme conditions. Of all the gardens made in Britain in the late 20th century, this is the one that was both deeply in touch with the spirit of the time and managed to make something beautiful of it.

INFORMATION

Location Elmstead Market, Colchester CO7 7DB, Essex; ¼m E of Elmstead Market by A133
Tel 01206 822007
Email info@bethchatto.fsnet.co.uk
Website www.bethchatto.co.uk
Owner Mrs Beth Chatto
Open Mar to Oct, daily except Sun 9–5; Nov to Feb, Mon–Fri 9–4 (closed for two weeks over Christmas and New Year)
Area 5 acres/2 hectares

Docwra's Manor

A LIVELY GARDEN MADE BY TWO EXPERT AMATEUR PLANT-COLLECTORS, FULL OF THEIR FINDS

The house is a very pretty one – 17th-century but with a gentlemanly early 18th-century façade facing the village. John and Faith Raven came here when they married in 1954, and started to remake the garden. Both keen botanists, they preferred the wild species to cultivars and many plants were introduced into the garden as a result of their own collecting, especially in the eastern Mediterranean. At Docwra's they found very low rainfall, alkaline soil, excellent drainage and protection provided by old brick walls and outhouses.

Touches of formality at Docwra's Manor

ENCLOSED SPACES

The Ravens created a garden of compartments, adding hedges to the existing enclosures and fashioning spaces of very different moods. To the east and north of the house is a large uncluttered lawn edged with a winding walk and good trees, leading to a wilder area where there is a hidden garden of shrub roses, Japanese maples and *Koelreuteria paniculata*.

West and north-west of the house lies a labyrinth of enclosures, entered by crossing a lawn and squeezing through a slit in a curved beech hedge. Here, where the profusion of plants all but engulfs paths, there are touches of formality – L-shapes of clipped yew and cones of gold variegated box. Here you will find many artemisias, cistus, clematis, eryngiums, euphorbias, hellebores, peonies and roses (species or those of wild character). Passing a glasshouse and a paved area with flowering cherries and *Cornus controversa*

'Variegata', you come to a walk of espaliered apples, and dahlias in the autumn. From here a narrow passage through a yew hedge leads to a series of arches of pears and clematis flanked with asparagus and pampas grass (*Cortaderia sellowiana*). An especially protected enclosed space has *Carpenteria californica*, pelargoniums, salvias and cones of clipped rosemary.

The garden at Docwra's Manor is both a delight to be in and absorbing. One great advantage of a botanical approach to gardening (provided it is not obsessed with mere rarity) is that it allows one to study groups of plants uninfluenced by horticultural fashion. Nature proposes a much wider range than even the largest garden centre, and is uninfluenced by notions of shelf-life and ease of mass propagation.

INFORMATION

Location Shepreth, nr Royston SG8 6PS, Cambridgeshire In Shepreth village; 8m S of Cambridge off A10
Tel 01763 260677
Website www.docwrasmanorgarden.co.uk
Owner Mrs John Raven
Open Wed and Fri 10–4 (Feb to Nov, also 1st Sun in month 2–4)
Area 2½ acres/1 hectare

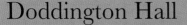

Doddington Hall

NOBLE ELIZABETHAN GARDENS WITH MODERN PLANTING, FINE TREES AND LOVELY SPRING BULBS

Doddington is a wonderful house – late Elizabethan, almost certainly designed by Robert Smythson and miraculously unchanged in outward appearance since it was built. The entrance forecourt, with its dashing gabled gatehouse on one side and the dazzlingly ornamental house on the other, needs little ornament of a horticultural kind. Here today are plain lawns, low box hedges and gravel paths with cones of clipped yew about the perimeter, and a pair of free-standing *Magnolia grandiflora* flanking the entrance. Mounds of pink hydrangea billow against the walls of the house, with plumes of *Aruncus dioicus*, and close to the front door are topiary box unicorns holding shields. The upper part of the west court behind the house has a knot garden of box and compartments filled with plantings of a single colour – irises, catmint and white or yellow roses. At the lower level two octagonal pools with water jets are surrounded by beds of purple irises. Borders run round the walls of the court, filled with alliums, campanulas, daylilies, echinops, peonies, phlox and sedums, with much repetition. Clematis,

honeysuckle and roses are trained on the walls. In spring these beds are filled with red and yellow crown imperials, thoroughly naturalised here.

FINE TREES AND BULBS

An 18th-century Italian wrought-iron gate leads to an avenue of Irish yews underplanted in spring with sheets of *Crocus tommasinianus* and *C. sieberi*. The wild garden opens out to the north, with many flowering cherries, a group of ancient yews, a walk of rowans and a handsome *Catalpa bignonioides*. Close to the edge of the garden an open Tuscan rotunda, a Temple of the Winds, has fine views over countryside and back towards the house. A huge cedar of Lebanon, planted in 1845, stands nearby. Closer to the house a croquet lawn is overlooked by a group of remarkable sweet chestnuts, sprawling and ancient. In late summer drifts of *Cyclamen hederifolium* gleam in the shade, and in the spring more crown imperials do the same.

The framework of beautiful old walls, much decorative planting, and good individual specimens of trees and other plants make the garden at Doddington a most attractive place. The house, rising above it with superb aplomb, is breathtaking. The old walled kitchen garden was restored in 2007.

The west court at Doddington

INFORMATION

Location Doddington, nr Lincoln LN6 4RU, Lincolnshire; 5m W of Lincoln by B1190, signposted off A46 Lincoln bypass
Tel 01522 694308
Email info@doddingtonhall.com
Website www.doddingtonhall.com
English Heritage Register Grade II*
Owner Mr and Mrs J.J.Birch
Open mid Feb to Apr, Sun 1–5 (open Easter Mon); May to Sept, Wed, Sun and Bank Hol Mon 12–5
Area 12 acres/4.8 hectares

The Fairhaven Garden

EXQUISITE WOODLAND GARDEN IN THE MAGICAL SETTING OF THE NORFOLK BROADS, SURROUNDED BY NATURE

The natural spirit of the place is so strong at the Fairhaven Woodland and Water Garden that it makes gardening seem almost an act of vandalism. This ancient piece of woodland, threaded by streams and creeks, is one of the most beautiful things of its kind that you could imagine. Henry Broughton, later 2nd Lord Fairhaven, whose family made the garden at Anglesey Abbey (*see page 230*), came here in 1947 and with the greatest tact unostentatiously animated the place. It was the Debbage family who did the work, and until recently George Debbage was still in charge of the garden. Lord Fairhaven left the garden to a trust in 1973 and it opened to the public in 1975.

Waterside planting at Fairhaven

A SENSE OF SECRECY

Exotic plantings – azaleas, berberis, cherries. dogwoods, gaultherias and hydrangeas – were gently slipped in among the beautiful old beeches and oaks, and much underplanting now lines the banks of the streams and pools or flows about the feet of shrubs and trees – *Cardiocrinum giganteum*, ferns, irises, lysichitons and sheaves of dazzling candelabra primulas which now form probably the largest community of naturalised candelabra primulas in the UK. In spring the exotics intermingle with spreads of native wood anemones, bluebells and primroses. The place has a delicious sense of innocent secrecy. Bosky paths suddenly emerge in clearings of dappled light or, most exhilaratingly, open out to give serene views of South Walsham Broad lined with reeds and bulrushes. Suddenly revealed by the path is a superlative ancient oak, the "King Oak", said to be 950 years old. No garden I know has so many quacks,

twitterings, splashes and flutterings of birds. Indeed, there is a bird sanctuary here alongside the garden – an odd idea, for the garden itself seems to provide all the sanctuary that could be desired, with 95 species having been seen in the garden.

Many gardens give pleasure in a more or less detached way as you wander admiringly in them. Here, a spirit of contentment seems to descend almost as soon as you enter; it would be hard to imagine anyone having a really nasty argument in these surroundings, and if every community had access to such a place, thousands of social workers would become redundant overnight.

INFORMATION

Location School Road, South Walsham, Norwich NR13 6EA, Norfolk; E of South Walsham village, 9m NE of Norwich by B1140
Tel 01603 270449
Email enquiries@fairhavengarden.co.uk
Website www.fairhavengarden.co.uk
Owner The Fairhaven Garden Trust
Open daily 10–5 (closes 9 Wed and Thur May to Aug; closed 25 Dec)
Area 131 acres/53 hectares

The Gibberd Garden

A SUBLIME GARDEN FULL OF BEAUTY, POETRY AND SURPRISES – IDIOSYNCRATIC AND ORIGINAL

The architect Sir Frederick Gibberd came to live here in 1956. He inherited some fine garden features, the most striking of which was a lime avenue descending the slope north of the house. The garden he made is an amalgam of different styles.

GARDEN ORNAMENTS

Terraces and patios, ornamented with sculptures and pots, surround the house, and a narrow lawn and pool strike northwards, forming strong parallel axes. An octagonal mirador rises at the end of the pool. To the west the mirador commands handsome views over a lawn planted with amelanchiers, silver birches and cherries with sheets of daffodils in spring. On the other side is the lime avenue which continues the axis of the lawn garden deeper into the woods. The limes are planted close together, forming a nave of trunks, underplanted with bluebells, wood anemones and wood spurge.

The garden provides a home for a large collection of sculptures varying sharply both in quality and the skill with which they are used. A tormented nude figure of a girl by Gerda Rubinstein, for example, is placed as the focal point of a charming walk of coppiced hazels prettily underplanted with silver deadnettle and blue squills. But the statue is both coarse and shrill while the woodland planting with which it is associated is subtle and simple. Alongside it, on the other hand, a handsome broad-bellied stoneware pot by Monica Young stands in a spiral pool of gravel. The most memorable use of architectural fragments is in a glade in the north-western corner of the garden where a pair of soaring fluted stone columns rise from a mossy plinth. A few broken fragments lie in the grass and a row of swagged Coadestone urns perch on stone coping nearby. These were all rescued from the demolition of the old Coutts bank in the Strand in London – here, among trees, they have a lovely Arcadian presence.

The Gibberd Garden is like no other and, despite the criticism I have made, has the distinctive charm of an entirely personal approach to garden making which, at its best, produces effects of great and original beauty.

Columns and urns at the Gibberd Garden

INFORMATION

Location Marsh Lane, Gilden Way, Harlow CM17 0NA, Essex; E of the centre of Harlow, signed off B183 (Gilden Way), Jct 7 of M11
Tel 01279 442112
Email enquiries@ thegibberdgarden.co.uk
Website www. thegibberdgarden.co.uk
Owner The Gibberd Garden Trust
Open Apr to Sept, Sat, Sun and Bank Hol Mon 2–6
Area 16 acres/6.4 hectares

Glen Chantry

A BRILLIANTLY PLANTED GARDEN, SUPERBLY MAINTAINED BY PERFECTIONISTS, WITH AN EXCELLENT NURSERY TOO

Although plants rule in this garden, the layout is thoughtfully designed and the best is made of an awkward site. It is awkward in as many ways as a site can be awkward, in terms of the poverty of the soil (slightly acid but stuffed with stone); its exposure on top of a windy hill; lack of water (for this is just about the driest corner of England); and a gawkily sloping terrain. Any one of these problems might have deterred gardeners of less gumption than Wol and Sue Staines but, with the greatest aplomb, they have remedied the defects that are possible to remedy and learned to live with the others – a universal recipe for happiness among gardeners.

HAPPY PLANTS

Apart from some formal parts of the garden close to the house, the layout they adopted follows the flow of the land, with sweeping expanses of lawn curving about beds. Below the house is a rare feature: a modern rock garden of limestone and tufa richly planted with alpine plants. A naturalistic-looking

Glen Chantry stream garden

pool and streams have been created, which provide sites for such moisture-loving plants as hostas, rodgersias and primulas, while trees and shrubs give essential shade to plants such as anemones, erythroniums, hellebores, lilies and trilliums. I have seen few gardens in which ordinary plants look so healthy and more difficult ones seem so remarkably happy. For example, fritillaries grow superlatively here – not the everyday crown imperials or snake's head fritillaries with which almost any gardener may have some success, but trickier customers such as *F. michailovskyi* or *F. pallidiflora*. Species of another exceptionally attractive genus, the peonies, also seem completely at home – such as the tender *Paeonia cambessedesii* from Mallorca, one of the loveliest of them all in leaf and in flower and not at all easy to please. All this is achieved by very hard work – above all by the regular addition of lavish quantities of compost – and the standards of practical gardening here are of the highest. It is inspiring to see gardens of this sort but also dispiriting, for when you go home you will find that your own garden seems by comparison horribly neglected. The Staineses also find time to run an admirable nursery selling herbaceous perennials.

INFORMATION

Location Isham's Chase, Wickham Bishop CM8 3LG, Essex; 1m W of Wickham Bishop, 8m NW of Chelmsford by A12
Tel 01621 891342
Website www.glenchantry. demon.co.uk
Owner Wol and Sue Staines
Open Apr to end Sept, Fri and Sat 10–4 (also opens for NGS)
Area 3½ acres/1.4 hectares

Grimsthorpe Castle

GRAND PERIOD GARDENS – FLOWERS, FORMALITY AND SUPERB PARKLAND VIEWS FOR A GRAND PRIVATE ESTATE

Of the castle first built for Gilbert de Gant in the early 13th century, only a fragment survives. Since the early 16th century the estate has belonged to the Willoughby de Eresby family who altered the castle later in the 16th century, again in the late 17th century, and in the 18th century when Sir John Vanbrugh rebuilt the north front.

A FEELING OF THE PAST

The gardens were laid out in around 1680 by George London and much of what he did determines the pattern of the garden today. With many of the enclosures planned by London still in position, there is a powerful feeling of the past. To the east of the house is a parterre in which the compartments of a regular pattern of box-edged beds are filled with a single variety of rose or with lavender. The parterre is ornamented with fine stone urns, variegated holly clipped into domes and a lead figure of a warrior. To the east is a kitchen garden designed in 1965 by Lady Ancaster and John Fowler. This is a pioneer formal potager with beautifully clipped cones and domes of box and an orchard with trees planted in a pattern of triangular lawns. Old medlars and quinces are shaped into ornamental domes. The south court is divided into three with gravel paths and plain lawns decorated with old urns with finials carved to resemble flames. To its south are two gardens enclosed in yew hedges decorated with fanciful topiary. Inside is a pool with a fountain and lawns.

South-west of the house a long grass path is flanked with herbaceous borders, backed by yew hedges enlivened with buttresses of yew. The hedges swoop down between the buttresses to reveal an immense expanse of parkland and a lake spreading out below. The borders are planted in bold blocks of a single variety – pale yellow achillea, golden or rust-coloured daylilies, white leucanthemums, *Romneya coulteri* and sedums. Immediately to the west of the house a deep lawn runs the whole width of the house, with benches overlooking the park. Beyond the lawn the same swooping yew hedge is continued, now with a long border of shrub roses.

INFORMATION

Location Grimsthorpe, nr Bourne PE10 0LY, Lincolnshire; 4m W of Bourne on A151
Tel 01778 591205
Email ray@grimsthorpe.co.uk
Website www.grimsthorpe.co.uk
English Heritage Register Grade I
Owner Grimsthorpe and Drummond Castle Trust Ltd
Open Apr to May, Sun, Thurs and Bank Hol Mon 12–6; June to Sept, Sun to Thurs 12–6
Area 3,000 acres/1,214 hectares

The parterre at Grimsthorpe

Hatfield House

MAGNIFICENT 20TH-CENTURY GARDENS FOLLOW ANCIENT PATTERNS BELOW A TUDOR PALACE AND A JACOBEAN HOUSE

Here is a great private estate, maintained in old-fashioned seigneurial splendour, yet throwing its gates open to a public which relishes it. The house was built between 1607 and 1612 to the designs of Robert Lyminge for Robert Cecil, later Lord Salisbury. His descendant, the 7th Marquess of Salisbury, lives here today.

THE GARDENS' HISTORY

Work on the gardens started at the same time as the building of the house. The Cecils were great gardeners and they employed John Tradescant the Elder, one of the greatest plantsmen of the day (who later became royal gardener to King Charles I). Also

The knot garden at Hatfield

involved was the elusive but fascinating Salomon de Caus, the French water engineer and garden designer who was involved in several famous European gardens. In the early 17th century Hatfield was one of the great gardens of its age, but in the 18th century, as was so often the case, the elaborately inventive formal gardens were disposed of and a landscape park, running up to the very walls of the house, was put in place. In the 19th century new formal gardens were made, but it would be fair to say that only in the late 20th century, under the inspiration of the 6th Marchioness of Salisbury, did the gardens resume the distinction of the past. Lady Salisbury, who as Viscountess Cranborne had revitalised the remarkable gardens at Cranborne

Manor (*see page 35*), came to Hatfield in 1972. She was an experienced gardener, a knowledgeable garden historian and plantswoman, and above all she had the vitality and imagination needed to give the gardens at Hatfield new focus.

LADY SALISBURY

Immediately beside the early Tudor Old Palace, on the site of a 19th-century rose garden, Lady Salisbury created a new four-part knot garden of lively decorative inventiveness. Here is a maze and three "closed knots" filled with plants of a Tradescantian kind, including those introduced by the two Tradescants, father and son, such as goat's beard (*Aruncus dioicus*) and Michaelmas daisy (*Aster lateriflorus*, formerly *A. tradescantii*).

The main house's Victorian Privy Garden, enclosed in an 18th-century lime walk, was replanted with sprightly mixed borders, and a Scented Garden with camomile paths is heady with the perfume of honeysuckles, lavender,

lilies, Guernsey stock (*Matthiola incana*) and waves of roses. To the south is the Wilderness Garden, a marvellous spread of trees and shrubs with huge quantities of spring-flowering plants in the grass beneath them – cowslips, crocuses, fritillaries, scillas and tulips.

In the East Garden a formal arrangement had been reinstated in the 1840s with an unconvincing "Jacobean" layout of elaborately fussy beds disposed on a large square of lawn overlooked by a terrace and a grand double staircase. The L-shaped beds have gone and in their place are sixteen square box-edged beds of mixed planting which have an avenue of topiary yew shapes down the middle. On either side of the lawn are double rows of clipped mop-headed holm oaks forming shady walks. This great tapestry of plants and patterns, immediately beneath the house's façade, was designed to be seen from above.

The Woodland Garden further to the east and close to the New Pond, which dates from Tradescant's time, has been made since 1990. Here is a spectacular display of snowdrops beneath superb old oaks, and flowering shrubs are being introduced along the paths. In 2002 a totally new garden was made below the south front of the house, with a sunken parterre, a rose walk and box topiary.

Hatfield is an old-fashioned garden, executed with panache. In one regard it is old fashioned in a particularly modern way, for it is gardened organically throughout; Lady Salisbury was a pioneer member of HDRA.

INFORMATION

Location Hatfield AL9 5NQ, Hertfordshire; in the centre of Hatfield, 20m N of London, Jct 3 of A1(M)

Tel 01707 287010

Email visitors@hatfield-house.co.uk,

Website www.hatfield-house.co.uk

English Heritage Register Grade I

Owner The Marquess of Salisbury

Open early Apr to end Sept, daily 11–5 (East Garden open only Thur)

Area 30 acres/12 hectares

Helmingham Hall

MOATED HOUSE AND FLOWER GARDENS OF DREAMLIKE BEAUTY, RUN BY A PERFECTIONIST

The approach to Helmingham Hall is one of the loveliest of any house in England. The drive curves across an ancient deer park, still with fallow and red deer and studded with remarkable old oaks. The beautiful brick house, started in 1480 for John Tollemache, stands confidently, protected by its moat. South-west of the house is a walled garden, also enclosed by a moat. The present garden has 18th-century brick walls but it may even pre-date the house. However, although there are traces of earlier gardens, most of what we see today dates from the 20th century.

The borders at Helmingham

FLOWERY EXUBERANCE

The moated garden opens with a burst of decorative exuberance. A box parterre whose compartments are filled with *Santolina incana* and ornamented with stone urns on plinths, is enclosed on three sides by brick walls. About the walls are borders edged in lavender and filled with Hybrid Musk roses underplanted with London pride, *Campanula lactiflora* and *Alstroemeria ligtu* hybrids. The roses, sweetly scented and flowering throughout the summer, flank wrought-iron gates which lead into the walled kitchen garden. Here, a path runs the whole length of the garden between narrow herbaceous borders, forming a chasm of flowers. The garden is divided into eight partitions (as it has been since the 16th century), separated by paths and by tunnels festooned with sweet peas, ornamental gourds or runner beans. The beds are still used for fruit and vegetables but Lady Tollemache keeps making encroachments for decorative purposes. All in all it is one of the loveliest examples in the country of an ornamental kitchen garden.

A new garden north-east of the house was laid out from 1982 by Lady

Tollemache. Here is a knot of herbs and, beyond it, a four-part pattern of rose beds edged in billowing lavender or hyssop. The roses, chiefly old shrub varieties or species are lavishly underplanted with *Alchemilla mollis*, blue and white *Campanula persicifolia*, geraniums and violas. David Austin roses and later-flowering perennials prolong the flowering season. The whole area, except on the house side, is enclosed in finely detailed yew hedges with piers and arched openings. In the park a new woodland garden is evolving with rare species of trees and shrubs.

The gardens at Helmingham make reference to the formality of Tudor garden design, and their flowery exuberance is also true to the Tudor spirit. The whole ensemble – park, house and gardens – is remarkably beautiful.

INFORMATION

Location nr Stowmarket IP14 6EF, Suffolk; 9m N of Ipswich by B1077

Tel 01473 890363 **Fax** 01473 890776

Email events@helmingham.com

Website www.helmingham.com

English Heritage Register Grade I

Owner Lord and Lady Tollemache

Open May to mid Sept, Sun 2–6 (also groups by appointment on Wed 2–5; individuals may join a Wed group if one has been booked)

Area 10 acres/4 hectares

Houghton Hall

HISTORIC ESTATE WITH LIVELY NEW ORNAMENTAL GARDENS FOR A GRAND WALLED KITCHEN GARDEN

Houghton Hall was built in the 1720s for Sir Robert Walpole. There was an elaborate formal garden here in the early 18th century. Surviving from that time is the Water House, an elegant classical building with a first-floor loggia that housed a horse-powered pump which provided water for the stables and outhouses. It stands today at the head of a double avenue of horse chestnuts, commanding beautiful views of the house to the south.

A NEW GARDEN

A completely new garden has been made at Houghton in recent years in the old brick-walled kitchen garden to one side of the house. Here, largely designed by Julian and Isabel Bannerman, is a sprightly layout of flowers and formality. A pair of herbaceous borders forms the chief axis, running north to south. At the southern end a rustic pavilion of unbarked wood has a grand pediment filled with deers' antlers. Inside is a

The rose garden at Houghton

noble bench, painted chocolate brown and gold – a William Kent design echoing his work on the interior of the house. In the south-east corner of the garden, hedged in yew and screened by pleached limes, is a formal orchard of plums. The only other ornament is a bench and an urn standing out against the dark yew. The effect is simple, elegant and beautiful.

A rose garden has box-edged beds, each filled with a single variety of rose and with occasional standard roses at the centre. Statues of classical deities stand among the flowery profusion and at the heart of the garden is a sunken pool and fountain. On the west side of the garden a walk of flowering cherries runs along beds of *Iris pallida* 'Argentea Variegata'. To one side a raised pool edged in box has a fountain which leaps and falls rhythmically. It is flanked by beds of box and lavender which trace the initials S C – commemorating Sybil Cholmondeley, the present Marquess of Cholmondeley's grandmother. A croquet lawn with a Kentian wooden pavilion is enclosed in yew hedges pierced on one side by openings containing Janus busts which look both ways through the hedge. This is a charming garden, full of delight and decoration – a contrast to the more sombre and serious parkland that provides the setting for the house.

INFORMATION

Location Houghton, King's Lynn PE31 6UE, Norfolk; 11m NE of King's Lynn by A148
Tel 01485 528569
Email enquiries@houghtonhall.com
Website www.houghtonhall.com
English Heritage Register Grade I
Owner The Marquess of Cholmondeley
Open Easter Sun to Sept, Wed, Thur, Sun and Bank Hol Mon 11–5.30
Area (Walled garden) 5 acres/2 hectares

Hyde Hall

A GARDEN THAT SHOWS WHAT IS POSSIBLE ON TOP OF A WINDY HILL IN THE DRIEST CORNER OF ENGLAND

Mr and Mrs R.H.M. Robinson came to farm at Hyde Hall in 1955. The house is on the top of a hill (by Essex standards a veritable Himalaya) in a windswept part of the country that is also just about the driest place in England. They made a garden from scratch and filled it with an astonishing array of plants. They formed the Hyde Hall Trust which, in 1993, gave the estate to the Royal Horticultural Society.

The Dry Garden at Hyde Hall

RHS INNOVATIONS

The RHS has built on the Robinsons' garden. A pergola, clothed in clematis and white wisteria, now leads into the garden, and a handsome rose garden has two rows of rectangular beds edged in box or yew and a central walk with tall obelisks of climbing roses. At the entrance to the house an elegant parterre has plants of ornamental foliage. The former farmyard pond is now a gently formalised lily pool with ornamental fish and a cascade.

Part of the Robinsons' original garden, Hermione's Garden, takes advantage of a boggy site and the shade of an old ash to grow ferns, hellebores, hostas, ligularias and rheums. In the Woodland Garden the Robinsons established a windbreak and made the naturally neutral soil sufficiently acid to cultivate rhododendrons. The species grown include some of the tender large-leafed kinds such as *R. macabeanum* and *R. sinogrande*. South-east of the house the Robinsons laid out a series of island beds (often with substantial ornamental trees) and borders of winter interest (with grasses and heathers). On the edge of this area they made a long border of shrub roses underplanted with foxtail lilies (*Eremurus robustus*).

One of the most successful creations of the RHS is the Dry Garden where rocks rise above gravel and paths wind about the undulating site. Here, in a scheme no doubt inspired by another Essex gardener, Beth Chatto (*see page 237*), is a wide range of plants that thrive in the driest conditions, many of which will form self-supporting colonies – cistuses, euphorbias, lavenders, penstemons, salvias, sedums and verbenas. Ornamental grasses, including some of the larger species of *Cortaderia*, New Zealand flax (*Phormium* species) and yuccas, make strong punctuation marks. It is delightful and very effective – a desert garden on a hilltop in Essex.

INFORMATION

Location Buckhatch Lane, Rettendon, Chelmsford CM3 8ET, Essex; 7m SE of Chelmsford by A130 and minor road
Tel 01245 400256
Email hydehall@rhs.org.uk
Website www.rhs.org.uk
Owner The Royal Horticultural Society
Open daily (except 25 Dec) April to Sept 10–6; Oct to Mar, 10–5 (or dusk)
Area 136 acres/55 hectares

The Old Vicarage Garden

SPECTACULAR FORMAL GARDENS WITH MAGNIFICENT PLANTS FLAWLESSLY CULTIVATED BY PERFECTIONIST GARDENERS

In recent years every visit to the Old Vicarage Garden has revealed new splendours as Alan Gray and Graham Robeson have extended their intricate and opulently planted garden. They bought the Arts and Crafts vicarage in 1973, at first using it for weekends and holidays; but since 1986 they have lived here full-time. There was no garden then and the garden they have made obeys the principle of consulting the genius of the place.

LAVISH PLANTING

Greg and Robeson built brick walls and buildings (they seemingly employed a full-time bricklayer) sympathetic to the Arts and Crafts spirit, while opening vistas onto the external landscape and drawing in church towers as eyecatchers. The proximity of the sea – which is only 1½ miles/2.4km away – has a pronounced effect on the climate, allowing (provided protection is given from the wind) the cultivation of many tender plants. The soil here is richly fertile loam which gives their lavish planting an extra luxuriance.

A strong southerly axis extends from the house – a long grassy walk of hedges starts with an avenue of yew pyramids and ends with a tall-roofed pavilion overlooking the Mediterranean Garden in which plants like *Beschorneria yuccoides* grow with abandon. This axis provides a backbone for the framework of the garden. Long straight walks, with yew or holm oak hedges, an avenue of acacias, or rows of apples underplanted with catmint guide the eye to the different parts of the garden. The Mediterranean Garden takes advantage of the drainage afforded by gravelly soil to grow a sumptuous array of cistus, echiums, lavenders, rosemary and yucca. An Exotic Garden has sumptuous borders of bananas and palms underplanted with cannas, dahlias, grasses and salvias overlooked by an oriental-style pavilion. In high summer the planting looks natural – in fact much of it has to be bedded out and some of the tender plants require winter protection. A garden inspired by the Arizona desert resembles a dry river bed and is planted with agaves, aloes, dasylirions and swathes of self-sown *Eschscholzia californica*.

Throughout the garden there is evidence of much skill in planting and cultivation. There are cool and restrained corners but overall this is a garden of surprise and drama, of explosive colour and form – the rumble of a symphony orchestra rather than the tootling of a flute.

The desert Garden at the Old Vicarage

INFORMATION

Location East Ruston, Norwich NR12 9HN, Norfolk; nr East Ruston church, off A149, signposted Bacton, Happisburgh; left at T junction and ignore three signs to East Ruston
Tel 01692 650432 **Fax** 01692 650233
Email erov@btinternet.com
Website www.e-ruston-oldvicaragegardens. co.uk
Owner Alan Gray and Graham Robeson
Open end Mar to end Oct, Sat, Sun, Wed, Fri and Bank Hol Mon 2–5.30
Area 12 acres/4.8 hectares

Peckover House

BUSTLING TOWN GARDEN WITH EXCELLENT TREES, BORDERS, ROSE ARBOUR AND GLASSHOUSES

This is a rare opportunity to see a notable town garden. Peckover House is a beautiful early Georgian house, built before 1727. The walled garden is as decorative as the house, its variety and charm appearing all the more attractive for its unexpected position in the middle of a busy market town. There are some remarkably large trees here – a noble *Gingko biloba*, a *Liriodendron tulipifera* and a splendid *Sophora japonica*.

Close to the house, a 19th-century feature, Alexa's Rose Garden, has been reconstructed from an old photograph. A circle of metal arches supports some of the swooniest of all climbing roses – 'Madame Isaac Pereire', 'Climbing Souvenir de la Malmaison', 'Sanders' White Rambler', 'Blush Noisette' and 'Madame Grégoire Staechelin'. At its

Topiary peacocks at Peckover

centre a circular lily pool is surrounded by curved beds cut into the turf and planted with tulips and violets in the spring and cannas and coleus in summer.

SCORNFUL OF FASHION

Near the rose garden a green and white painted summerhouse overlooks an oval lily pool. A pair of topiary peacocks rise above an opening in a yew hedge leading to a gravel path running between borders with mixed plantings of acanthus, buddleias, *Clematis recta*, crocosmia, euphorbias, Japanese anemones and roses. Sections are divided by hedges of *Viburnum opulus* 'Compactum', *Hydrangea arborescens* subsp. *discolor* 'Sterilis' or hibiscus. An arbour of roses spans the path and beyond it a glasshouse contains three large orange trees. A fern house alongside protects tender ferns and orchids and is heavy with the ponderous scent of stephanotis; its narrow passage brings visitors unusually close to the plants. A range of cold frames and compost bins is hidden behind a hedge of golden privet and against a wall is a swashbuckling Victorian arrangement: a ribbon border in which alternate circles of pale pink and hot cerise busy lizzies are edged with loops of thrift on one side and santolina on the other. Much of the charm of the garden comes from an unemphatic idiosyncrasy which seems to scorn fashion.

INFORMATION

Location North Brink, Wisbech PE13 1JR, Cambridgeshire; in the centre of Wisbech, well signed in the town
Tel and fax 01945 583463
Email peckover@nationaltrust.org.uk
English Heritage Register Grade II
Owner The National Trust
Open mid Mar to Oct, Sat to Wed 12–5
Area 2 acres/0.8 hectare

Saling Hall

A SPLENDID COLLECTION OF TREES IN A FINE PARKLAND SETTING, AND CHARMING WALLED GARDENS

The garden of the amateur – in the true sense of that word – is often of quite special attraction. Hugh Johnson is probably most famous as the man who invented modern wine-writing, but he also loves gardens and plants (especially trees), and has written memorably on both. He and his wife, Judy, came here in 1970, to a delightful 17th-century house with a pretty garden that needed refocussing. Furthermore, this was the time when Dutch elm disease was about to sweep across the country, devastating the landscape, not least the woodland of Saling Hall. The urge to plant trees was given even more pressing significance. An old walled garden, built at the same time as the house, with herring-bone paths of brick and rows of old apple trees clipped into mushroom shapes, makes a fine flower garden – formality blurred by profusion but with firm lines. Bold pyramids of box mark the corners of four central beds filled with roses, daylilies, irises, delphiniums, geraniums, and phlomis, and a splendid blowsy lead figure of Flora stands at the centre, enclosed by a metal arbour. A procession of Irish junipers (*Juniperus communis* 'Hibernica') marches down the centre of each of these beds. Mixed beds under the walls are large enough for such ornamental trees as *Koelreuteria paniculata* and *Gleditsia triacanthos* 'Sunburst'.

The walled garden at Saling Hall

THE ARBORETUM

These pleasures are an *hors d'oeuvre* for the main course which is the aboretum that lies beyond the walls. Elms and poplars ruled here before the Johnsons came, but now the land has been transformed into a miniature landscape park enriched with marvellous trees woven skilfully into the scene. Eyecatchers – a giant stone ball, a pedimented temple, a Japanese arch, a stag on a plinth, a millennium menhir – draw you on but not for long, for you will be sidetracked to savour some tree. Birches, maples, oaks, pines, willows, wingnuts and countless others grow as they should – not as exhibits in a museum but as part of a beguiling landscape. A private garden of this kind has only to honour its surroundings and please its owners and their friends. The garden at Saling Hall is animated by a sense of the pleasure that gardening brings – and this in turn has a palpable effect on the spirit of the place.

INFORMATION

Location Great Saling, nr Braintree CM7 5DT, Essex; 6m NW of Braintree by A120
Tel 01371 850141 **Fax** 01371 850274
Email hugh@salinghall.com
English Heritage Register Grade II
Owner Hugh Johnson
Open May to Jul, Wed 2–5
Area 12 acres/4.8 hectares

Sandringham House

STATELY VICTORIAN LAKESIDE PLANTINGS AND A FINE FORMAL FLOWER GARDEN FOR A ROYAL HOUSE

The estate at Sandringham goes back to the 18th century. The old house was demolished after 1862 (except for a conservatory, built in 1854 by S.S. Teulon for the Hon. Charles Spencer Cowper, now a billiard room) when the estate was bought as a country house for Albert Edward, Prince of Wales. The house was rebuilt in what Pevsner calls "frenetic Jacobean". The estate remains in the possession of the royal family who use it chiefly for holidays and shooting.

The gardens, apart from a few old trees, date from the 1870s onwards; they were designed by William Broderick Thomas whose nephew, the architect and garden designer Francis Inigo Thomas, said of him: "[he] gave up fox-hunting for laying out the places of country gentlefolk in the prevailing 'landscape' manner." Thomas gave the pleasure grounds of Sandringham the essential character they possess today. He moved a lake further from the house to the south-west and made a new lake to the south. The banks of the upper lake are shrouded in trees, with a Pulhamite boathouse/grotto on its north bank and, in a prominent position on its east bank, the Nest, a curious

The upper lake at Sandringham

gingerbread pavilion of rustic stone, standing on top of a rock garden. This, with its pretty panelled interior, was built in 1915 for Edward VII's Queen, Alexandra, and has an inscription, "The Queen's Nest. A small offering to the blessed lady from her beloved majesty's devoted old servant General Probin".

SUBTLE FORMAL GARDEN

North of the house is a subtle and refined formal garden designed in 1947 by Sir Geoffrey Jellicoe. A series of compartments threaded along a gravel path and enclosed in high box hedges contain mixed borders of buddleias, Brompton stocks, echinaceas, eupatorium, geraniums, irises, rosemary and roses, with judicious sprinklings of annuals. Four of the compartments contain nothing at all except a flawless square lawn. At their northern end is an 18th-century figure of winged Father Time. The whole arrangement is flanked by double pleached lime walks, one of which culminates in a splendid plump gilt Buddha guarded by Chinese lions.

The entrance courtyard east of the house has magnificent yew hedges with finely tailored bays for benches on either side. Splendid trees, especially conifers dating from Thomas's time, crowd in.

INFORMATION

Location Sandringham, King's Lynn PE35 6EN, Norfolk; 9m NE of King's Lynn by B1440

Tel 01553 612908

Email visits@ sandringhamestate.co.uk

Website www. sandringhamestate.co.uk

English Heritage Register Grade II*

Owner HM The Queen

Open Apr to Oct (closed late Jul and early Aug; phone for details), daily 11–4.45

Area 60 acres/24 hectares

Sheringham Park

A BRILLIANTLY SIMPLE LANDSCAPE PARK BY HUMPHRY REPTON, MAKING THE MOST OF A LOVELY SETTING

Sheringham is the last work of Humphry Repton and it gave him special pleasure for it lies in his own home county. His client was a rich young man, Abbot Upcher, who died in 1817 before work was completed. The site chosen was a lovely combe, near the coast and with fine sea views – Repton thought that it possessed "more of what my predecessor called Capabilities" than any place he had seen in fifty years. Repton was also asked to design a new, grander house to replace the existing farmhouse. He and his son John built a vaguely Italianate villa, tucked away behind rising land to protect it from the fierce coastal winds from the north. Repton also devised a drive that would curl round from the south and reveal the house with its wooded hill behind and the sea and ships displayed to the east.

Repton's Red Book of proposals for Sheringham shows a domed rotunda on a vantage point to the east of the drive, commanding wide views of the whole estate. This was not built until 1975 when a design was commisioned from the architect James Fletcher-Watson based on Repton's original.

STUNNING VIEWS

The route that visitors take through the park today only gradually reveals the character of the place. The path plunges into woodland, with oaks, Scots pines and sycamores most in evidence, but with much underplanting of rhododendrons. Then, after skirting a wood – with views of the house across the valley to the east and of cattle grazing in pastures – a path leads across a field, where you may have to dodge the cows, and comes to the temple on a wooded eminence. The view from the temple is extraordinarily beautiful. The house is seen far across the valley, partly enclosed in trees, and behind it the sea is revealed in the distance – a sliver of blue between two sweeps of trees on the horizon. Repton himself wrote that "This may be considered my most favourite work" and it is indeed a place that is very easy to love.

INFORMATION

Location Upper Sheringham, Sheringham NR26 8TL, Norfolk; 2m SW of Sheringham by A148
Tel 01263 820550
Email sheringhampark@nationaltrust.org.uk
English Heritage Register Grade II*
Owner The National Trust
Open daily dawn–dusk
Area 90 acres/36 hectares

The Sheringham temple

Somerleyton Hall

GRAND VICTORIAN GARDENS WITH FINE TREES, WALLED GARDEN, BORDERS, GLASSHOUSES AND A MAGNIFICENT MAZE

This is one of the most enjoyable and interesting gardens in Suffolk. At a quick glance it seems entirely Victorian. However, the estate was established by the 17th century when it was described as having a "variety of seats, statues, fish ponds, a house for pleasure newly erected and diverse other rarities". No traces of this remain but in the early 18th century avenues were made of which traces are visible.

In 1844 a new house was built for a new owner, Morton Peto, an archetypal Victorian self-made man who started as a bricklayer, was by his thirties an immensely wealthy building tycoon, and was knighted in 1855. To the Italianate mansion he added gardens largely designed by W.A. Nesfield. A formal garden west of the house was laid out in 1846 – now much simplified – with urns, rose beds and clipped shapes of golden and common yew. North of the house are lawns and fine trees (oaks, cedars of Lebanon and sweet chestnuts) and a statue of Atalanta gathering the golden apples.

THE KITCHEN GARDEN

A dramatic Wellingtonia with wide-spreading branches stands at the front of the entrance to the walled kitchen garden. The entrance to the kitchen garden is itself scarcely less dramatic – an arched opening in a screen of brick and stone with niches carrying urns of flowers, richly carved ornament over wrought-iron gates, and the whole crowned with a pair of bronze agaves in stone troughs. Inside, glasshouses run the whole length of the south-facing wall on each side of the entrance – the original peach houses. Running across the garden are magnificent ridge and furrow vine houses, probably designed by Sir Joseph Paxton. A cross walk leads

The kitchen garden at Somerleyton Hall

under a long pergola with grapevines, roses and an ancient wisteria, to a maze of yew hedges designed by W.A. Nesfield – infuriatingly difficult.

Any visitor to Somerleyton should also visit the village which Sir Morton Peto rebuilt in picturesque style with half-timbered cottages *ornés* crowned by high-rising bogus Tudor chimney stacks. Peto went bankrupt in 1866 and the estate was bought by Sir Francis Crossley whose descendant, the Hon. Hugh Crossley, still owns it. The garden is finely cared for and very little has changed in it since the 19th century, making it one of the outstanding survivors of its period in the country.

INFORMATION

Location Somerleyton, Lowestoft NR32 5QQ, Suffolk; 5m NW of Lowestoft by B1074
Tel 08712 224244
Email enquiries@somerleyton.co.uk
Website www.somerleyton.co.uk
English Heritage Register Grade II*
Owner Hon. Hugh Crossley
Open Apr to Oct, Thur, Sun, and Bank Hol Fri, Sun and Mon (also Tue and Wed in Jul and Aug) 10–5; Nov, Sun 10–5
Area 12 acres/4.8 hectares

Wimpole Hall

SUPERB PARKLAND AND RESTORED EARLY 19TH-CENTURY FLOWER GARDENS IN A WONDERFUL SETTING

The first house at Wimpole was built for Sir Thomas Chicheley in the 1640s. Kip's engraving in *Britannia Illustrata* of 1707 shows a formal garden of immense grandeur and complexity. Daniel Defoe, when it was still very new, described it as being filled with "all the most exquisite Contrivances which the best Heads cou'd invent". This garden was possibly the work of George London and Henry Wise and was made even grander in the 1720s when Charles Bridgeman added an elaborate pattern of avenues.

AN ARCADIAN SETTING

Most of the formal garden was dismantled in the 18th century, chiefly by Capability Brown from 1767 onwards, leaving Wimpole Hall by the end of the century enclosed in a naturalistic landscape park with traces of earlier avenues, new billowing belts of trees and serpentine lakes. Brown did, however, leave the spectacular double avenue of elms to the south of the house, which survived until Dutch elm disease destroyed it in the 1970s. A ruinous eyecatcher, to the design of

Sanderson Miller, was built in 1768 – "foolish, fantastic mock ruins", Col John Byng called it on his visit to Wimpole in 1790. In 1801 Humphry Repton produced a Red Book for Wimpole but apart from a formal flower garden below the house's north façade few of his proposals were put into force.

One of the most attractive features of Wimpole today is the beauty of the house's position – an open site on an airy eminence commanding distant views. To the south, gliding down the hill in front of the house, is a double avenue of limes – a replacement of the ancient elm avenue. Behind the house a mid 19th-century flower parterre is tricked out with brilliant bedding plants. This garden is enclosed by railings (a suggestion of Repton's), beyond which sheep or cattle graze in parkland studded with trees, with Sanderson Miller's ruin rising in the distance. Repton had the ingenious idea of framing this view of Brown's park with a pair of gate piers capped with splendid early 18th-century urns, and they are still in place. The park provides exactly the kind of Arcadian setting for the classical house that the 18th-century landscaper so desired.

The flower parterre at Wimpole Hall

INFORMATION

Location Arrington, Royston
SG8 0BW, Hertfordshire;
SW of Cambridge by A603
Tel 01223 206000
Email wimpolehall@
nationaltrust.org.uk
Website www.wimpole.org
English Heritage Register
Grade I
Owner The National Trust
Open mid Mar to Oct, Sun to
Wed 10.30–5; (also open
Thurs, mid Jul to Aug); phone/
see website for winter
openings
Area 20 acres/8 hectares

Wrest Park

GRAND EARLY 18TH-CENTURY GARDENS WITH SPLENDID LATE VICTORIAN ADDITIONS FORM A THRILLING LANDSCAPE

The de Grey family came to live at Silsoe in the 13th century. In the late 17th century Anthony de Grey, 11th Earl of Kent, rebuilt the medieval and Tudor house and made grand new formal gardens. Kip's engraving in *Britannia Illustrata* (1707) shows a walled garden south of the house, parterres with circular pools, and two mazes of different designs. The central axis of the walled garden is continued beyond gates in the wall by the Long Water – a canal flanked by hedges. Further formal gardens lie to the east of the house and there is a second canal at an angle to the south-east of the house.

A MIXTURE OF STYLES

All this was greatly extended by the 12th Earl (who became the first Duke in 1710). His Great Garden introduced woodland threaded with formal rides on each side of the Long Water, new

canals at right-angles to it and, as a magnificent eyecatcher at its southern end, the Pavilion – a beautiful domed building by Thomas Archer, built between 1709 and 1711. Later in the century, between 1758 and 1760, Capability Brown was consulted by Jemima, Marchioness Grey, and his work is commemorated by a tall stone column topped by an acorn, with an inscription that acknowledges "the professional assistance of Lancelot Brown, Esq., 1758" in the beautifying of the gardens. In the 1830s Thomas, Earl de Grey, demolished the old house and built in its place (to his own designs) a mansion in extravagant French 18th-century style. He also laid out suitably flamboyant parterres on its south side, and these, with swirling patterns of cut turf, curved box-edged beds of annuals, and statues of Venus and Adonis and Diana and Endymion, are still in place.

The great charm of Wrest Park comes from the most unlikely mixture

The Pavilion and canal at Wrest Park

of ingredients in which features from the gardens of different periods, and of very different character, live cheek by jowl.

ORNAMENTAL BUILDINGS

Archer's Pavilion is still a dominant ornament in the landscape (Horace Walpole saw it in 1771 and much disliked "the frightful Temple designed by Mr Archer"), rearing up confidently at the far end of a canal, with a fine lead statue of King William III, possibly by Henry Cheere. East of the canal, a serpentine stream winds its way through the woods with an elegant Chinese pavilion (a 19th-century reconstruction of an 18th-century original) on its bank. The stream here, spanned by an arched "Chinese" bridge (1876), was a canal in the 1st Duke's garden and presumably made informal by Capability Brown.

The woodland gardens on either side of the Long Water are divided with a curious mixture of straight rides, sometimes leading to Archer's Pavilion, and winding walks. In the north-west corner of the woodland is a bowling green overlooked by a grand pillared building with a pretty interior. This was built for the 1st Duke and possibly designed by Batty Langley.

The Chinese pavilion at Wrest Park

One of the oddest surviving buildings at Wrest is a monumental bath house, or hermitage, partly thatched and fashioned of massive blocks of uncut stone. Horace Walpole thought that it was designed by Capability Brown and approved of its "bold good taste". In fact it was built in 1770 and designed by Edward Stephens to resemble a semi-ruined classical building. This lies on the far west side of the garden, behind the handsome Frenchified orangery which, like the house, was designed by the Earl de Grey in Louis XVth style, and built under the supervision of James Clephan between 1836 and 1839.

The Wrest Park estate remained in the family until 1917, and after World War II was bought by the Ministry of Public Building and Works, who passed it in due course to English Heritage. The house, retaining all its splendour, is let out. Fortunately the gardens and their beautiful buildings – one of the most alluring living anthologies of English garden taste – are open to the public.

INFORMATION

Location Silsoe MK45 4HS, Bedfordshire; ¾m E of Silsoe by A6
Tel 01525 860152
Website www.english-heritage.org.uk/visits
English Heritage Register Grade I
Owner English Heritage
Open Apr to Jun, Sept to Oct, Sat, Sun and Bank Hol Mon 10–6; Jul to Aug, Thurs to Mon 10–6
Area 80 acres/32 hectares

NORTH of ENGLAND

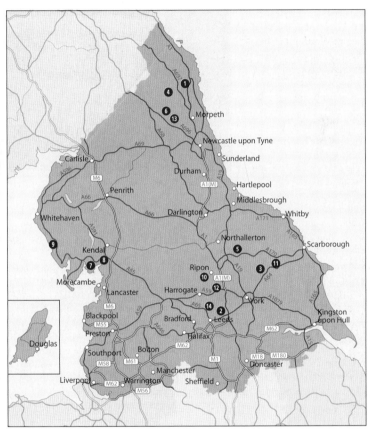

GARDENS TO VISIT

1. Alnwick Castle
2. BramhamPark
3. Castle Howard
4. Cragside House
5. Duncombe Park
6. Herterton House Gardens
7. Holker Hall
8. Levens Hall
9. Muncaster Castle
10. Newby Hall Gardens
11. Scampston Walled Garden
12. Studley Royal
13. Wallington
14. York Gate

Alnwick Castle

A DAZZLING MODERN GARDEN FOR THE ANCIENT CASTLE OF ALNWICK WITH FINE PLANTING AND SURPRISES

The medieval castle at Alnwick, built near the river Aln, is the home of the Dukes of Northumberland. From 2000 an 18th-century walled garden has been spectacularly transformed as the Alnwick Garden, designed by Jacques Wirtz and his son Peter.

The site is steeply sloping and the dominating, indeed overwhelming, feature at its heart is a gigantic cascade in which lively patterns of water jets play. Outlined in sinuous stone edging, the cascade has paths and serpentine tunnels of hornbeam on either side. Patterns of water jets play about the cascade. Behind the hornbeam tunnels, circular pools are ringed with fastigiate oaks (*Quercus robur* 'Fastigiata') and each pool has a soaring water jet.

The cascade at Alnwick

THE WALLED GARDEN

Above the cascade lies the walled Ornamental Garden, linked by its use of water but quite different in mood. Water from a square raised pool in the centre falls into rills one of which takes it down to the Cascade and others to circular pools at the centre of circular gardens hedged in yew. A pergola with clematis and roses surrounds the central pool and a pattern of square box-hedged beds spread out on either side. Each is framed with a screen of crab-apples (*Malus* 'Red Sentinel') high up on a framework of bamboos. Here are many roses, often planted with fruit – the pink rose 'Ballerina' is underplanted with neat rows of 'Yellow Wonder' strawberries and *Rosa* 'Albertine' (standard trained) is underplanted with different cultivars of blueberry. Deep, generously planted, mixed borders run under the walls, with substantial ornamental trees – among them *Koelreuteria paniculata, Malus sargentii* or *Ptelea trifoliata* – rising high.

To one side of the lower garden a rose garden has densely planted beds, tunnels and arbours of roses, with many David Austin English Roses, old shrub and climbing roses and winding paths. On the opposite side of the garden is the Poison Garden where two curving tunnels of ivy wind among poisonous plants which range from the exotic, like belladonna and cannabis, to the familiar like laburnum.

Further gardens are to be added – Alnwick is a developing project. Already it is one of the grandest and most enjoyable gardens in the country, immensely attractive to the thousands of visitors who come.

INFORMATION

Location Denwick Lane, Alnwick NE66 1YU, Northumberland; in Alnwick, 1½m W of A1
Tel 01665 511350
Fax 01665 510876
Email info@alnwickgarden.com
Website www.alnwickgarden.com
Owner The Duke of Northumberland
Open daily 10–5 (closed 25 Dec)
Area 12 acres/4.8 hectares

Bramham Park

SUPERB EARLY 18TH-CENTURY FORMAL LANDSCAPE GARDEN WITH BEAUTIFUL BUILDINGS AND GIANT VISTAS

The garden was laid out in the very early 18th century for Robert Benson, 1st Lord Bingley, who in all likelihood designed his own remarkably attractive house as well as the grandiose formal landscape that provides its spectacular setting. Benson had been on the Grand Tour and saw the latest French gardens. Under their influence he laid out giant patterns of walks lined with beech hedges and animated with ornamental buildings and ornaments. Unlike a French garden, however, there is no rigidly geometric frame to the layout: straight vistas, sometimes of vast size, shoot off at unaccountable angles and something surprising – a temple, an obelisk or a distant view back to the house – is suddenly revealed. The land rises and falls: a long walk appears to end in a distant stone urn (and you fail to realise how far away it is because you are not used to urns 12ft/3.6m high) but when you finally arrive at the urn you will find that the walk continues down the slope beyond it, seemingly without destination but revealing delicious views over the rural landscape.

Fine buildings, which are all rather later than the garden's original layout, are woven into the landscape. James Paine's summerhouse of around 1760 marks the opening of an immense vista which runs past the garden front of the house, past a noble formal water garden, past a domed Ionic temple (also, possibly by James Paine), to culminate in a soaring obelisk which, in turn, is at the centre of an explosion of five radiating avenues.

A GARDEN TO SAVOUR

The architect Colen Campbell, seeing Bramham in its heyday, admired the "curious gardens laid out with great judgement". Visitors may easily share his admiration but Bramham requires an entirely different kind of attention from that which you would give to a pretty garden of flowers. The only way to appreciate it to the full is to take a long walk and gradually submit to the atmosphere of the place. You will need at least two or three hours to get to grips with the vast landscape, pausing from time to time to relish its beauty from different angles and to think about the sources of its charms. Having seen it once, properly, you will not forget it.

The tree-lined walks at Bramham Park

INFORMATION

Location nr Wetherby LS23 6ND, West Yorkshire; 5m S of Wetherby by A1

Tel 01937 846000

Fax 01937 846007

Email enquiries@ bramhampark.co.uk

Website www. bramhampark. co.uk

English Heritage Register Grade I

Owner Nick Lane Fox

Open Apr to Sept, daily 11.30– 4.30 (closed on certain days in June and Aug, phone/see website for details)

Area 66 acres/27 hectares

Castle Howard

DRAMATIC LANDSCAPE, A BEAUTIFUL WOODLAND GARDEN AND FINE ORNAMENTS FOR A GREAT ESTATE

Approaching Castle Howard, the majestic scale of its setting creeps up on you. The natural surroundings, pretty grand in themselves, merge with a designed landscape covering 1,000 acres/404 hectares. Obelisks and temples rise from the moors, with the astonishing castle at the centre of it all. The castle was the work of Sir John Vanbrugh, with Nicholas Hawksmoor, from 1699, for Charles Howard, 3rd Earl of Carlisle. Vanbrugh also designed many of the great buildings and ornaments in the grounds.

DRAMATIC APPROACHES

Visitors arrive by an avenue of beech and lime over three miles long. Along the avenue, from south to north, are the Monument designed by F.P. Cockerell (1870); Carrmire Gate designed by Nicholas Hawksmoor c.1730; the Gatehouse designed by Vanbrugh in 1719; and the Obelisk by Vanbrugh (1714). South of the castle is the Pyramid by Hawksmoor (1728) and, nearby, Vanbrugh's Temple of the Four Winds (1724–34). South-east of the castle is Hawksmoor's domed and pillared Mausoleum (1726–44) which

inspired Horace Walpole to write: " [it] would tempt one to be buried alive."

The greater landscape with its dramatic approaches and buildings largely survives, but the formal gardens close to the castle have radically changed. Ray Wood, east of the house, was made in about 1718 into a semi-formal woodland garden with winding gravel walks and statues. Today it is a woodland garden of a completely different kind – a wonderful collection of trees and shrubs built up from 1968 under the supervision of a remarkable plantsman, James Russell, and now one of the finest collections of acid-loving trees and shrubs in the country.

South of the castle are formal gardens, designed in 1850 by W.A. Nesfield, sporting a grand fountain with a figure of Atlas supported by Tritons, enclosed in yew hedges. Nearby, the 18th-century walled former kitchen garden is divided into three – The Venus Gardens, The Sundial Garden, and Lady Cecilia's Garden with a magnificent collection of roses. In 2006 an ornamental kitchen garden was laid out in the Sundial Garden. In any other context these formal gardens might be the chief beauty of the landscape. At Castle Howard the setting of the house is conceived on such a grandiose scale, with such sublime monuments, that flower beds and statuary find it hard to engage the attention.

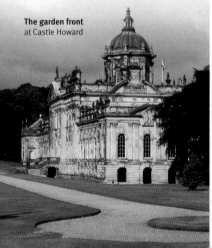

The garden front at Castle Howard

INFORMATION

Location nr York YO60 7DA, North Yorkshire; 14m NE of York by A64
Tel 01653 648333
Email house@castlehoward.co.uk
Website www.castlehoward.co.uk
English Heritage Register Grade I
Owner The Hon. Simon Howard
Open daily (except 25 Dec) 10–4.30
Area 50 acres/20 hectares

Cragside House

A PLUNGING PLANT-FILLED RAVINE, GLASSHOUSES WITH FRUIT TREES ON ROTATING PLATFORMS AND A DAHLIA WALK

The name Cragside gives some idea of what to expect here. Sir William Armstrong commissioned the architect Norman Shaw to transform a modest sporting lodge in wild heathland into a towered and turreted extravaganza suitable for one of the great industrial tycoons of the day. The house, finished in 1884, soars on a stony cliff above the Debdon burn whose water Armstrong harnessed to provide hydraulic power for all sorts of gadgets in the house (including a lift) and in the garden (in a glasshouse it was used to rotate fruit trees in pots so that the fruit would ripen evenly). By 1900 Armstrong owned almost 30,000 acres/12,145 hectares and had planted 7,000,000 trees; his pleasure gardens covered 1,000 acres/405 hectares, with plantings of rhododendrons on a heroic scale.

The ravine garden at Cragside

PLANTED SLOPES

The most eloquent view of the place is from the banks of the burn below the house where a steel bridge arches elegantly over the water. Among the cascade of rocks that seem to tumble down from the house are wild plantings of rhododendrons and rowans underplanted with small conifers, ferns, heather, saxifrages and sedums. By the burn a pinetum provides exactly the right note of coniferous gloom. Tree planting started here in the 1860s and many have grown to enormous size, especially North American species like the western hemlock (*Tsuga heterophylla*) and Low's white fir (*Abies concolor* var. *lowiana*) – the latter, at over 150ft/45m, the tallest specimen in the country. The soaring shapes of these trees provide the perfect growing counterpoint to the soaring mansion above.

On the far side of the Debdon valley are glasshouses and formal gardens.

The fruit-turning platforms in the glasshouses have been restored and a great range of different fruits, all superbly trained, is cultivated. To one side, magnificent displays of carpet bedding are spread out on beds angled to display them at their best. There is a fernery in a splendid winding rustic rockery, and glasshouses protect tender plants. On the slopes below is a long terraced dahlia walk with clipped shapes of golden variegated holly. Yet, attractive as these are, they are as the tinkling of piano music after the thunder of the symphony being played in the rocky ravine below.

INFORMATION

Location Rothbury, Morpeth NE65 7PX, Northumberland; 13m SW of Alnwick by B6341
Tel 01669 620333
Email cragside@nationaltrust.org.uk
English Heritage Register Grade II*
Owner The National Trust
Open mid Mar to early Nov, daily except Mon (open Bank Hol Mon) 10.30–5.30; early Nov to mid Dec, Wed to Sun 11–4
Area 1000 acres/405 hectares

Duncombe Park

REMARKABLE 18TH-CENTURY TERRACES AND TEMPLES AND PRETTY VICTORIAN FLOWER PARTERRES

Arthur Young in his *A six months tour through the North of England* (1770) wrote of Duncombe that it was "the place in this country by far the most worth the attention of the curious traveller, [it] cannot be viewed without the most exquisite enjoyment." The house is Baroque and surprisingly grand, with a distinct touch of the Castle Howards about it, and indeed there is a possibility that it was designed with help from Sir John Vanbrugh. At all events, it was begun around 1713 and built by William Wakefield for Thomas Duncombe. It occupies a wonderful site on land high above the rooftops of Helmsley, where the remains of the 13th-century castle provide a memorable if ruinous ornament, with the river Rye winding past far below.

This view dominates the garden, which is designed specifically to display it to its greatest picturesque effect.

THE GREAT TERRACE

Immediately to the east of the house a plain square of lawn is ornamented with a splendid figure of Father Time stooping over a sundial (early 18th-century and possibly by John Van Nost). Beyond it there opens out one of the grandest garden views in England: a huge, gently curving grassy terrace, half a mile long, running both north and south and overlooking the wooded valley of the Rye, whose waters are occasionally glimpsed gleaming through the branches far below. Each end of this

The Doric temple
at Duncombe Park

East Terrace is marked by a domed and pillared temple of about 1730 – an Ionic Temple to the north (possibly by Vanbrugh) and a Doric Temple to the south (possibly by Sir Thomas Robinson). The Ionic temple is an open rotunda and commands wonderful views to the north and east over Helmsley. The Doric temple at the southern end of the terrace is surrounded by wildflowers. It also has a surprise: it marks the beginning of a further South Terrace running due west. From near the western end of this terrace the Broadwalk cuts back north through woodland towards the east façade of the house, ending north-east of the house in a very old yew walk and a monumental serpentine ha-ha. This has been attributed to Vanbrugh, possibly with the involvement of Charles Bridgeman, but there is no archival evidence. Vanbrugh may also have laid out the terraces. At Blenheim

Palace (*see page 78*) he had tried to persuade the Duchess of Marlborough to preserve the ruins of Woodstock Palace as a picturesque landscape ornament; he would certainly have recognised the potential of Helmsley Castle in a similar role. All the work on both house and garden, begun in 1713, was completed by 1730. The terraces, and the emphasis on the picturesque attributes of the landscape, are true pioneers in garden design.

UNFORGETTABLE VIEWS

There are other attractive things to see in the garden at Duncombe – Victorian sunken parterres, possibly by W.A. Nesfield, flanking the house, and an attractive but decaying conservatory (1851, designed by the younger Charles Barry and R.R. Banks) hidden in the woods behind the South Terrace – but it is the unforgettable terraces and their views that command attention. Thomas Duncombe's son, another Thomas, went on to design a similar terrace at Rievaulx, two miles away, in about 1758 and a carriage drive was made between the two estates so that visitors could also view the terrace at Rievaulx.

The terraces at Duncombe and Rievaulx are magnificent. Christopher Hussey in his *English Gardens and Landscapes* 1700–1750 (1967) described them as "unique, and perhaps the most spectacularly beautiful among English landscape conceptions of the 18th century". Having seen them in their grand simplicity you may return to your own garden, with its fiddly borders and tedious views, and experience a certain depressing sense of inconsequence.

INFORMATION

Location Helmsley YO62 5EB, North Yorkshire; on the W edge of Helmsley, 12m E of Thirsk
Tel 01439 772625 **Fax** 01439 771114
Email liz@duncombepark.com
Website www.duncombepark.com
English Heritage Register Grade I
Owner Lord Feversham
Open Easter to end Oct, Sun to Thur 11–5.30
Area 485 acres/196 hectares

Herterton House Gardens

A RARE PRIVATE GARDEN OF FLOWERY ENCLOSURES AND TOPIARY WITH A MAGICAL ATMOSPHERE

Herterton is a precious example of a garden whose owners, two expert gardeners, plough their own furrow. It is a rare original, although inspired by many different influences – the cottage-garden planting of Margery Fish at East Lambrook Manor (*see page 39*), the tidily formal Shakespearean gardens recreated at New Place in Stratford-upon-Avon and, surprisingly, avant-garde art of the early 20th century.

FLOWERY ENCLOSURES

In 1975 Frank and Marjorie Lawley took a lease on a derelict village house belonging to the National Trust. They rebuilt the stone house and made a garden in which they "considered design and planting, rather than dabbling improvisation". It was to be a garden of compartments, with no repetition of mood but with repetition of such basic structural plants as box, holly and yew.

At the front are hedges and topiary of box with intervening spaces carpeted with different varieties of dicentra. A secret Physic Garden, hidden by walls, has a giant totem of clipped weeping silver pear (*Pyrus salicifolia* 'Pendula'). Intricately shaped beds are filled with native and medicinal plants. Behind the house the Flower Garden is a maze of paths, hedges and topiary, overflowing in high summer with herbaceous plants. As the flowers extend from the house, their colours change from cool yellows and whites to orange and blue at the centre, and finally to rich reds and purples. A Fancy Garden connects to the Flower Garden, sharing its central axis. A high-rising stone gazebo built against the boundary wall rears up at the end of this axis, facing inwards into the garden and outwards over the pastures and wooded countryside. The Fancy Garden has a symmetrical pattern of stone-flagged paths and box-edged beds with a central, noble stone basin. A topiary yew house to enclose a bench was well under way in 2007.

The various enclosures of the garden enfold the visitor – in the Flower Garden you are engulfed in flowers – which gives the place a revivifying intimacy. Are gardens good for you? I don't know, but I do know that I always arrive at Herterton, as I leave it, with a spring in my step.

The Flower Garden
at Herterton House

INFORMATION

Location Hartington, nr Cambo NE61 6BN, Northumberland; 2m N of Cambo by B6342
Tel 01670774278
Owner Frank and Marjorie Lawley
Open Apr to Sept, Fri to Mon, and Wed 1.30–5.30
Area 1 acre/0.4 hectare

Holker Hall

FINE TREES AND SHRUBS, PRETTY FORMAL GARDENS AND A WILDFLOWER MEADOW WITH A LABYRINTH

Holker Hall goes back to the 17th century but in the late 19th century, after a fire, a new east wing was built in lively neo-Elizabethan style. Formal gardens were made for Sir Thomas Lowther in the 1720s, embellished with statues brought from London by sea. Sir Thomas married Lady Elizabeth Cavendish, a sister of the 3rd Duke of Devonshire, and the estate subsequently passed to the Cavendishes, who still own it. There was landscaping in the late 18th century and adjustments to the formal gardens about the house in the early 20th century by Thomas Mawson, who laid out a formal rose garden. This was at the time of Lady Moyra Cavendish who also greatly enriched the plantings of trees and shrubs.

The cascades and fountain at Holker Hall

A FEAST OF PLANTS

Today, the formal gardens by the house give way gradually to wooded informality. The formal gardens immediately south of the house are attractive, with much finely judged decorative planting, but for me the excitement at Holker starts when you arrive at the 19th-century fountain and pool, with a pebble walk shaded by *Cornus kousa* var. *chinensis*. This walk leads to a flight of steps flanked with cascades like those in an Islamic garden, shaded by large tree rhododendrons and, at the top, a 17th-century Italian statue of Neptune.

If you now turn back towards the house you can walk past a splendid lead figure of Inigo Jones and embark on a looping anti-clockwise amble through the pleasure grounds. On the grassy slopes is a marvellous feast of trees and shrubs with a backdrop of beautiful old beeches and oaks. The soil here is acid, the rainfall high, and the proximity to the sea creates a benign microclimate. A National Collection of four genera of the Styracaceae family is kept here (*Halesia*, *Pterostyrax*, *Sinojackia* and *Styrax*). Some of these are among the loveliest of garden plants, such as *Styrax japonicus* with its hanging white bell-like flowers, and the graceful *Pterostyrax hispida*. Here, too, are dogwoods, magnolias, rowans, rhododendrons, stewartias and oaks.

Halfway through your amble you will pass Mawson's rose garden, curiously isolated from the rest of the formal gardens. West of the garden is a wildflower meadow and in a field beyond a remarkable modern sundial. An even more recent addition is a fine labyrinth with 12 slate monoliths.

INFORMATION

Location Cark-in-Cartmel, nr Grange-over-Sands LA11 7PL, Cumbria; 4m W of Grange-over-Sands by B5277
Tel 01539 558328
Email publicopening@holker.co.uk
Website www.holker-hall.co.uk
English Heritage Register Grade II
Owner Lord Cavendish of Furness
Open Apr to Oct, daily except Sat 10.30–5.30
Area 24 acres/10 hectares

Levens Hall

SPECTACULAR TOPIARY GARDEN OF WONDERFUL CHARACTER – A GARDEN ICON OF MARVELLOUS BEAUTY

Famous gardens can often become overburdened by their renown and fail to live up to their reputation. Nothing could be less true of the gardens at Levens Hall, which breathe a spirit of entrancing lightheartedness – a suitable setting for one of Mozart's funnier operas: *The Marriage of Figaro*, perhaps. Still privately owned, it is lovingly maintained to the highest standards. Historians treasure it because it is such a rare survival of its time, and garden visitors love it because it is so entertaining.

The topiary garden at Levens Hall

TOPIARY AND A HA-HA

The garden was made from 1694 for Col James Grahme by a mysterious Frenchman, Guillaume Beaumont. As a setting for the house, with its sombre 13th-century pele tower, Beaumont laid out a feast of topiary, chiefly of yew. He also made a dramatic passage of beech hedges which open out half way down into a spacious rondel. Lastly, he made the first ha-ha in England – no laughing matter. All this survives, and age has given topiary and hedges a new and wonderful identity. The topiary has become gigantic, deformed into phantasmagoric shapes of the wildest imaginings: "a peacock here, a huge umbrella-like construction there, an archway, a lion . . . and a host of other such adornments all shaped out of ductile yew", as *Country Life* put it in 1899. Some of the topiary goes back to the original plantings; some has been renewed, sometimes using the newly fashionable 19th-century gold-leafed cultivar of yew. The trees stand in beds edged in box and recently have been underplanted with colourful seasonal schemes – tulips and pansies in spring, verbenas and silver-leafed helichrysum in summer. The beech hedges, too, have become gigantic, so wide that you may inspect the interior, lavishly carpeted with wild garlic in spring. The ha-ha, which allows an unbroken view of grazing sheep and cattle, and an avenue of sycamore marching away across the pastures, is mentioned in a letter of April 1695 as "the Ditch behind the Garden" – the earliest known reference in England to a ha-ha.

The present owners have added new borders and a fountain and also all the necessary offices of a tourist attraction. However, the rare old garden comes first and its delightful character is impeccably preserved.

INFORMATION

Location Kendal LA8 0PD, Cumbria; 5m S of Kendal by A591 and A6
Tel 01539 560321
Email houseopening@levenshall.co.uk
Website www.levenshall.co.uk
English Heritage Register Grade I
Owner C.H. Bagot
Open Apr to mid Oct, Sun to Thurs 10–5
Area 6 acres/2 hectares

Muncaster Castle

OUTSTANDING RHODODENDRONS AND A GRAND TERRACE WALK OVERLOOKING THE RIVER ESK

The castle – commanding a bluff overlooking the Esk valley – is very ancient. A medieval pele tower, built here on Roman foundations, was later much expanded and then suavely Victorianised by Anthony Salvin between 1862 and 1866. The Penningtons are newcomers; they have lived here only since the 13th century.

There was much tree planting here in the 18th century, today providing precious wind protection to the west. As you enter, the drive curves through woods enriched with splendid mature rhododendrons, a chief interest of the garden. Sir John Ramsden, grandfather of the present owner, saw that the acid soil, high rainfall and mild climate here would be perfect for rhododendrons. Between the wars he subscribed to the plant-collecting expeditions of Frank Ludlow, George Sherriff and Frank Kingdon Ward, enriching the garden with their new introductions.

On the far side of the castle the land drops briskly and wonderful views of the Esk estuary form a spectacular panorama. The wooded slopes here are densely planted with broad-leafed trees and dazzle with rhododendrons in spring and early summer.

A TERRACED WALK

Running along the lip of the wooded slopes is a remarkable terraced walk snaking away from the castle. Its outer edge is hedged in box, with regular piers of golden or Irish yew rising higher than the box, echoing the castle's castellations. The inner side of the walk is densely planted with cherries, maples, magnolias, pieris and rhododendrons. The view across the valley, with Scafell and the other lakeland hills rising on the far side, is of the greatest splendour. The terrace is in two parts, separated by a ravine; the part furthest from the house is referred to as the "new" terrace in a drawing of 1810. If you follow the terrace to its end you will pass by a charming Victorian summerhouse with a high pointed roof of wooden shingles and panels of rustic work. Retracing your steps new views reveal themselves, with the castle suddenly emerging from the woods. There are few flower beds at Muncaster and nothing is on a small scale. The pleasures here come from the castle, with views of its beautiful landscape, and the bold plantings of fine trees and shrubs.

The Esk valley from Muncaster

INFORMATION

Location Ravenglass CA18 1RQ, Cumbria; 1m SE of Ravenglass by A595
Tel 01229 717614
Email info@muncaster.co.uk
Website www.muncaster.co.uk
English Heritage Register Grade II*
Owner Mrs Phyllida Gordon-Duff-Pennington
Open daily (closed in January) 10.30–6 (or dusk if earlier)
Area 77 acres/31 hectares

Newby Hall Gardens

A GREAT YORKSHIRE GARDEN – FORMALITY, EXCELLENT TREES AND MAGNIFICENT BORDERS IN A SUPERB SETTING

Newby is one of the most attractive and enjoyable gardens in England. Its pleasures are various: it has a strong and harmonious design, excellent and sometimes rare plants, and a delightful atmosphere. The house is exceptional – late 17th-century of brick and stone, spectacularly added to by Robert Adam in 1767. There was a notable garden here by the end of the 17th century and Kip's engraving in *Britannia Illustrata* (1707) shows a splendid formal layout with avenues radiating from the west façade of the house. The head gardener was Peter Aram who had formerly worked for London and Wise and they supplied trees for Newby from their Brompton nursery. Of the subsequent history of the garden there are only tantalising glimpses. J.C. Loudon writing in *The Gardener's Magazine* in 1837 in a bilious mood, did not think much of it – "A mass of flower beds have nothing to recommend them . . . it is seen at a glance that they have no business where they are." Late in the 19th century the architect William Burges, who built the church in the grounds, advised on the garden, restoring some of its formal ingredients. The garden today owes its chief character to two generations of the Compton family – Major Edward Compton, a friend of Lawrence Johnston of Hidcote, and his son Robin Compton, the father of the present owner, Richard Compton.

COMPARTMENTS

The garden that the Comptons made is divided into compartments but on a much grander scale than Hidcote and spiced with informal interludes. It is firmly connected to the house and

The great borders
at Newby Hall

arranged about a strong T-shaped axis – a long descending walk south from the house flanked by herbaceous borders, and the handsome Statue Walk (reputedly designed by William Burges) running east and west below the lily pond in front of the house. Formal enclosures find logical positions in relation to these axes – Sylvia's Garden, the Rose Garden, the Autumn Garden and others, all of which have been restored in recent years. These are interspersed with gardens of woodland character threaded with winding walks.

NOTABLE PLANTS

Wherever you walk there are notable plants to admire. A National Collection of dogwoods is held here, many grouped west of the Rose Garden. It is surprising to see among them *Cornus capitata*, a tender species from the Himalayan, looking so vigorous in North Yorkshire. There are other tender plants here (*Drimys winteri* is one) and they are testimony to the Comptons' skill in understanding their site.

It would be all too easy to embark on lists of plants but suffice it to say that you are likely to make many new discoveries here, and that there are specialist collections of particular species. Richard's brother, James Compton, is a distinguished plantsman with a special interest in, among other plants, salvias. (A remarkably fine collection is deployed in the garden.)

It is a pleasure at Newby to wander in the garden, gasp from time to time at the beauty of the house, plunge into the woodland areas, emerge into the Autumn Garden (where you can sit on a bench), fill your notebook with the new plants you have seen, and go home resolving to improve your own garden.

INFORMATION

Location nr Ripon HG4 5AE, North Yorkshire; 4m SE of Ripon by B6265
Tel 0845 4504068
Email info@newbyhall.co.uk
Website www.newbyhall.com
English Heritage Register Grade II*
Owner Richard Compton
Open April to Sept, daily except Mon (open Bank Hol Mon and Mon in Jul and Aug) 11–5.30
Area 25 acres/10 hectares

Scampston Walled Garden

A BRILLIANT WALLED GARDEN COMBINING VARIETY AND FORMALITY DESIGNED BY PIET OUDOLF

Scampston Hall is a handsome late 18th-century house in fine wooded parkland. At a little distance from the house is a 4½-acre walled garden built in the mid 18th century, which in recent times had been used for growing Christmas trees. In 1998 Sir Charles and Lady Legard met, by chance, the Dutch garden designer Piet Oudolf and asked him to create a new layout for the walled garden. Work started in 1999 and was essentially complete in 2003.

VIRTUOSO PLANTING

The garden that Oudolf made is a dazzling sequence of hedged enclosures with virtuoso planting and a masterly orchestration of different atmospheres. A path leads round three walls of the garden with borders of bold and varied mixed planting against the walls and high beech hedges topped with pleached limes on the other side. A central opening in the hedge reveals a grove of katsuras (*Cercidiphyllum japonicum*) embracing an oval bed of the beautiful grass *Molinia* subsp. *arundinacea* 'Transparent'. Beyond is an oval pool at the centre of a four-part "perennial meadow" overlooked by a decorative 19th-century glasshouse. On each side of these gardens other intriguing enclosures beckon the visitor.

The Serpentine Garden has twisting yew hedges and monumental clover-shaped yew topiary, the whole embraced by a U-shaped pattern of shrub borders. Alongside, a grove of *Prunus* x *yedoensis* has, at its centre, a high mount from whose top is a delicious view of the whole patterned garden. At the other end of the garden the Silent Garden has a central square pool with seats and rows of solemn columns of clipped yew. A border of shrubs with herbaceous underplanting runs down one side. Beyond it, Drifts of Grass is an enclosure of subtle austerity where rows of sinuous beds of Molinia grass are separated by curving sweeps of turf, with a group of the decorative tree *Phellodendron chinense*. The Spring Box Garden nearby has a procession of large box cubes and a boisterous border of amsonia, astrantia, catmint, geraniums, *Iris sibirica* and opium poppies.

The triumph of Oudolf's design is to produce variety without jumble. A lavishly, even explosively, planted area is often succeeded by a green space of topiary and calm. There is room enough, too, to have large spaces as well as much more intimate areas. It is a masterpiece of garden design.

The conservatory at Scampston

INFORMATION

Location Malton YO17 8NG, Yorkshire; 4 miles east of Malton off A64
Tel 01944 759111
Email info@scampston.co.uk
Website www.scampston.co.uk
Owner Sir Charles and Lady Legard
Open early April to Oct, daily except Mon (open bank Hol Mon) 10–5
Area 4½ acres/1.8 hectares

Studley Royal

REMARKABLE 18TH-CENTURY VALLEY GARDEN WITH OUTSTANDING WATER GARDENS AND GREAT BUILDINGS

The garden was started in 1674 by George Aislabie whose son, John Aislabie, from 1718 created a visionary semi-formal water garden incorporating the river Skell in its lovely wooded valley. He laid out a circular Moon Pond (and the Temple of Piety on its bank) with attendant crescent ponds on each side, all embellished with statues of stone or lead. On the wooded heights above the pools he built a banqueting house (1728–32 by Colen Campbell) and an octagonal tower (1728, originally built in classical style but lavishly Gothicised ten years later). These buildings command delicious views over the landscape and also serve as eyecatchers in prominent positions.

The Moon Pond at Studley Royal

FOUNTAINS ABBEY

William Aislabie succeeded his father in 1742 and extended the estate further along the valley in 1767 when he acquired Fountains Hall and the ruins of the 12th-century Cistercian Fountains Abbey. William Aislabie was responsible for the surprise view of the abbey from Anne Boleyn's seat high in the woods above a curve of the river, and for smoothing the banks of the river Skell as it approached the abbey ruins, so that its shorn turf ran down to the water. After William Aislabie's death the estate passed to his daughter and then to a niece. It remained intact, remarkably little changed, to modern times. The great Palladian house, however, built by John Aislabie between 1728 and 1732 and possibly designed by Colen Campbell, was severely damaged by fire in 1946 and demolished. Only the stable block survives, also possibly by Campbell and now in separate ownership. The Vyners, descendants of the Aislabies, sold the estate to West Riding County Council in 1966 and the National Trust acquired it in 1983.

Visitors today approach the garden by way of the abbey. This is delightfully revealed through the trees as you descend the hill but the pleasure of its sudden, astonishing revelation from the other end of the garden as you pass a bend in the valley is lost. However, the whole landscape of Studley Royal is of enchanting beauty and also a painless lesson in garden history from the semi-formal stirrings of the landscape movement in the early years of the 18th century to the full-blown picturesque romanticism of the later years.

INFORMATION

Location Fountains, Ripon HG4 3DY, North Yorkshire
Infoline 01765 608888
Email fountainsenquiries@nationaltrust.org.uk
Website www.fountainsabbey.org.uk
English Heritage Register Grade I
Owner The National Trust
Open Mar to Oct, daily 10–5; Nov to Feb, daily except Fri 10–4 (closed 24 and 25 Dec)
Area 900 acres/364 hectares

Wallington

The house at Wallington is essentially 17th and 18th century, built for the Blackett family, though it was altered in the 19th century with the advice of John Ruskin for the Trevelyans, who gave the estate to the National Trust in 1942.

The walled garden at Wallington

The chief garden interest lies on the other side of the road from the house where a gate leads into old woodland. A semi-formal lake is at the heart of the wood, with the delightful prospect of the mid 18th-century pedimented Portico House rising on the slopes above the lake's north bank. Almost immediately, however, you come to the surprise in the woods – a walled garden, built in 1760 and sloping south and east in a most unusual dog-leg shape.

PACKED WITH PLANTS

The planting here is almost entirely the work of the National Trust since 1958. The garden is packed with plants and incidents – fairly higgledy-piggledy but finely maintained and constrained only by the enclosing walls. At the entrance is a surprisingly grand but rustic double staircase, curving back to enclose a pool and fountain. The upper terrace ends in a glasshouse with the elegant Owl House, an 18th-century pavilion, rising behind it. Alongside the glasshouse a new, brilliantly coloured late-summer border bursts with cannas, crocosmias, flamboyant dahlias and kniphofias. Below it an old brick path runs downhill between yew hedges and under arches of honeysuckle and 'Perle d'Azur' clematis. A hidden paved enclosure has seats, an urn filled with summer bedding and fringed with lambs' lugs,

and pots filled with pink mallows and petunias. An orchard-like little arboretum has a large collection of elders (a National Collection), flowering cherries and mountain ash. Against the north-facing lower wall a deep border is planted with campanulas, hostas, hydrangeas, potentillas, pulmonaria and sedums. In the middle of the lawn a sprawling arrangement of conifers and heathers has a decidedly retro flavour.

The unexpectedness of the walled garden, the curious lie of the land, the raised terrace along the top wall and the eccentricity of the garden's shape are what stick in my mind rather than any notable beauty of planting. On several occasions I have walked through the noble gloom of the woods to emerge in the brilliant sun and colour of the walled garden – a contrast to relish.

INFORMATION

Location Cambo, Morpeth NE61 4AR, Northumberland; 12m W of Morpeth by B6343
Tel 01670 774283 **Fax** 01670 774420
English Heritage Register Grade II*
Owner The National Trust
Open Apr to Oct, daily 10–7 (closes 6 in Oct); Nov to Mar, daily 10–4
Area 100 acres/40 hectare

York Gate

A BRILLIANTLY DESIGNED AND PLANTED 20TH-CENTURY GARDEN WITH IDEAS FOR ALL GARDENERS

York Gate was a farmhouse when Frederick and Sybil Spencer bought it in 1951. They, with their son, Robin, made a new garden on the site of a small orchard. They devised a layout of intimate enclosures filled with lively, often original planting animated by a strong decorative sense. Although full of ideas beautifully carried out, and an enchanting garden to be in, York Gate has never had the fame it deserves.

The enclosures flow about the house on three sides, harmoniously linked but with no overall dominating pattern. A pair of ethereal white and silver borders are full of *Campanula lactiflora*, *Rosa* 'White Pet', giant *Onopordum acanthium* and *Viola cornuta* Alba Group. At their head, a curious stone sundial marks a junction with the Allée, a stone path flanked with strips of turf and hedged in beech. The Allée is also linked with the herb garden, one of the best parts of the garden, with a central path of gravel edged with granite setts and interrupted in the middle by an old

millstone set in the ground. Borders on each side, backed by yew hedges, are filled with herbs and punctuated by tall spirals of clipped box. In high summer the scent of the herbs, intensified by the enclosing hedges, suffuses the loggia, and the garden is loud with the buzzing of bees. At the far end of the borders a monumental opening is formed of square columns of yew surmounted by generous yew spheres. A walk leads off at an angle and this too has a beautiful path – a lattice-work pattern of setts laid in gravel – which leads to an open pavilion with a high pitched roof.

EYE-CATCHING DETAILS

Decorative details catch the eye at every turn. *Cedrus libani* subsp. *atlantica* 'Glauca' is deftly espaliered against a dry stone wall to form long ribbons of colour against the stone; a gap in a hedge looks over a miniature ha-ha to reveal the open countryside – all the more effective in a garden otherwise largely inward-looking; a giant cast-iron urn is filled with crocuses, the mass of delicate flowers holding their own in the bold container; a paved area close to the house was made into a bonsai court and still has some ancient specimens.

Path of setts at York Gate

INFORMATION

Location Back Church Lane, Adel, Leeds LS16 8DW, West Yorkshire; 5m NW of Leeds, close to Adel church E of the Leeds-Otley road (A660)
Tel 0113 267 8240
Website www.perennial.org. uk/yorkgate.html
Owner Perennial (The Gardeners' Royal Benevolent Society)
Open Easter to Sept, Thur, Sun and Bank Hol Mon 2–5
Area 1 acre/0.4 hectare

SCOTLAND

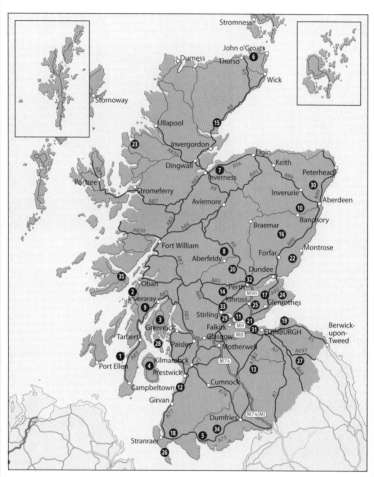

GARDENS TO VISIT

1. Achamore
2. Arduaine Garden
3. Benmore Botanic Garden
4. Brodick Castle
5. Broughton House and Garden
6. Castle of Mey
7. Cawdor Castle
8. Cluny House Gardens
9. Crarae Garden
10. Crathes Castle
11. Culross Palace
12. Culzean Castle
13. Dawyck Botanic Gardens
14. Drummond Castle Gardens
15. Dunrobin Castle Gardens
16. Edzell Castle
17. Falkland Palace
18. Glenwhan Garden
19. Greywalls
20. The Hermitage
21. Hopetoun House
22. House of Pitmuies
23. Inverewe
24. Kellie Castle
25. Kinross House
26. Logan Botanic Garden
27. Mellerstain
28. Mount Stuart
29. The Pineapple
30. Pitmedden
31. Royal Botanic Garden Edinburgh
32. Scone Palace
33. Stirling Castle
34. Threave Garden
35. Torosay Castle

Image *Dawyck Botanic Gardens*

Achamore

ON THE ISLAND OF GIGHA, A GARDEN WITH EXCEPTIONAL RHODODENDRONS AND OTHER FLOWERING SHRUBS

Visiting Achamore is always exciting – the difficulty of access, slipping across the sound in a boat, increases the excitement. Sir James Horlick came to Gigha in 1944 to an existing sporting estate that had the priceless asset of mature trees, chiefly spruce and sycamore, which had been established by his predecessor, Captain William Scarlett (3rd Lord Abinger), to provide protection for game. Although the climate is mild here, strongly influenced by the Gulf Stream, westerly gales and salt-laden air make gardening possible only with windbreaks. Sir James wanted to plant rhododendrons and at Achamore, with its mild climate, high rainfall, acid soil and existing protection of trees, he found the perfect site. Today they are wonderful to see.

Woodland glade at Achamore

WOODLAND GLADES

In laying out the garden Sir James was helped by Kitty Lloyd Jones, and they built up a marvellous collection of rhododendrons, mostly propagated or bred here at Achamore. These are grouped according to their categories: *R. griersonianum* and *R. thomsonii* hybrids, for example – both of which are among the most prolific of hybridisers. Rhododendrons loom large, providing brilliant spring colour, but the garden is rich in other trees and shrubs – southern beeches (*Nothofagus* species), *Cercidiphyllum japonicum*, embothriums, eucryphias, rowans, styrax and viburnums. The north walled garden houses a collection of conifers, among them such rarities as the Formosan fir (*Abies kawakami*). Herbaceous planting

includes hostas, lilies, meconopsis, narcissi, Asiatic primulas and much else.

The manner of planting is most attractive. This is, in effect, a garden of compartments, but compartments formed not of the architectural hedges and walls of an Arts and Crafts layout but mostly of glades cleared in the existing woods. The experience of wandering from glade to glade is delightful. It is a big garden and there is much to see, but a useful sketch plan is available and routes of different lengths are waymarked. If you go past the walled garden to the south and climb the gently rising land of Spring Bank you will come to the garden's highest point, with delicious views westwards of the islands of Islay and Jura.

In 2002, after some uncertainty about the future of the island, Gigha was bought by its inhabitants.

INFORMATION

Location Isle of Gigha PA41 7AD, Argyll; off the W coast of Kintyre, ferry from Tayinloan
Tel 01583 505254 **Fax** 01583 505244
Website www.isle-of-gigha.co.uk
Owner Island of Gigha Heritage Trust
Open daily dawn–dusk
Area 50 acres/20 hectares

Arduaine Garden

IN AN IDYLLIC SETTING CLOSE TO THE SEA, MARVELLOUS HERBACEOUS PLANTS AMONG TREES AND SHRUBS

The estate at Arduaine was bought in 1897 by James Arthur Campbell, a tea planter and friend of Osgood Mackenzie of Inverewe (*see page 302*). Campbell built a house and began to make a garden a little distance from the house, choosing as his site an area close to the sea (thus strongly affected by the Gulf Stream, with Asknish Bay to the south and Loch Melfort to the north). For protection, he planted a shelter belt to the west, chiefly of larch.

THRILLING RARITIES

James Campbell's collection of species rhododendrons is of outstanding quality. His tea-planting connections provided the seed of a Ceylon rhododendron, *R. arboreum* subsp. *zeylanicum*, which came to Arduaine in a chest of tea; specimens here of this tree rhododendron are the largest in the British Isles. Other species include plants propagated by seed gathered in

Himalayan hillside at Arduaine

the wild (such as the late-flowering evergreen *R. auriculatum* from Hupeh, China), species which were among the first to flower in the west at Arduaine (such as *R. protistum* var. *giganteum*), and many other rarities which not only flourish but, on the sloping upper reaches of the garden, look as much at home as in their homeland. Other outstanding flowering trees and shrubs include eucryphias, magnolias and rowans. Among the many herbaceous plants, especially in the lower garden with its streams and pools, are marvellous spreads of *Cardiocrinum giganteum*, Chatham Island forget-me-not (*Myosotidium hortensia*), meconopsis and Asiatic primulas. Throughout the garden are fine specimens of plants which in any other garden would be regarded as notable. Here, however, the various berberis, cedars of Lebanon, *Gunnera manicata*, Monterey cypresses and New Zealand flaxes seem positively humdrum alongside the thrilling and beautifully grown rarities.

After James Campbell's death in 1929 the estate passed to his son and grandson but in 1964 everything except the garden was sold. The house became the Loch Melfort Hotel and the garden, still owned by the Campbell family, was neglected until 1971 when it was bought by Edmund and Harry Wright, retired nurserymen who devoted themselves to its revitalisation. Now well cared for in the hands of the National Trust for Scotland its future seems secure.

INFORMATION

Location Arduaine, by Oban PA34 4XQ, Argyll; 20m S of Oban by A4816
Tel and **fax** 01852 200366
Scottish Inventory Listed
Owner The National Trust for Scotland
Open daily 9.30–sunset
Area 20 acres/8 hectares

Benmore Botanic Garden

AN OUTSTANDING COLLECTION OF PLANTS IN A WILD AND DRAMATIC SETTING WITH SPECTACULAR VIEWS

The garden starts with a splendid fanfare – a triumphant avenue of Wellingtonias planted in 1863 and now all over 130ft/39m high. The first notable plantings were made by Ross Wilson in 1820, of which some Scots pines still survive. Subsequent owners made their mark, in particular James Duncan who, in 1871–83, planted 1,622 acres/656 hectares with well over 6,000,000 trees. Henry Younger from 1889 greatly added to the ornamental planting, as did his son Harry. In 1925 part of the estate was taken over by the Royal Botanic Garden Edinburgh, since when the garden has been spectacularly enriched; it now forms one of the finest plant collections in Britain.

THE EFFECT OF CLIMATE

The climate at Benmore is fairly benign, with mild winters and very high rainfall. Wind, whose potential for damage has been mitigated by dense planting, can still have devastating effect – in the winter of 1968 more than 500 trees of over 120ft/36m were blown down. The surroundings are beautiful, and whether you look uphill or down there is always something to admire.

The planting throughout the garden is naturalistic, with the exception of the Formal Garden in the old walled garden with its collection of around 300 cultivars of conifers. The rest of the garden is preeminently a garden for walking in – excellent maps will help you to find your way. Plants are grouped either by habitat, for example the Chilean Rainforest, or by type of plant, such as the collection of garden conifers in the Formal Garden or the over 650 species and cultivars of rhododendron. Some plant collections, grouped by habitat, have splendid settings – the Bhutanese Glade is alongside the rocky Massan Cliff and plants such as *Abies densa*, *Betula utilis* and *Sorbus thibetica* look entirely at home.

The garden is also rich in ornamental shrubs – cotoneasters, enkianthus, eucryphias, magnolias, osmanthus, pieris and stewartias. Conifers loom large (200 species) but there are also excellent deciduous trees – acers, birches, *Cercidiphyllum japonicum*, nothofagus, rowans and *Styrax japonicus*. Among non-flowering plants are some lovely ferns, native and exotic, and many lichens, liverworts and mosses.

The wild and beautiful setting makes Benmore exceptional. Although other British botanic gardens have notable collections of plants, none has a natural site of such beauty.

Benmore in its wild setting

INFORMATION

Location Benmore, Dunoon PA23 8QU, Argyll; 7m N of Dunoon by A815
Tel 01369 706261
Email benmore@rbge.org.uk
Website www.rbge.org.uk
Scottish Inventory Listed
Owner Trustees of the Royal Botanic Garden Edinburgh
Open Apr to Sept, daily 10–6; Mar and Oct, daily 10–5
Area 120 acres/48 hectares

Brodick Castle

ON THE BEAUTIFUL ISLE OF ARRAN, A FINE WOODLAND GARDEN FOR A HISTORIC ESTATE

The castle, a fortified tower dating back to the 13th century, has a superb position facing southwards over Brodick Bay. Many later alterations include additions in the mid 19th century. The island was crown property until 1503 when James IV gave it to his cousin, John Hamilton, 1st Earl of Arran. The Hamilton heiress, Mary Louise, married James Graham, later 6th Duke of Montrose, in 1905. Their descendants gave the estate to the National Trust for Scotland in 1958.

The site is a splendid one for a garden – protected from westerly winds and enjoying south-facing slopes which run down to the sea. High rainfall and the Gulf Stream favour the cultivation of marvellous woodland plants. The fine walled garden south-east of the castle dates from 1710. This, gently terraced, must have been the kitchen garden but is now turned over to ornamental purposes with a cruciform pattern of paths, Victorian style carpet bedding, mixed borders and a fortissimo display of roses in beds and on arbours.

TENDER SHRUBS

The great distinction of Brodick lies in the woodland garden to the west and south-west. In the early 20th century the Duchess of Montrose started to plant lavishly, inspired by the expeditions to the Himalayas of George Forrest and Frank Kingdon Ward. Long walks run through the woodland and everywhere there are wonderful plants. Such tender rhododendrons as *R. protistum* var. *giganteum* (a Forrest introduction of 1926) and *R. magnificum* (a Kingdon Ward introduction of 1935) burst magnificently into flower in March. Another Forrest introduction is the delightful *R. taggianum*, rarely seen growing out of doors in British gardens.

The woodland garden at Brodick

There are many other distinguished shrubs here, many of which are tender and often rare: the scented Madeiran lily-of-the-valley tree (*Clethra arborea*); eucryphias of great splendour; the most dramatic of all buddleias, *B. colvilei*; and magnificent camellias.

At the southernmost tip of the garden, close to the shore of Brodick Bay, is a rare and enchanting garden building – the Bavarian summerhouse. This rustic pavilion was built in 1845 to celebrate the marriage of the 10th Duke of Hamilton's son to Princess Marie von Baden. The interior is beautifully fashioned with intricate patterns of pine cones and strips of larch, and the exterior swarms with artificial climbers, giving it the appearance of emerging from the undergrowth.

INFORMATION

Location Isle of Arran KA27 8HY; 2m from Brodick ferry
Tel 01770 302202 **Fax** 01770 302312
Scottish Inventory Listed
Owner The National Trust for Scotland
Open (Walled garden) end Mar to end Oct, daily 10–5; (Country park) daily 9.30–sunset
Area (Walled garden) 3 acres/1.2 hectares; (Country park) 891 acres/360 hectares

Broughton House and Garden

AN ARTIST'S ENCHANTING GARDEN, PACKED WITH PLANTS, FOR AN 18TH-CENTURY TOWN HOUSE

With its harbour on the estuary of the river Dee, Kircudbright is a delightful town with excellent architecture. It became a favoured resort of artists in the 1880s, one of whom, the "Glasgow boy" E.A. Hornel (whose family originally came from Kircudbright), bought Broughton House in 1901. Between 1901 and 1933 he adorned the fine 18th-century house with an enchanting garden. Hornel died in 1933 and the house and garden were passed to a trust until the National Trust for Scotland took over in 1994.

The garden, long and narrow, runs down westwards behind the house. The first part, busy with ornament, is a crowded garden with a Japanese feel. Here are clipped conifers, a spreading Japanese maple, bamboos, a bronze bell, troughs and mysterious shapes of stone. Such distinguished trees as *Acer griseum* and *Cornus controversa* 'Variegata' cast their shade over moss-covered rocks and a miniature ferny ravine. A little pool is crossed by stepping stones and spanned by a scarlet railing doing visual duty as a Japanese bridge. A bed

has azaleas, epimediums, ferns and shapes of clipped box. A second pool has a bronze crane overlooked by a cast-iron bench in a bower of Japanese anemones and hydrangeas.

A CHANGE OF MOOD

The visit to Japan, although brief, is memorable; but an entirely different kind of garden now spreads out before you. A long narrow paved path edged with box runs the full length of the garden and on each side enclosures of different kinds are revealed. A lawn is shaded by a sprawling magnolia and has a summerhouse fringed with hellebores and hydrangeas. A larger lawn has a sundial, a spectacular old apple tree, *Cytisus battandieri*, abutilons and eucalyptus. An oval parterre is full of roses with a medlar and a *Cercidiphyllum japonicum* to one side. An arbour of gnarled wisteria spans a path and a long mixed border backed by a wall is brilliant with eucryphias in late summer. Paths dart off here and there, old apple trees rise hither and yon, and the odd soaring tender echium stands in a corner. You eventually emerge to find yourself in the shade of a large old cherry tree with an elevated view of yachts lying tranquilly at anchor in the harbour below.

The rose parterre at Broughton House

INFORMATION

Location 12 High Street, Kircudbright DG6 4JX, Kirkcudbrightshire; in the centre of Kircudbright
Tel 01557 330437
Scottish Inventory Listed
Owner The National Trust for Scotland
Open Feb to Mar, Mon to Fri 11–4; Apr to Oct, Thur to Mon 12–5 (Jul to Aug, daily)
Area 2 acres/0.8 hectare

Castle of Mey

WALLED GARDEN OF QUEEN ELIZABETH, THE QUEEN MOTHER, ON THE WILD COAST OF CAITHNESS

The castle was built in the second half of the 16th century, with alterations made in the 19th and 20th centuries. The estate changed hands more than once before being bought in 1952 by Queen Elizabeth, the Queen Mother, who used it as a holiday home until her death in 2002.

Built of pinkish stone, the Castle of Mey is a characteristic Scottish fortified tower house with towers and castellations. Close to the sea, it faces north across the Pentland Firth towards Orkney. Violent salt-laden winds off the sea and a very short growing season severely restrict gardening possibilities. Most of the ornamental gardening is done in the protection of a walled kitchen garden which was probably made in the 17th century. The north, seaward, wall of this garden rises to a height of 12ft/3.6m and gives much protection, as do shelter belts of sycamores close to the castle. No tree grows well here, nor any plant of much size, without wind protection.

The walled garden at the Castle of Mey

PROTECTED PLANTINGS

The space within the walled garden is divided into many compartments, with hedges made of a charming jumble of plants – berberis, blackcurrant, fuchsia, hawthorn, honeysuckle, privet and sycamore, a shifting tapestry of intermingled foliage, fruit and flowers. A gravel path round the perimeter of the garden is lined with borders and its inner side is planted with annuals and ramparts of sweet peas. A glasshouse overlooks a rose garden with oval beds of bedding roses. This is still, at least in part, a working kitchen garden and there are espaliered fruit against the walls, fruit cages and beds of vegetables.

Close to the castle is a bed named "Windy Corner Rosebed", planted with rugosa roses to celebrate the Queen Mother's 100th birthday. Beyond the castle, a pair of mixed borders, walled on two sides and protected by sycamores, is filled with astilbes, buddleias, fuchsias, potentillas, shrub roses and weigelas. Many visitors will come here because of the Castle of Mey's association with an admired member of the royal family, but it is a charming place and the garden is a fine example of what may be achieved in a most unpropitious environment. It is also a period piece, containing plants that are beyond fashion, of the sort that the Queen Mother especially enjoyed.

INFORMATION

Location Mey, nr Thurso KW14 8XH, Caithness; 6m W of John O'Groats by A836, 12m E of Thurso by A836
Tel 01847 851473
Email castleofmey@totalise.co.uk
Website www.castleofmey.org.uk
Scottish Inventory Listed
Owner The Queen Elizabeth Castle of Mey Trust
Open end May to Sept, daily 10.30–4 (closed for 2 weeks, end Jul to early Aug)
Area 100 acres/40 hectares

Cawdor Castle

AN 18TH-CENTURY FLOWER GARDEN AND INTRIGUING LATE 20TH-CENTURY GARDENS FOR A SPLENDID CASTLE

The castle at Cawdor was built for the Campbell family (later Thanes of Cawdor and later still Earls of Cawdor) in the 14th century and much altered in the 17th and 19th centuries. Together with its handsome crow-stepped outhouses, the castle makes a deliciously romantic group at the heart of the gardens.

This part of Scotland is famous fruit-growing country and the castle archives show that orchards were cultivated at Cawdor in 1635. A kitchen garden also existed in the first half of the 17th century; later in the century this included such exotics as French sorrel and lamb's lettuce and the first flowering ornamentals (among them a double-flowered hollyhock).

THE FLOWER GARDEN

The walled Flower Garden was laid out in about 1710 by Sir Archibald Campbell, the brother of the 15th Thane of Cawdor. This garden, hard by the southern façade of the castle, was redesigned in 1850 by the 1st Countess Cawdor who came from a notable gardening family – the Thynnes of Longleat (Wiltshire). Its Victorian character survives today, with a broad turf path running down the centre and deep herbaceous borders on each side backed by old apple trees. These borders were painted by George Elgood in 1905 and have retained their ebullient character, with aconitums, astilbes, delphiniums, lilies and monardas enriched with additions of summer bedding plants. Such borders in 19th-century Scottish gardens were often planned to be at their peak in August when the house would have been full of guests for the shooting season. Countess Cawdor also laid out a formal pattern of oval rose beds edged

in lavender and with Irish yews, both golden and common, which is still in place. Nearby, enclosed in yew hedges splashed with the scarlet flowers of *Tropaeolum speciosum*, is a box parterre whose compartments are filled with red or yellow begonias. Most memorable in August is an ethereal bed of white *Galtonia candicans* intermingled with orange tiger lilies.

A gate in the Flower Garden wall leads through to a hidden woodland garden on the slopes running down to the Cawdor burn with its high-arched stone bridge. This part of the garden was developed in the 19th century and further planting was done in the late 20th century. Here are azaleas and rhododendrons, ornamental maples and rowans and some fine old trees from 19th-century plantings, among them a spectacular Wellingtonia.

NEW FORMAL GARDENS

North-east of the castle, in the old walled Lower Garden, some of whose walls go back to the middle ages, the present Dowager Countess Cawdor laid out new formal gardens. A holly maze is enclosed on two sides by cloisters of pleached laburnum and by hedges of field maple and yew. A parterre of medicinal and culinary herbs, sweetly scented in high summer, has a central star of low box hedges filled with pinks and chamomile, flanked by elaborately patterned beds of artichokes, herbs and lavender. Cones of yew and lollipops of gooseberries are underplanted with irises and lavender. At the centre of a Paradise Garden, enclosed in a circle of high yew hedges and entered by the narrowest of openings (the eye of the needle?), is a beautiful fountain – a bronze column with a sweeping relief pattern, veiled by a film of water that flows over it. It lies at the centre of a circular bed of thyme scattered with bronze cockle shells. The surrounding beds are filled with many white-flowered plants – campanulas, feverfew, heathers, hydrangeas, philadelphus and shrub roses.

Cawdor is an admirable example of an easy and harmonious intermingling of ingredients of different periods. Here, there are no dramatic flights of horticultural fancy but everything seems appropriate to the place.

INFORMATION

Location Cawdor IV12 5RD, Nairnshire; 11m N of Inverness by A96 and B9090
Tel 01667 404401
Email info@cawdorcastle.com
Website www.cawdorcastle.com
Scottish Inventory Listed
Owner The Dowager Countess Cawdor
Open May to mid Oct, daily 10–5.30 (open in winter to groups by appointment)
Area 20 acres/8 hectares

The Flower Garden
at Cawdor Castle

Cluny House Gardens

A PRIVATE GARDEN WITH A WONDERFUL COLLECTION OF PRIMULAS AND OTHER HERBACEOUS PERENNIALS

As naturalistic gardens go, few give the appearance of so little human intervention as Cluny – in fact such convincing wildness only comes as the result of much hard work. The site is paramount here – 600ft/180m up in fine wooded country that slopes down southwards towards the river Tay. The country has an alpine character and the name Cluny means in Gaelic "meadow place". The soil has patches of deep, natural peat; the rainfall is around 40in/100cm per annum; and the woodland provides protection and a perfect environment for marvellous herbaceous plants and shrubs – many of them Himalayan exotics planted by Bobby and Betty Masterton who started the garden in 1950. After the death of the Mastertons the garden was taken over by their daughter and son-in-law, Mr and Mrs Mattingley.

Asiatic primulas at Cluny

GIANT SPECIMENS

The house at Cluny was built in around 1800 and woodland was developed in the 19th century. Some of the trees are giant specimens, among them a vast Wellingtonia whose girth is 36ft/11m, the largest girth of any conifer in Britain, and a beautiful old fern-leafed beech (*Fagus sylvatica* var. *heterophylla* 'Aspleniifolia'). These provide a distinguished background to many smaller ornamental trees – acers, birches, dogwoods and rowans – with such shrubs as embothriums, eucryphias, hoherias, magnolias and rhododendrons. But to my eye the greatest splendour of Cluny is the herbaceous planting in the shade of these trees and shrubs. The Mattingleys hold a National Collection of over 100 species of Asiatic primulas and few such collections are so beautifully displayed. They interbreed freely here (infuriating for the more austere botanist but delightful for the gardener), colonising the land with their often decorative rosettes of foliage and graceful stems of flowers – yellow, dusty red, violet, pale orangey-brown, pink and magenta. In May and June they are a marvel to see. The garden is especiallly rich in bulbous woodland plants – magnificent *Cardiocrinum giganteum*, spring and autumn crocuses, fritillaries, lilies, superb nomocharis and trilliums.

The maintenance of a garden of this sort is arduous. It is gardened organically and all weeding must be done meticulously by hand to preserve precious seedlings. As the plants naturalise they show the gardener the conditions they prefer and in this way the plants themselves gradually enter into the management of the garden.

INFORMATION

Location by Aberfeldy PH15 2JT, Perthshire; 3½m NE of Aberfeldy, W from Aberfeldy to bridge over Tay, turn R at Weem–Strathtay road
Tel 01887 820795
Email mattingley@dial.pipex.com
Scottish Inventory Listed
Owner Mr J. and Mrs W. Mattingley
Open Mar to Oct, daily 10–6
Area 6 acres/2.4 hectares

Crarae Garden

A RAVINE GARDEN WITH BEAUTIFUL VIEWS OF LOCH FYNE AND MARVELLOUS FLOWERING SHRUBS

Crarae Garden has a wonderful site in a precipitous wooded glen on the west bank of Loch Fyne. A mountain stream, the Crarae burn, cascades down the ravine, occasionally crossed by bridges from which there are also marvellous views.

The garden was effectively started in 1912 by Grace, the wife of Sir Archibald Campbell (the 5th baronet), whose nephew was the plant collector and pioneer rock-gardener Reginald Farrer. In 1914 Farrer came to Crarae, bringing eucalyptus, conifers and rhododendrons for the garden. Lady Campbell had embarked on a garden but it was her son, Sir George, the 6th baronet, who from 1925 embellished the landscape with fine shrubs and trees from all over the temperate world. His son, Sir Ilay, continued the collection and then passed it on to the Crarae Gardens Charitable Trust, which increasingly found itself unable to fund the garden. Its future hung perilously in the balance until, after a breakneck public appeal, it was acquired for the National Trust for Scotland in 2002.

The garden has a large collection of rhododendrons (over 400 species and cultivars) but they form only part of much richer and more diverse planting. Conifers include *Cunninghamia lanceolata* from China; *Picea omorika*, the Serbian spruce from eastern Europe, which forms a tall slender shape; *Saxegothaea conspicua*, a yew-like tree from Chile; and *Tsuga mertensiana*, the mountain hemlock from the Sierra Nevada in California.

EPHEMERAL DELIGHTS

These, together with other evergreen trees such as eucalyptus and southern beeches (*Nothofagus* species), form a wonderful permanent background to the ephemeral delights of the flowering shrubs which include, apart from the rhododendrons, camellias, drimys, embothriums, eucryphias, magnolias and osmanthus – and also the Japanese *Disanthus cercidifolius* which has unexciting flowers but brilliant autumn colour ("the rich hue of vintage port in candlelight", according to Sir Ilay). The garden is rich, too, in ornamental deciduous trees, among them acers, cercidiphyllum, cornus, malus, rowans and styrax. All these are naturalistically disposed on the banks of the burn or, splendidly, on the rocky heights above.

Crarae has a rare collection of plants chosen to suit the special microclimate of high rainfall and mild winters, and the planting in this sublime landscape makes wonderful use of the natural dramatic topography.

The ravine at Crarae

INFORMATION

Location Crarae, by Inveraray PA32 8YA, Argyll; 10m S of Inveraray by A83
Tel and fax 01546 886614
Scottish Inventory Listed
Owner The National Trust for Scotland
Open daily 9.30–sunset
Area 50 acres/20 hectares

Crathes Castle

WALLED GARDENS WITH EARLY 18TH-CENTURY YEW HEDGES AND DAZZLING 20TH-CENTURY BORDERS

The castle at Crathes was built chiefly in the 16th century for the Burnetts of Leys who owned the estate until it was given to the National Trust for Scotland in 1952. The detail of the gardens is for the most part of the 20th century but much of their character and charm comes from the past – in particular, the beautiful early 18th-century yew hedges.

When Gertrude Jekyll visited Crathes in 1895 she wrote: "The brilliancy of colour masses in these gardens is something remarkable." Most modern visitors, especially those used to gardens further south, will have the same response. At the latitude of 57° N Crathes is well north of Moscow and the long hours of summer daylight encourage border perennials to grow with remarkable vigour.

The Walled Garden at Crathes

BOLD USE OF COLOUR

The present planting of the garden is dominated, from 1926 onwards, by the influence of Lady (Sybil) Burnett of Leys. The Colour, or Upper Pool, Garden shows the boldness of her ideas. Four right-angles of yew hedges clasp a square pool and the surrounding beds are planted in brilliant reds, oranges and yellows, subdued by occasional sombre notes of purple foliage from berberis, cotinus and fennel. A strong layout, a disciplined if occasionally raucous colour scheme, and much repeat planting create an atmosphere of explosive harmony. In the lower part of the walled garden an old clipped Portugal laurel (*Prunus lusitanica*) rises like a beacon among the borders. Lady Burnett's white borders, dating from 1936 and predating the more famous ones made by Vita Sackville-West for Sissinghurst (*see page 149*), are planted with hydrangea,

philadelphus and spiraea, underplanted with white-flowered *Aruncus dioica*, campanulas, geraniums, lychnis, musk mallow and pulmonaria. However, as Gertrude Jekyll recommended, the whiteness is spiked from time to time with another colour – the purple of orach leaves and the dusky red of *Astrantia* 'Ruby Wedding'. Since the National Trust took over, other colour-themed borders have been introduced – purple and red, gold and yellow and blue, purple and silver. All are exceptionally well cared for by an outstanding team of gardeners.

The garden is open on every day of the year and is worth visiting in any season. In late summer and autumn, however, the borders in their explosive exuberance offer one of the most memorable pleasures of any garden.

INFORMATION

Location nr Banchory AB31 3QJ, Kincardineshire; 3m E of Banchory and 15m SW of Aberdeen by A93
Tel 01330 844525 **Fax** 01330 844797
Scottish Inventory Listed
Owner The National Trust for Scotland
Open daily 9–sunset
Area 92 acres/37 hectares

Culross Palace

CHARMING RECONSTRUCTED 17TH-CENTURY TOWN GARDEN OF FLOWERS, FRUIT AND VEGETABLES

This is the smallest garden owned by the National Trust for Scotland and one of the most unusual. Culross is an ancient and enchanting place, with the remains of a 13th-century Cistercian monastery (now the parish church) and a rare ensemble of houses from the 16th century onwards. Its wealth grew as a result of James VI making it a royal burgh in 1592 and granting it a monopoly for the manufacture of cast-iron griddles.

PERIOD GARDENS

Culross Palace is not a palace at all, but the house of a mine-owner, George Bruce, who had a smart town house built in the late 16th and early 17th centuries. It has been finely restored and behind it, on sloping ground, the National Trust had the attractive idea of laying out a terraced period garden in keeping with the house, intermingling useful and ornamental plants. The lowermost terrace is a kitchen garden with six raised beds separated by paths of finely crushed seashells. In the beds containing vegetables occasional strips of roughly cut grass are decorated with wild achillea, borage and oxeye daisies. Fruit

trees are pleached against a south-facing wall and below this are medicinal and culinary plants such as horehound (*Marrubium vulgare*), southernwood (*Artemisia abrotanum*), valerian (*Valeriana officinalis*) and Welsh onion (*Allium fistulosum*). There is also a tunnel of pleached mulberry and the ornamental grapevine 'La Ciotat'. An upper terrace is planted with a long hedge of rosemary and lavender and ornamental native plants such as the oyster plant (*Mertensia maritima*), wallflowers (*Erysimum cheiri*) and bearded iris (*I. germanica* var. *florentina*). A vertiginous flight of stone steps leads to an even higher and narrower terrace with a little wattle fence entwined with clematis, honeysuckle and hop, and blackberries trained on the wall behind. The view from this point (not for vertigo sufferers) is enchanting: southwards over the garden and the jumbled pantiled rooftops of the village to the waters of the Forth beyond.

INFORMATION

Location Culross KY12 8JH, Fife; in the centre of Culross, 14m SE of Stirling by A907 and B9037
Tel 01383 880359 **Fax** 01383 882675
Owner The National Trust for Scotland
Open daily 10–6 (or dusk if earlier)
Area ¼ acre/0.10 hectare

The garden at Culross

Culzean Castle

CLIFFTOP GOTHIC PALACE DESIGNED BY ROBERT ADAM, WITH MARVELLOUS TERRACED, WALLED AND WOODLAND GARDENS

Few houses have so dramatic or romantic a setting as Culzean, and Robert Adam designed his Gothic castle to extract every ounce of drama from its cliff-top position looking west across the sea. The Kennedy family (later Earls of Cassilis, and Marquesses of Ailsa) had lived here since the 14th century, but the present castle was built for the 10th Earl during 1777–92.

"VERY PRETTY" GARDENS

The castle faces inland over terraced gardens described at the time of their origin in the 17th century as "very pretty". The top terrace is a simple walk with a castellated wall, with views of the ornamental terraces below. A long gravel walk on the first of these terraces runs along a deep mixed border below the retaining wall, planted with *Acca sellowiana*, callistemons, *Hoheria glabrata*, *Olearia paniculata*, penstemons and drifts of *Watsonia candicans*; the walls above are garlanded with clematis, the beautiful but tender *Mutisia decurrens* and *Vitis coignetiae*. In the border against the retaining wall of the terrace below are *Aralia elata* 'Variegata', bananas,

The fountain garden at Culzean

crocosmias, *Macleaya cordata*, *Melianthus major* and clumps of blue *Salvia guaranitica*. In the middle of this terrace is a lawn with a grand scalloped pool and central fountain.

South of the castle is an exquisite early 19th-century camellia house with tall tracery windows, battlements and finials. Here, a grand 18th-century walled garden is divided into two parts. The first has a late 19th-century vinery with grape cultivars of the period; a picturesque rockery grotto planted with alpines and ferns; and a number of good trees, among them a *Catalpa bignonioides*, a grand cedar of Lebanon and magnolias. The second walled garden is divided into four by herbaceous borders – part of it is a formal orchard and part a nursery. Deeper into woodland is one of the most attractive and unusual parts of the garden – the 13-acre/5-hectare Swan Pond overlooked by a Gothic cottage with ornamental verandah and porch. At the head of an uphill grass ride is the Pagoda, of vaguely oriental character, built in 1814.

Culzean also has hundreds of acres of woodland, which was originally wild moorland but planted with trees in the 18th and 19th centuries (when the 3rd Marquess of Ailsa is reckoned to have planted 5,000,000 trees). Under the National Trust for Scotland Culzean became Scotland's first country park and provides miles of wonderful walks.

INFORMATION

Location Maybole KA19 8LE, Ayrshire; 4m W of Maybole by B7023 and A719, 12m S of Ayr by A719
Tel 01655 884455 **Fax** 01655 884503
Email culzean@nts.org.uk
Scottish Inventory Listed
Owner The National Trust for Scotland
Open (Walled garden) Apr to Oct, daily 10.30–5; (Country park) daily 9.30–sunset
Area 560 acres/226 hectares

Dawyck Botanic Gardens

ANCIENT ESTATE WITH A REMARKABLE TREE COLLECTION IN A PICTURESQUE SETTING OF GREAT CHARACTER

From the 13th to the 17th century the Dawyck estate was owned by the Veitch family. By the 15th century it was "ringed with trees", and in the 17th century the Veitches planted the first horse chestnut grown in Scotland and also introduced silver firs (*Abies alba*), some of which still survive.

In 1691 the estate was acquired by James Naesmyth whose son, Sir James Naesmyth, introduced the first European larches (*Larix decidua*) to be planted in Scotland. His grandson, Sir John Murray Naesmyth, rebuilt the house in 1830 and laid out Italianate terraces with lawns and stone urns in front of the house. In 1897 the estate was bought by Mrs Alexander Balfour whose son, Frederick, continued the tradition of tree planting. In 1978 his son, Alastair, gave the woodland garden, which contains the most important part of the collection, to the Secretary of State for Scotland, from whom it passed to the Royal Botanic Garden Edinburgh.

The burn garden at Dawyck

NEW CONIFERS

The undulating site is densely wooded, with the Scrape burn tumbling down a ravine spanned by a high-arched stone bridge. The soil is a rich acid loam and with shelter belts trees grow well. In the 19th century many conifers were raised from seed collected in the wild for Sir John Murray Naesmyth by such collectors as David Douglas who in 1827 introduced the Douglas fir, of which several specimens at Dawyck survive from the 1835 planting. The slender fastigiate Dawyck beech (*Fagus sylvatica* 'Dawyck') was found in about 1850 by Sir John Murray Naesmyth. The original survives, now over 100ft/33m high. Under the Balfours many rhododendrons were planted, in particular those introduced from China by E.H. Wilson. The woodland garden is planted with birches, cercidiphyllums, cherries, maples and rowans with a brilliant display of daffodils – for twenty years Frederick Balfour planted a ton a year. Among those smaller ornamental plants for which Scottish gardens are specially noted are beautiful meconopsis and marvellous trilliums.

INFORMATION

Location Stobo EH45 9JU, Peeblesshire; 8m SW of Peebles by A72
Tel 01721 760254
Email dawyck@rbge.org.uk
Owner Royal Botanic Garden Edinburgh
Open Feb to Nov, daily 10–6 (Feb and Nov, closes 4; Mar and Oct closes 5)
Area 60 acres/24 hectares

Drummond Castle Gardens

A GIANT AND BREATHTAKING TERRACED PARTERRE GARDEN FOR A GREAT 17TH-CENTURY HOUSE

After her visit to Drummond Castle in 1842, Queen Victoria wrote in her diary: "We walked in the garden which is really very fine, with terraces, like an old French garden." There is indeed a dash of French formality here but it is heavily overlaid with elaborate 19th-century complications, made slightly less elaborate in the 20th century.

The first castle was built here in the 15th century by the 1st Lord Drummond whose family later became Earls of Perth. In the 1630s the 2nd Earl of Perth built a new house in renaissance style, designed by Charles I's master mason, John Mylne, and added elaborate terraced gardens. In around 1675 a gardener called John Reid was employed here; he later wrote the first book on gardening published in Scotland, *The Scots Gard'ner* (1683). In 1807 the Drummond heiress, Sarah, married Peter Burrell

who later became the 21st Baron Willoughby de Eresby. In 1818 the garden designer Lewis Kennedy became factor of the Drummond estate and from 1820 supervised a new terraced garden which J.C. Loudon in his *Encyclopaedia of Gardening* (1822) describes: "the grounds extended and highly improved by the present owner, assisted by his ingenious steward Lewis Kennedy." The work was completed by 1838 but the architect Sir Charles Barry did a watercolour in 1828 showing a proposed remodelling of the castle with ornate terraced gardens, and possibly he also had a hand in the new garden.

The garden that survives today is very much as it was seen by Queen Victoria, though it is now slightly less elaborate. South of the castle a terrace leads to a very grand double descending staircase. The immense formal garden below has the appearance of a giant parterre, dominated by a St Andrews cross of paths. At first sight one reacts with astonishment: it is so large an area – 1,000ft x 300ft/300m x 90m – and so relentlessly patterned and primped. I am not sure that it could be called beautiful but it is undeniably remarkable. A central path runs straight across the garden to a classical arcade with a pool and niches containing a figure of Pan and a boy with a dog, and a grotto wall behind the central arch. This, dating from the 18th century, was originally at Grimsthorpe Castle (*see page 243*). In the centre of the garden is a multi-faceted sundial designed by John Mylne and dated 1630. Lawns, criss-crossed by further paths, are ornamented with box-edged beds shaped like great fans or triangles and filled with permanent and seasonal plantings – *Anaphalis triplinervis*, antirrhinums, bedding roses, lambs' lugs, lavender. The whole garden is studded with a profusion of shaped trees and topiary in copper beech, common and gold variegated holly, purple-leafed plum (*Prunus cerasifera* 'Nigra'), juniper and yew (both common and golden), intermingled with statues and urns. The modern planting is, however, very different from the original 19th-century scheme, in which, as we know from photographs and descriptions, most of the large compartments were densely planted with small trees and shrubs, with occasional smaller beds of brilliant annuals. Laying the garden out must have been a nightmare, for the site is far from even. You are unaware of this until you walk among the parterres when you see that the walks swoop up and down with writhing abandon.

A LESS FORMAL GARDEN

To the east, the garden becomes less formal. On the grassy slope below the castle is a scattered group of venerable clipped Portugal laurels, like a herd of exotic creatures, and a fine statue is almost engulfed in a spreading mound of clipped yew (apparently a single plant but in fact several whose canopies now merge into a vast roof). The gully below is spanned by a magnificent four-arched castellated bridge, with ornamental woodland spreading beyond.

No other British garden has a parterre like that at Drummond. Extraordinary as it is, it does possess a kind of gawkily attractive charm, and there remains a hint of the much more restrained and harmonious renaissance idea of a stately terraced garden spread out below the windows of the house. Something else of renaissance character can be seen as you leave the parterre: a grotto-like niche in the great stairs, decorated with rustication and shells and a mask of Neptune in a keystone.

The great parterre
at Drummond

INFORMATION

Location Muthill, nr Crieff PH7 4HZ, Perthshire; 2m S of Crieff by A822
Tel 01764 681433
Email the.gardens@drummondcastle.sol.co.uk
Website www.drummondcastlegardens.co.uk
Scottish Inventory Listed
Owner Grimsthorpe and Drummond Castle Trust
Open Easter weekend and May to Oct, daily 1–6
Area 15 acres/6 hectares

Dunrobin Castle Gardens

DELIGHTFUL FORMAL GARDENS FOR A FRENCH-STYLE CHÂTEAU WITH SPLENDID SEA VIEWS

The castle, with origins in the 13th century, was designed in the 19th century by Sir Charles Barry for the Duke of Sutherland (who had also designed Trentham for the 1st Duke of Sutherland; *see page 224*) but it became a collaboration between the Duke himself, Barry and the architect William Leslie. It is a delightful confection: a jolly château of beautiful pale stone with round towers crowned with swooping witches' hats, balustrades and machicolations. It rises high on a terrace with rounded bastions, looking out confidently over the Moray Firth.

The west parterre at Dunrobin

A PAIR OF PARTERRES

By far the most notable feature of the landscape, however, is the pair of parterres laid out between the castle and the sea, in part designed by Sir Charles Barry in around 1850. The west parterre has a circular fountain pool surrounded by four circular box-edged beds, each planted with *Aralia chinensis*. Further beds are filled with hardy geraniums underplanted with tulips in spring and lilies for late summer. Beyond this four square beds have tall wooden pyramids, trained with *Actinidia kolomikta*, roses and sweet peas. Narrow beds edging the squares have achilleas, bergamot, catmint, daylilies, geraniums and tradescantia, with mop-headed quinces rising at intervals. A second circular pool, with a water jet, is surrounded by segmental beds, each filled in summer with a single variety of antirrhinum, and with a conical hornbeam in each corner.

The east parterre is an enormous circular lawn. At its centre a circular pool with a fountain is surrounded by round box-edged beds planted with *Aralia chinensis*. Outside it, a concentric circle of clipped Irish yews is edged

with more box-edged beds, each one containing either white *Potentilla fruticosa* or scarlet dahlias. East of the parterre is a summerhouse, built in 1732 for William, Lord Strathnaver (later 17th Earl of Sutherland) and now housing a delightful small museum which contains, among much else, several extraordinary carved Pictish stones.

Dunrobin offers two very different views: from the castle, the lively patterns of the parterres are finely displayed, with long views of the sea beyond; from below, as you stand in the parterres surrounded by brilliant colours and the splashing of water, there are wonderful views up to the castle on its cliff above.

INFORMATION

Location Golspie KW10 6SF, Sutherland; 1m N of Golspie by A9
Tel 01408 633177
Email info@dunrobincastle.net
Website www.highlandescape.com
Scottish Inventory Listed
Owner The Sutherland Trust
Open Apr to mid Oct, daily 10.30–5.30 (Apr, May and Oct, closes 4.30 and opens 12 on Sun)
Area 5 acres/2 hectares

Edzell Castle

AN ORNAMENTAL RENAISSANCE WALLED GARDEN AND 20TH-CENTURY PLANTING ADORN A MEDIEVAL CASTLE

There are few gardens so small, and so sketchily planted, that have so strong an atmosphere as the walled garden at Edzell. The remains of a 15th-century fortified house was, in the early years of the 17th century, provided with an ornamental "pleasaunce" by the Lindsay family, Earls of Crawford, who had lived here since 1358.

LIVELY DECORATION

The roofless tower house, garden walls and fragments of other buildings with crow-step gables present a picturesque scene across a meadow. The garden walls bear a carved stone plaque with the arms of David Lindsay, Lord Edzell, and the date 1604. Three walls are decorated with a series of carved stone panels in relief, showing the Planetary Deities with their symbolic attributes: Mars in full armour carrying a sword, Venus with a flaming heart and a flouncy skirt, Mercury with winged sandals and staff entwined with snakes, and so on. Further panels depict the Liberal Arts (Grammatica, Rhetorica, and so on) and the Cardinal

Virtues (faith, hope, justice, etc). They are beautifully carved and full of liveliness and humour.

At the centre is a sunken garden which was reconstructed just before World War II. A parterre of low box hedges was made here, into which Lindsay mottoes are worked from clipped box – *Dum Spiro Spero* (as long as I breathe I hope) and *Endure Forte* (hold firm). Four angled beds each contain a block of a single cultivar of floribunda rose – scarlet 'Lilli Marlene' or yellow 'Old Gold' – and at the corners triangular beds contain a thistle, rose or fleur-de-lys; a clipped drum of yew at the centre is surrounded by mounds of yew. This thoroughly 20th-century arrangement does have something of the lively decorative spirit that characterises the enclosing walls.

Built into a corner of the garden walls is a pretty summerhouse of the same date as the garden, with crow-stepped gable, finely carved window surrounds and a niche. In English gardens of this period such garden buildings were often used as banqueting houses in which post-prandial sweetmeats were eaten. Despite its fragmentary state, and sometimes coarse modern planting, Edzell Castle gives much pleasure, and the rare decorations of its garden walls, a unique survival of its period, give it unusual distinction.

Edzell's walled "pleasaunce"

INFORMATION

Location Edzell, nr Brechin DD9 7UE, Angus; 1m W of the village of Edzell, 6m N of Brechin by A90 and B966
Tel 01356 648631
Scottish Inventory Listed
Owner Historic Scotland
Open Apr to Sept, daily 9.30–6.30; Oct to Mar, Sat to Wed 9.30–4.30
Area 1 acre/0.4 hectare

Falkland Palace

FINE FLOWER GARDENS ON A GRAND SCALE DESIGNED BY
PERCY CANE FOR A MAGNIFICENT ROYAL PALACE

A much older house here was acquired by King James II in 1458 and turned into a royal palace. In the 16th century, under James IV and James V, it took on its dazzling renaissance character. James V was married to Madeleine de Valois, who died young, and subsequently to Marie de Guise. As a result of this connection, French stone masons came to Falkland and almost certainly created the lovely detail of the palace. After James VI became King of England in 1603 the palace was no longer the home of monarchs. In 1887 it was acquired by John Crichton Stuart, 3rd Marquess of Bute, who began a wholesale programme of restoration. In 1947 his grandson, Major Michael Crichton Stuart, commissioned a new garden from Percy Cane.

A GRAND SCALE

Percy Cane was not concerned with history – his response was an aesthetic one to the drama of the architectural setting. To one side of the palace he laid out a giant lawn with island beds about its perimeter and flower borders between the island beds and the enclosing walls. The planting within the island beds is on a grand scale, with ornamental trees and shrubs at the centre, and herbaceous planting about the edges. Many of the trees are now overgrown and their shape distorted due to crowding, but the design is effective, especially because of the generous spaces of lawn at the centre. Here you may saunter along what is in effect a very broad grass path with sinuous edges. To the west the palace rises splendidly above the ornamental trees and to the east there are intermittent glimpses of Cane's deep mixed border along the boundary wall (590ft/180m long), with its passages of brilliant colour, especially in late summer.

Percy Cane laid out two further areas of the garden. By the north range of the palace a little formal garden has blocks of clipped golden yew backed with cushions of clipped *Brachyglottis greyi* and symmetrical beds planted with blocks of red and yellow roses. At the northern end of the garden, behind a tall yew hedge, is a piece of bold post-World War II modernism: a water garden with two rectangular lily pools flanked by processions of fastigiate junipers (*Juniperus communis* 'Hibernica') and prostrate golden juniper (*J. x pfitzeriana* 'Pfitzeriana Aurea') – not for the faint-hearted.

The mixed border at Falkland

INFORMATION

Location Falkland KY7 7BU, Fife; in the village of Falkland, 11m N of Kirkcaldy by A912
Tel 0131 243 9300
Email information@nts.org.uk
Website www.nts.org.uk
Scottish Inventory Listed
Owner The National Trust for Scotland
Open Mar to Oct, daily 10–5 (opens 1 on Sun)
Area 7 acres/2.8 hectares

Glenwhan Garden

PLANTSWOMAN'S LAVISHLY PLANTED HILL-TOP GARDEN IN A BEAUTIFUL SETTING FILLED WITH FINE PLANTS

In the late 1970s the Knotts came with their young family to Glenwhan to farm. When they arrived there was nothing here except gorse and bracken. The site, with beautiful views over Luce Bay and the Mull of Galloway, is 300ft/90m above sea level, close to the sea, and often swept by violent coastal winds. However, the influence of the Gulf Stream is strongly felt here, rainfall is around 40in/100cm per annum and the soil is acid.

The lochans at Glenwhan

Starting in 1979, Tessa Knott planted shelter belts of conifers and deciduous trees, and broke up the space with thickets of willows. Two pools (lochans as they are called in these parts) were excavated, fed by a rushing stream, and stocked with brown trout and Koi carp.

DENSE PLANTING

Almost thirty years later the garden is densely planted. The lochans are at the heart of the garden, with rising land behind them and flatter ground to the south, where the house is. A perimeter walk girdles the garden, with subsidiary paths darting off to particular areas. The style of planting is naturalistic and the range of plants is immense. Space is set aside for particular groups of plants – birches, maples, camellias, heathers, hollies, hydrangeas, willows and so on. Otherwise, plants of different kinds come thick and fast. As in some idiosyncratic zoo, exotics are intermingled with perfectly ordinary plants – a soaring eucalyptus, for example, rising among Scots pines, heather and rowans. Where the perimeter walk starts, you come in quick succession to *Eucryphia milligani*, a cistus, *Crinodendron hookerianum*, hydrangeas, lilacs, *Quercus robur* 'Hungaria' and rhododendrons. Trees and shrubs form the main meal but there are lovely *hors d'oeuvres* of smaller ornamental plantings – agapanthus, erythroniums, meconopsis, narcissi, tricyrtis and trilliums.

Above the lochans, on the highest slopes of the garden, are sitting places and viewpoints from which the garden is seen spread out below with a distant and lovely panorama of the sea. The dark varnished surface of the lochans is occasionally ruffled by ducks or fish, and on the banks are fronds of cortaderia, scarlet crocosmia, bulrushes and irises. The design of the garden is light-handed – it is essentially a happy home for plants, making the most of the handsome topography and the climate.

INFORMATION

Location Dunragit, by Stranraer DG9 8PH, Wigtownshire; 7m E of Stranraer by A75
Tel 01581 400222
Email tess@glenwhan.freeserve.co.uk
Website www.glenwhangardens.co.uk
Owner Tessa and William Knott
Open Apr to Sept, daily 10–5 (at other times by appointment)
Area 12 acres/4.8 hectares

Greywalls

EDWIN LUTYENS'S EXQUISITE GARDEN DESIGN FOR A GOLF-
LINKS HOLIDAY HOME WITH FINE BORDERS

Greywalls was built for the Hon. Alfred Lyttelton in 1901 to the designs of Sir Edwin Lutyens. On the southern edge of Muirfield golf course, overlooking the Firth of Forth, it was conceived as a holiday house and golfing base. It is an enchanting house which gave Lutyens every opportunity to show his characteristic charm and ingenuity.

A SEQUENCE OF SPACES

Lutyens also laid out the garden, which flows in a sequence of deftly planned spaces. The southern entrance façade of the house is concave, sweeping about a turning circle at one corner of a square forecourt. To one side, immediately south of a wing of the house, a paved terrace edged with deep beds of lavender overlooks a walled garden. A broad paved path leads between a symmetrical pattern of beds of acanthus, heuchera, kniphofias, *Lychnis coronaria*, sedums and thalictrum, with much repetition of plants and identical planting on either side. Doors open on each side, one leading to the entrance forecourt and the other to a croquet lawn. The axis opened by the paved path continues southwards along a grass walk edged in stone which runs between rows of rowans rising from box-edged beds filled with periwinkles. On each side of the walk are secret gardens hedged in thornless holly (*Ilex aquifolium* 'J.C. van Tol') and planted with cherry trees in lawns. At the head of the walk, in the boundary wall, a pedimented alcove seat with an opening in its back forms a *claire-voie*, giving views out of the garden to the Lothian hills.

On either side of the holly-enclosed beds which flank the central walk are semicircular spaces enclosed in stone walls. Each has paths radiating across lawns to doors in the walls whose openings are surrounded by typical Lutyens patterns of terracotta tiles laid edge on. The eastern enclosure is lined with a narrow herbaceous border and has a Lutyens seat in an arbour of clematis and roses; the western one has a lawn with a weeping silver pear (*Pyrus salicifolia* 'Pendula') and, along its straight side, a border of purple-leafed *Cotinus coggygria* Rubrifolius Group underplanted with lavender and edged in *Lonicera nitida* 'Baggesen's Gold'.

To stay in the hotel, or simply eat a meal, and walk in this garden is a wonderful pleasure, perfect for gardeners who are also keen on golf.

INFORMATION

Location Muirfield, Gullane EH31 2EG, East Lothian; 5m W of North Berwick by A198
Tel 01620 842144
Email hotel@greywalls.co.uk
Website www.greywalls.co.uk
Open to guests of the hotel
Area 11 acres/4.4 hectares

Greywall's south garden

The Hermitage

A WOODLAND WALK WITH GRAND TREES, A SPECTACULAR CASCADE AND AN 18TH-CENTURY PAVILION

This is a bosky and mysterious place – the atmospheric remains of the 2nd Duke of Atholl's 18th-century romantic landscape. Originally part of the Dunkeld House estate, it was given to the National Trust for Scotland by the 8th Duchess of Atholl in 1943.

An apparently aimless path leads into coniferous woods following the bank of the rushing river Braan. The woods are filled with rare specimens of Douglas fir (*Pseudotsuga menziesii*), some of them of giant size. David Douglas was born nearby at Scone and introduced this fir from the Pacific coast of North America in 1826. Visible from the Hermitage woods, but just over the boundary in the Forestry Commission land of Craigvinean Forest, is the fourth tallest specimen in the British Isles, at 194ft/ 59m – a self-sown seedling dating from around 1887. Progressing in the cool shade of these great trees, you soon see a handsomely arched 18th-century stone bridge and hear a mighty rushing of water. To one side of the bridge is a stone pavilion. Penetrate the gloom, and the roaring of the water becomes even greater. You see light at the far end of the room and emerge onto a viewing platform overlooking a marvellous waterfall in the river below – broad and rocky, with the water cascading down to be trapped in a narrow channel where it rushes below the bridge.

The cascade at the Hermitage

"THE TOUCH OF MAGIC"

In 1805 William Wordsworth and his sister Dorothy visited the pavilion (or Ossian's Hall as it was then called – built in 1785 and later renamed the Hermitage) escorted by the Duke's gardener. Dorothy wrote of their visit: "The gardener desired us to look at a painting of the figure of Ossian, which . . . disappeared, parting in the middle, flying asunder as if by the touch of magic, and lo! we are at the entrance of a splendid room, which was almost dizzy with waterfalls, that tumbled in all directions – the great cascade, which was opposite to the window that faced us, being reflected in innumerable mirrors upon the ceiling and against the walls." The experience is not as impeccably stage-managed today but the waterfall is every bit as dramatic. Nearby, hidden in the woods, is a rustic grotto of the same date: Ossian's Cave. This is all that remains of a garden which in its day was one of the great Scottish beauty spots. Dorothy also describes "quaintly intersected walks" and gardens of "fine flowers among the rocks". All this detail has gone but the vivid character of the setting remains.

INFORMATION

Location 1m W of Dunkeld, 16m N of Perth, signed off the A9
Tel 01796 473233
Scottish Inventory Listed
Owner The National Trust for Scotland
Open daily dawn–dusk
Area 37 acres/15 hectares

Hopetoun House

A GREAT HOUSE ON THE BANKS OF THE FIRTH OF FORTH WITH FINE WOODLAND AND A SUPERB TERRACED WALK BY THE SEA

The palatial house at Hopetoun was started by Sir William Bruce in 1699 and much enlarged from 1721 by William Adam. It was built for Charles Hope, the 1st Earl of Hopetoun, whose descendants (later Marquesses of Linlithgow) have continued to live here. There is no garden here now but the wooded grounds are of exceptional interest and charm and provide a magnificent setting for the house.

A formal garden was laid out by Sir William Bruce and Alexander Edwards when the house was built, which John Mackay described in his *A Journey Through Scotland* (1728): "The parterre fronting the saloon hath a large bason of water at bottom, it's also adorned with a multitude of statues on pedestals. From the Terras to the north of this Parterre is the finest view I ever saw anywhere." The west lawn, overlooked by the drawing room of the house, still has a pool, now a large disc of water with a splendid jet. The "terras" mentioned by Mackay is still very much present and the view from it is indeed magnificent. This terraced walk, edged in a neatly clipped yew hedge about 4ft/1.2m high, curves along the Firth of Forth with grand views over the water to the coast of Fife. Below the terrace the ground swoops down – at its western end is a deer park with a herd of Red Deer. The best route here leads through a beautiful avenue of old lime trees and thence into the woodland that lies behind the terrace walk.

HOPE'S WALK

A stream, the Cornie Burn, flows through the woodland where there are some exceptional trees – ancient oaks, a giant yew (the oldest tree at Hopetoun, said to be 550 years old) and a gigantic old beech with vast spreading branches. On the site of Abercorn Castle (keep of the Clan Douglas in the 13th century) is a spectacular group of three immense cedars of Lebanon. Hope's Walk was laid out as a place of recreation where the ladies of the household could walk along the Cornie Burn and admire the rhododendrons, laurels and crab apples on their after-dinner walks. Walking back towards the house, splendid views of it are framed by the trees.

Hopetoun House is famous but its marvellous wooded landscape setting should be better known.

The west lawn at Hopetoun

INFORMATION

Location South Queensferry, near Edinburgh, West Lothian EH30 9SL; 12m W of Edinburgh, 2½ m W of the Forth Road Bridge

Tel 0131 331 2451

Email marketing@ hopetounhouse.com

Website www. hopetounhouse.com

Owner Hopetoun House Preservation Trust

Open Easter to Sept, daily 10.30–5 (open out of season to groups by appointment)

Area 100 acres/40 hectares

House of Pitmuies

OUTSTANDING FLOWER GARDENS, PRETTY KITCHEN GARDEN AND RIVERSIDE WALKS BEAUTIFULLY MAINTAINED

The House of Pitmuies is a handsome 18th-century house with fine contemporary outhouses and walled gardens surrounded by well-wooded policies. The distinction of its garden comes chiefly from its present owner, Margaret Ogilvie, who is a skilled and original gardener. The former kitchen garden, retaining a mixture of the ornamental and productive, with beds of fruit and vegetables, lavish garlands of honeysuckle, roses on trelliswork, and cordons of sweetpeas, is delightful but unexceptional. The real excitement comes in the adjacent walled garden which spreads out in front of the house.

Walled garden borders at Pitmuies

A FLORIFEROUS CHASM

Aligned with the gate into the garden is an arch of clipped silver pear (*Pyrus salicifolia* 'Pendula') which frames a view of a long pair of herbaceous borders separated by a narrow turf path running right across the garden. The colour scheme is dominated by purple and pink from such plants as *Geranium psilostemon*, *Silene dioica* 'Flore Pleno', *Stachys byzantina* and *Sidalcea* 'Sussex Beauty', intermingled with plenty of white-flowered and silver-leafed plants. The borders are narrow and the planting rises on either side of the grass path, forming a floriferous chasm. Parallel to these borders is another pair, aligned with a window of the drawing room, whose ethereal colours of blue, cream, white and yellow are chosen to match the colour scheme of the room within. Both sets of borders are hedged in walls of coppiced *Prunus cerasifera* 'Pissardii' whose fresh pink new foliage in spring becomes increasingly purple and sombre as the season passes, forming in high summer an excellent background to the lively colours of the borders. A cross-axis is formed by a distinguished avenue of Tibetan cherry (*Prunus serrula*). There are many other pleasures here – excellent shrub roses, a good collection of *Potentilla fruticosa* cultivars and some remarkable old delphinium cultivars.

The final treat at Pitmuies is a walk in the woods, past a decorative Gothic dovecote and along the banks of the Vinny water. The dovecote is dated 1643 with the Gothic detailing probably added in the 19th century. There are good trees here, the most memorable being a magnificent old *Acer griseum*. Everything seems just right at Pitmuies. Margaret Ogilvie knows her plants and shows a rare sense of atmosphere.

INFORMATION

Location Guthrie, by Forfar DD8 2SN, Forfarshire; 7m E of Forfar by A932
Tel 01241 828245
Email ogilvie@pitmuies.com
Website www.pitmuies.com
Scottish Inventory Listed
Owner Mrs Farquhar Ogilvie
Open Apr to Oct, daily 10–5
Area 25 acres/10 hectares

Inverewe

EXTRAORDINARY WOODLAND GARDEN ON THE COAST – ONE MAN'S REMARKABLE ACHIEVEMENT

When Osgood Mackenzie came here in 1862 the tallest plant he could see was a scrubby willow 3ft/1m feet high, and any remotely edible vegetation was instantly consumed by sheep. He fenced off a promontory of land that juts out into Loch Ewe and gradually started to establish evergreen windbreaks of Austrian, Corsican and Scots pine. It was fifteen years before he was able to begin planting the tender exotics for which the garden became famous. The land was almost bereft of humus so fertile soil had to be brought laboriously by sea and carried in creels on men's backs. The coast, however, benefits from the benign influence of the Gulf Stream with high rainfall of up to 60 in/150cm a year.

The coastal walk at Inverewe

Once protection from the salt-laden wind was established and the soil improved, an immense range of temperate plants was able to be grown and Mackenzie built up his collection. Shortly before World War I he was visited by the famous W.J. Bean from Kew – "I had the pleasure of showing him my tricuspidarias, embothriums and eucryphias, my trees of *Abutilon vitifolium*, my palms, loquats, drimys, Sikkim rhododendrons, my giant olearias, senecios, veronicas, leptospermums, my metrosideros, mitrarias, etc." He adds, "I have, too, some of the less common varieties" and proceeds to list the real rarities of the collection. Mackenzie died in 1922 and his daughter Mairi (later Mairi Sawyer) took over the running of the garden, which she left to the National Trust for Scotland on her death in 1953.

A MESMERISING JUNGLE

The visitor to Inverewe today will be bewildered and enchanted by the extraordinary plants grown in scenes of jungle-like beauty. Three National Collections of plants are kept here – of brachyglottis (formerly senecio), olearias and *Rhododendron barbata*. The bark of old Scots pines, like that of giant myrtles, eucalyptus and rhododendrons, is marvellously ornamental; and everywhere there is much strange and beautiful foliage. The mesmerising jungle is laced with paths, sometimes narrow and often precipitous, with occasional delicious views of the loch.

Visitors will also relish Osgood Mackenzie's kitchen garden. On terraced slopes near the entrance to the garden below the house, protected by a long curving wall of stone, are beds of fruit and vegetables interspersed with enchanting ornamental planting – all maintained to impeccable standards.

INFORMATION

Location Poolewe IV22 2LG, Ross and Cromarty; 6m NE of Gairloch by A832
Tel 01445 781200 **Fax** 01445 781497
Scottish Inventory Owner The National Trust for Scotland
Open Apr to Sept, daily 9.30–5; Oct, daily 10–4; Jan to Mar, daily 9.30–4
Area 62 acres/25 hectares

Kellie Castle

INTIMATE WALLED FLOWER GARDEN FOR A HISTORIC ESTATE WITH LIVELY ARTS AND CRAFTS CHARACTER

Kellie Castle stands in the Neuk of Fife and enjoys splendid distant views of the Firth of Forth. The castle is essentially a fortified tower house of the 16th and 17th centuries, although a house has existed here at least since the 15th century. The walled garden immediately alongside it dates from the 17th and 18th centuries. The modern garden history of Kellie starts in 1878 when the estate was bought by Professor James Lorimer who restored the then abandoned castle. His son Robert became a distinguished architect and garden designer, and as a sixteen-year-old schoolboy in 1880 laid out a delightful walled garden for Kellie Castle. A painting of 1892 by John Henry Lorimer shows great thickets of *Lilium longiflorum* rising below apple trees, and when George Elgood painted the garden in 1899 he showed gravel walks and box-edged beds filled with hollyhocks, poppies and roses. The planting is essentially Victorian in character but Lorimer's design already shows his fondness for what he later described as the essential spirit of 17th-century Scottish gardens – "great intersecting walks of shaven grass, on either side borders of brightest flowers backed by low espaliers hanging with shining apples".

AN INTIMATE GARDEN

The walled garden lies hard against the castle walls. A cruciform pattern of paths of gravel and mown grass divides the space with strong and simple axes. Herbaceous borders edged with box flank the vista aligned with the entrance. Lemon-yellow achilleas, violet-blue *Echinops ritro*, orange heleniums and lavender goat's rue (*Galega officinalis*) are planted in bold drifts, with espaliered pears trained on wires at the back. The vista is closed by a bench with an arched back of Arts and Crafts style, designed by Hew Lorimer (Robert Lorimer's nephew). A grass path forming a cross-axis passes between beds of gallica roses and lavender (with great drifts of *Galtonia candicans* in late summer), under an arch of roses to a fine armillary sphere on a plinth. Beds about the walls are largely given over to the cultivation of fruit, vegetables and herbs. Robert Lorimer also designed a delightful little gardener's bothy in one corner, surmounted by a jaunty carved stone bird. It is a delightful place – a vision of a cottage garden suitable for a castle.

The walled garden at Kellie Castle

INFORMATION

Location nr Pittenweem KY10 2RF, Fife; 3m NW of Pittenweem by B9171
Tel 01333 720271 **Fax** 01333 720326
Owner National Trust for Scotland
Open daily 9.30–5.30
Area 1½ acres/0.6 hectare

Kinross House

OUTSTANDING 17TH-CENTURY FORMAL GARDENS BY SIR WILLIAM BRUCE FOR HIS OWN HOUSE

The garden at Kinross is a marvellous survival from the late 17th century – one of the grandest and most attractive gardens in Scotland. It was created in the 1680s by Sir William Bruce for his own use, and surviving plans show that the relationship of the garden to the house was planned from the start. Bruce had bought land here in 1675, much attracted by the romantic lake, Loch Leven, with its ruined medieval castle on an island at its centre – one of the many places where Mary Queen of Scots is thought to have been imprisoned. Bruce made it the focal point of both house and garden.

A SINGLE AXIS

Bruce's magnificent classical mansion and its garden are united about a single axis. This started with the old High Street of the town of Kinross, which led up to the entrance lodges of Bruce's estate, and although the High Street has now been cut off, the remainder of the axis remains intact. From the lodges it runs straight to the front door of the house, and on the other side it continues in the form of a path to the boundary wall of the garden where it appears to end at an iron gate with a magnificently decorated stone surround. But the visual axis in fact continues for, centred on the gate, is the prospect of the ruins of Loch Leven Castle in the middle of the loch.

When Inigo Triggs visited Kinross House to research his *Formal Gardens in England and Scotland* (1902) he found "The whole place, which has not been inhabited since the year 1819, has now a very desolate and ruinous aspect." The estate and gardens were restored in the early 20th century by the Montgomery family, whose plantings follow the firm

structure of Bruce's layout. Excellent mixed borders under the walls, with their beautiful architectural detailing, are broken from time to time by buttresses of clipped yew in keeping with the architecture of the walls. The path running from the house towards the loch passes through a rose garden ornamented with helical shapes of clipped yew and then between a pair of mixed borders, backed by hedges of clipped purple beech, whose colours modulate from whites to purples and blues, then to yellows and finally to a triumphant flourish of rich reds – red *Persicaria affinis* and scarlet *Crocosmia* 'Lucifer'. The wrought-iron gate ending the path is flanked by tall piers capped

Herbaceous border at Kinross

with putti gambolling with dolphins, and the arch above the gate is topped by a stone urn filled with fish (seven identifiable species of fish which were found in the loch in the 17th century). Closer to the house the walls are interrupted by boldly carved and decorated piers which flank openings. On one side they frame a path ("Kirk Wynd") which led to a church that no longer survives, and on the other they opened a view of an arcadian grove of trees. These were both part of Bruce's original design and, in the same spirit as the framed view of Loch Leven Castle, borrowed the landscape outside the garden and thus enriched the garden.

HIDDEN GARDEN

Close to the house is a garden hidden behind yew hedges. Here, a summerhouse with a sweeping ogee-shaped roof overlooks beds of roses and a fine statue of Atlas shouldering the universe. The garden wall is decorated with finials and a multi-faceted sundial of the kind that was popular in 17th-century Scottish gardens.

Kinross is still privately owned, by the family that restored it, and both house and garden are impeccably maintained. Visitors are welcome in the garden but there is no trace of the heritage industry; the entrance charge is by an honesty box and when you are there you have the impression of being a privileged guest in a private and splendid domain. It is easily one of the finest gardens in Scotland.

INFORMATION

Location Kinross KY13 7ET, Kinross-shire; In the centre of the town of Kinross
Email jm@kinrosshouse.com
Website www.kinrosshouse.com
Scottish Inventory Listed
Owner Mrs James Montgomery
Open Apr to Sept, daily 10–7
Area 4 acres/1.6 hectares

Logan Botanic Garden

MARVELLOUS PLANTS, MANY OF THEM RARITIES, IN A GARDEN OF MUCH BEAUTY WITH A SUBTROPICAL CLIMATE

Logan Botanic Garden is part of the Royal Botanic Garden Edinburgh. Because of its privileged climate (affected by the Gulf Stream but also by the peculiar lie of the land, making it mild and wet), it is able to cultivate all kinds of tender plants, especially those of the southern hemisphere.

Cordyline avenue at Port Logan

SUBTROPICAL EXOTICISM

Logan's chief attraction to the visitor will be the prospect of seeing unfamiliar plants flourishing in the open air, giving the garden an atmosphere of subtropical exoticism. At the heart of the garden is an irregular walled area with such traces of formality as the garden possesses. Wilder woodland lies outside the walls. A lily pool is flanked by rows of *Cordyline australis* and a border alongside is full of *Gladiolus papilio*, kniphofias and watsonias, with a huge spread of blue and white agapanthus. Magnificent tree ferns are underplanted with different species of herbaceous ferns, with the occasional eruption of *Fascicularia bicolor* – an ornamental grass with startling crimson blades among its foliage. A flight of stone steps curves up to the terrace, freckled with the Mexican daisy *Erigeron karvinskianus*, and the statuesque leaves of the Madeiran *Echium pininana* rise on one side, backed by thickets of ceanothus with electric blue flowers. The terrace walls are draped with such tender climbers as pale yellow *Jasminum mesnyi*, *Mutisia ilicifolia* with fragile-looking palest pink flowers, and the glowing cerise bell-flowers of *Lapageria rosea*. In the bed below are the Californian white sage (*Salvia apiana*), *Cedronella canariensis* (whose aromatic leaves smell of cedar), a shrubby foxglove from Madeira (*Isoplexis sceptrum*), and much else that is exotic and tender.

The northern part of the walled garden has lawns and informal plantings of trees and shrubs. Among them are superb old eucryphias and rhododendrons, and a giant *Magnolia sprengeri* – a noble sight. The rows of cabbage palms (*Cordyline australis*) make something exotic of a conventional garden feature. Here they reach their full potential, flowering profusely and producing creamy clouds of blossom whose rich scent pervades the walled garden in summer. There is something irresistible, too, in the sight of a tricky exotic – waves of the Chatham Island forget-me-not (*Myosotidum hortensia*), for example – grown in lavish profusion rather than lonely pampered splendour.

INFORMATION

Location Port Logan, Stranraer DG9 9ND, Wigtownshire; 12m S of Stranraer by A716
Tel 01776 860231
Email logan@rbge.org.uk
Website www.rbge.org.uk
Scottish Inventory Listed
Owner Trustees of the Royal Botanic Garden Edinburgh
Open Mar to Oct, daily 10–6 (closes 5 in Mar and Oct)
Area 30 acres/12 hectares

Mellerstain

MAGNIFICENT ROSE TERRACES, A GRAND LANDSCAPE AND A SURPRISING COTTAGE GARDEN

The house was designed by William Adam in 1725 to 1726 and by his son, Robert Adam, who between 1770 and 1778 gave it its present gently castellated appearance. William Adam was also probably responsible for laying out the parkland, in particular the two axes which divide the land, meeting north of the house. Early 18th-century formal gardens were removed in the landscaping craze later in the century. A version of them, however, was put back in 1909 by Sir Reginald Blomfield, and his grand scheme is the chief landscape ornament today.

Blomfield's terraced gardens lie below the south façade of the house where the ground falls away, giving wonderful views over woodland to the Cheviot Hills. A grass terrace below the house, with tall cones of clipped yew and a mixed border, curves round at each end to provide side views over the lower terraces. From here, a double balustraded staircase leads to a lower terrace with a rose garden planned as a giant parterre. Shaped beds cut into the turf are filled with catmint or with a single variety of white, pink or red bedding roses with box topiary disposed between the beds. A second double staircase, embracing a pool of irises and waterlilies, leads down to a simple grass terrace with a classical statue facing back towards the house.

A CURIOUS EYECATCHER

The lawn slopes southwards, edged with beech hedges, towards a distant pool fringed with trees. As you descend you suddenly find the incline becoming steeper, with the land scooped out in a vast amphitheatre of turf. At the bottom the pool turns out to be the head of a canal, enclosed in a curving balustrade. The canal penetrates the woodland, through which there are walks, and on rising land above the woods, centred on the canal, is a curious eyecatcher – Hundy Mundy – like the west front of a medieval cathedral with two pointed gables and a central arch.

In the wooded policies north of the house is a charming curiosity: a thatched cottage *orné*, part of which is a round tower, formerly a dovecote. It has a garden of a cottagey kind – swooping beds edged in box, Irish yews, wigwams of runner beans and drifts of irises, pelargoniums, phlox and roses.

The terraced gardens at Mellerstain

INFORMATION

Location nr Gordon TD3 6LG, Berwickshire; 7m NW of Kelso by A6089

Tel 01573 410225

Email enquiries@mellerstain. com

Website www.mellerstain.com

Owner The Earl of Haddington

Open May to Sept, Sun, Wed and Bank Hol Mon (also Mon and Thur July to Aug) 11.30– 5.30; phone/see website for other openings

Area 50 acres/20 hectares

Mount Stuart

AN 18TH-CENTURY WOODED LANDSCAPE GARDEN WITH NOTABLE TREES AND A FINE PINETUM

The Stuarts (now Crichton-Stuarts and Marquesses of Bute) have lived on Bute since 1385. The early 18th-century house was largely destroyed by fire in 1877 and a new house, a Gothic palace of marvellous splendour, was designed by Robert Rowand Anderson. (All visitors should see it, with its sumptuous and dramatic interior of marble vaults, painted ceilings, stained glass and magnificent contents.)

Gardens were made here in the early 18th century under the 2nd Earl of Bute. At this time the family lived in Rothesay but planting had already begun in the garden before 1722. By 1759, in the time of the 3rd Earl, a plan showed a parterre and bowling green close to the house, and avenues and rides through woods dividing the landscape – a pattern which survives to this day. The 3rd Earl, a confidant of George III and of his mother, the Princess Augusta, helped lay out their garden at Kew and was thus one of the founders of the Royal Botanic Gardens (*see page 142*). At Mount Stuart the Earl kept a collection of dahlias long before their hybridisation made them into a fashionable garden plant.

The best way to visit the gardens is to start at the 19th-century pinetum just

Mount Stuart from the great lawn

beyond the handsome kitchen garden (designed by Rosemary Verey and redesigned by James Alexander-Sinclair) at the bottom of the drive. Here is a splendid collection of conifers, chiefly new introductions from the north-west coast of America – Wellingtonias (*Sequoiadendron giganteum*), Douglas firs (*Pseudotsuga menziesii*), western hemlocks (*Tsuga heterophylla*) – all grown to great size. A new arboretum forms part of the Royal Botanic Garden Edinburgh's International Conifer Conservation Project.

An amazing avenue of 18th-century lime trees and rides through woodland now become apparent – six rides converge on a triumphant stone column dedicated to Princess Augusta. From here the pink stone of the astonishing house is seen, gleaming through the trees across an enormous lawn.

PRETTY ROCK GARDEN

Behind the house is a pretty rock garden designed by Thomas Mawson in the 1890s; south-west of the house, the Wee Garden, made in 1823, has tender exotics from the southern hemisphere. These are attractive but they are tinkly chamber music in relation to the symphonic resonance of the views of the dream-like pink palace in its formidable landscape of lawn and trees.

INFORMATION

Location nr Rothesay PA20 9LR, Isle of Bute; 5m S of Rothesay by A844
Tel 01700 503877
Email contactus@ mountstuart.com
Website www.mountstuart. com
Scottish Inventory Listed
Owner The Mount Stuart Trust
Open May to Sept, daily 10–6
Area 300 acres/121 hectares

The Pineapple

THE LOVELIEST GARDEN PAVILION EVER MADE, IN AN 18TH-CENTURY WALLED ORCHARD OF CRAB APPLE TREES

The Dunmore Pineapple must surely be one of the most beautiful of all garden buildings. It was built in 1761 as a banqueting house for the 4th Earl of Dunmore, who later became Governor of New York. Dunmore Castle fell into disuse, the estate was subsequently dismembered and the Pineapple survived only by the skin of its teeth. It was bought by the Earl and Countess of Perth in 1974 and presented to the National Trust for Scotland.

MAGNIFICENT CARVING

The Pineapple is built into the south-facing wall of a 6-acre/2.4-hectare walled kitchen garden – ornamental buildings are often integrated into walls in Scottish gardens in this way. On the garden side a pedimented portico with a Palladian entrance rises to exactly the height of the garden wall. Above it, forming the base of The Pineapple, is a circle of seven windows with ogee-shaped frames and finely carved surrounds which burst into flames at each apex. Between each window a pilaster rises into the lower pineapple leaves. The Pineapple itself is magnificently carved in stone and each of the extravagantly curving leaves is drained internally to avoid damage by frost. It was in the past flanked by ranges of glasshouses against the wall.

No-one knows whether there is any particular significance in pineapples for Dunmore. They were certainly grown in Scottish gardens by the mid 18th century – the earliest date for their cultivation is 1732 when they were grown by James Justice of Midlothian. They may have been grown here at Dunmore – certainly the former glasshouses on either side of The Pineapple were heated, with the flues emerging through ornamental urns

The Dunmore Pineapple

which can still be seen running along the crest of the wall.

The National Trust has planted a formal orchard in the mown grass that now fills the kitchen garden, but in all truth the magnificent Pineapple itself is of such consuming interest and beauty that almost any planting would fade into irrelevance. The interior of The Pineapple, by contrast, is relatively restrained and has been finely restored. You may not visit it; however, you may rent The Pineapple as a holiday house through the Landmark Trust.

INFORMATION

Location Dunmore, nr Stirling, Stirlingshire; on the Dunmore estate (enter by East Lodge) 6m SE of Stirling by A905
Tel 0844 4932132
Website www.nts.org.uk
Scottish Inventory Listed
Owner The National Trust for Scotland
Open daily 9.30–sunset
Area 6 acres/2.4 hectares

Pitmedden

DELIGHTFUL 20TH-CENTURY FLOWER PARTERRES FOR A SUPERB 17TH-CENTURY WALLED GARDEN

The Great Garden is a walled enclosure with fine architectural detail. It is one of the very rare dated gardens in Scotland – the entrance bears the date 2 May 1675 and the cipher of its maker, Sir Alexander Seton, together with that of his wife, Dame Margaret Lauder. The old house at Pitmedden was destroyed by fire in 1818, together with all its contents; no documentary evidence survived to indicate the design of the original garden here.

The Great Garden at Pitmedden

In 1951 the Pitmedden estate was given to the National Trust for Scotland by Major James Keith. The National Trust recreated a formal garden in keeping with the spirit of the period and the character of the Great Garden. They laid out box-edged parterres inspired by a mid 17th-century design for the parterres at Holyroodhouse in Edinburgh. The compartments of the parterres are planted with thousands of bedding plants, in blocks of a single colour, and in one parterre the Seton arms are traced in plants.

The Great Garden is sunken, and on three sides you may look down on it from a walk along the retaining walls. The seductive mixture of patterned formality, brilliant colours and lively ornament, all superlatively maintained, is a thrilling sight. A walk of yew pyramids runs across the garden from an elegant double staircase to a gate in the opposite wall. The western wall of the garden, by which you enter, is planted with a series of yew buttresses, clipped into swooping ogee curves and topped with a dashing topknot. At each end of the wall is an elegant pavilion whose roof is also shaped in ogee curves

– a common feature of Scottish 17th-century architecture. Excellent herbaceous borders run along the south- and west-facing walls, and on the walls behind are apples superbly trained in espaliers, goblets and fans, looking exactly like illustrations from an old manual of fruit growing.

OLD SCOTTISH APPLES

Leading up to the Great Garden, new gardens have been added. Yew topiaries march towards the entrance, with a circular pool and two formal enclosures hedged in beech or pleached lime screens and box parterres at the centre. Nearby a tunnel of apples is a showcase for old Scottish varieties – with marvellously appetising names – 'Galloway Pippin', 'Lass O'Gowrie' and 'Howgate Wonder'.

INFORMATION

Location nr Pitmedden, Ellon, Aberdeenshire AB4 0PD; 14m N of Aberdeen by A920 and B999
Tel 0844 4932177
Website www.ngs.org.uk
Scottish Inventory Listed
Owner The National Trust for Scotland
Open May to Sept, daily 10–5.30
Area 4¾ acres/2 hectares

Royal Botanic Garden Edinburgh

ONE OF THE BEST, MOST ATTRACTIVE, BOTANIC GARDENS IN THE WORLD – FABULOUS PLANTS ON A BEAUTIFUL, HILLY SITE

Citizens of Edinburgh love the Royal Botanic Garden, referring to it affectionately as "The Botanics". Its history goes back to 1670 when it was founded as a garden of medicinal plants attached to the university. In 1820 it moved from Leith Walk to its present site – high and airy, and commanding splendid views northwards across the Firth of Forth to the hills of Fife. The curator was William McNab who devised an ingenious cart to transport mature trees across Edinburgh to the new site – creating an instant garden. McNab's son James became regius keeper of the garden and in 1870 created the rock garden. He also took great pains in the landscaping of the whole garden, establishing a superb layout on this undulating site.

Later in the 19th century, one of the greatest plant collectors, George Forrest, came to work here. He made six expeditions to China, bringing back immense numbers of new plants – over 300 species of rhododendrons, over 150 species of primula, and dozens of buddleias, irises, honeysuckles and lilies. This was the start of the garden's special interest in Chinese plants. In 1993 the Pringle Chinese Garden was made – a stream and pool overlooked by a scarlet pavilion and a rising bank of Chinese plants disposed in naturalistic profusion.

FABULOUS COLLECTIONS

The grassy slopes of the botanic garden are clothed in trees – so many species and such fine specimens. Here are excellent examples of every genus of hardy tree; many non-hardy species are found in one or another of the 11 glasshouses. The collection of rhododendrons includes most of the species hardy in a temperate climate. An immense deep herbaceous border, 500ft/150m long, runs below huge beech hedges, and behind it is an admirable demonstration garden. James McNab's rock garden presents a dazzling sight, especially in spring, with erythroniums, fritillaries, trilliums and the exquisite nomocharis lilies grown to perfection; even trickier alpines are cosseted in the alpine house and its courtyard of troughs and raised beds.

As a place in which to study plants, learn about gardening, push a pram, or merely wander in a magical landscape, the Royal Botanic Garden Edinburgh is outstanding. Its only rival in Britain is Kew – and there is no admission charge to the cherished "Botanics".

The rock garden at the Royal Botanic Garden

INFORMATION

Location Inverleith Row, Edinburgh EH3 5LR; 1m N of the city centre
Tel 0131 552 7171
Email info@rbge.org.uk
Website www.rbge.org.uk
Scottish Inventory Listed
Owner Trustees of the Royal Botanic Garden Edinburgh
Open Mar and Oct, daily 10–6; Apr to Sept, daily 10–7; Nov to Feb, daily 10–4 (closed 25 Dec and 1 Jan);
Area 67 acres/27 hectares

Scone Palace

BEAUTIFUL PARKLAND AND A REMARKABLE 19TH-CENTURY PINETUM FOR A HISTORIC ESTATE

For many non-Scots the first thing to learn about Scone is how to pronounce the place – scoon, unlike the delicious baked scone (scon) which is invariably best eaten in Scotland. The great house at Scone dates back to the early 17th century but now has a comprehensively Gothicised appearance – the work of William Atkinson in the early 19th century.

The park was landscaped by Thomas White between 1781 and 1786 with unhappy results. In 1804 J.C. Loudon was asked to come and improve on the work, in particular to break up White's many tight clumps of trees into a more naturalistic arrangement. Loudon described Scone in his *Encyclopaedia of Gardening* (1822): "one of the finest situations in Scotland, with a lawn in front of great extent, washed by the Tay, and backed by rising grounds covered with wood".

A REMARKABLE PINETUM

In the middle of the 19th century, at the height of the craze for such things, the 4th Earl of Mansfield started to plant a pinetum. The interest in conifers had been stimulated by the introduction of new species from the American Pacific coast, and many of these had been discovered by a local man, David Douglas, who was born at Old Scone and became a gardener's boy at Scone Palace. A majestic Douglas fir (*Pseudotsuga menziesii*), propagated from the first seeds brought back by Douglas in 1826, is a wonderful sight.

The pinetum includes over 50 species of conifer, some of which go back to the 1848 plantings, and has mature specimens of often remarkable trees of great character: the Chinese fir (*Cunninghamia lanceolata*) with glowing cinnamon-coloured bark and gleaming

The pinetum at Scone

fronds of foliage like demented bottle-brushes; a lovely old western hemlock (*Tsuga heterophylla*) with a deeply gnarled trunk and wide spreading branches, introduced to Scotland in 1852, planted at Scone in 1866 and now one of the largest specimens in Britain; Brewer's spruce (*Picea breweriana*) with wonderfully ornamental and gracefully cascading branches sweeping to the ground.

There are sketchy ornamental flower plantings at Scone but it is the old pinetum that is the object of exceptional horticultural interest. The site is as beautiful as Loudon had described it and the parkland on the slopes below the castle is exceptional.

INFORMATION

Location Scone, Perth PH2 6BD, Perthshire; 2m NE of Perth on A93
Tel 01738 552300
Email visits@scone-palace.co.uk
Website www.scone-palace.co.uk
Scottish Inventory Listed
Owner The Earl of Mansfield
Open Apr to Oct, daily 9.30–6
Area 100 acres/40 hectares

Stirling Castle

RARE AND DELIGHTFUL 17TH-CENTURY KING'S KNOT GARDEN FOR A MAGNIFICENT CASTLE ON A DRAMATIC SITE

Stirling Castle is built on top of a great rock whose western face forms a vertiginous cliff. It was started at the beginning of the 12th century when Alexander I built a chapel here, and by 1174 there was enough of a castle for it to be surrendered to Henry II of England under the Treaty of Falaise. The modern appearance of the castle dates from the 15th century during the reign of James IV.

By the 15th century there were gardens here on the flat ground below the cliff on the western side of the castle rock. This is an area that had long been known as the King's Park and a new garden was put in place here for the visit of Charles I in 1633. The English gardener William Watts was working at Stirling in 1625 and work was done on the King's Garden and orchard between 1628 and 1629. A painting of the castle by Johannes Vorsterman, made around the late 1670s, shows a great rectangular walled enclosure with a central circle or oval from which paths radiate out directly to each side, and the whole lavishly embellished with tall statues. This, or something like it, is described in the Ordnance Survey *Gazetteer* of 1882: "Near the extreme SW side of the gardens is an octagonal earthen mound with terraces and a depressed centre known as the King's Knot, and probably the place where the old game called The Round Table was played."

THE KING'S KNOT TODAY

If the modern visitor stands on the raised walk that edges the Bowling Green below the palace at Stirling Castle, an astonishing view opens out. At the foot of the cliff the King's Knot is plainly to be seen, covered in close-mown turf and traced by changes in level. At its centre is an octagonal mound on two levels within a rectangle. This does not precisely correspond with the Vorstermann painting and when exactly it was made is not known – but it is still a wonderful sight. Almost as wonderful is the view to the south, across the Dumbarton road, to the ancient King's Park. It is remarkably unspoilt although, where deer once grazed, golfers now swing their clubs.

INFORMATION

Location Castle Wynd, Stirling FK8 1EJ, Stirlingshire; in the centre of Stirling
Tel 01786 450000 **Fax** 01786 464678
Scottish Inventory Listed
Owner Historic Scotland
Open Apr to Sept, daily 9.30–6; Oct to Mar, daily 9.30–5
Area 20 acres/8 hectares

The King's Knot at Stirling

Threave Garden

A WALLED KITCHEN AND ORNAMENTAL GARDEN WITH EXCELLENT PLANTS IN A LOVELY WOODED LANDSCAPE

Threave House was built in Scottish baronial style for William Gordon in 1872. The estate was given by Major Alan Gordon to the National Trust for Scotland in 1957, and since 1960 it has been the base of a school of gardening. It is the gardening students who have been largely responsible for creating and maintaining the garden.

WINDING PATHS

The undulating site is well wooded with beeches, conifers and oaks, many of which go back to plantings made shortly after the house was built. There is no strong pattern of design to the garden; areas are linked by winding paths, with always something interesting or attractive to see. From the entrance a path leads among beds of mostly shrub roses, which include several varieties of the lovely wild Scottish Burnet rose (*Rosa pimpinellifolia*). Below, the old kitchen garden is enclosed in stone walls and divided into four by a central broad

The kitchen garden at Threave

gravel walk flanked by deep herbaceous borders, and a cross-walk of beds of 'New Dawn' roses trained on pillars and underplanted with *Salvia* x *superba*. Each quarter of the garden is under cultivation with fruit or vegetables and a large glasshouse contains tender ornamentals, splendidly displayed.

Close to the walled garden the path leads to a pool and cascade whose banks are planted with *Gunnera manicata*, hostas, *Iris sibirica*, meconopsis, primulas and rodgersias. The house rises among trees on a slope which in spring is covered in thousands of narcissi. Bold herbaceous borders run along the path at the foot of the slope and a laburnum arbour leads to a hidden garden with walks among shrubs and trees which include several varieties of maple. On lawns nearby are raised rockeries and a large collection of plants of an alpine kind. A shelter here is thatched in heather (a once traditional material) which has now grown a deep eiderdown of moss. From here there are grand views of the lovely rolling wooded landscape. On the slopes above the house is a youthful arboretum and a collection of heathers laid out in great swathes in the grass.

Threave is a particularly attractive garden with a fine collection of plants excellently grown in a beautiful setting, a treat for all gardeners.

INFORMATION

Location Stewartry, Castle Douglas DG7 1RX, Kircudbrightshire; 1m SW of Castle Douglas by A75
Tel 0844 4932245
Email Threave@nts.org.uk
Website www.nts.org.uk
Scottish Inventory Listed
Owner The National Trust for Scotland
Open daily 9.30–5
Area 65 acres/26 hectares

Torosay Castle

IDYLLIC GARDEN ON THE ISLAND OF MULL WITH TERRACES, TENDER PLANTS, FINE STATUARY AND ROMANTIC SEA VIEWS

The castle is a Scottish baronial mansion built on a superb site in the 1850s. In the very early years of the 20th century a new terraced garden was built below the south façade of the house, possibly designed by Robert Lorimer. The uppermost terrace has a circular pond at its centre and narrow borders about its perimeter, with a balustrade and a battlemented gazebo at each end. The enticing terrace ingeniously leads the visitor into the garden which lies beyond and below. But, having walked out onto the terrace, you see to one side something far more beautiful than any garden. Beyond the romantic castle on Duart Point and across the Lynn of Lorne are breathtaking views over the water to the mountains of Ben Nevis and Glen Coe on the mainland to the east. Suddenly revealed to one side in this way, the combination of surprise and borrowed landscape is unforgettable.

The lion terrace at Torosay

THE STATUE WALK

From the terrace, steps lead into the garden proper with, to one side, the statue walk – a procession of statues emerging from thickets of fuchsia. These, the work of Antonio Bonazzo (1698–1765), from a ruined villa at Padua, depict estate workers – the gamekeeper, gardener and so forth. The statue walk leads, at an angle, to the lion terrace, with two recumbent marble lions ("Growler" and "Smiler") gazing down at a sunken lawn. Below the lion terrace is the original 18th-century walled kitchen garden, now turned over to ornamental purposes. Here are yew hedges and a grand colonnade festooned with clematis, *Vitis coignetiae* and wisteria, and ending in a domed rotunda.

The garden is rich in good plants, among which are some remarkable ancient western red cedars (*Thuja plicata*). The climate is mild here and a tender *Cornus capitata* by the statue walk has grown to great size and beauty. A woodland garden is bright with Himalayan poppies and primulas and there is a fine specimen of *Stewartia pseudocamellia*. A slightly perfunctory oriental garden on the eastern margin of the garden is an example of exactly what not to do; it serves no purpose here and could scarcely be less appropriate for its beautiful setting, with views eastwards across the sea.

INFORMATION

Location Craignure, Isle of Mull PA65 6AY, Argyll; 1m SE of Craignure by A849
Tel 01680 812421
Email torosay@aol.com
Website www.torosay.com
Scottish Inventory Listed
Owner Chris James
Open daily 9–7 (closes dusk in winter)
Area 11 acres/4.4 hectares

IRELAND

GARDENS TO VISIT

Image *Annes Grove*

Altamont Garden

DISTINGUISHED PLANTING IN AN ATMOSPHERIC SETTING,
WITH FORMAL GARDENS, LAKE AND WOODLAND WALKS

Altamont is an ancient place and the present house, largely dating from the mid 18th century, has foundations that go back at least to the 16th century. The garden here was started by Feilding Lecky Watson who rented the house in 1923 and subsequently, finding it so much to his taste (in particular the fine acid soil), bought the estate. Watson started to build up a collection of plants, especially of rhododendrons, with the help of Sir Frederick Moore, the director of the National Botanic Garden at Glasnevin. Watson died in 1943 and shortly after World War II his daughter Corona (Corona North after her marriage in 1966) took charge of the garden, rescued it from wartime neglect and started to add much new planting of her own. After her death in 1999 the garden passed to Dúchas, The Heritage Service.

Such formality as the garden possesses starts immediately behind the house where three more or less parallel walks lead down to a lake. The central Broad Walk is overarched from time to time by 19th-century Irish yews trained to meet in the middle. On either side borders are rich in shrub roses. In Mrs North's day the lawns that flank the walk, decorated with many good trees, were also often ornamented with clucking chickens, giving the impression of a dashingly aristocratic farmyard.

THE LAKE

The lake is the heart of the garden and was dug in the 1850s, after the Famine, to provide labour for the local unemployed. The banks are lavishly planted with trees and shrubs, especially rhododendrons added by Mrs North's father. Walks about the edge of the lake give delicious views back towards the house and lead into woodland on land which slopes down to the river Slaney. Here are an arboretum, a bog garden and a most remarkable Ice Age glen whose air of ancient wilderness is occasionally contradicted by some distinguished rhododendron. A flight of granite steps (100 of them) leads back from the river towards the house where paths skirt a field with exquisite views of the rural landscape and the Wicklow Hills. The charm of Altamont lies in the subtle focus of attention on the natural beauties of the land, enlivened by distinguished planting.

The lake at Altamont

INFORMATION

Location Tullow, County Carlow, Republic of Ireland; 9km S of Tullow on the Bunclody road, signed off N80 and N81
Tel (00353) (0) 59 915444
Email altamontgarden@eircom.net
Website www.altamontgarden.com
Owner Dúchas, The Heritage Service
Open daily 9–7.30
Area 40 acres/16 hectares

Annes Grove

ON THE BANKS OF A RIVER, ONE OF THE BEST WILD GARDENS IN IRELAND, AND A PRETTY WALLED FLOWER GARDEN

Annes Grove preserves a deliciously secretive and private air, untouched by the heritage industry. The site is delightful, with the river Awbeg forming one of the chief ornaments of the landscape. The fame of the garden was due to Richard Grove Annesley who started to garden here in 1907. Inheriting an essentially Victorian layout rich in conifers and with an ornamental flower garden, Annesley discovered the land running along the Awbeg valley was of fine acid soil, perfect for the kind of woodland gardening in which he was interested.

The walled garden at Annes Grove

RIVER PATHS

A long walk winds through woods north of the house with the river valley falling away along its eastern edge. The path is lined with fine plants – dogwoods, embothriums, enkianthus, myrtle (*Luma apiculata*), rhododendrons, magnolias and much else. An occasional slithery path or rustic moss-bearded flight of stone steps leads down past flowering shrubs to the river, its dark and glassy waters flowing under alder and ash. Paths along the river are mown through long grass, bracken, cow parsley and the occasional glowing forest of yellow flag iris. A rocky outcrop juts out from the valley side, covered in valerian and with a grove of white foxgloves. Above it the largely coniferous trees which clothe the slope are illuminated in spring and early summer with bursts of colour from rhododendrons. Further downstream the planting is denser and more exotic: majestic clumps of *Gunnera manicata* and lysichiton, with Himalayan primulas spread out below *Cercidiphyllum japonicum*, cabbage palms (*Cordyline*

australis) and *Drimys winteri*. The occasional rustic bridge spans the water.

Nearer the house a walled garden enclosed in stone walls and yew hedges, probably an orchard in the 18th century, today preserves a decorative 19th-century character. Here a flagstoned path forming a central axis is flanked by herbaceous borders backed with yew hedges, with a pergola of honeysuckles and roses running off at an angle. A rose garden has a pattern of symmetrical beds cut into a lawn and a series of yew-edged beds contain mounds of multi-coloured lupins. More herbaceous borders run under the walls with the occasional distinguished shrub such as *Hoheria glabrata*. In the north part of the garden are beautiful magnolias with hostas, lilies, pulmonaria and rodgersias in their shade.

INFORMATION

Location Castletownroche, County Cork, Republic of Ireland; 1.6km N of Castletownroche, signed from the town centre
Tel (00353) (0)22 26145
Email annesgrove@eircom.net
Website www.annesgrovegardens.com
Owner Patrick Annesley
Open mid Mar to Sept, daily 10–5 (Sun 1–6) and by appointment
Area 40 acres/16 hectares

Ballinlough Castle

A ROMANTIC HOUSE IN A SPLENDID PARKLAND SETTING ADORNED WITH RESTORED WALLED GARDENS

Ballinlough Castle was built in the 17th century on the site of a medieval tower house and was given its cheerfully castellated air in the late 18th century. In the mid 19th century a lake divided by an isthmus and a bridge was made below the house, giving the impression of an 18th-century landscape park. The water comes from a canal crossed by a rockwork bridge. Walks about the canal and lake are punctuated by good trees, especially several fine Turkey oaks (*Quercus cerris*), and by views up the hill towards the most castle-like façade of the house.

The rose garden at Ballinlough

LARGE WALLED GARDEN

From 1994 the garden was restored by Sir John and Lady Nugent. The very large walled former kitchen garden has been thoroughly refashioned, much of it turned to decorative purposes. A pair of herbaceous borders backed by beech hedges forms the chief axis. Behind the borders lawns are planted with flowering cherries, a magnolia walk and other ornamental shrubs. A former sunken garden has been made into a formal pool shaded by cherries and ornamented with urns of the pink-flowered strawberry (*Fragaria* 'Panda'). A rose garden is divided into four by paths meeting at a central arbour swathed with honeysuckle (*Lonicera etrusca* 'Michael Rosse'), *Clematis viticella* 'Purpurea Plena Elegans' and *Rosa filipes* 'Kiftsgate'. The paths are lined with beds of shrub roses and lavender. Leading off it is a secret garden with mixed borders against three sides and a deep paved area running against a south-facing wall. There are clematises, *Cytisus battandieri*, *Euphorbia mellifera* and

roses against the wall, and *Alchemilla mollis*, *Potentilla atropurpurea*, strawberries and thymes in the cracks between the paving stones. A Gothic bench is half concealed by a billowing bush of yellow tree lupin. A very large formal orchard is planted with espaliered fruit against the walls and free-standing damsons, medlars, mulberries, pears and plums.

Between house and walled garden is a decorative old stable yard. Those interested in Irish social history will note the large arched entrance to a tunnel which connects the yard to the kitchen quarters of the house – the only entrance apart from the front door. This arrangement, common in old Irish country houses, permitted servants to go about their business invisible to the fastidious eyes of the gentry.

INFORMATION

Location Clonmellon, County Westmeath, Republic of Ireland; 25km W of Navan by N51 and R154, or by Kells and N52

Tel (00353) (0)46 9433234/9433268

Email castle@ballinloughcastle.ie

Website www.ballinloughcastle.ie

Owner Nick and Alice Nugent

Open May to Sept, Sat and Sun by appointment only

Area 40 acres/16 hectares

Ballymaloe Cookery School Gardens

FORMAL HERB, FRUIT AND KITCHEN GARDENS EMBELLISHED WITH HERBACEOUS BORDERS AND AN EXQUISITE SHELLHOUSE

Tim and Darina Allen started the cookery school alongside their own house at Shanagarry in a peacefully rural setting. They restored the 19th-century garden and made new additions of their own. A wide range of fruit, vegetables and herbs is cultivated to meet the needs of the cookery school and this seems perfectly to suit the rhythm of life at Ballymaloe.

Close to the school buildings is a maze-like formal fruit garden with apples, apricots, grapes, peaches, pears and pomegranates. A formal vegetable garden is laid out like a parterre, with herring-bone brick paths and hedges of box with lapping waves of nasturtiums, edgings of chives or marigolds and lollipops of clipped bay.

At a distance two 19th-century enclosures are handsomely hedged in beech. Lydia's Garden has lawns, herbaceous borders and a summerhouse with a delightful mosaic floor of broken china artfully disposed and dated 1912. This is linked to a herb garden enclosed in the same superb beech hedges – a herb parterre on the grand scale, with a symmetrical pattern of interlocking intricately shaped beds edged in box, each bed containing a generous block of a single kind of herb with the occasional angelica, artichoke or giant fennel forming an emphatic plume at its centre. The whole is overlooked by a wooden viewing platform arrived at by scrambling up a precipitous flight of wooden steps.

EXQUISITE SHELLWORK

To the south of this, a spanking new double herbaceous border, separated by a broad grass path and backed with yew hedges, leads to a dashing summerhouse with a tall pointed roof. The planting is a curious mixture of the coarsely cottagey, with plants such as yellow loosestrife and the fashionable, even trendy, oriental poppy, *Papaver orientale* 'Patty's Plum'. The summerhouse, however, is a rare masterpiece. It has an anonymous air until you enter and its stunning interior bursts upon you – a gleaming extravagance of shellwork exquisitely arranged in endlessly inventive patterns by the grotto artist Blot Kerr-Wilson. Each wall, and the surrounds of the door and Gothic windows, is encrusted with virtuoso arrangements; each bay is separated by a pilaster formed of alternate vertical stripes of mussels and limpets; the high vaulted ceiling is patterned with stripes made of cockles and mussels.

The herb garden at Ballymaloe

INFORMATION

Location Shanagarry, Midleton, County Cork, Republic of Ireland; 30km E of Cork by N25 and R632
Tel (00353) (0)21 464 6785
Website www.cookingisfun.ie
Owner Tim and Darina Allen
Open May to Sept, daily 11–6
Area 10 acres/4 hectares

Bantry House

AN 18TH-CENTURY HOUSE IN A WONDERFUL POSITION OVERLOOKING BANTRY BAY WITH FINE FORMAL GARDENS

Bantry House has a remarkably beautiful position on rising ground above Bantry Bay, looking north-west over Whiddy Island to the Caha Mountains. The early 18th-century house was bought in 1750 by Richard White (later 1st Earl of Bantry) whose family still lives here. The traveller and garden connoisseur Prince Pückler-Muskau came here in 1828 and was especially struck by the tender plants that flourished and by walls "garlanded by ivy and roses antiquely picturesque". Lord Bantry's heir, another Richard, did the Grand Tour, sending all sorts of

treasures back to Bantry House between 1820 and 1840. He also developed a taste for Italian gardens and in the 1840s, under their inspiration, created the essential lines of the garden as we see it today. In accordance with the principles he had imbibed on the Continent, he determined that the garden and house should live in harmony together, and the garden he made is one of the most outstanding and attractive formal gardens of its period in Britain or Ireland.

In the early 19th century the new Cork road had been built along the coast below the house. The 2nd Earl obscured it by terracing the land above

The terraces at Bantry House

it and forming a wide viewing platform to take advantage of the grand view north over the bay. On the other, south, side of the house he laid out an "Italian parterre" with a central pool. He also built on a new room, the library, whose chief window is exactly aligned on the centre of the parterre and, beyond, on vertiginous flights of stone steps linking terraces on the steep slope above.

GARDEN RESTORATION

Restoration of the garden began in 1997, and a further programme of restoration is under way. The terraces overlooking the bay have, once again, their original 19th-century arrangement of fourteen large circular beds, hedged in box and planted alternately with blocks of red hot poker (*Kniphofia* 'Nancy's Red', an old Irish variety) and of *Perovskia atriplicifolia*. This whole area

is enclosed in balustrading, now restored, and ornamented with statues and urns. The Italian parterre has been replanted with hedges of common and golden yew, its compartments filled with Brompton stocks and irises. The central pool is enclosed in a circular arbour entwined with wisteria, and the edges of the pool are encrusted with rockwork; at its centre a rockwork mount is decorated with shells and crowned with a pair of fish and a water spout. A balustraded terrace overlooks the parterre on three sides and the flights of steps up the hill are once again ornamented with beautiful basketwork terracotta pots, copied by an Italian pottery from a surviving 19th-century original.

More work needs to be done at Bantry – including the restoration of a magnificent walled garden at a distance from the house, where a formal orchard has been reinstated. But enough has been done to show how the garden takes such exceptional advantage of its site. The walk up to the top of the steps rewards the climber with one of the loveliest views in Ireland. An intriguing further attraction at Bantry House is the Armada Museum. This tells the story of a historical event with which many will be unfamiliar. In 1796 a French naval fleet of 50 ships carrying 15,000 soldiers sailed from Brest towards Cork in an attempt to end British rule in Ireland and restore independence. They were thwarted by violent storms, in which several ships were lost, including one, the Surveillante, in Bantry Bay, and the rest turned tail.

INFORMATION

Location Bantry, County Cork, Republic of Ireland; on the western outskirts of Bantry on the N71
Tel (00353) (0)27 50047
Email info@bantryhouse.com
Website www.bantryhouse.com
Owner Mr and Mrs Egerton Shelswell-White
Open mid Mar to Oct, daily 10–6
Area 45 acres/18 hectares

Birr Castle Demesne

A SUPERB COLLECTION OF TREES AND SHRUBS, PICTURESQUE RIVERSIDE WALKS AND A MAGNIFICENT WALLED GARDEN

The castle at Birr was originally built in the 17th century by the Parsons family (who became the Earls of Rosse), but was heavily Gothicised in the 19th century. The demesne has a marvellous site, with the river Camcor – spanned by an elegant iron suspension bridge – running below the castle and fine trees everywhere. The 5th Earl subscribed to the plant-hunting expeditions of E.H. Wilson between 1907 and 1911, and a superb collection of magnolias dates from this time. He also terraced the precipitous slope running down to the river close to the castle, making lawns set with ornamental trees and shrubs and picturesque walks along both banks.

A GREAT COLLECTION

The 6th Earl, Michael, married Anne Messel who was brought up at Nymans in Sussex, and together they developed the garden. Today Birr has over 1,000 species of woody plants, making it one of the finest collections in Ireland.

Rose arbour at Birr Castle

Michael and Anne Rosse also laid out a beautiful formal garden. This was well restored in 2000 by their son Brendan, the 7th Earl, and has been renamed The Millennium Gardens. Enclosed by stone walls and hedges of yew, with "cloisters" of pleached hornbeam, it has fine statues and urns. Here is a fine collection of old shrub roses, a lively border planted in blue, white and yellow, box parterres and a path edged with intertwined patterns of box and pyramids of yew.

A remarkable curiosity is the 3rd Earl's great telescope, "Leviathan", built in the 1840s; at that time the largest in the world, it is housed in a Gothic building to match the castle. The 3rd Earl was the first man to observe, in 1845, the spiral form of the galaxies. His descendant, the present Earl, commemorated the 150th anniversary of this discovery by laying out a spiral walk of limes (*Tilia cordata*).

Further west, across a fine meadow, is a superlative old English oak planted in the 16th century. Beyond it is a shapely lake, the arboretum and a fernery. It is the great collection of trees and shrubs, and the lie of the land (especially by the banks of the river and lake), that are the most memorable aspects of the garden at Birr. It is also touched by a far from disagreeable idiosyncrasy. Birr is a splendid historic estate full of interest.

INFORMATION

Location Birr, County Offaly, Republic of Ireland; on the edge of the town of Birr, 40km S of Athlone by N52
Tel (00353) (0)509 20336
Email mail@birrcastle.com
Website www.birrcastle.com
Owner The Earl of Rosse
Open mid Mar to Oct, daily 9–6; Nov to Feb, daily 10–4
Area 120 acres/49 hectares

Castle Ward

A GRAND HOUSE IN A WOODED DEMESNE ON THE BANKS OF STRANGFORD LOUGH, WITH FORMAL TERRACED GARDENS

The position of Castle Ward on undulating ground at the southern tip of Strangford Lough looking down a wooded valley towards the water is memorably beautiful. Mrs Delany saw it when it was recently built and thought that "it hath every advantage from Nature that can be desired". The house, built in around 1763, is delightfully two-faced – coolly classical on the entrance side and boisterously Gothic where it looks towards the lough. The stylistic clash is continued in the interior, reflecting a difference in taste between its builder, Bernard Ward, later 1st Earl of Bangor, and his wife, Lady Anne, who had what Mrs Delany described as "whimsical" taste which inclined towards Strawberry Hill Gothic. The designer was probably an English architect and the house is faced in Bath stone brought from Bristol in Mr Ward's own ship.

Castle Ward from the west

VICTORIAN CHARACTER

By the time Mrs Delany saw Castle Ward there had already been much planting in the demesne. A watercolour by her shows the early 18th-century Palladian garden temple, possibly designed by Robert Morris, on the wooded slopes above Temple Water, a formal canal (today rather informal), dug in 1724. It is close to the remains of Audley's Castle, a 15th-century towerhouse built to guard the entrance to the lough. Strikingly visible from the lough side of Castle Ward, rising above the trees, the tower is as neatly placed as a purpose-built picturesque ruin.

Apart from surviving earlier trees the chief character of the garden is Victorian. Close to the house is a walled terraced garden with much exotic planting – *Acca sellowiana*, *Beschorneria yuccoides*, large old plants of cabbage palm (*Cordyline australis*) and substantial hummocks of *Melianthus major*. A sunken lawn has a circular lily pool with a splendid figure of Neptune at the centre, brandishing a gold-tipped trident. Behind a screen of Irish yews a rock garden with dwarf conifers runs along one side of a mid 19th-century pinetum with immense Wellingtonias, a piquant contrast. But the best things at Castle Ward are the grand walks in the huge demesne. It is the larger landscape, with delicious views of trees and lough enlivened by the occasional building – not least the irresistible house itself – that constitute the greatest pleasure of this delightful and rare place.

INFORMATION

Location Strangford, Downpatrick BT30 7LS, County Down, Northern Ireland; 7m NE of Downpatrick on A25

Tel (028) 4488 1204

Email castleward@nationaltrust.org.uk

Owner The National Trust

Open Apr to Sept, daily 10–8; Oct to Mar, daily 10–4

Area 750 acres/303 hectares

Castlewellan National Arboretum

AN EXCEPTIONAL COLLECTION OF TREES AND SHRUBS AND AN 18TH-CENTURY WALLED ORNAMENTAL GARDEN

The castle was built in the 1850s, a granite castellated house for the 4th Earl Annesley, to the designs of William Burn. Beneath its south façade it preserves a terrace walk of distinctly Victorian kind, with a parade of giant mounds of Portugal laurel and spreading shapes of golden yew.

The fountain borders at Castlewellan

The arboretum was started in the 1870s by the 5th Earl Annesley, incorporating a fine walled garden of 12 acres/5 hectares, now called the Annesley Garden, which had been made in the mid 18th century. This, with a further 96 acres/39 hectares of woodland outside the walls, in particular the beautiful land spreading along the north bank of Castlewellan Lake, constitutes the National Arboretum. The whole is set in the context of the Castewellan Forest Park.

NOTABLE SPECIES

The walled Annesley Garden, on a gently south-facing slope, is essentially a garden of trees and shrubs but at its heart is a pair of herbaceous borders backed by yew hedges and interrupted by a splendid fountain. Throughout the garden are notable species which are often tender and frequently rare. Here are fine collections of pines, Japanese maples, many different species and cultivars of cypress (including such tender plants as the beautiful *Cupressus cashmeriana*), spruces and many plants from the southern hemisphere (especially New Zealand).

Just outside the Annesley Garden beds of dwarf conifers, not today as fashionable as once they were, now have the character of a period piece. Here too is a spring garden with

flowering cherries and crab apples and attractive planting about a group of pools. In the woods nearby a large collection of rhododendrons is grown among evergreen and deciduous trees. Autumn Wood, on the bank of the lake immediately west of the castle, has a collection of trees and shrubs with especially fine autumn colour – birches, *Cercidiphyllum japonicum*, dogwoods, maples, the American red oak (*Quercus rubra*), thorns and much else.

The fame of Castlewellan lies in its outstanding collection of trees and shrubs (with 34 champion trees of the British Isles and 18 oldest specimens of their species). But the landscape is very beautiful too, with lovely views from the castle terrace southwards over the lake towards the distant Mourne Mountains.

INFORMATION

Location Castlewellan BT31 9BU, County Down, Northern Ireland; on the edge of the town of Castlewellan, 30m S of Belfast by A24

Tel (028) 4377 8664

Email customer.forestservice@dardni.gov.uk

Website www.forestserviceni.gov.uk

Owner Department of Agriculture (Northern Ireland)

Open daily 10–dusk

Area 1,136 acres/460 hectares (including the Castlewellan Forest Park)

Derreen Garden

A WILD WOODLAND GARDEN OF TREMENDOUS CHARACTER, FILLED WITH GOOD PLANTS AND WITH EXQUISITE VIEWS

The 5th Marquess of Lansdowne inherited Derreen in 1866, made it his summer home and started laying out a garden. The high rainfall and mild climate made it the perfect place for growing tender exotics. The garden occupies a promontory of rocky land overlooking the estuary of the Kenmare river, and the setting adds much to the beauty of the place. The estate belongs today to the 5th Marquess's great-grandson who in recent years has done much work on the garden.

WELL PLANNED PATHS

Derreen is a woodland garden of walks planned to take in the beauties of the landscape and to guide the visitor to the many notable trees and shrubs that find their home here. An excellent leaflet has a map of the paths and also indicates especially notable plants and vantage points. The Broad Walk follows the edge of the promontory, with delicious shifting views of Kilmakilloge Harbour. From it, several paths lead into the

A grove of tree ferns at Derreen

jungly hinterland. One path, the unforgettably named King's Oozy, plunges into a flourishing grove of tree ferns (*Dicksonia antarctica*) of the greatest splendour. First planted at Derreen in around 1900, these ferns now look completely natural, popping up elsewhere in the garden and becoming part of the scenery because the climate suits them so well. They show how marvellous such plants are when grown in this way rather than struggling for survival, pathetically swaddled in sacking and straw, in gardens whose climate does not remotely suit them.

The planting is often so dense that you must look upwards to identify a tree or shrub. Every walk reveals its beauties, with many excellent rhododendrons, exceptional specimens of such trees as *Cryptomeria japonica* 'Elegans', deodar (*Cedrus deodara*), silver fir (*Abies alba*) and *Styrax japonicus*. There is also much recent planting of camellias and of rarities like *Dacrydium franklinii*.

The landscape is punctuated by dramatic outcrops of rocks, usually clothed in moss. Away from the coast the land rises, offering fine prospects of the surrounding landscape. Froude's Seat is a simple bench in an elevated meadow full of buttercups, with a stately 'Loderi' rhododendron close by and a grand view of Kilmakilloge Harbour. The Knockatee Seat rises even higher and looks out, high above rhododendrons, towards the peak of Knockatee mountain to the north.

INFORMATION

Location Lauragh, County Kerry, Republic of Ireland; 25km SW of Kenmare by N71 and R571
Tel (00353) (0)64 83588
Owner The Hon David Bigham
Open Apr to Oct, daily 10–6 (closed Mon to Thur in Aug except by appointment);
Area 80 acres/32 hectares

The Dillon Garden

A RAVISHING TOWN GARDEN LAID OUT AND PLANTED BY ONE OF THE GREAT GARDEN MAGICIANS OF THE DAY

Helen Dillon is one of the best gardeners of her day, and 45 Sandford Road is a showcase for her skills. The front garden and that behind the house are of very different character.

The front garden is free-flowing, abundant and inviting, with plants straying over onto surfaces of gravel or stone paving. There is much yellow – euphorbias, honeysuckle, phlomis, roses, Welsh poppies – which glows in the early morning light. On either side of the steps leading up to the front door are little beds filled with the plant treasures that Helen Dillon loves – arisaemas, celmisias, dactylorhizas, erythoniums, *Onychium japonicum* and other small and often rare exotics.

A DAZZLING REVELATION

The garden behind the house is a dazzling revelation. At its centre is a splendid canal, long and narrow and edged in grey Kilkenny limestone. The canal, a big feature in a small garden, has the paradoxical effect of making the garden seem larger. It lies at the heart of a garden which, though it has formal interludes, is essentially rambling and informal, and is flanked by superb mixed borders, predominantly red on one side and blue on the other. Behind the borders paths wind among dense planting, with the occasional raised border to give sharp drainage or to bring some treasure a little closer to the eye. There are touches of formality – for example a sketch of a parterre with crisp hedges and spheres of box but with compartments planted informally.

At the end of the canal an arcade of clipped gold variegated ivy provides the opening to a tunnel of clematis, *Akebia quinata*, fruit trees and roses. In a corner there is a splendid old Bramley apple tree with deeply gnarled trunk and limbs, a reminder that the commonplace can be beautiful too. Throughout the garden decorative details emerge amid the profusion – a beautiful metal trellis screen, an armless concrete Venus, a handsome sundial, fine urns, a pair of sphinxes, and pots of rarities in odd corners. The garden is magnificently maintained, the plants bursting with vigour. Once you know it you will want to revisit. You will anticipate the pleasure, always see new things, and leave invigorated, with a spring in your step.

The canal in the Dillon Garden

INFORMATION

Location 45 Sandford Road, Ranelagh, Dublin 6, Republic of Ireland; 2km S of city centre

Tel and Fax (00353) (0)1 497 1308

Email helen@dillongarden. com

Website www.dillongarden. com

Owner Val and Helen Dillon

Open Mar, Jul to Aug, daily 2–6; Apr to Jun, Sun 2–6; also parties by appointment

Area ¾ acre/0.3 hectare

Downhill Castle

THE SKETCHY BUT UNFORGETTABLE REMAINS OF AN 18TH-CENTURY LANDSCAPE GARDEN WITH A CLIFF-TOP TEMPLE

Occupying one of the grandest landscapes in the British Isles, but with an address of suburban reticence, Downhill sits on a splendid promontory jutting out high over the Atlantic waves. It was the creation of Frederick Augustus Hervey, Bishop of Derry and 3rd Earl of Bristol. The house was gutted by fire in 1851 and although rebuilt was subsequently dismantled between the two world wars. What remains today, with sheep and cattle grazing peacefully among the ruins, is still a landscape of drama and melancholy beauty.

The Mussenden Temple

SPECTACULAR VIEWS

The most complete surviving building is the Mussenden Temple, circular in plan, and domed and pillared. The Earl–Bishop dedicated it to his cousin Frideswide Mussenden who died at the age of twenty-two before the temple was completed. It stands on the very brink of a cliff, with Magilligan Strand washed by the Atlantic rollers 200 ft/60m below. The interior was fitted out as a library, with a crypt below where the Earl–Bishop's catholic staff could worship. The Temple, now without its library fittings, may be visited and the views from its windows are spectacular. On a stormy day the roar of the wind, the cry of buffeted seagulls and the crashing of waves far below evokes the sublime drama which 18th-century landscapers so relished.

Nearby, the beautiful masonry shell of the house has something of the character of a Piranesi etching, standing serenely on a grassy island enclosed by a ha-ha. On wild moorland in the hinterland a high domed mausoleum rises up – a monument to the Earl–Bishop's elder brother, the 2nd Earl and the absentee Lord Lieutenant of Ireland to whom the Earl–Bishop owed his preferment and wealth. Built between 1779 and 1783 it was badly damaged in the "big wind" of 1839 which toppled the life-size figure that crowned it. The decapitated body lies today forlorn among bushes of escallonia and myrtle at the entrance lodge to the garden.

In more recent times the gardens by the lodge were lovingly tended by Miss Jan Eccles, who came to live in the Gothic lodge house in 1962. Here she laid out a charming flower garden with hellebores, Himalayan poppies, candelabra primulas, ferns and the fairy-foxglove (*Erinus alpinus*), a native of the Burren in her native County Clare.

INFORMATION

Location 42 Mussenden Road, Castle Rock, Coleraine BT51 4RP, County Londonderry, Northern Ireland; 5m NW of Coleraine on A2
Tel (028) 2073 1582
Email downhilldemesne@nationaltrust.org.uk
Owner The National Trust
Open daily dawn–dusk
Area 147 acres/59 hectares

Dunloe Castle Gardens

CHOICE TREES AND SHRUBS BEAUTIFULLY DISPLAYED IN THE SETTING OF A 13-CENTURY CASTLE

The original castle at Dunloe, a fortress guarding the river Laune, was built by the Fitzgeralds in 1215, later passed to the O'Sullivan family, and was largely destroyed in the late 16th century. In the 20th century an American, Howard Harrington, came to live in a house near the castle ruins and in the 1920s started a collection of exotic trees. These have been preserved and added to by the current owners who have established a large five-star hotel in the grounds. It is rare for a hotel to have a plant collection of such distinction in a setting that is so beautiful – over the river to the south are views of the Gap of Dunloe and the mountains of Macgillycuddy's Reeks.

TREE COLLECTION

The garden is essentially a collection of trees although it does have its moments of attractive design. The Gothic tower of the old castle, for example, is drawn into the garden as an eyecatcher by an enticing walk of decorative trees and

Old Dunloe Castle

shrubs leading up to it. The path is lined with camellias, *Elaeagnus* 'Quicksilver', eucalyptus, *Rhododendron* 'Fragrantissimum' (the climate is very mild here) and golden yews. At the opening of the path is a rarely seen evergreen tree from Japan, *Castanopsis cuspidata*. A few older trees also survive, such as a pair of 17th-century yews of tremendous character – they are male and female, christened Adam and Eve, and plainly planted as a decorative pair. But the tree collection is the main attraction. Some are of specifically Irish interest such as the beautiful example of an unusual hornbeam, *Carpinus henryana*, from western China, discovered by the great Irish plant collector Augustine Henry.

The very mild microclimate allows the cultivation of such tender trees as the lovely *Cupressus torulosa* 'Cashmeriana' and the South American *Lomatia ferruginea* with fern-like evergreen foliage. (W.J. Bean describes the latter as "one of the handsomest trees that have come from S. America".) Another outstanding evergreen is the Chinese swamp cypress (*Glyptostrobus pensilis*) whose falling leaves turn glowing red. Many good hotels have well-kept gardens but few have such an enticing collection of plants set in scenery so lovely.

INFORMATION

Location Dunloe, County Kerry, Republic of Ireland; 8km NW of Killarney by R582
Tel (00353) (0)64 44111
Owner Hotel Dunloe Castle
Open May to Sept, daily dawn–dusk
Area 3 acres/1.2 hectares

Florence Court

AN 18TH-CENTURY LANDSCAPE FOR A GREAT HOUSE, WITH 19TH-CENTURY PLEASURE GROUNDS AND SUMMERHOUSE

The house was built in the 18th century for John Cole MP (later 1st Lord Mountflorence) and for his son William (1st Earl of Enniskillen). It has a lovely position on rising land and is itself the most prominent feature of the landscape. In the late 18th century William King worked on a landscape park here, enclosing the whole park with belts of trees threaded with a drive, and dividing the interior parkland with three long belts of trees. The pleasure grounds were laid out by James Fraser (or Frazer) on the slopes beyond the house in the 1840s, and they have a strong 19th-century character, with a beautiful fern-leafed beech (*Fagus sylvatica* var. *heterophylla* 'Asplenifolia'), magnolias, monkey puzzles and giant tree rhododendrons.

Victorian summerhouse at Florence Court

A rustic summerhouse here, dating from before 1860, with thatched roof and walls patterned with twigs, was restored in 1993. If you sit in it today, in one of the pretty rustic chairs, you may be puzzled by the sound of a soft mechanical groaning which turns out to be a waterwheel powering a sawmill hidden behind trees.

THE ORIGINAL IRISH YEW

At the foot of the slope old meadow land is dazzling in spring and early summer with wild flowers, especially orchids. Beyond it are woodland walks and a remarkable tree – the original Irish yew, a chance seedling, one of two discovered in the 19th century by George Willis, a farmer on the estate. He planted one in his own garden, which died in 1865, and gave the other to his landlord. All Irish yews are

descended from this single plant which is female, and thus all true Irish yews, whose identity will persist only when propagated by cuttings, are female.

The 18th-century walled kitchen garden to the far side of the house is a curiosity, more a garden with walls than a walled garden for it is not fully enclosed and some of the walls are freestanding. It has now been turned over to ornamental purposes. One wall is crowned with a pediment and festooned with roses. A very long pergola is covered in clematis, roses and wisteria and underplanted with astrantias, bergenias, hellebores and hostas. A rose garden of Victorian flavour has shaped beds and climbing roses trained on an arbour and on rope swags. Nearby is a grove of flowering cherries.

INFORMATION

Location Enniskillen BT92 1DB, County Fermanagh, Northern Ireland; 8m SW of Enniskillen by A4 and A32
Tel 028 6634 8249 **Fax** 028 6634 8873
Email florencecourt@ntrust.org.uk
Owner The National Trust
Open Apr to Sept, daily 10–8; Oct to Mar, daily 10–4
Area 21 acres/8 hectares

Fota Arboretum

MAGNIFICENT TREES AND SHRUBS, A 19TH-CENTURY FERNERY AND A GRAND WALLED FLOWER GARDEN

The estate of Fota Island formed part of the lands granted to Phillip de Barri by Henry II in the late 12th century. The position of the demesne is unusual, and unusually beautiful, occupying an island in the estuary of the river Lee which opens out into the harbour of Cobh. Although it is now linked to the mainland by a causeway it still retains a remote atmosphere. The house at Fota was built first as a hunting box in the early 18th century by the Hon. John Smith-Barry and immensely extended in around 1820 to the designs of Richard Morrison, acquiring a refined Regency character. The chief maker of the garden was James Hugh Smith-Barry who in the first part of the 19th century built formal gardens about

A fern-leafed beech at Fota

the house. The remains of these gardens can be seen: plain, unadorned terraces to the east and south of the house that originally had an elaborately patterned parterre of shaped beds. He added large numbers of distinguished plants and also built a Gothic sham castle, designed by the Cork architect John Hargrave, with castellated round towers overlooking the estuary. After various changes of ownership in the late 20th century the demesne is now in the care of Duchás, The Heritage Service.

RICH IN PLANTS

Much restoration work has been done in recent years and a grand walled garden to the east, the former kitchen garden, is now rich in plants, with a rare collection of Irish bred narcissi (163 varieties), many roses and beds of

agapanthus, crocosmia, kniphofia and phormium. Venerable thickets of cabbage palm (*Cordyline australis*) have hanging bunches of flowers which perfume the whole garden in high summer, and against a wall is a pretty domed alcove which must date from the early 19th century. A broad gravel walk leads to a handsome vaulted orangery with fine stone urns on the parapet and a collection of oranges and lemons inside. It is flanked by a pair of date palms (*Phoenix dactylifera*) – evidence of how mild the microclimate is here.

A long walk ending in a monumental stone bench links a garden door on the south side of the house to James Smith-Barry's arboretum. That is the most direct route but it is far better to zigzag across impeccable lawns and marvel at the magnificent trees that stand all about. These range from splendid examples of common trees, like the Durmast oak (*Quercus petraea*) close to the house, to outstanding examples of less common ones like the Crimean

pine (*Pinus nigra* var. *caramanica*) a little further away. Some of the plants at Fota, while perfectly hardy in many parts of southern England, will never attain the size and distinction that they do here. A *Drimys winteri*, for example, here forms a magnificent upright cascade of gleaming foliage. The beautiful evergreen *Hoheria populnea*, with its lavish clusters of white flowers, at Fota assumes the dimensions of a stately tree.

FERNERY AND LAKE

A fernery, in the shade of an old sweet chestnut, dates from the mid 19th century. Its mossy rocks and colonies of mother-of-thousands (*Saxifraga stolonifera*) form a jungly background to a remarkable collection of old tree ferns (*Dicksonia antarctica*). An irregular lake, dappled with waterlilies and fringed with arum lilies and reeds, also has notable trees. Some of these are 19th-century conifers, including some very big Wellingtonias, but others are good examples of less familiar trees. A notable group of *Cornus controversa* is a rarity. Its variegated form was one of the most fashionable trees of the late 20th century but the plainer, and more distinguished, type is seldom seen – at Fota it flowers prodigiously.

Now owned by the state, Fota is an immensely popular place to push prams and take the air, yet it retains the character of a private estate. The magnificent old trees are well cared for and, just as important, much new planting has been done to provide replacements for the future.

INFORMATION

Location Fota Island, Carricktwohill, County Cork, Republic of Ireland; 15km E of Cork by N25 and R624
Tel (00353) (0)21 481 5543
Email info@fotahouse.com
Website www.fotahouse.com
Owner Dúchas, The Heritage Service
Open Apr to Sept, daily 10–5 (opens 11 on Sun); Oct to Mar, daily 11–4
Area 32 acres/13 hectares

Glenveagh Castle

AT THE HEART OF A NATIONAL PARK, A DRAMATIC 19TH-
CENTURY CASTLE WITH EXQUISITE FLOWER GARDENS

In wild, remote and beautiful country, the castle was built between 1870 and 1873 by John Adair who married an American heiress and accumulated an estate of 24,700 acres/10,000 hectares. The estate had further American connections, being bought in in 1937 by Henry McIlhenny of the Tabasco Sauce family, who restored the castle and made the gardens. He gave castle and gardens to the Irish state in 1974.

Gothic orangery at Glenveigh

A BEAUTIFUL SITE

The site of the castle is very beautiful – facing north-west on a promontory jutting out into Lough Veagh. In Mrs Adair's time the grounds to the east of the castle running down to the banks of the lough were developed as pleasure grounds and many trees planted as windbreaks. Henry McIlhenny carried out much new planting and planning of new features. In the planting he had the advice of James Russell, the great connoisseur of trees and shrubs, who for the pleasure grounds suggested, among much else, the fine large-leafed species rhododendrons like *R. falconeri* and *R. sinogrande* and the sweetly scented late-flowering *R. maddenii*. This area, with a long lawn surrounded by dense planting, has today an outstanding collection of trees and shrubs which do best in acid soil in a very wet but mild climate – acers, camellias, eucryphias, nothofagus, podocarpus and stewartias. Forming the southern boundary of the pleasure grounds, the Belgian Walk, named after convalescent Belgian soldiers who stayed here in World War I, is dazzling with flowering shrubs.

Behind the castle, on sloping ground, is a walled kitchen garden which has been given an ornamental character. Box hedges and domes divide the compartments, and flowery borders run across the middle with catmint, dahlias, *Eryngium alpinum*, repeated clumps of *Geranium psilostemon* and loosestrife. Against the castle wall are a long lean-to glasshouse and a high, airy Gothic orangery designed by the artist Philippe Jullian in 1958. Decorative lead statues, urns and elegant cast-iron benches create a lighthearted atmosphere below the stern walls of the castle. The little Italian Garden concealed in woods beside the castle is also rich in ornament. Guarded by sphinxes, it is enclosed in hedges of griselinia, above which rise stone statues. Walks up the steep slopes above the castle give astonishing views of the lough and the barren rocky slopes that rise above it.

INFORMATION

Location Churchill, Letterkenny, County Donegal, Republic of Ireland; 16km NW of Letterkenny by N56 and R255
Infoline (00353) (0)74 37090
Fax (00353) (0)74 37072
Owner Dúchas, The Heritage Service
Open mid Mar to early Nov, daily 10–6.30
Area 28 acres/11 hectares

Heywood

A MASTERPIECE BY SIR EDWIN LUTYENS – A GIANT OVAL WALLED GARDEN, TERRACES AND HEDGED FLOWER GARDENS

The house at Heywood was built in 1773 for Michael Trench to his own designs, probably with the help of James Gandon. A lithograph of 1818 shows an 18th-century landscape garden embowered in woods running down to a lake, and picturesque ornament from this time still enriches the scene: on the drive a Gothic sham castle stands alongside a sham ruin with tracery windows, but only the ruins of a bridge over the lake survive.

In 1906 a new garden close to the house was laid out, designed by Sir Edwin Lutyens with planting by Gertrude Jekyll. This beautiful and ingenious garden survives almost entirely intact, although the planting is sketchy. Immediately below the site of the 18th-century house – gutted by fire and later demolished – is a deep terrace, with stone columns finely carved with swags. Below this is a second, lower terrace, beyond which the ground drops away with idyllic views over parkland. At the west end of these terraces Lutyens built a pergola on two

levels which both closes off the formal gardens on this side and gives delicious views to the north and west. At the other end of the upper terrace is Lutyens's Italian Garden. A huge oval walled space has concentric oval terraces descending to an oval pool with a monumental stone basin. About its edge are hemispheres of stone on which crouch bronze turtles.

MIXED PLANTINGS

Each terrace has borders along the flagstoned paths: a ring of pink roses on the uppermost terrace and mixed plantings of blocks of bergenias, catmint, hostas, kniphofias or sage on the others. The garden would be improved if this planting were more generous and if the interior walls were also clothed in plants – as they originally were. In 2007 replanting was underway.

From the top terrace a beautiful curving flight of steps penetrates the wall to an upper level where there is a maze of yew-hedged enclosures with paved paths and herbaceous borders. From this upper vantage point a grand view opens out, over the oval garden and far into the countryside beyond its walls. The garden at Heywood shows Lutyens at his most irrepressible, deftly making the best of the site at every turn.

Lutyens's oval garden at Heywood

INFORMATION

Location Ballinakill, County Laois, Republic of Ireland; on the edge of Ballinakill village, 8km SE of Abbeyleix

Tel (00353) (0)502 33563

Owner Dúchas, The Heritage Service

Open daily dawn–dusk

Area 45 acres/18 hectares

Ilnacullin

A DREAM-LIKE GARDEN ON GARINISH ISLAND, DESIGNED BY HAROLD PETO AND PLANTED WITH RARE EXOTICS

Garinish Island, with its Martello Tower built in 1805 to protect Ireland from possible attack by Napoleon, was bought in 1910 by a Belfast-born East India Merchant, John Annan Bryce. Between 1911 and 1914 a hundred men worked to make a garden, blasting rock, importing soil from the mainland and planting trees for windbreaks.

ITALIANATE BUILDINGS

Bryce commissioned garden buildings from Harold Peto who designed two Italianate buildings close to the western coast: the Casita overlooking a sunken garden with a rectangular pool and, on its far side, an elegant arcaded open pavilion leading to a balustraded viewing platform looking towards the mainland and the pointed peaks of the Caha Mountains. The island scenery was gently animated by other architectural features: a dramatic flight of stone steps runs up a slope to an open-columned Greek Temple (also with views to the mainland) and similar steps were made to the Martello Tower. Peto also laid out a large walled garden.

The Casita at Ilnacullin

In contrast to the architectural formality, the planting is wild and naturalistic. The very high rainfall – more than 70in/180cm per annum is usual – and a site strongly influenced by the Gulf Stream, allow the cultivation of plants unfamiliar to gardeners from dryer, cooler parts. Rarities from the southern hemisphere are well represented. Here are *Acacia pravissima* from Australia; the Kauri pine (*Agathis australis*) from New Zealand, one of many tender conifers; the beautiful tree fern *Cyathea dealbata*, also from New Zealand; *Taiwania cryptomerioides* from south-west China; and many other rare, curious or beautiful trees and shrubs. There is also a very large collection of rhododendrons, the species being particularly well represented. The walled garden has a pair of long borders, the closest that Ilnacullin gets to conventional gardening, and the walls themselves are, naturally, festooned with countless plants.

The charm of Peto's buildings, the heady range of exotic plants and the beauty of the natural scenery make Ilnacullin an exceptional place. Even getting there is special – slipping across the water in a small boat, passing on the way a miniature island on which seals sleepily sprawl as the charms of Ilnacullin come gradually into focus, makes this one of the most memorable journeys to any garden.

INFORMATION

Location Garinish Island, Glengarriff, County Cork, Republic of Ireland; on an island in Bantry Bay, boats from Glegarriff
Tel (00353) (0)27 63040
Owner Dúchas, The Heritage Service
Open Mar and Oct, daily 10–4.30 (Sun 1–5); Apr to May, Sept, daily 10–6.30 (Sun 1–7); Jul to Aug, daily 9.30–6.30 (Sun 11–7)
Area 37 acres/15 hectares

The Irish National Stud

A LIVELY JAPANESE GARDEN ALONGSIDE AN OUTSTANDING MODERN GARDEN CELEBRATING THE LIFE OF ST FIACHRA

The stud is one of the world's centres of racehorse breeding and the beautiful horses may be seen grazing in their paddocks or being led from the stables to exercise. It was founded in 1915 by Col William Hall-Walker (later Lord Wavertree). He was also a keen gardener and in 1906 commissioned a Japanese gardener, Tassa Eida, to make a Japanese garden at Tully. It traces an individual's journey from the gate of oblivion to the gateway of eternity with all sorts of indecisions, torments and temptations at every turn. Here are a pool and stream, rocky outcrops, a teahouse, an arched bridge painted scarlet, snow lanterns, flowering cherries and clipped evergreens. There is also a collection of magnificent bonsai distributed about a flawless lawn close to the bridge. After Eida's time further elements of Japanese inspiration were added: the Garden of Eternity, a dry landscape of rocks and gravel with a splendid *Cercidiphyllum japonicum* at the centre, and a Zen meditation garden.

St Fiachra's Garden at the Irish National Stud

ST FIACHRA'S GARDEN

An entirely new garden, St Fiachra's garden, was made to celebrate the millennium and completed in 1999 to the designs of Professor Martin Hallinan. St Fiachra was a 7th-century Irish monk who later lived in France and became the patron saint of gardening. The garden is one of water, woods and rocks. At its heart are two domed monks' cells, beautifully fashioned of stone, situated in ground shaped into mysterious mounds and undulations where huge shapes of stone rise up to embrace a path. A very narrow passage leads to an interior with a glowing Waterford crystal "garden" of glass plants and rocks let into the floor and illuminated by fibreoptics.

Outside, on an outcrop of rock jutting out into the waters of a lake, is a bronze figure of St Fiachra contemplating a seed clasped in his hand. Water-worn slabs of stone emerge from the lake and paths wind about the banks among alders and ashes. A second lake, at a lower level, is joined to the first by a spectacular broad but shallow waterfall. In the waters below are 5,000-year-old bog oaks, blackened and preserved by the acidic water, whose jagged shapes rise dramatically from the water. The place has potent character, with drama, mystery and beauty evoked by the simplest of means.

INFORMATION

Location Tully, Kildare, County Kildare, Republic of Ireland; on the SE side of Kildare town signed from the centre, 50km W of Dublin by N7 and M7
Tel (00353) (0)45 521 617
Email japanesegardens@eircom.net
Website www.irish-national-stud.ie
Owner Irish National Stud
Open mid Feb to mid Nov, daily 9.30–5
Area 5¼ acres/2 hectares

Kilfane Glen

AN 18TH-CENTURY WOODLAND GARDEN WITH CASCADE AND COTTAGE ORNÉ, AND MODERN FORMAL GARDENS

In 1819 Louisa Beaufort wrote to Sophy Edgeworth, "Mr B, Pa, Ma and I in the inside jaunting car and Richard on horseback all went to Kilfayne, Mr Power's, a very pretty place." In the 1790s Sir John Power had made a picturesque garden in a natural ravine in the demesne of Kilfane. In woodland of beech, larch, pine and sweet chestnut Power had built a cottage *orné* beside a rushing stream and, opposite it, a spectacular cascade erupting from the cliffside and tumbling into a pool far below.

Susan and Nicholas Mosse knew nothing of this garden when they came to live here. Only when they saw some drawings of 1804 did they discover what sort of garden had been here. They located the site of the cottage, whose foundations survived, and rebuilt it at the bottom of the valley on a grassy clearing at the edge of the stream. In spring, you see it from afar as you wind down the precipitous path through the leafless woods. It has a

thickly thatched roof, a verandah with rustic columns and a floor inlaid with pebbles, and it is furnished with charming rustic furniture. From the ground-floor room, now a tea-room for visitors, are views through lattice windows to the restored cascade. Much clearing of the woodland has allowed anemones, ferns, narcissi and wood anemones to flourish. The Kilfane glen is a perfect piece of garden restoration, giving the visitor the delightful feeling of straying into the picturesque past.

SCULPTURE GARDEN

The Mosses have also created new formal gardens for their house above the glen. Here are a waterlily pool, a pergola of clematis and roses, a garden of grasses, a pale garden of white flowers and silver or variegated foliage, a formal orchard with circles of crab apples, and a fernery ending in a mysterious distorting mirror. Here and in the adjacent woodland are works of art by such artists as William Pye, James Turrell, Bill Woodrow and many others, with new works being added regularly.

In this upper garden there is, too, a recent restoration of a vista focused on the peak of Slievenamon. So homage is paid to the past but the present is also alive and kicking.

The cottage *orné* at Kilfane

INFORMATION

Location nr Thomastown, County Kilkenny, Republic of Ireland; 6km N of Thomastown signposted on the N9
Tel (00353) 56772 4558
Owner Susan and Nicholas Mosse
Open Jul and Aug, daily 11–6
Area 15 acres/6 hectares

Killruddery

A 17TH-CENTURY ESTATE WITH A RARE EARLY 18TH-CENTURY FORMAL GARDEN AND PRETTY VICTORIAN GARDENS

The Killruddery estate was acquired in 1618 by Sir William Brabazon, later 1st Earl of Meath. The house was built for the 10th Earl to the designs of Richard Morrison in around 1820 in dashing neo-Elizabethan style but incorporating parts from the 17th century. In the 1680s at the time of the 4th Earl, a Frenchman, Bonet, laid out a remarkable formal garden which was completed by the early 18th century

Behind the house two parallel canals, with a single water jet at the end, point towards an avenue which sweeps away up a hill. To one side is a symmetrical pattern of walks hedged in beech, hornbeam and lime and ornamented with statues at meeting points – known as "the Angles" and similar to the bosquets of 17th-century French gardens. Close by is a circular pool with a jet and the remains of formal cascades. On the far side of the canals the Wilderness has the sketchy remains of straight rides through the woodland and a few statues, among them a stricken warrior and a Venus standing high on a plinth.

The stricken warrior at Killruddery

A GREEN THEATRE

Closer to the house a pretty *théâtre de verdure* (green theatre) with turf seats is enclosed in hedges of bay. Nearby, a circular space enclosed with vast beech hedges encompasses a huge circular pool with tritons spouting water and a fountain of birds among reeds. A similar but rectangular enclosure has a statue of frolicking putti, and a magnificent conservatory, vaulted and spectacularly domed, built in about 1850, houses a collection of statues. Below the conservatory a Victorian parterre has box-hedged beds filled with bedding roses and lavender, decorated with a central scalloped pool. An ornamental octagonal dairy, with a pretty interior, has stained glass windows with Gothic tracery and a verandah swathed in clematis.

In 1843 the gardens were restored by Daniel Robertson and it is possible that the handsome turf terraces that flank the drive and spread out to one side of the house date from this time. Killruddery intermingles features of different periods with success, but the most memorable part of the garden is the bold axis of the two canals flanked by their intriguing hedges and rides. This is the only extensive formal garden of its type and period surviving in Ireland.

INFORMATION

Location Bray, County Wicklow, Republic of Ireland; 20km SE of Dublin by N11/M11
Tel (00353) (0)404 46024
Email info@killruddery.com
Website www.killruddery.com
Owner The Earl and Countess of Meath
Open Apr, Sat and Sun 1–5; May to Sept, daily 1–5
Area 41 acres/17 hectares

Kylemore Abbey

A GREAT WALLED KITCHEN GARDEN, NOW SPLENDIDLY
RESTORED, IN A SETTING OF DAZZLING BEAUTY

Kylemore Castle was built from
1864 for a Manchester merchant,
Mitchell Henry MP, to the designs of
James Franklin Fuller – a wildly
romantic confection deploying the full
vocabulary of the Gothic decorated
style in which every parapet has its
battlements and no tower is left
unmachicolated. Its position on the
northern bank of Lough Pollacappul
surrounded by the Connemara
mountains is wonderfully romantic in
itself, and Henry built a causeway
across the lough to give visitors a
marvellous distant prospect of his house.

Henry was a devoted gardener and
he set out to make a garden where no-
one had gardened before, draining bogs
and clothing the desolate, violently
windswept hills with many thousands of
trees. At some distance from the house,
linked by a pinetum, he built a great
walled garden on a sloping and
irregular site. It was used both as a
kitchen garden and as an ornamental
garden. Its most spectacular feature was
a range of glasshouses on the grandest
possible scale – 18 of them, used to
cultivate bananas, figs, grapes, melons
and much else. Henry died in 1910 and
ten years later the estate was bought by
Irish Benedictine Nuns. This order,
known as the Irish Dames, had been
established in Ypres, Flanders, in the
17th century but was forced to leave
during World War I.

The nuns continued to cultivate the
walled garden, in particular the kitchen
garden, but with reduced labour the
ornamental gardens and glasshouses
were not maintained. In 1996, with the
help of outside funds and a restoration
committee, restoration of the walled
garden began. Excellent photographs
and other documentary evidence, as
well as an archaeological dig, has made
it possible to reconstruct the garden,
and it opened to the public in 1999.
The hugely expensive rebuilding of the
glasshouses is still not complete but it is
plain how impressive they were.

THE RESTORED GARDENS

The garden slopes from north to south
and a wild stream and trees form the
north–south boundary separating the
ornamental from the productive
garden. The ornamental garden is
dominated by two lawns sloping down
to meet at a gravel path. Here,
elaborate crescent-shaped beds cut in
the turf brim with bedding plants, and
old plants of cabbage palm (*Cordyline
australis*) stand on either side. Above, to

Kylemore Abbey kitchen garden

the north, is the site of the 19th-century glasshouses. At the heart of the glasshouse complex, a circle of metal posts linked by metal arches is decorated with flower baskets hanging from each arch and crowning each post. Within the circle is a bed with segments of turf radiating from its centre, symmetrical patterns of bedding and a mound crowned by a monkey puzzle – these were often used as short-term bedding plants and were moved when they threatened to become too big. Two of the glasshouses have already been reinstated – a vinery with a curved roof, and a lean-to for general purposes. Close by is the charming head gardener's house, now restored and furnished, giving a good idea of the status a head gardener had in a great Victorian estate. It commands fine views over the garden.

The kitchen garden is spread out above and below an axial path flanked with herbaceous borders. Beds of vegetables are edged in box and the view of them from the top of the garden is unforgettable. A pattern of productive beds is always a delightful sight but from this vantage point you see over the walls to the countryside beyond – to looming mountains, often shrouded in mist, giving a vivid idea of the desolation of the place before Mitchell Henry came here.

There are other pleasures to sample at Kylemore, not least the astonishing abbey itself. There are fine walks along the banks of the lough, and the nuns, continuing the tree-planting tradition established by Henry, have already planted 10,000 ash and oaks.

INFORMATION

Location Connemara, County Galway, Republic of Ireland; 116km NW of Galway by N59 and R344
Tel (00353) (0)95 41146
Email info@kylemoreabbey.ie
Website www.kylemoreabbey.com
Owner The Benedictine Order of Nuns
Open mid Mar to Oct, daily 10–4.30
Area 6 acres/2.4 hectares (walled garden)

Lismore Castle

A MAGNIFICENT 17TH-CENTURY TERRACED GARDEN WITH FINE MODERN SCULPTURES AND GOOD PLANTING

Richard Boyle, 1st Earl of Cork, bought Lismore in 1602. It passed by marriage to the 4th Duke of Devonshire in 1753 and has remained in that family. The present building is a 19th-century reworking of an essentially 17th-century house standing on a wonderfully romantic site, a wooded bluff high above the Blackwater river.

The garden falls into two quite separate parts. The lower garden on the slopes below the castle is informally planted with trees and shrubs in grass – especially notable are the magnolias. Immediately below the castle wall is a circular pool and an avenue of eucryphias (*E.* x *intermedia* 'Rostrevor') with at its end a soaring bronze statue by Eilís O'Conell. The most memorable plants in the lower garden are ancient yews (possibly planted in 1707) in a double procession, forming a narrow shady passage at whose far end is a perfectly placed, still figure – a bronze statue of a man by Antony Gormley.

THE UPPER GARDEN

The terraced upper garden – the original kitchen garden – was laid out after the 1st Earl of Cork came to live here in 1620 and is the earliest surviving garden of its kind in Ireland. A long axial walk descending the terraces is exactly aligned on the slender spire of the Cathedral of St Carthage, and the top terrace, backed by a castellated wall, has a broad grass walk. Marking the end of the walk is a sculpture by Simon Thomas, a cool oval of white Carrara marble with delicately carved convolutions on one side. A border runs along the top terrace wall, filled with cistus, euphorbia, lilies, Melianthus major, mimosa (*Acacia dealbata*) and myrtle (*Myrtus luma*). Mixed borders

The Antony Gormley statue at Lismore

backed by yew hedges follow the descending axis of the garden, with cross-walks and borders catching the eye. There is still a substantial kitchen garden here, with areas of vegetables, soft fruit and espaliered fruit trees as well as the large orchard.

Lismore is an attractive garden with a remarkable setting and history, and the addition of a number of excellent modern sculptures has given it a new excitement. Furthermore, at Lismore someone has taken much trouble to place them where they both show to advantage and add to the existing character of the place.

INFORMATION

Location Lismore, County Waterford, Republic of Ireland; In Lismore town, 79km NE of Cork by N8 and N72
Tel (00353) (0)58 54424
Email lismoreestates@eircom.net
Website www.lismorecastle.com
Owner The Trustees of the Lismore Estate
Open Apr to Sept, daily 1.45–4.45 (Jun to Aug, opens 11)
Area 7 acres/2.8 hectares

Mount Congreve

THE WORK OF A 20TH-CENTURY MASTER GARDENER – A VAST AND EXQUISITE WOODLAND GARDEN PACKED WITH RARITIES

The house at Mount Congreve was built in the early 18th century and was, like the garden, greatly extended by the present owner, Ambrose Congreve, in the 1960s. There had been a simple terraced garden with woodland of ilexes and sweet chestnuts on the slopes that lead towards the river Suir. Ambrose Congreve took advantage of the woodland, and its fine site, to make one of the most extraordinary gardens of the 20th century.

LARGE GROUPS OF PLANTS

This is the garden of a perfectionist collector, especially of trees and shrubs; and with acid soil, relatively high rainfall and a mild microclimate a wide range of plants can be grown. Ambrose Congreve despises "dotty" planting and repeat planting, believing that a single spectacular group best conveys a plant's essence. Immaculate paths wander through the woodland, usually edged with vast quantities of a single plant – hummocks of Japanese maple or seas of white azaleas, fronted perhaps with a deep ribbon of hostas. Quite small herbaceous plants are also used in

prodigal quantities – carpets of *Omphalodes cappadocica* or epimediums, for example, about the trunks of trees. A rare straight path is the half-mile (1km) long river walk which runs down to the Suir. It is lined with 100 *Magnolia campbellii* on one side and 100 *Magnolia sargentiana* var. *robusta* on the other, with vast numbers of *Magnolia soulangeana* in front and hydrangeas in front of them.

Fine native trees, especially oaks and beeches, are used with deliberation and respect. A group of magnificent beeches stands in a glade on a flawless lawn edged with ramparts of maples and rhododendrons. The trees themselves are frequently used as supports for climbing plants skilfully trained – clematis and roses in quantity but also really large-scale climbers like *Actinidia kolomikta* or *Vitis coignetiae*.

There are one or two pieces of decorative formality here – a Chinese pavilion and a pillared temple, for example – as well as a very large walled garden with finely kept borders and vast ranges of glasshouses. However, it is the brilliantly novel approach to what might be considered a fairly exhausted tradition of woodland planting that is thrilling at Mount Congreve. Here is a far wider range of plants than you have ever seen in a private garden, deployed in an entirely unfamiliar fashion.

Spring at Mount Congreve

INFORMATION

Location Kilmeaden, County Waterford, Republic of Ireland; 8km W of Waterford by N25
Tel (00353) (0)51 384 115
Email congreve@eircom.ie
Owner Ambrose Congreve
Open Apr to Sept, daily 9–4.30 (groups by appointment only)
Area 180 acres/73 hectares

Mount Stewart

A DAZZLING AND IDIOSYNCRATIC GARDEN WITH FORMALITY, FINE PLANTING AND DELICIOUS LAKESIDE WALKS

The house, replacing an 18th-century one, was built in the early 19th century for the 1st Marquess of Londonderry. The gardens close to the house are the creation from 1921 of Edith, the wife of the 7th Marquess. About the house she devised an idiosyncratic series of formal gardens executed with flamboyant panache.

The Italian Garden at Mount Stewart

The Italian Garden south of the house is in the form of a giant parterre with beds edged in startling golden thuja or smouldering purple berberis. The east parterre has an explosion of carmine or yellow crocosmias, scarlet lobelia, purple delphiniums and yellow figwort (*Phygelius aequalis*). Things cool down a little to the west where the planting is blue, lavender and grey, with the occasional jolt of magenta. Tall pillars on the south side of the garden are crowned with monkeys made of cement, each sitting on the shoulders of a grotesque figure. A whole menagerie of cement animals parades on the Dodo Terrace to one side.

A SUNKEN GARDEN

West of the house the sunken garden is surrounded on three sides by a fine pergola with stone pillars planted with clematis, honeysuckle and roses. The garden sinks to two lower levels, with monumental tree heathers, giant clipped mushrooms of purple sycamore, orange-red azaleas and herbaceous borders. Irish yews flank the entrance to the Shamrock Garden where the red hand of Ulster is picked out in red begonias. Gertrude Jekyll is said to have had a hand in the planting of the sunken garden, which certainly displays skilful planting. The Shamrock Garden,

however, teeters on the verge of kitsch. North of the house is a landscape of an entirely different character, with noble trees planted in greensward that leads gently uphill away from the house.

The revelation of a lake beyond the summit of the slope comes as a surprise, for a lake is usually at the bottom of a declivity, not at its top. Laid out in the 19th century, it has been finely restored by the National Trust. Lakeside walks pass ornamental trees and glades. The banks of the lake are planted with long drifts of arum lily (*Zantedeschia aethiopica*), crocosmias and *Iris laevigata*. To the north, shrouded in trees and shrubs, is Tir Nan Og, the Londonderry family burial ground. Here are many tender shrubs – banksias, callistemons, hakeas and leptospermums – with communities of self-sown echiums.

INFORMATION

Location Newtownards BT22 2AD, County Down, Northern Ireland; 15m E of Belfast by A20
Tel 028 4278 8387
Email mountstewart@nationaltrust.org.uk
Owner The National Trust
Open Mar (from 2nd week), Mon to Fri, 10–4; Apr, daily 11–6; May to Sept, daily 10–8; Oct, daily 10–6
Area 78 acres/32 hectares

Mount Usher Gardens

A RARE AND RAVISHING 19TH-CENTURY WOODLAND GARDEN ON THE BANKS OF THE RIVER VARTRY

The estate – a mill and an acre of land – was bought by Edward Walpole in 1868. He and his three sons acquired more land and started to lay out their garden. They had the advice of some of the great plantsmen of the 19th century, among them E.A. Bowles, the great plant collector Augustine Henry, and Sir Frederick Moore of the National Botanic Garden in Dublin. A Walpole son, Thomas, was an engineer and he made the weirs which are such a vital part of the garden. The falls are ornamental in themselves but their crucial role is to provide the calm pools which mirror the plantings of trees and shrubs that crowd about the banks. Thomas Walpole was responsible also for the delightful iron bridges that span the river from time to time.

A path leads down into the valley where the grassy banks of the river are richly planted on either side – here are at least 3,000 species of plants. The climate is mild, the valley gives added protection, and the rainfall is fairly high. There are notable collections of acers, eucalyptus, eucryphias and southern beeches (*Nothofagus* species) –

The river garden at Mount Usher

often propagated by seed direct from the site of origin. (Seeds of over 60 different kinds of eucalyptus came from the Melbourne or Sydney Botanical Gardens.) Also from the southern hemisphere are the Kauri pine (*Agathis australis*) from New Zealand, *Bowkeria gerrardiana* from South Africa, and *Telopea truncata* from Tasmania. The woody plants command the chief attention but there is also much excellent herbaceous planting – orchids such as *Dactylorhiza* and *Orchis maderensis*, the spectacular giant lily *Cardiocrinum giganteum*, martagon lilies, swathes of Asiatic primulas, and real rarities like the Chilean *Tecophilea cyanocrocus*, now almost extinct in the wild.

PLANT-LOVER'S PARADISE

Mount Usher may be enjoyed in many different ways. It is a plant-lover's paradise but anyone will relish the lovely riverside walks, with brilliant colours and strange shapes reflected in the placid water of the weir pools. Unlike a botanical garden where plants are ordered according to genus, the plants here are disposed on the basis of appearance or of appropriateness of site. The devoted plant-spotter, however expert, will see unfamiliar and wonderful plants and will often see them when least expecting it.

INFORMATION

Location Ashford, County Wicklow, Republic of Ireland; in Ashford village, 50km S of Dublin by N11
Tel (00353) (0)404 40205
Website homepage.eircom. net/~gardens
Owner Mrs Madelaine Jay
Open Mar to Oct, daily 10.30–6
Area 20 acres/8 hectares

Powerscourt Gardens

A SUPERB IRISH SHOWPIECE – GRAND TERRACED GARDENS, A LAKE, A JAPANESE GARDEN AND OUTSTANDING TREES

The house at Powerscourt was built between 1731 and 1741 for Richard Wingfield, later 1st Viscount Powerscourt, to the designs of Richard Castle. It was gutted by fire in 1974, and all its contents destroyed. Some of the rooms have been reinstated and others are used as a visitor centre. The site is magnificent. From the brow of a hill the land swoops down and there are sublime views of Sugarloaf Mountain in the Wicklow hills. A series of terraces and parterres descends to a large circular lake with its triumphant jet of water.

A LAKE AND WOODLAND

The top terrace is ornamented with fine stonework, urns and statues of Diana, Apollo and the Angels of Fame and Victory. An ornate flight of steps, with beautiful wrought iron and decorative pebble paving, leads down, ending in a flourish where it approaches the lake, with a pair of pegasi rearing up – the pegasus is the crest of the Wingfield family. Lawns on each side of the terrace steps have bedding schemes in 19th-century style, with clipped mushrooms of Portugal laurel.

At the centre of the lake a figure of Triton blows his single jet high into the air, and woodland presses in on three sides. Here is a further surprise – a delightful sketch of a Japanese garden laid out for the 8th Viscount in 1908, with snow lanterns, a scarlet bridge, Japanese maples and flowering cherries.

The demesne of Powerscourt is exceptionally well wooded. In the 19th century the 6th and 7th Viscounts indulged in a frenzy of tree planting. Each year between 1870 and 1880 an average of 400,000 trees was planted in one part of the estate – the Ballyreagh Plantation. Within the gardens are magnificent conifers – fine specimens of cedar, cryptomeria, Douglas fir (*Pseudotsuga menziesii*), monkey puzzle, spruce, Wellingtonia and others. Among these are distinguished deciduous trees, some of them very rare, like the excruciatingly slow-growing cutleaf oak (*Quercus robur* 'Filicifolia').

Powerscourt is one of the great Irish showpieces and is much visited. Such places are not necessarily agreeable but here, even in high summer, there will always be a fine tree, beautiful stonework or wrought-ironwork, a refreshing woodland glade or an exhilarating prospect of the Wicklow countryside to please the visitor.

The lake at Powerscourt

INFORMATION

Location Enniskerry, County Wicklow, Republic of Ireland; 20km S of Dublin by N11
Tel (00353) (0)1 204 6000
Fax (00353) (0)1 204 6900
Email carmel.byrne@ powerscourt.net
Website www.powerscourt.ie
Owner Powerscourt Estate
Open daily 9.30–5.30 (dusk in winter; closed 25 and 26 Dec)
Area 47 acres/19 hectares

Rowallane Garden

A ROMANTIC AND MYSTERIOUS GARDEN WITH A WONDERFUL WALLED FLOWER GARDEN AND MAGNIFICENT ROCK GARDEN

The house at Rowallane was built in 1861 for the Revd John Moore. The garden is largely the 20th-century creation of his nephew, the plantsman Hugh Armytage Moore. After Moore's death in 1954 the estate was acquired by the National Trust.

The first experience of Rowallane as you proceed down the drive is one of mystery. Lugubrious conifers and old rhododendrons form a dark tunnel and, flanking the drive, mossy rocks erupt from the ground, interspersed from time to time with curious conical cairns of round stones. This slightly sinister introduction scarcely prepares you for the flower-filled spectacle to come.

The walled garden at Rowallane

LIVELIEST GARDENING

The walled garden is the scene of the liveliest gardening here. Mixed borders are stuffed with big old shrubs – *Hoheria lyallii*, several venerable magnolias, tree peonies and huge thickets of *Rosa moyesii*. The occasional startling, and rare, rhododendron animates the scene – such as *R. cinnabarinum* var. *blandfordiiflorum* with explosive trumpets of red and yellow. Astilbes, hostas, *Kirengeshoma palmata*, meconopsis, primulas, rodgersias and much else form the underplanting. There are touches of formality – cones of clipped yew, garlanded in summer with the scarlet flowers of *Tropaeolum speciosum*; a parterre with drums and hedges of clipped box; and a shaped magnolia at the centre of the parterre, planted with a pattern of penstemons. The walled garden has a kind of inner sanctum, a secondary compartment quite different in character from the rest, where a lawn is planted with specimen trees and shrubs, including the cultivar *Viburnum plicatum* 'Rowallane' which originated here. Steps lead down to a pool flanked by fine stone urns, which is edged in sheaves of *Iris pseudoacorus* and shaded by a *Davidia involucrata*.

Outside the walled gardens a long walk leads across Spring Ground, with ramparts of rhododendrons echoing the rolling contours of the land. You come eventually to a rock garden where natural outcrops of rock are planted with azaleas, daphnes, olearias and pieris, underplanted with beautiful celmisias, meconopsis and primulas. By 2007 much of the nearby Rock Garden Wood had been restored. A curiosity in the wooded pleasure grounds behind the house is a 19th-century bandstand which, threatened with demolition in Newcastle, was rescued by the National Trust and erected on an existing plinth from which, it is said, the Revd John Moore used to practise his sermons.

INFORMATION

Location Saintfield, Ballynahinch BT24 7LH, County Down, Northern Ireland; 11m SE of Belfast by A7
Tel 028 9751 0131
Email rowallane@nationaltrust.org.uk
Owner The National Trust
Open Mar to Feb, daily 10–8 (closes 4 from Mar to mid Apr and mid Sept to Feb; closed 24 Dec to 1 Jan)
Area 51 acres/21 hectares

Index